WORKING
THROUGH
NARCISSISM

WORKING THROUGH NARCISSISM

Treating its Sadomasochistic Structure

Maria Carmen Gear, M.D.
Melvyn A. Hill, Ph.D.
Ernesto Cesar Liendo, M.D.

NEW YORK   ARONSON   LONDON

Library of Congress Cataloging in Publication Data

Gear, Maria Carmen.
    Working through narcissism.

    Bibliography
    Includes index.
    1. Sadism—Therapy. 2. Masochism—Therapy. 3. Narcissism
—Etiology. I. Hill, Melvyn A. II. Liendo, Ernesto César.
III. Title. [DNLM: 1. Narcissism. WM 460.5.E3 G292w]
RC560.S23G4   616.85′83506   81-65688
ISBN 0-87668-448-7   AACR2

Manufactured in the United States of America.

"But the casual relation between the determining psychical trauma and the hysterical phenomenon is not of a kind implying that the trauma merely acts like an *agent provocateur* in releasing the symptom, which thereafter leads an independent existence. We must presume rather that the psychical trauma—or more precisely the memory of the trauma—acts like a *foreign body* which long after its entry must continue to be regarded *as an agent that is still at work*; and we find the evidence for this in a highly remarkable phenomenon which at the same time lends an important practical interest to our findings.

For we found, to our great surprise at first, that each individual hysterical symptom immediately and permanently disappeared when we had succeeded in bringing clearly to light the memory of the event by which it was provoked and in arousing its accompanying affect, and when the patient had described that event in the greatest possible detail and had put the affects into words."

Sigmund Freud, *Studies on Hysteria*

Contents

Preface

In this book we propose a mode of psychoanalytic treatment that aims at the etiology rather than the symptoms of mental illness, that endeavors to treat the unconscious structures of the pathology rather than particular elements or conflicts that contribute to it. We regard the recent concern with the treatment of narcissism in psychoanalysis as a move in this direction.

The view of narcissism as self-sufficient in nature—a trait that blocks the way to productive and satisfying relationships and activities—bars the hope for a successful treatment. This conception retains Freud's negative prognosis that narcissism constitutes a virtually autistic barrier to therapeutic influence. Instead, we offer a concept of narcissism that shows how it is inherently accessible to the interventions and influence of a therapist. We believe narcissism should be viewed as an unconscious, bipolar structure that consists of the intrapsychic representations of an ego and an alter. One of these poles is invariably transferred in the course of therapy, thereby making the whole structure accessible to influence. In terms of the Greek myth, we include not only Narcissus but also his image reflected off the water-mirror, as well as the voice of the nymph Echo.

Narcissism is a psychic structure that unconsciously governs the relationship between the subject and his or her "others" so that they serve as each other's reflecting mirror. This structure can be traced back to the earliest relationship of the child to its parents—the "others" who first served as reflecting mirrors and demanded their reflection back in return. In the therapeutic relationship the dynamic of mirroring is once more at issue in the transference–countertransference process, where the subject makes every effort to seduce or compel the therapist into becoming a mirror for the reflection that the subject projects onto him.

In order to design a treatment that helps the analysand transform the narcissistic controller of his interactions, it is first necessary to describe and understand the reciprocal mirrored interaction of the subject and his "others" that drives him into mental illness. Only then can the process be reversed through a precise, powerful, and specific treatment based on the etiology of the illness. In this book we concentrate on the introjected and continuously projected narcissistic structure that consists of a pathogenic, bipolar, mirror relationship with an alter.

There are two fundamental variables in the constitution of this kind of structure between the ego and the generalized other, or alter. First, economic control is vested in one of the partners and classifies the ego or the alter as either a controlling agent or a controlled patient within the relationship. Second, affective control classifies the ego as either a dominant sadist or a dominated masochist of the complementary alter. Thus Narcissus can be a sadistic agent who controls and dominates the alter, a masochistic patient who is controlled and dominated by the alter, a masochistic agent who controls but is dominated by the alter, or a sadistic patient who is controlled but dominates the alter. The one who exercises economic control is not always the one who exercises affective control, but it does appear that the exercise of economic control in the relationship is the more important of the two. Therefore we have used it as the criterion to discriminate between agents and patients.

In our view the agent, whether a masochist or a sadist, is chiefly responsible for transmitting and perpetuating mental illness with the unconscious complicity of the patient. This pattern is the key to our psychoanalytic epidemiology; since it is activated again in the transference and countertransference, we are able to work through it and reverse its effects. The analysand transfers onto the therapist what was previously his own countertransference reflection. He was a mirror for the transference of the original alters who operated as sadistic or masochistic agents at a time when he or she depended on them biologically and economically. The success of the therapy depends on whether the therapist is able to transform this mirrored, sadomasochistic structure that unfolds in the trans-ference–countertransference relationship and not become "alterized"; that is, contaminate or be contaminated in the therapeutic situation.

When Lasegue and Folret first postulated a folie à deux kind of relationship, they described three elements:
1. The clinical characteristics of the delusional lunatic, or agent, that provokes the delire à deux.
2. The clinical characteristics of the rational lunatic who always accompanies him.
3. The characteristics of the delusional pact, consisting of the mutual compromises that push them into the communicated insanity.
We have dedicated this book to the careful description of these three elements in the psychopathology of provoking agents and provoked patients and the pact between them.

If the therapist intends to help the analysand transform this kind of narcissistic structure, he or she must always have in mind both poles of this reciprocal relationship as they function intrapsychically and interpersonally. The therapist becomes the rational alter who mirrors the two reflecting mirrors, and he or she must constantly take care not to fall into the role of the rational lunatic who, instead of interrupting and healing the chain of interactions whereby mental illness is transmitted, becomes yet another link in it. To help in this task we have drawn on linguistics and semiotics in order to provide maximum precision and sophistication in the analysis of the subtle and powerful structure of verbal and nonverbal mirrors. We have also drawn on concepts from structuralism and political theory and have focused on developing a model of psychoanalytic treatment that is illustrated throughout the book with precise clinical material.

Acknowledgments

We would like to acknowledge the help and inspiration of some of those who have contributed to our work and made it possible: Hannah Arendt, David Bakan, Morris Eagle, Mauricio Goldenberg, André Green, Leon Grinberg, Anne Leslie Hill, Juan Miguel Hoffmann, Kathy Johnston, David Liberman, Robert Martin, Jorge Posadas, Harry Prosen, Eugene Supinski, and Lila Vega.

INTRODUCTION
The Sadomasochistic Quality of the Narcissistic Mirror

Psychoanalysis is pursued in many different parts of the world, and the elaboration and clarification of its theory and practice varies with the influence of cultural traditions and institutional arrangements. Given the constraints of time and difficulties of communication that limit the contact between the different schools of psychoanalysis, it is not surprising to find that colleagues in different parts of the world may be working on a similar set of problems without having the chance to benefit from each other's efforts. It seems as if a series of discrete national and even regional versions of psychoanalysis have been created and that they have little of interest to say to one another; yet in fact there are extremely valuable gains to be made by anyone who takes the trouble to compare the various contributions.

We have attempted to integrate certain features of the European and American schools of psychoanalysis in order to solve what are universally recognized as the most resistant problems in the field today. Our hope has been that, with the benefit of a clear and precise theory, we would be able to develop a more effective mode of therapy. The reader will probably be curious to know which European influences, in particular, we have taken into account. Without going into detailed explanation—which is provided in the course of our book—we can give some indication of what we have included.

1

If one looks at the extensive body of psychoanalytic literature it becomes apparent that most psychoanalytic writing consists of a search for a more profound angle of interpretation—one that multiplies continuously without reaching a resolution, as if there were some underlying depth or complexity still to be plumbed. Unfortunately, this quest is doomed to fail unless one realizes that it is the unifying structure (and not its virtually infinite aspects or variations) that constitutes the key to unconscious overdeterminations of pathology. This is the basic insight of the structural psychoanalysis founded in France by Jacques Lacan, and influenced by the structural linguistics of Ferdinand de Saussure and by the structural anthropology of Claude Lévi-Strauss. Some of the works of the French school have been translated in recent years, largely in response to the interests of persons working in such fields as anthropology and literary criticism; but because of its apparent obscurity and lack of clinical applicability it has had little influence in the mental health disciplines. One of the tasks we have undertaken is to make the contribution of structuralism accessible to the practitioner both theoretically and practically. The same applies to the richness of the Kleinian school in England, with its own theoretical development, which has had a minimal influence in the United States.

At the same time we have been able to integrate recent developments in semiotics, communications theory, and political theory in order to clarify and simplify the psychoanalytic model and to codify psychoanalytic technique, so that clinical discoveries can be more easily transmitted.

Narcissism: A Fundamental Concept

Along with many psychoanalysts around the world, we have found that the fundamental problem yet to be resolved in psychoanalysis is that of narcissism (Freud 1914); in pragmatic terms this is the problem of how to get through to the analysand. It is the source of much frustration to the analyst to find that despite diligently following the rules of procedure and conscientiously working through the analysis, no change really takes place in the analysand's psychic structure or his compulsive patterns of behavior.

In the recent American literature on the subject, the work of Otto Kernberg (1975) and Heinz Kohut (1971) stands out. Both attempt to tackle this issue, albeit from different perspectives. Kernberg emphasizes the role of pathological narcissism as a defense against infantile sadism and the identification system that goes along with it, whereas Kohut sees the problem of narcissism largely as a traumatic fixation at an otherwise normal stage of development.

The implications of these new attempts to solve the problem of narcissism have already emerged in the debate between Kernberg and Kohut themselves. From our point of view there are two initial observations.

The first is that Kernberg has absorbed the Kleinian prejudice in favor of infantile sadism as an explanation, overlooking infantile masochism, a possibility noted by Freud (1924). This tends to give Kernberg's theory a bias that would be reflected in a differential outcome in the treatment of sadistic and masochistic analysands, both of whom are in fact narcissistic. Our second observation is that Kohut's recommendation for the treatment of a narcissistic analysand would put the analyst always in the position of an indulgent mother. With a sadistic analysand, this would simply satisfy his narcissistic demands, thereby confirming him in his neurosis while compelling the analyst to become masochistic in relation to him. The masochistic analysand would be stabilized by this form of treatment, but would not be likely to work through his deepest conflicts.

In our view (Gear and Liendo 1975a,b), narcissism is a structural condition and is neither a defense nor a fixation but a bipolar organization of the psychic apparatus that always alternates between a sadistic and a masochistic position, each being the necessary complement and mirror of the other. Our theory explains narcissism as a bipolar structure with sadism and masochism as the two poles and provides a detailed method of analyzing the narcissistic analysand, whether he presents himself as a sadist or as a masochist (Gear and Liendo 1980a).

THE CONCEPT OF NARCISSISM AS A PHENOMENON OF NARCISSISM

During the last decade, the problem of narcissism has emerged as a focus of concern in American social theory and American psychoanalytic circles. This renewed interest in narcissism (which was introduced as early as 1914 by Freud) has grown out of an increasing sense that something has been missing from conventional North

American social psychology and psychoanalysis. An obvious sense of frustration informs the literature, and an intense search has begun for a new approach that will provide the missing intellectual and therapeutic link.

The concept of narcissism has been used to explain the persistence of social and psychic structures that are neither adaptive nor transformable, but the development of the concept in America has so far failed to provide the means to overcome this persistence. Rather, American psychoanalysis tends to reify the phenomenon even as it appears to explain it. The veil of narcissism, although perceived, has yet to be lifted.

Ironically, insofar as the theory of narcissism fails to resolve the underlying issue, it becomes an unconscious rationalization of the problem it is supposed to solve. In the same way, an ineffectual psychoanalysis becomes an end in itself: "the disease of which it professes to be the cure," in the words of Karl Kraus. We could say that, in some sense, the theory of narcissism is the phenomenon of which it professes to be the concept.

What is missing in the current theory of narcissism is the recognition of power and authority and their role in the pathological structures of social institutions and interpersonal relations. This lack of awareness of power and authority in the analytic setting is also the source of the therapeutic inefficacy of psychoanalysis. Without a clear understanding of the role of power and authority in maintaining the legitimacy of a structure it is impossible to analyze how and why the structure persists, let alone to change it successfully.

Because of the inadequacy of psychoanalysis both as a field of inquiry and as a therapeutic institution, it has lost prestige in North American culture. For the most part it is seen as passé—an esoteric and expensive method of contemplation that becomes an end in itself for those inclined to the solipsistic cultivation of their intellectual self-consciousness.

Like the contemplative disciplines of earlier eras—the meditations of the philosopher seeking consolation, the monk's pursuit of salvation, or the Renaissance man's cultivation of an internal harmony—psychoanalysis is perceived as an unrewarding withdrawal from mundane concerns into a rarefied pursuit of truths which lie buried in the deepest layers of subjectivity. Only those with time and money to spare can afford to indulge themselves in the search;

the rest are compelled to take care of the pressing concerns of everyday life, or to attend to immediate affective needs. The one exception is the group of analysands who have entered psychoanalysis for the advancement of a career in the mental health professions. This exception only proves the rule that one would have to be an incipient navel-gazer to go into psychoanalysis, unless one has a "real" motive for doing so. In other words, psychoanalysis itself has become identified with narcissism in the culture.

The most common understanding of narcissism is the belief that it is a self-contained structure. A narcissistic person is seen as someone so involved with himself that he does not respond to others, and in that sense impervious to influence. It is precisely this kind of person who (since Freud) we are told presents the greatest resistance to psychoanalysis, and who enjoys the greatest chance of success within the social institutions currently prevailing (see Kohut 1971, Lasch 1979).

Because they can see no reason to be open with others, narcissists seem to be immune to the influence of power; yet, paradoxically, power accrues to them because, by contrast, everyone else is involved in transferences and countertransferences that keep them on a constant treadmill of human interaction. To some extent this model of the narcissistic personality is a sophisticated rendering of the ideal of independence, autonomy, and self-sufficiency in the cultural ideology.

We wish to introduce a recognition of the importance of power and authority into psychoanalytic theory and practice in the hope of opening up the persistent narcissistic structures—of both personality and human interaction—to effective therapeutic change and the possibility of freedom.

The whole picture of narcissism changes and the structure itself is transformed if one breaks through the myth of its self-containment or self-sufficiency. For instance, a narcissistic analysand who is dismissed as unanalyzable after several years of analysis can hardly be described as "self-contained," since he has been engaged in seeking help from another on whom he has depended all that time. Here, in the domain of narcissism, we can clearly see both transference and countertransference at work, although the conventional theory of narcissism would tell us that the analysand is unanalyzable because he does not transfer. The analysand has simply transferred impotence onto the analyst who has countertransferred omnipotence onto the analysand. In our view the omnipotence (self-containment) of the analysand has in fact been sustained by the impotence that he induced in his analyst.

The so-called narcissist, who, according to Christopher Lasch (1979), can maneuver himself into a dominant position in our social institutions, is self-contained only in the sense that others also transfer this kind of omnipotence onto him while accepting his countertransference of impotence. Underlying the appearance of narcissistic self-sufficiency and unconcern about others is an extremely subtle arrangement that has been negotiated with them. The success of the antisocial personality is only a specific kind of social relationship; once it is recognized as such, it loses its fascinating hold on the observer and becomes accessible to theoretical understanding and practical thinking.

Once we recognize the underlying relationships that inform narcissistic structures, we discover that they are power structures that generate an authority which obstructs freedom of action for everyone involved. Only by applying a different kind of power can the authority of the narcissistic alignment of power be overcome, and the possibility of using power to act freely be introduced.

THE NARCISSISTIC FINESSE OF PSYCHOANALYSIS

In our view, narcissism revolves around a fundamental bipolar structure that has traditionally been described as sadomasochistic in psychoanalysis, and as the master-slave dialectic in philosophy. What has not been clear in psychoanalysis is the fact that this structure turns on the partnership between a sadist and a masochist (French psychiatry calls this *folie à deux*, a term coined by Lasègue and Falret [1873]). Psychoanalysis has extended the concept of sadomasochism beyond the perversions described by sexologists, and stressed not only the isomorphism and complementarity between the two perversions but denoted a pair of opposites just as fundamental to the evolution of instinctual life as its manifestations. In brief, *sadomasochism seems to be a universal and basic way of dealing with destructiveness in order to avoid the disorganization of the psychic apparatus.*

The conventional narcissist as defined in social theory and in psychoanalysis basically conforms to our concept of the sadist, who looks for his own satisfaction at the expense of the frustration of others. We think that the masochist is equally narcissistic but is immune to his own suffering (the frustration provoked by the satisfaction of others) rather than immune to his own insecurity, like the sadist. The self-containment of either partner in the sadomasochistic relationship is made possible by the mirror that the other partner constantly holds up—a mirror in which he sees the reflection of himself as he wants to be seen. He thereby confirms the myth of his self-containment as a sadist or his helplessness as a masochist.

In narcissism, as in any form of personality structure, it is only through the other that one can have an identity confirmed. What obscures this in the case of a narcissistic partnership is that the other does not confirm one's identity through himself, but rather by holding up a mirror to the other, as Echo does for Narcissus. Thus, the analyst who finds his analysand immune to analysis fails to realize that their real relationship (as well as what has been transferred and countertransferred) remains unanalyzed: it has been conducted through the looking-glass. We can argue that "identity" can be defined and acquire meaning only through opposition and difference with *alterity*: our image depends not only on the image that we have of ourselves but also on the image that others have of themselves and of us. Identity and alterity always form a bipolar structure.

Analysts are particularly vulnerable to the narcissistic invitations (inducements) of their analysands because one of the basic rules of analytic practice requires that the analyst be a mirror to the analysand. This meets all too well the basic requirements of a narcissistic relationship where one is (induced to be) the mirror to the other.

Of course there is a distinction between Freud's concept of the analytic mirror (1914) and that of the narcissistic looking-glass. The analyst-as-mirror is supposed to reflect an accurate articulation of the analysand's pathological inducements. The narcissist-as-mirror-to-another narcissist is only supposed to reflect the opposite of his partner's inducements. The masochist accepts the sadist's dependence on him but reflects an image of him as independent, while the sadist accepts the masochist's independence but reflects an image of him as dependent. Neither sees the mirror that the other holds because each believes the confirming reflection in it to be true.

Unless the analyst is aware of the narcissistic mirror-function, his analytic mirror-function will be finessed. This is only a variation of the finessing that ordinarily occurs in narcissistic partnerships where the mutual exchange of identity and alterity (of self and other and object) is short-circuited and the relationship becomes a nonmutual structure consisting of superior and inferior, or of a master and slave.

We are using the term *finesse* as it is applied in the game of bridge, where one induces an opponent to play his most powerful card in a suit and then trumps it with an even more powerful card, one that the opponent does not suspect will be played. Applying this analogy to the analytic situation, one could say that the unsuspecting analyst plays his most powerful card to form what he believes to be a therapeutic relationship with the analysand (in the classical sense), only to fall victim to the analysand's unconscious finesse of the analytic relationship. This finesse induces the analyst's narcissistic partnership, thereby trumping his card.

Obviously the analyst must become aware of the analysand's unconscious finessing of the analytic process. This is the first step toward a transformation, but it is not sufficient in itself. In our view the narcissistic structure that the analysand presents is a constellation of power, and can be transformed only by the application of counter-vailing powers. Theoretically, this means that the analyst will be aware of the possible narcissistic ploys of the analysand so that he may strategically pull the analysand out of the sadomasochistic pattern. (In chapter 9 we will provide an overview of the specific initiatives that the analyst can take to countervail the narcissistic power of the analysand's attempts to transform him into a sadistic or a masochistic mirror.)

There are a range of antinarcissistic interventions based on the specific use of therapeutic power. These do not constitute a set of options to be adapted for the sake of a personal style of analysis; on the contrary, they become essential wherever the analyst encounters the analysand's immunity. The basis of the narcissistic structure is built and held together by the dissuasion of a pathological other and can therefore only be dissolved if the analytic interpretations are supported by the power of therapeutic counterdissuasions. These counterdissuasions must be perceived by the analysand as more powerful in the present situation than the continuously repeated narcissistic interaction with the destructive other. This may be clarified by a brief discussion of the compulsion to repeat that is manifest in the analysand's pattern of acting-out.

From Compulsion to Action

Our meaning of the term acting-out is not confined to uncontrolled, irresponsible, impulsive behavior, but refers to typical actions of the analysand that are constantly self-defeating in view of his long-term goals. Let us start from the simple observation that in nonpathological behavior one adopts a goal and acts (through specific actions) in order to obtain it. We will use the concept of "specific action"—developed by Freud (1895) in his "Project"—to describe free, healthy, conscious actions. In some ways, it is the opposite of the concept of acting-out used to describe compulsive, pathological, unconscious actions. In the case of acting-out, however, the analysand is deflected from his goal—the analytic cure, for instance—by a compelling inner pressure exerted by the introjected other. We might call this *compelling-out* rather than acting-out, and we might say that the impulses behind an acting-out are really *compulses.*

It is precisely against the acting-out as compelling-out that the analyst must direct his therapeutic counterpressures, and avoid provoking a pathological counter-compelling-out. A clear example is Freud's (1918) intervention in the case of the Wolf Man, where, after realizing that the analysis was not progressing (because he was compelled to act as a nullifying overprotector), he decided to apply a strategic therapeutic counterpressure by setting an arbitrary time limit to the analytic process if the analysand did not make some specific changes. This pressure not only led the Wolf Man to overcome his phobic reaction to the real world, but also, as Freud himself comments, to a most productive working-through of the analysis. Up to this point the Wolf Man, subject to internal compulsions, had pressured Freud to allow him to maintain a masochistic position in their relationship. This pressure was undermining the analytic work, and the analysand was using the analytic relationship for the sake of a narcissistic repetition in which he pushed Freud into the position of an overprotector who could then be accused of castrating him.

Consequently, just as the concept of a superego implies that power is a relevant factor, the concept of compulsion to repeat refers to a power relationship between a compeller and a compelled. The compelled pole could be the ego, for example, and the compeller could be any of its three masters: the superego, the id, or the external world. But, at the same time, the ego itself can be a compeller of others whom it would like to transform into its narcissistic mirrors.

THE PSYCHOANALYTIC FINESSE OF NARCISSISM

The theoretical development of this book may appear somewhat strange and difficult to follow to the reader because it depends upon a number of fields that one does not commonly integrate into psychoanalysis. We offer the following brief explanation of our theory to reassure our readers that our purpose is a practical one: to increase the therapeutic power of psychoanalysis.

Chapter 1 presents the clinical evidence for distinguishing between four classes of analysands. We argue that the analyst must approach each class in a different way and that a metapsychology must be developed to accommodate this distinction.

In our view the traditional metapsychology primarily defines the intrapsychic situation of the sadist. It does not, however, suggest specific means for analyzing sadists. On the contrary, we find that the sadistic "agent" as an analysand tends to transform his analyst into a masochistic "patient." The classical approach also tends to induce the analyst to become a sadistic agent in relation to those analysands who are masochistic patients, thereby reinforcing their pathology. In both instances, therefore, we see the iatrogenic potential of psychoanalysis at work. Our intention is to rework the metapsychology and the recommendations for treatment in order to reverse these situations.

Chapter 2 is devoted to developing a semiotic model of the psychic apparatus (Gear and Liendo 1975a) based on Freud's topographic model (1900) and his theory of psychic representation. "Semiotic" here means that we understand psychic representations both as significations and communications; we are concerned to show how both the sadistic and the masochistic organization can be understood in terms of the first Freudian model. By "semiotic model" we mean that the psychic apparatus can be conceived as a system of signs, or symbolic representations of the subject himself as well as the others.

In chapter 3 we demonstrate how semiotics, as an instrument and not merely as a model, permits a systematic analysis of the speech, actions, and affects of the analysand. Two new technical instruments—the psychotomogram and psychic flowchart—are developed which allow the analyst to arrive at a comprehensive breakdown of both the analysand's intrapsychic structure and its reflection in the sequential patterns of interaction typical of his compulsion to repeat.

The first three chapters of the book represent a summation of work previously published by us in Spanish, French, and Italian (Gear and Liendo 1975a,b; 1976; 1977; 1979; 1980a,b).

The second section of this book is based on the second Freudian model—the structural theory—in which Freud (1923) himself gave a second meaning to the concept of psychic representations—namely, that these are also political representations that reflect the relations of power obtaining between the ego and its significant others when the ego tries to satisfy its desires at the expense of others, and vice versa. In our work this becomes the semiotic representation of the political representation which culminates in the concept of superego.

Freud recognized that the issue of sadomasochism is central to the functioning of the psychic apparatus, but assumed that where it was pathological, the superego would be the sadistic agent and the ego its masochistic partner. *We argue that this describes the psychological makeup of the masochistic patient only. We believe that in the case of the sadistic agent the relations of power are reversed and that the ego is sadistic, while the superego* (as the introjected parents) *is masochistic. Thus, in the case of a sadistic agent, the introjected others cannot properly be called a superego since they are in an inferior position with respect to the ego. In the terminology we will adopt, the sadist's introjected others will be called an inferalter.* (See Figure 0-1 (a)).

In chapters 4, 5, 6, and 8 a general psychoanalytic theory is developed; this theory proceeds from an empirical basis to the theoretical model and defines the rules of correspondence between the two. In chapter 7 we reconstruct the relationship between topog-

	SADIST	MASOCHIST
SUPER	EGO	ALTER
INFER	ALTER	EGO

Figure 0-1 (a).   The positions of ego and alter

raphy and defense in the development of psychoanalysis in order to explain the theoretical background of our model.

To help the reader orient himself we provide Figure 0-1 (b), which shows where the original Freudian concepts are located in terms of our new model of the unconscious representations of ego and alter. This diagram indicates the unconscious structure of representation of the ego and the alter for the sadist and the masochist. We will show how these are reversed in consciousness. Thus the conscious representation of ego and alter is precisely the opposite of its unconscious representation. Here we are taking a position that disagrees with an ego psychology in which the inversion between the conscious and unconscious representations of the ego (or the alter) is overlooked in favor of a simple representation of each. In our view that would lead to acceptance of the analysand's distorted conscious representations of himself and others, leading to a therapeutic stalemate. There is a conscious identity (and alterity) as well as reversed unconscious one.

In chapter 9 we attempt to integrate an analysis of the social and political dimensions of sadomasochism with the expectations of analytic treatment and in chapter 10 we redefine the classical recommendations for analytic treatment based on what we perceive are the requirements of an effective psychoanalysis—one that can transform the intrapsychic and interpersonal narcissistic power relationships central to the psychoanalytic model of the psychic apparatus. In dealing with these relationships, the analyst should arrive—through "negotiations" with the inner and outer agents of mental illness—at a

	SADIST	MASOCHIST
SUPER	EGO [Grandiose Ideal Ego]	ALTER [Proscribing Superego + Prescribing Ego Ideal]
INFER	ALTER	EGO

Figure 0-1 (b).   The positions of ego and alter

common course of therapeutic action which would be supported by all the parties involved. This would create a new source of analytic power which would enable the analyst and patient to undertake deeper and broader joint action and transform their closed narcissistic system into an open one, transforming the psychic slavery imposed by the pleasure principle into the psychic freedom allowed by the reality principle.

At the basis of our model of the psychic apparatus is a theory of transmission. The theory of psychic bipolarity is not intended to be a description and explanation of psychic structure which, however subtle and sophisticated, ends up suggesting that the deepest problems are intrinsic to the individual's constitution. So often psychoanalysts come to this conclusion because they despair of finding an answer to the ultimate source of the problem. The result is always that, however dialectical the approach seems to be—a dialectic between the drives, between subject and object, between pleasure and reality—the key to the problem turns out to be the psychic monad, which is nothing more than the common understanding of narcissism as the source of all intractable problems, and, one could say, of all evil.

We believe, however, that the problem of narcissism can only be understood and resolved in terms of its dialectical structure. To see the narcissist as the monadic source of his own problem is in some sense to confer a legitimacy on his narcissism that cannot be challenged in theory or in practice. The result of this is profound pessimism in both psychotherapy and social science. This monadic theory of narcissism protects the very problem that it identifies, and in the end one has to conclude that it is also protecting the theorist's or the practitioner's own narcissisim.

Once narcissism is understood not to be the characteristic of particular individuals but rather of a structure of binary opposition, it can be analyzed and overcome. But this means that the partners to a narcissistic bond (including a narcissistic bond between analyst and analysand) cannot blame each other, or, for that matter, blame such impersonal constitutional factors as temperament, tolerance for anxiety, or drive level. Thus the phenomenon of transmission becomes central to our model of the psychic apparatus. Narcissism is transmitted by induction between the two or three people (who can be reduced to two, as we will show), and does not arise from the mysterious depths of nature.

The inspiration for our theory of transmission has come from structuralism, which presents culture as a set of structures organized on the axis of binary oppositions. These structures attempt to contain a fundamental contradiction within an opposition that appears to organize it logically. Lévi-Strauss (1963) takes as his point of departure the contradiction between nature and culture that gives constant rise to myths which attempt to overcome it by a series of logical oppositions inherent in the representations of nature. Lacan (1966) first applied this theory at the psychological level, because implicit in the contradiction between nature and culture is the contradiction between body and mind—the point of departure for psychoanalysis. Freud himself makes this clear when he attributes the vulnerability of the psychic apparatus to the relative prematurity of the human neonate, or to the simple fact that the apparatus is not given at birth but has to be organized in order to adapt the infant (and later the child) to the demands of reality as defined by culture and society.

The survival and pleasure of the infant depends entirely on the aid that it receives from the mother and father. It is in this bipolar relationship, where the initiative rests primarily with the parent (since the infant is dependent), that the narcissistic structure may originate if the mother and father fail to recognize the desire of the infant but instead induce in it the complement to their own unconscious and repressed desire. Thus, the child is educated to be a mirror and to find others who will in turn mirror its own repressed, unconscious desire.

With this concept of the inducement to enter a narcissistic structure, narcissism loses its apparent self-containment and inaccessible monadism. Consequently, we believe that our theory of psychic bipolarity offers a more optimistic view of the future of psychotherapy and social relations.

REFERENCES

Freud, S. (1895). Project for a scientific psychology. *Standard Edition* 1: 281-397.
—— (1900). The interpretation of dreams. *Standard Edition* 4/5.
—— (1905). Fragment of an analysis of a case of hysteria. *Standard Edition* 7:7-122.
—— (1909). Analysis of a phobia in a five-year-old boy. *Standard Edition* 10:3-149.
—— (1914). On narcissism: an introduction. *Standard Edition* 14:67-102.
—— (1918). From the history of an infantile neurosis. *Standard Edition* 17:3-122.
—— (1923). The ego and the id. *Standard Edition* 19:3-66.
—— (1924). The economic problem of masochism. *Standard Edition* 19:159-173.
—— (1930). Civilization and its Discontents. *Standard Edition* 21:59-145.
Gear, M. C., and Liendo, E. C. (1975a). *Sémiologie psychanalytique.* Paris: Minuit.
—— (1975b). *Psicoterapia della coppia e del gruppo familiare.* Florence: del Riccio.
—— (1976). *Psicoanálisis del paciente y de su ambiente.* Buenos Aires: Nueva Visión.
—— (1977). *Informática psicoanalitica.* Buenos Aires: Nueva Visión.
—— (1979). *Action psychanalytique.* Paris: Minuit.
—— (1980a). *Psicoanálisis del paciente y de su agente.* Buenos Aires: Nueva Visión.
—— (1980b). *Matemática psicoanalitica.* Buenos Aires: Nueva Visión.
Kernberg, O. (1975). *Borderline Conditions and Pathological Narcissism.* New York: Jason Aronson.
Kohut, H. (1971). *The Analysis of the Self.* New York: International Universities Press.
Lasègue, C., and Falret, J. (1873). La folie à deux ou folie communiquée. *American Journal of Psychiatry* 4:1-23, 1964.
Lacan, J. (1966). *Ecrits.* Paris: Editions du Seuil.
Lasch, C. (1979). *The Culture of Narcissism.* New York: Warner Books.
Lévi-Strauss, C. (1963). *Structural Anthropology.* New York: Basic Books.

1
The Sadomasochistic Chain of Mental Illness

The Four Classes of Analysands

Many years devoted to intense and varied psychoanalytical clinical work led us to the inescapable (and alarming) conclusion that our theory was suffering from a fundamental fault that affected our technique and practice. It was not just a "split" between theory and practice, or a lack of scientific systematization or technical rationalizations. It seemed rather a question of contradictions and paradoxes (Russell 1927)—some of them true logical antinomies, between the sophistication of our explanations of the patients' behaviors and the efficiency of our therapeutic operations.

One of the principal methodological, theoretical and technological discoveries (Gear and Liendo 1979b) that resulted was that the universe of mentally sick persons is made up not only of the "patients" suffering the anxieties and mutilation of mental illness, but also of the "agents" that unconsciously or preconsciously reinforce and transmit such anxieties and mutilations. We discovered that neither the phenomenology nor the deep dynamic understanding of "patients" was identical to that of "agents." It was a question of "class" and "complement," and not just a single-member class: there exist persons who, as carriers, permanently reproduce and transmit psychic damage, and there also exist others who are the receivers of this damage. These observations led us to revise our ideas about the transmission and perpetuation of mental illness.

17

Analyzing the record of the psychoanalytic experience with transference and countertransference neuroses (Freud 1914a), we realized that we frequently used a theory and technology of *victims* of mental illness to understand and modify the *transmitters* of mental illness. When this mismanagement occurred we had the potential to become iatrogenic agents of mental illness, including our own, instead of agents of mental health (Gear and Liendo 1975). If we treated patients as if they were agents, we became reinforcing agents. Conversely, if we treated agents as if they were patients, we were assuming the position of the patients.

Apart from this, we overlooked an operational classification of the patient which would allow a better understanding of his psychopathology and epidemiology. Our psychoanalytical theory of psychic bipolarity is a tentative ordering and integrating of the main intra- and interdisciplinary clinical and operative hypotheses that we use each day with different classes of the sick population: the patients and agents of patients who, voluntarily or involuntarily, consult us. We tried to approach the phenomena with a different epidemiological mentality, taking into consideration the agent, the whole cycle of contamination, and the susceptibility of the different types of patients. Then we were able to study the psychopathological disturbances which result from the three main sickness-producing factors: censorship, dependency, and blackmail (Schelling 1960).

When we analyzed the values and objectives of patients and agents we found that their mental illness was due, to a considerable degree, to their lack of knowledge about both the cognitive structure of the psychic system and the symbolic complexities of the corresponding social environment (Lévi-Strauss 1963). They were unable to correlate the signals with their traumatic consequences. In the same way that an aphasic driver fails to interpret a warning signal and react accordingly, the patients showed a poor semiotic understanding of the warning signals of the external world. For instance, the phobic patient will do his best to avoid irrational danger but will be easily seduced by the complementary agent who will continue to destroy him by way of fear-provoking protection. At the same time, the agent will not be aware of the destructive interaction because he will feel that he is helping without recognizing the systematic disqualification of the patient's capabilities. The agent and the patient both believe that overprotection and dependence are sources of pleasure. This kind of interaction stultifies them to the point where they conceive human relations as being ruled by a perverted pleasure principle, which provides a very inferior quality of enjoyment. So, the pathological communication "from unconscious to unconscious" (Freud 1914) is not merely a deceitful communication; it is also subliminal and incomplete.

In short, we may state that the psychoanalyst is an interpreter of the deep psychic signs and that he must follow the Socratic method in order to be a thorough interpreter: he discovers and teaches *per via di levare* (Freud 1914c) the limitations of the symbolic and meta-symbolic universe of the sick (Gear and Liendo 1975). The sick person must learn to reinterpret his own conscious and unconscious signs, having previously learned his conscious and unconscious values and objectives together with his conscious and unconscious compulsive and repetitive intellectual limitations.

The way to this disalienating process is to make the analysand aware of his own defense mechanisms, so that patients understand their tendency to melancholic identifications and agents understand how their projections operate in an attempt to get rid of painful affects.

In this chapter we proceed to set out a series of fairly rigid distinctions between the sadistic agent and the masochistic patient, or between the masochistic agent and the sadistic patient, as they become manifest in terms of character and also in the analytic setting. In doing so we do not mean to give the impression that we are dismissing the valuable work that has been done in the classification of psychopathological syndromes at either a clinical or an operational level. Nor are we insisting that our hypotheses are the only ones required in psychoanalysis. On the contrary, we are offering these hypotheses in order to strengthen the hand of the psychoanalyst in his efforts to classify the psychopathological disposition of his analysands and to develop a strategy specifically designed for their therapeutic needs.

Our point of departure was the discovery that the systems of classification already in use did not adequately take into account the power structure that obtains in the psychic apparatus and that interacts with the various styles of defense, creating an asymmetrical relationship between the ego and the superego critical to the structure of the personality and the outcome of the analytic process.

What we are now proposing as an additional and crucial dimension is the classification of analysands according to two new sets of variables superimposed upon the various neurotic styles. It first must be determined whether the analysand is an *agent* or a *patient* in terms of the distribution of power in his significant object relations. The agent is in charge of reality in his relationships (he makes the economic decisions, he can make the other obey by persuasion or dissuasion, etc.); the patient is subject to the rule of his agent. The patient and the agent constitute a structure of mutual dependency, although only the former appears to be dependent. The sadist obtains pleasure at the expense of his significant others and is unconcerned about security. The masochist, on the other hand, is primarily concerned with security, and in order to obtain it sacrifices his pleasure to satisfy his significant other.

As Figure 1-1 shows, there are essentially four classes of analysands: the sadistic agent, the masochistic patient, the masochistic agent, and the sadistic patient. (Later in this chapter we will explain why we consider the last two classes as "borderliner" and "borderlined," as shown in the figure.) This suggests that for the hysterical agent (who seduces) there is an hysterical patient (who is seduced), and so on with respect to the other neurotic concerns. Also, in terms of interventions, it is the patients who respond most readily to interpretations while the agents need the additional interventions (parameters) in order to be analyzed according to the basic rule.

By unifying psychoanalytic theory at a new level of abstraction, our object has been to make it easier to grasp, especially as a guide

	SADISM	MASOCHISM
AGENT	SADIST	BORDERLINER
PATIENT	BORDERLINED	MASOCHIST

Figure 1-1.   The four classes of analysands

to practice. We consider the clinical data in their psychoanalytic setting, their setting of significant object relations that both affect and are affected by the psychoanalysis, and their setting in society. These observable data are the clinical descriptions of the ways in which the interdependence between sadistic and masochistic persons perpetuates the transmission of mental illness.

One of the principle clinical consequences of the development and integration of the three theoretical levels is the classification of different types of diagnosis, prognosis, treatment and prophylaxis of patients and agents of mental illness. The topics, dynamics, and economics are different and, in fact, complementary. Agents are, in a way, the inverted mirror of patients, just as the water and the nymph Echo are the visual and auditory mirrors of Narcissus.

Clinical Differences between Patients and Agents

Freud's case histories reveal how he attributed the role of "external agents" of the neurotic perturbations of his patients (Freud 1914b) to parents, teachers, and society at large. These external agents were internalized, following Freud's hypothesis, as the superego, or "ideal of the ego" (Freud 1923): that is, as "internal agents" of mental illness who were projected or later transferred to new external objects. In this way a vicious circle was closed, and mental illness was perpetuated.

After many years of observing the analysand-analyst interaction, we arrived at a clinical hypothesis (Gear and Liendo 1979b) which holds that analysands can be classified into two groups clearly different with respect to how they deal with their conflicts and anxieties. Some analysands (masochistic patients) tend not only to retain and exaggerate their own anxieties and conflicts, but also to introject the analyst's conflicts and anxieties. Other analysands (sadistic agents) tend not only to project their own anxieties and conflicts onto the analyst but also to exaggerate the analyst's conflicts and anxieties.

Which group a given patient belongs to can be determined quite simply by a differential diagnositic test. If in the course of the first interview (or in any session) the analyst remains silent for fifteen or twenty minutes, for example, masochistic patients will start disqualifying (denigrating) themselves and overqualifying (idealizing) the analyst: they will say, for instance, that the analyst is not speaking because he must be bored with the nonsense that the analysand is speaking, etc. On the other hand, when analysands who are sadistic agents are faced with the same situation, they will start disqualifying the analyst while overqualifying themselves: they will say, for instance, that the analyst is not speaking because he is an inferior analyst who has no idea of what is going on, who is unable to understand the sophisticated level on which the analysand is speaking, etc.

As is well known (Freud 1914c), the analysand-analyst relationship not only has a sequential dimension, called "transference-countertransference neurosis" but also a cross-sectional dimension, called simply "transference-countertransference." In studying the transference-countertransference dimension (that is, in a broad sense, how the analysand and the analyst speak, act, and feel in a given moment within the analytic setting), there are many clear differences between the clinical behavior of the masochistic patient and of the sadistic agent.

CLINICAL TRAITS OF MASOCHISTIC PATIENTS

According to purely empirical observations, the masochistic patient can be defined by the following clinical features, which could be compared to those of the "victim" of a pathogenic "double bind" situation (Bateson 1972).

1. He is pathologically dependent, because he cannot (or he thinks he cannot) survive without the extra help of the analyst. He is a crippled, overprotected person who tends to depend on "protectors" who torture him. He thinks that the analyst will punish by abandonment any attempt at independence and autonomy.

2. He tends to disqualify and to denigrate himself as being "bad," "stupid," or "crazy." He describes himself as a victimizer of the analyst (and of others).

3. He tends to overqualify and to idealize the analyst (and others) as being "good," "clever," or "sensible." He describes the analyst as his victim.

4. He tends to induce the analyst (and others) to mistreat and torture him. He acts as a victim of the analyst.

5. He tends to induce the analyst to overqualify himself and to disqualify him. He gives the analyst the role of a judge, of a wise adult, of his own superego, while he takes the role of an accused, stupid child who must make excuses for himself.

6. He constantly tries to justify and excuse himself.

7. He avoids thinking or making big decisions regarding his survival. He expects that the analyst will take care of them. In the outside world he leaves his financial problems in the hands of others, even if the others cheat him.

8. He is constantly fearful for his survival. He accepts any kind of mistreatment on the part of the analyst provided that the analyst (or others) takes care of him.

9. He avoids being powerful, because that implies losing the protection of the analyst or of other powerful protectors.

10. He does not tolerate any dependence of the analyst (or others) on him. He punishes anybody who tries to depend on him on big issues. He is reliable only on small ones.

11. He is selectively naive: he falls constantly into the same trap that others (the analyst included) set in order to control and exploit him.

12. He is very obedient to the analyst (or others) or, in a negative way, systematically opposed to him. He tends to be "dependently independent."

13. He is a conformist, in the sense that he accepts any kind of discomfort or humiliation, if he is promised security in return.

14. He tends to be dependent solely upon the analyst because he thinks that if he does not isolate himself from other possibilities, the analyst will punish him with abandonment. He fears that he will lose the analyst as a sadistic source of security.

15. He is a hostage of the analyst because he thinks that the analyst is a jealous controller who advises him that other persons are not reliable. Moreover, he thinks that the analyst will accuse him of plotting with others against the treatment if he establishes any reliable, friendly alliances with them.

16. He is unable to take care of his reputation; he cannot form any kind of favorable consensus because he has an unconscious

"ability" to show himself socially as bad, crazy, or stupid. He turns the "neutral" witnesses against him and in favor of the analyst.

17. He is censored by himself and (he thinks) by his analyst; he feels he cannot make any unfavorable comment regarding the analytic relationship, even if that relationship is an unhealthy one.

18. He feels that he is a powerless, blackmailed person because he thinks that he is forced by his analyst to accept destructive dependency, disqualification, crippling isolation, and exploitation. He fears that the analyst will withdraw his protection and will punish him socially if he does not behave masochistically.

19. He tends to be abused by the analyst because he is a naive negotiator who always loses the battle for pleasure that he thinks he has with the analyst: he is always offering himself as a source of pleasure for the analyst provided the analyst functions as a source of overprotection for him.

20. He is a blind, affectively exploited, autodestructive puppet, narrow-minded and manipulated because he cannot conceive of any kind of pleasure and security other than that based on his giving up his pleasure, while believing in false promises and threats concerning his survival.

With Respect to the Analytic Treatment Itself, the Masochistic Patient:

21. Does not tolerate the idea that the analyst does not denigrate and disqualify him: he thinks that he is deceiving the analyst or that the analyst is just being compassionate if the analyst does not devalue him.

22. Does not tolerate the idea that the analyst does not idealize and overqualify himself: he thinks that the analyst is weak, or guilty, or unable to protect him.

23. Does not tolerate the idea that the analyst does not mistreat him in a sadistic way.

24. Has a compulsive idealized transference while splitting his negative transference and expressing it through other persons (sadistic agents) or through somatizations. He always fears that he will lose the idealized analyst.

25. Provokes an omnipotent countertransference: the analyst feels that he is a powerful master of the analysand and that he is responsible for his destiny.

26. Is addicted to the treatment and fears constantly that it might be catastrophically interrupted.

The following passage shows a typical analytic interaction with a masochistic patient. She is a twenty-eight-year-old medical doctor who is very dependent on her analyst and on her boyfriend. She came to treatment because she was feeling depressed. She has five sessions weekly.

Fragment from the Tuesday Session
(*Third Month of Analysis*)

Analysand: I even have difficulty thinking clearly, but when listening to you I think I have hope. To fight that thing that drags me down . . . that doesn't let me sleep . . . takes away the meaning of life . . . that makes me feel that everything I do is harmful and meaningless, as if I were "bad" and really useless and incurable. I don't feel like working or studying . . . Over and over, depressing ideas come into my mind. I'm not interested in anything in life. Besides not feeling well, I enjoy saying it. I can't tell anybody about the good things or when I'm feeling better.

Analyst: Maybe you're asking me to allow you to grow up, to analyze yourself, but all this is in secret without your mother or even yourself knowing it. Letting you grow up, but also allowing you to complain about it, as if you didn't have any interest in doing so. In fact, you have shown interest in the treatment beyond your discouragement.

Analysand: Yes . . . but just to be able to complain . . . although your point about it being a secret might be important. Yesterday I had a talk with Juan Carlos and confided to him some of my future plans and my fears of not being able to accomplish them. He said that I was like an ambitious little girl and that he couldn't see how I would be able to do any of those things, that I expected things for which I was not prepared. He always advises and takes care of me. I don't know what I would do without him, although when I'm okay and talk with him, everything gets worse. He likes to protect me, and I like that too. He is so sure of himself.

Fragment From the Wednesday Session

Analysand: This morning I had a discussion with Juan Carlos in relation to our sex life. It all started because I didn't want to go to bed with him. When that happens he says I'm a homosexual, sickly and dependent on my mother. But when I go *along and have sexual relations he becomes serious, distant, contemptuous . . . as if he was saying that I'm a prostitute, and further, if I don't reach an orgasm he calls me frigid, while if I climax he says I am a libertine and that surely I would like to go to bed with other men. And I think he is totally right.*

Analyst: *You are trying to convince me that Juan Carlos is very bad to you so that I will defend you. But despite how bad he seems to be, you can't break with him. In the same way that you can't break with the internal and external relationship that you keep with your mother, from whom you'd also like me to defend you.*

Analysand: *I have no cure, this is similar to what happens to me with Amalia. She complains about my being unfaithful to our friendship, but when I stay with her she says I am dependent, and that I shouldn't bother her asking continuously for protection and advice.*

Analyst: *Something similar to what you told me on Monday about the old secretary in the hospital.*

Analysand: *Since I'm not a valuable person, I try to be with valuable people, secure in themselves. I insist that you are wrong, that you think I'm better than what I really am, or simply that you are trying to cheer me up . . .*

Analyst: *Yes, but now you are telling me that I don't have anything valuable to give, that I can only feed you illusions or tell you polite lies.*

CLINICAL TRAITS OF SADISTIC AGENTS

The sadistic agent can be defined by the following clinical features, comparable to those of the "victimizer" of a pathogenic double-bind situation (Bateson 1951).

1. He is a nullifying dependency-maker because he tries to castrate or cripple the analyst through overprotection or by some other method. He thinks that the analyst will punish any attempt on his part at being dependent. It can be said that he is pathologically independent.

2. He tends to overqualify, to idealize himself, as being "good" (generous), "clever," or "sensible." He describes himself as a victim of the analyst (and of others).

3. He tends to disqualify and denigrate the analyst (and others) as being "bad," "stupid," or "crazy." He describes the analyst as victimizing him. He is an astute disqualifier, a judge who accuses the analyst of making a subtle alliance with the analysand's superego. In fact, he tries to function as a superego of the analyst.

4. He tends to induce the analyst (and others) to be mistreated or tortured by him. He acts as a victimizer of the analyst.

5. He tends to induce the analyst (and others) to disqualify himself and to overqualify him. He gives the analyst the role of one who is accused—of a stupid, bad child—who must excuse himself, while he takes the role of a judge—of a wise, blaming adult. He disguises himself as the superego of others.

6. He constantly tries to blame and accuse the analyst by criticizing his work, etc.

7. He tries to take control of all big decisions regarding not only his own survival but the survival of the analyst. He tries to "coach" the analyst in financial and political issues.

8. He is constantly fearful about his unpleasure. He accepts overprotecting the analyst, provided that the analyst (or others) functions as a masochistic source of pleasure for himself. That is, the analyst must provide hedonistic, cognitive, and ethical unpleasure in order to allow him the corresponding pleasures.

9. He avoids being powerless, because that implies losing control over the analyst (or others) as a source of pleasure and becoming a suffering, dependent little child tortured by a sadistic, powerful adult.

10. He does not tolerate any independence of the analyst (or of others) from him. He punishes anybody who tries to be independent of him on big issues by withdrawing his overprotection or by other dissuading methods.

11. He is selectively astute: he constantly sets the same trap for others (the analyst included) in order to control and exploit them.

12. He is very bossy with the analyst (and others) in a covert or an overt way. He is the one who says or suggests what must be done in the treatment.

13. He is very demanding, in the sense that he does not accept any kind of discomfort or humiliation, even if continuation of the treatment is threatened.

14. He tends to make the analyst dependent solely upon him because he thinks that if he does not isolate the analyst from other

sources of dependence, he will lose the analyst as a masochistic source of pleasure.

15. He is a kidnapper of the analyst, acting as a jealous controller who attacks any link of the analyst with others, blaming him for plotting with others against himself, particularly if the analyst establishes any casual, friendly connection with the family of the analysand. He tries to convince the analyst that the other persons (with the exception of himself) are not reliable, and that they are enemies. He is a social isolator who harshly punishes any "infidelity" of the analyst (or others).

16. He constantly attacks (or threatens to attack) the reputation of the analyst. He is a remarkable consensus-maker, because he has the ability to disqualify, torture, and exploit the analyst (and other victims) privately; but at the same time, he is able to consistently show "public opinion" that he is really a victim of the badness, craziness, or stupidity of his analyst (or others). He is the one who plots with neutral witnesses against his analyst, so he can press him, intrapsychically through the analyst's superego, and socially through professional consensus.

17. He is a censor of the analyst because he criticizes and punishes any comment by the analyst about his castrating, disqualifying, isolating, and exploitive attitude: if the analyst denounces him, he accuses the analyst again of being bad, stupid, or crazy.

18. He is a powerful blackmailer of the analyst because he tries to achieve a position from which he can force the analyst to accept a masochistic role by threatening him with withdrawal of his financial overprotection (particularly if the analyst is young), with moral criticism, and with social shame or punishment (attacks on the analyst's reputation).

19. He tries to abuse the analyst because he is dirty, tricky negotiator who always wins the battle for pleasure by forcing the analyst (and other victims) to accept a very disadvantaged master-servant agreement with him. He tries to function as a "godfather" by offering himself as a source of security for the analyst, provided the analyst functions as a masochistic source of sadistic pleasure.

20. He is a narrow-minded destructive puppeteer who tries to exploit the analyst affectively because he cannot conceive of any kind of human relations other than those based on the affective abuse of others through false promises or threats to their security.

With Respect to the Analytic Treatment Itself, the Sadistic Agent:

21. Does not tolerate the idea that the analyst does not idealize or overqualify him: he thinks that the analyst is attacking or devaluating him if he does not idealize him.

22. Does not tolerate the idea that the analyst does not disqualify or denigrate himself: he thinks that the analyst is cheating him or hiding his own deficiencies if the analyst does not devaluate himself.

23. Does not tolerate the idea that the analyst will not let him be a sadistic, mistreating analysand.

24. Has a compulsive, negative transference and splits his idealized transference by expressing it through other persons (masochistic patients) or through somatizations. He always mistrusts the devalued analyst who he thinks is tricky.

25. Provokes an impotent countertransference: the analyst feels that he is a powerless, helpless, hopeless servant of the powerful analysand who has the analyst's professional future in his hands.

26. Has a very superficial link with the treatment and is constantly threatening to abandon it.

We will now present a typical analytic interaction with a sadistic agent. He is a forty-year-old engineer who dominates his wife. He has been sent for treatment by his wife's analyst. Her analysis was not progressing because of the pathological couple relationship. The analysand continuously enrages and depresses his wife and then pleads innocence.

In the first interview, the rules of the setting were described and explained, particularly the necessity for the fundamental rule of limiting the therapeutic contact, if possible, to free associations and interpretations during the analytic hours.

The Beginning of the First Session

Analysand: I was thinking of what you told me about restricting our contact as much as possible to the analytic work . . . But I think that today I have a very special situation. You see, I forgot to tell my poor wife that I was coming to the session. She'll be expecting my phone call, and you know how nervous she is. Can you please make an exception and let me use your phone just for a few moments?

Analyst [disoriented]: *Let's see . . . Can you please elaborate a little more on that?*

Analysand: *Well . . . I don't really have too much to elaborate on that . . . Things are as simple as that . . . I don't want my wife to be concerned about my not calling her as I usually do. She doesn't know that I'm in session now.*

Analyst [disoriented]: (*Silence.*)

Analysand [after waiting for a few moments]: *Well? What do you say? Will you lend me your phone or not?* [Pause] *I see. You're like many other analysts, cold, inhuman . . . ridiculously rigid . . . I must remember that before asking you any special favor. I might have known that you wouldn't understand. It's too complicated for little minds.*

Analyst [disoriented]: (*Silence.*)

Analysand: *At least you might know that you're making my poor wife unhappy with your "technique"* [sarcastically]. *You need to be smart to be flexible . . . But I understand your position. You're afraid of doing something wrong. The poor thing . . .*

Analyst [angry]: *Let me tell you once more that, as I explained to you in our opening interviews, if we are restricting our contacts to associations and interpretations it's because we are trying to protect and enhance the analysis. On the other hand, it seems that you are trying to dump onto me your own feelings of guilt with respect to your wife: you're the one who forgot to tell her about the sessions, not me. And, moreover, it seems that not only does your wife not know that you are in session today, but that you don't know it either. You think that I should "phone" you and interpret and remind you of that. Because of your own rigidity, it is very difficult for you to accept that you are the one who is in treatment right now.*

Analysand [interrupting]: *Don't get angry, doctor. You should keep yourself under control. It seems that you don't understand that I'm not violating our agreement. It seems, moreover, that you understood literally that I was asking you for your phone. That's not true. I'm just associating about asking you for the phone. I didn't really mean that I really wanted to use your phone. As a specialist, you should know the actual meaning of your patient's words* [sarcastically].

Analyst: *I understood that you were asking me for the phone and not just associating, because you didn't make any clarification*

in this respect. By using this ambiguity you are trying, uncon-
sciously, to make me appear nervous, uncontrolled, naive and
dumb. Don't you think that this is something quite similar to
what must happen between you and your wife: when you are
trying to take care of her but she ends up crying and yelling at
you . . . depressed and feeling stupid?

The Sadomasochistic
Transference Neurosis

The narcissistic game is played between those who constantly manipulate and use consensus to make other people mentally sick, and
those who constantly manipulate and use consensus to get other
persons to make them sick: agents and patients. Agents unconsciously
blackmail patients by threatening them with the loss of their source
of survival, and patients unconsciously blackmail agents by threatening them with the loss of their source of pleasure. Patients try to
transform (transfer) their analysts into sadistic "masters" (agents of
mental illness instead of agents of mental health). They want them
to be a source of survival offered to them as a source of pleasure.
Conversely, agents try to transform (transfer) their analysts into
masochistic "servants"—into patients. They want them to be a source
of pleasure offered to them as a source of survival.

Consequently, the masochistic patient perceives his own masochism projected onto his analyst, even if he treats him as a "master-
analyst"; and the sadistic agent perceives his own sadism projected
onto his analyst even if he treats him as a "servant-analyst." Both
sadists and masochists participate in a narcissistic mirroring transference and provoke a narcissistic mirroring countertransference.
Kohut's description (1971) of a narcissistic personality disorder coincides entirely with our description of a masochistic patient: he has a
low self-esteem, a repressed dependence on his parents, and a split-
off and projected narcissistic omnipotence. On the other hand,
Kernberg's (1975) description of a narcissistic personality (the reverse
of Kohut's description) as a selfish, omnipotent person coincides
entirely with our description of a sadistic agent. It seems to us that
both authors are right but that they describe the two varieties (sadistic
and masochistic) of the same narcissistic phenomenon.

Finally, with regard to the classical North American description of borderline personalities, it seems that a special type of analysand is referred to—one who is dependent, like a masochistic patient, yet one who also tortures, like a sadistic agent. He has a diabolic ability to make the analyst responsible for all his acts and decisions and then, from this position, to behave in an irresponsible and destructive way that constantly overdemands and overconcerns the analyst. A pathogenic sequence exists that may finally lead to either an analytic cure or to an unconscious sadomasochistic agreement between the analysand and the analyst, if the latter is unable to analyze it properly. This sequence usually occurs between the masochistic patient and the sadistic agent. Of course, the sadistic agent's transference neurosis will go through a series of stages. These are opposite and complementary to the masochistic patient's transference neurosis.

As in every human story, characters are connected by specific relationships, and there is a plot sequence with an opening, development, climax, and a final agreement between the characters. This agreement can be altered afterwards by different types of crises.

The pathogenic sequence is initiated when the sadistic (or the masochistic) analysand selects his analyst; he then tries to compel the analyst to assume a powerless masochistic (or powerful sadistic) role. The analyst fights back; the analysand either resists the sadistic (or masochistic) pressures or surrenders to them. If he resists, the sadomasochism is overcome and the cure is reached. If he gives up (unconsciously, of course) he takes the position of a powerless masochistic patient (or of a powerful sadistic agent) and a final chronic, unconscious, sadomasochistic agreement is reached. This agreement can be altered by different types of crises, depending on the balance of power between the analysand and the analyst.

If the sequence is pathogenic, there will be a selecting-out (unconscious compulsive pathological object choice) and an acting-out (or compelling-out) on the part of the analysand, and a counteracting-out (or compelled-out) on the part of the analyst, until the sadomasochistic agreement is reached.

If the sequence is therapeutic, there will also be, initially, a selecting-out and an acting-out on the part of the analysand, but a specific therapeutic (antisadistic or antimasochistic) reaction on the part of the analyst followed by a specific (nonsadistic or nonmasochistic) therapeutic action from the analysand until a nonsadomasochistic therapeutic agreement is reached.

TRANSFERENCE NEUROSIS IN THE SADISTIC AGENT

We will now examine the sequential steps of the transference neurosis in the sadistic agent analysand.

1. Unconscious, compulsive choice of a masochistic analyst. The sadistic analysand will try to select someone who seems, because of his personality or his technique, a possible masochistic victim: naive, generous, hypertolerant, submitting to the attacks of his analysands, etc. This is the same type of unconscious choice that he has already made with his spouse and friends. This is called the sadistic *selecting-out*.

2. Unconscious testing of the analyst to determine if he is a masochist and whether he is the specific type of masochist needed to satisfy the specific type of sadism. A sadistic paranoid analysand will need a masochistic melancholic analyst; a sadistic counterphobic will need a masochistic phobic type, etc.

3. Unconscious seduction of the (supposed) masochistic analyst by offering himself to the analyst as an overprotecting provider of security. The sadistic analysand promises to take care of the financial and professional decisions and problems of the "poor" analyst.

4. Unconscious crippling of the (supposed) masochistic analyst by trying to relieve him of all important decisions, including the analytic ones: he will send new analysands to him, will suggest new and better ways to invest his money, etc.

5. Unconscious jealous attacks on all the good relationships that he supposes the analyst has: he will criticize bitterly the analyst's family, friends, colleagues, or internal objects; or he will express anger each time he perceives that the analyst is well-connected with his internal or external objects. In this way he tries to separate the analyst from all good objects with the exception of the analysand, until the analyst is monodependent on him.

6. Unconscious control of, or attacks on, the reputation of the analyst: he will speak (or threaten to speak) to others about how good, clever, or sensible he is as an analysand and how bad, stupid, or crazy the analyst is. This is particularly important in the case of young analysts to whom reputation is a crucial factor in developing a clientele. The sadistic analysand, generally speaking, is a very subtle and effective consensus-maker and lets this be known to the analyst as a form of dissuasion: he can negatively influence the

analyst's clientele and, consequently, threaten the analyst's professional survival.

7. Unconscious alliance with the analyst's (supposed) sadistic superego and (supposed) masochistic ego: after making the analyst dependent on him and isolating him from internal and external objects, the sadistic analysand will start disqualifying and denigrating the analyst for being bad, stupid, or crazy (negative transference), on the lines of the analyst's own superego disqualifications. The sadistic analysand has a particular ability to find the weak points, the masochistic soft spots of the analyst's ego, as well as the specific sadistic characteristics and accusations of the analyst's superego. For this reason, he will overqualify and idealize himself, just as the analyst's sadistic superego idealized itself. In this way he will function as a *super-other* of the analyst, who will be an *infer-subject*.

8. Unconscious attacks on the perception, memory, thinking, and feelings of the analyst: functioning as a sadistic super-other of the analyst, the sadistic analysand tries to distort the analyst's perception and memory of the analytic relationship, and the appropriate feelings and responses produced by the relationship. For example, the sadistic analysand will deny that he arrives late—not only to a particular session; he also will deny that he usually arrives late. Or, he will deny that the analyst's countertransferential feelings of depression are provoked by his disqualifications. He will suggest, in short, that the analyst is inventing a reality that does not exist: that the analyst is suffering from a delusion, or is hallucinating, or is mentally ill if he claims that he perceives correctly the sadistic behavior of the analysand.

9. Unconscious censorship of therapeutic descriptions of the sadistic behavior of the analysand. The sadistic analysand will try to block any objective comment from the analyst about his dependency-creating, isolating, disqualifying, jealous, controlling behavior by disqualifying those comments as bad, crazy, or stupid. He may threaten the analyst with attacks on his reputation or withdraw his "indispensable" support if the analyst insists on denouncing his sadism. Again, the sadistic analysand will make an alliance with the analyst's superego to block these therapeutic comments.

10. Unconscious attacks against every movement the analyst makes toward independence, toward reestablishing good internal or external relationships, or toward his own requalification (as not being bad, stupid, or crazy).

11. Unconscious imprisonment of the analyst. If the analyst surrenders to the sadistic attacks made by the analysand against his therapeutic comments, independence, social contacts, or requalifications, he finally becomes a "hostage." He will be totally in the hands of his analytic "kidnapper," isolated from his internal and external objects and with his survival in danger, depending only on the analysand.

12. Unconscious affective exploitation of the analyst. The sadistic analysand will try to use the analyst as a masochistic "container" for his own feelings of badness, stupidity, and craziness, while stealing from him his feelings of goodness, intelligence, and mental health.

13. Unconscious blackmail of the analyst if he resists being a masochistic container of painful feelings. The sadistic analysand, once he has "kidnapped" the analyst, will use the psychological and social pressures already described to keep him in the masochistic position. Mainly, he will exert pressure negatively through punishments or threats to the analyst's survival and positively through promises and rewards of protection.

14. Unconscious masochistic response of the analyst: if the analyst surrenders to the manipulations and pressures of the sadistic analysand, he unconsciously behaves in the masochistic style and fulfills the analysand's wishes. He finally responds with an unconscious masochistic counter-acting-out to the sadistic demands of the analysand.

15. Unconscious reward of the masochistic response of the analyst. Once the analyst starts behaving masochistically, the sadistic analysand "improves" clinically and eases (temporarily at least) his attacks and pressures against the analyst.

16. Unconscious sadomasochistic agreement between the sadistic analysand and the masochistic analyst. The analytic relationship stabilizes itself with a chronic sadistic acting-out on the part of the analysand, and a corresponding masochistic counter-acting-out on the part of the analyst. The analysand is constantly injecting unpleasure into the analyst while overprotecting him with respect to his survival. On the other hand, the analyst is constantly absorbing unpleasure while being overprotected by the analysand.

17. Possible crises within the sadomasochistic analytic regime provoked by an alteration in the balance of power. Crises of the sadomasochistic regime can appear either because the sadistic anal-

ysand does not want to be (or cannot be) sadistic any longer; because the masochistic analyst does not want to be (or cannot be) masochistic any longer; because the analysand is exceedingly sadistic and destroys the analyst; or because the analyst is exceedingly masochistic and destroys himself.

We have described the pathogenic evolution of the transference neurosis of the sadist—that is, the pathogenic sequence of the transmission of mental illness that begins with the sadistic agent analysand. The sequence will evolve in this sadomasochistic way only if the analyst surrenders to the sadistic attacks and pressures of the analysand. But, of course, if the analyst fights back in an antisadistic way, resisting and interpreting the sadistic pressures, the transference neurosis will have a quite different ending: either the analysand will not tolerate a nonmasochistic analyst (seen as a sadistic one) and will interrupt the treatment or, gradually he will give up his sadistic acting-out and start making a nonsadistic (and nonmasochistic) specific therapeutic action. This action will be in response to the specific antisadistic therapeutic reaction of the analyst until the analytic system is stablized in a "democratic," nonsadomasochistic agreement and the sadistic transference neurosis dissolved. (This therapeutic process will be described in detail in chapter 9.)

TRANSFERENCE NEUROSIS IN THE MASOCHISTIC PATIENT

The typical sequence of the transference neurosis in the masochistic type of analysand can be described as follows:

1. Unconscious compulsive choice of a sadistic analyst. The masochistic analysand will try to choose, just as he has already chosen his spouse and friends, someone who seems to be, because of his personality or his technique, a possible sadistic victimizer of himself: astute, selfish, demanding, cruel and intolerant of any attack from his analysands, etc. It is a masochistic "selecting-out."

2. Unconscious testing of the analyst to determine if he is a sadist and whether he is the specific type of sadist needed to satisfy the specific type of masochism: a masochistic phobic analysand will need a sadistic counterphobic analyst, etc.

3. Unconscious seduction of the (supposed) sadistic analyst by offering himself to the analyst as a very nice source of sadistic

pleasure. The masochistic analysand promises to give all kinds of hedonistic, ethical, or cognitive satisfactions to the sadistic analyst, even if these satisfactions imply his own frustration.

4. Unconscious crippling of himself by the (supposed) sadistic analyst by leaving all the important decisions of his life in the analyst's hands: he will "follow" blindly all the financial and personal directions that the analyst can "suggest" to him through interpretations.

5. Unconscious social and familial isolation of himself, believing that this isolation will please his (supposed) jealous, controlling analyst. From now on the analyst will be the only reliable source of security and advice against all the external "enemies," even if those enemies were close friends before the analysis began. He will become totally monodependent on the analyst.

6. Unconscious attacks on his own reputation. When speaking to others about his relationship with the analyst, he will say how good, clever or sensible the analyst is, and how bad, stupid, or crazy he is. This is particularly true if the analyst is famous (a well-known training analyst, for example) and the analysand is an "unimportant" person (a new, timid candidate, for example).

7. Unconscious identification with the (supposed) masochistic ego of the analyst which is under the cruel attack of the analyst's sadistic superego. After making himself totally dependent on the analyst and isolating himself from his internal and external objects, the masochistic analysand will try to function as a masochistic ego while trying to induce the analyst to function as a sadistic superego. This means that the analysand will start disqualifying and denigrating himself as being bad, stupid, or crazy, according to the analyst's original ego disqualifications.

At the same time he will start idealizing or overqualifying the analyst (idealized transference) as being good, clever, and sensible. The masochistic analysand has a particular ability to find and remark on the strong points of the analyst's ideal of the ego. In this way the analyst will function as a *super-other* of the analysand, who will be an *infer-subject*.

8. Unconscious interpretation of all the analyst's interventions as justified attacks against the analysand's perception, memory, thinking, and feeling: functioning as a masochistic *infer-other* of the analyst, the masochistic analysand supposes that the analyst is constantly "correcting" his own perception of reality, that the analyst is

not only interpreting new meanings but also suggesting that the analysand is inventing a reality that does not exist: that the analysand suffers from delusions or is hallucinating each time he perceives correctly what is going on in the analytic relationship. Moreover, the masochistic analysand tends to immediately accept as correct any disqualification of his perception, feeling, memory, or thinking that the analyst may make (or that the analysand thinks the analyst is making).

9. Unconscious censorship of his own descriptions about the (supposed or real) sadistic behavior of the analyst. The analysand will block—and will try to ensure that the analyst blocks too—any objective comment about his pathological dependency, isolation, or disqualification of himself and idealization of the analyst; or about the dependency-making, isolating, disqualifying behavior of the analyst. He will disqualify such comments as new evidence of his own badness, stupidity, or craziness.

10. Unconscious manipulation to ensure that the analyst attacks any movement towards independence, towards reestablishing good internal or external relationships, or towards his own requalification. The masochistic analysand constantly tries to present his independence as dangerous, his friends as bad and destructive, his own behavior as stupid or naive, etc., in such a way that the analyst must be very careful not to control, isolate, or disqualify him.

11. Unconscious punishment of any attempt on the part of the analyst to reply in any way to the analysand on important issues related to security and survival.

12. Unconscious imprisonment of the analysand. Once the masochistic analysand has achieved monodependence on the analyst, isolation of any source of security, disqualification and idealization of the analyst, he becomes a "hostage" of the analyst. This is especially true if he succeeds in transforming the analyst into an isolating, disqualifying dependency-maker, that is, into a "kidnapping" analyst who has in his hands the survival of the analysand.

13. Unconscious affective exploitation of the analyst: the masochistic analysand will try to use the analyst as a sadistic overprotector. He will offer himself as a "container" of the analyst's badness, stupidity, or craziness and as a source for the goodness, cleverness and mental health of the analyst; but at the same time he will deprive the analyst of any support in important issues. The

analyst has the obligation to take care of the survival of the analysand as a payment for the analysand's sacrifice of his pleasure.

14. Unconscious blackmail of the analyst if he resists being a sadistic "container" of feelings of insecurity. The masochistic analysand, once he has made the analyst "kidnap" him, will use psychological pressures to keep the analyst in the sadistic position. He will use threats or punishments against the analyst's pleasures as negative pressures, and promises and rewards of pleasure as positive ones.

15. Unconscious sadistic response of the analyst: if the analyst surrenders to the masochistic manipulations and pressures of the analysand, he unconsciously behaves in the sadistic style unconsciously requested by the analysand. Finally, he responds with an unconscious sadistic counter-acting-out to the masochistic demands of the analysand.

16. Unconscious reward of the sadistic response of the analyst. Once the analyst starts behaving sadistically, the masochistic analysand "improves" clinically and eases, temporarily at least, his attacks on himself and his pressures on the analyst.

17. Unconscious sadomasochistic agreement between the masochistic analysand and the sadistic analyst. The analytic relationship stabilizes itself with a chronic masochistic acting-out on the part of the analysand and a corresponding sadistic counter-acting-out on the part of the analyst: the analyst is constantly injecting unpleasure on the analysand while overprotecting him with respect to his survival. On the other hand, the analysand is constantly absorbing unpleasure while being overprotected by the analyst.

18. Possible crises within the sadomasochistic analytic regime provoked by an alteration in the balance of power: abandoning the sadistic or the masochistic position, or being oversadist or overmasochist can break down the sadomasochistic regime.

We have described the pathogenic sequence—started by a masochistic patient analysand—in which the analyst fails to overcome these masochistic pressures. If the analyst can succeed in taking an antimasochistic position, resisting and interpreting the masochistic manipulations, either the analysand will not tolerate a nonsadistic analyst (seen as a masochistic one) and will interrupt the treatment or gradually will give up his masochistic acting-out and start making a nonmasochistic (and nonsadistic) specific therapeutic action. This action will be in response to the specific antimasochistic therapeutic reaction of the analyst, until the analytic system is stabilized in a nonsadomasochistic agreement and the masochistic transference neurosis dissolved.

TRANSFERENCE NEUROSIS IN THE MASOCHISTIC AGENT AND THE SADISTIC PATIENT

In order to develop a clearer psychoanalytic epidemiology—that is, a psychoanalytic explanation of the transmission of mental illness—the name "patient" will be used to refer to the dependent person, while the "agent" refers to the dependency-maker. The "sadist" is the cruel torturer who says that he is tortured by others, while the "masochist" is the cruelly tortured one who says that he is a torturer of others.

In the structure of the narcissistic relationship we have so far distinguished the sadist, who frustrates but is satisfied, and the masochist, who satisfies but is frustrated. But there is an extra element that determines their relationship. Ironically, for a narcissistic structure, it consists of their specific relationship to reality. The question is which of the two is more powerful in terms of reality.

We call the partner who is more powerful in terms of economic and social status an agent, and his more dependent other, a patient. The agent has the power to control the relationship, and, in particular, to maintain its narcissistic structure. The irony, then, is that the agent uses his power in relation to reality not in order to facilitate real satisfactions, but rather to sustain the sadomasochistic structure.

The *borderline* type of analysand as described in the literature is dependent as a patient and cruel and torturous as a sadist. Thus, it can be said that this borderline type is a *sadistic patient*. On the other hand, the usual pathological partner of the borderline analysand is a tortured dependency-making, over-protecting, spoiling, and sadistic-making type of person—a *masochistic agent*.

If we state that the borderline phenomenon is always the product of a dyad (or a triad, etc.) that is, a *folie à deux*, it can be said that the sadistic patient (borderline) is always accompanied by a masochistic agent (*borderliner*, or borderline-maker).

Usually one would expect the sadist to be the more powerful partner in conformity with our conventional idea of the sadistic position as one of strength and independence. We assume that the masochist, on the other hand, would relate from a position of dependence and weakness. And yet the opposite occurs. The masochist can be more powerful in terms of reality, while the sadist is, in fact, in the dependent position. This, indeed, is the relative situation of the borderlined patient, who is weak and yet sadistic, and the borderliner agent, who is strong and yet masochistic. And with this pair we encounter the clinical description that has intrigued so many analysts recently. It is almost as if the borderline syndrome has replaced the neurotic syndrome in frequency of occurrence in the clinical literature.

The so-called discovery of the borderline syndrome, which is in our view the syndrome of the borderliner and the borderlined, is not, in fact, as novel as it appears providing one takes into account the variable of the patient and the agent in relation to that of the sadist and the masochist. In effect, we are suggesting that the Hegelian dialectic of master and servant has to be viewed both in relation to the question of frustration and satisfaction, and in relation to the question of work. The master who is incapable of work is, in this view, a patient, while the servant who has the capacity to produce is an agent. Not only does the novelty fade in the light of the philosophical concept, it also yields to the traditional theory of neurosis.

Properly understood, the hysteric is essentially the sadistic patient, or the borderlined, while the masochistic agent, or the borderliner, is basically the obsessional neurotic. We are grateful to the school of Lacan for preserving this distinction in its full significance (Schneidermann 1980). Thus, the hysteric is overprotected and indulged while being nevertheless angry at the other for frustrating him. He alternates between states of dependence and idealization at one time and fury at another. The obsessional, meanwhile, works very hard to achieve approval but does not really feel that he achieves it. In the process, nevertheless, he accrues considerable power in reality. And what does he do with it? If he is in a partnership with an hysteric, he uses it to indulge the other's demands for satisfaction at the price of his own frustration. Consequently, in assessing the analysand and planning the analysis, it is essential to give full value to two sets of interacting variables: first, who is satisfied and who is frustrated in action, as opposed to consciousness;

second, who is in charge, or who is the agent and who the patient. Both the master and the slave are enslaved to the desire of the master. In terms of the sadist and the masochist, this means that it is always the sadist's demand for indulgence, his insistence on being spoiled, that provides the axis of the relationship and consequently organizes both their efforts in reality. The constant goal is to create the conditions necessary to satisfy the unrealistic desires of the sadist.

In order to understand what holds each partner in the narcissistic bipolarity one has to compare the underlying anxieties that the relationship itself serves to contain. The sadistic agent fears the loss of his pleasure while the masochistic patient fears that he won't survive. The sadistic patient, on the other hand, fears being overwhelmed by frustration, while the masochistic agent fears complete loneliness. Either variety of the *folie à deux* can be understood metaphorically as the relationship between an addict and a pusher. The agent, whether sadistic or masochistic, plays the role of the pusher, and the patient that of his dependent addict. In the case of the borderline syndrome, the addiction has simply become more obvious, approaching a symbiosis.

Because of the similarities between the masochistic patient and the masochistic agent and between the sadistic agent and the sadistic patient, in this book we will fully develop only the analysis of the clinical behavior and metapsychological structure of the sadistic agent and the masochistic patient. The differences in the treatment of the sadistic patient and the masochistic agent will be dealt with in chapter 9.

Clinically, the characteristics of the transference and countertransference and the sequence of the transference and countertransference neurosis in the case of the sadist are opposite to those of the masochist. Consequently, the political, strategic, tactical, and technical approaches of the analytic treatment must also be opposite in terms of the therapeutic setting and in the style and content of the interpretations. Since the speech, actions, and affects of sadists are different from those of masochists, the therapeutic speech, actions, and affects of the analyst must be different with them too.

REFERENCES

Bateson, G., and Ruesch, J. (1945). *Communication: the Social Matrix of Psychiatry*. New York: Norton.
Bateson, G. (1972). *Steps to an Ecology of Mind*. San Francisco: Chandler.

Freud, A. (1954). The widening scope of indications for psycho-analysis, *Journal of the American Psychoanalytic Association* 2:607–620.
Eissler, K. R. (1953). The effect of the structure of the ego on psychoanalytic technique. *Journal of the American Psychoanalytic Association* 1:104–143.
Freud, S. (1912). Note on the unconscious in psycho-analysis. *Standard Edition* 12:255–266.
—— (1914a). The dynamics of transference. *Standard Edition* 12:97–108.
—— (1914b). On narcissism: an introduction. *Standard Edition* 14:67–102.
—— (1914c). Remembering, repeating and working through. *Standard Edition* 12:145–156.
—— (1923). The ego and the id. *Standard Edition* 19:3–66.
Gear, M. C., and Liendo, E. C. (1975). *Sémiologie psychanalytique.* Paris: Minuit.
—— (1979a). *Action psychanalytique.* Paris: Minuit.
—— (1979b). *Psicoanálisis del paciente y de su agente.* Buenos Aires: Nueva Visión.
Klein, M. (1952). *Contributions to Psychoanalysis, 1921–1945.* London: Hogarth Press.
Kohut, H. (1971). *The Analysis of the Self.* New York: International Universities Press.
Kernberg, O. (1975). *Borderline Conditions and Pathological Narcissism.* New York: Jason Aronson.
Lévi-Strauss, C. (1963). *Structural Anthropology.* New York: Basic Books.
Russell, B. (1927). *An Outline of Philosophy.* London: Allen and Unwin.
Schelling, T. C. (1960). *The Strategy of Conflict.* Cambridge: Harvard University Press.
Schneidermann, S. (1980). *Return to Freud.* New Haven: Yale University Press.
Stone, L. (1954). The widening scope of indications for psycho-analysis. *Journal of the American Psychoanalytic Association* 2:567–594.
Wynne, L. C., Rychoff, I. M., Day, J., and Mirsch, S. I. (1958). Pseudomutuality in the family relations of schizophrenics. *Psychiatry* 21.

2

A Semiotic Model of the Metapsychology of Sadism and Masochism

Isomorphisms between the Semiotic and Psychoanalytic Models

Psychoanalysis and semiotics are disciplines of the human sciences with different objects and methods of study. Semiotics concerns itself with the description, explanation, and prediction of the systems of signs;* psychoanalysis attempts to do the same with the psychic system. Each of these disciplines can be utilized by the other. There are certain similarities between their respective objects of study: the psychic structure of the observer will influence decisively the manner in which he interprets the signs he decodes, while the psychic structure is, on a certain level, a semiotic structure.† The discipline of psychosemiotics is dedicated to the study of the aspects common

---

*Following Ferdinand de Saussure's (1916) theory, we consider that a "sign" is a psychological entity formed by the association of an image (or signifier) and a concept (or signified). A traffic sign would be, for example, the association of the image "red" and the concept "danger."

†A seminotic structure is the combination of various signs (by difference and opposition). For example, the semiotic structure of the traffic light system is formed by the opposition and difference between "red" and "non-red" (green) and between "danger" and "non-danger."

45

to both disciplines. Each possesses a model or models that can be fruitfully transferred to the other.

Both disciplines use simplified models, or representations, of the real world designed to make the systems more accessible. A model is an abstraction of reality that may be physical, conceptual, or mathematical. Ironically, this abstraction can become much more real than it may at first seem. Although the objects in themselves cannot be directly known, their structure, or the structure of their relation with other objects, can be studied.

It could be said, from a logicomathematical point of view, that a "structure" is a group of mutual relations that can be symbolized. To decide if a structure (a system of signs, for example) can represent another structure, such as a psychic system, one must ask if one system fulfills the "conditions" of the other; that is, whether the elements of each and the relationship between them are comparable. Generally there are several modelistic structures that can fulfill each system's fundamental hypothesis and its derived hypotheses.

One structure can serve as a model for another when there is *isomorphism* between them—a one-to-one relationship. The convention or code prescribes the types of isomorphisms that are accepted in any science, which are, in fact, the basis of the majority of scientific modelistic techniques. Consequently, the modeling of the superficial and deep structure of the psychic system, for example, depends on the possible isomorphisms with such a system.

If the modeling is not one-to-one, the model will be *homomorphic*. Since the correspondence between the systems of signs and the psychic system is partial, a semiotic model of the psychic structure will be homomorphic.

A model may supply only a "metaphor," to avoid falling into a literal state in which one might confuse the syntactic structure of the model with its new semantic content. Thus, to postulate the existence of psychic "signs" does not imply that these necessarily have a neurophysiological correlate.

Freud generated many of his hypotheses by transferring homomorphic elements and relations from optics, hydrodynamics, biology, etc. Far from betraying a lack of imagination, this demonstrated an epistemological maturity which permitted him to purify concepts, strengthening their explanatory power (Eagle 1973), and provided him a foil for his clinical practice. Attempting to explain the directly observable (free associations, dreams, symptoms, etc.)

by way of the unobservable (as the economic, topographic, and dynamic models do) gave psychoanalysis access to an original field of inquiry in the human sciences. Although it is true that it followed the characteristic nineteenth-century scientific path of a Helmholtz or a Maxwell, it is also true that it anticipated the steps of modern science. In effect, both economics and political science today utilize a growing number of conceptual and mathematical models for the sake of their greater explanatory and predictive power. Freud (1900) constructed his theory concerning the psychic apparatus through isomorphism with an electrodynamic theory of physics, and so, too, Jacques Lacan (1966), Marshall Edelson (1977), and we ourselves are engaged in constructing a new version of Freud's theory of the internal and deep functioning of the psychic system through its homomorphism with semiotic theory.*

Freud used this kind of modeling repeatedly in the psychoanalytic field. He modeled the psychic function mechanically (1900), as if it were an optic apparatus; dynamically, as if it were a fluid (libido) with cathexis and countercathexis; and biologically, as if it were a cheese with a tough rind and a soft center, or an amoeba. And if it is true that from time to time Freud fell into the methodological trap of literal and concrete interpretation of the models, it is also true that he was constantly alert to (and alerted others to) that risk.

The fact that similarities exist between the methods and the objects of psychoanalysis and semiotics has permitted us to use semiotics as an instrument to refine the methods of observation and systematization of clinical psychoanalytic material, as well as to plan more sophisticated therapeutic psychoanalytic treatments. For example, the structural analysis of myths and the structural analysis of narratives are of great use for the observation and systematization of the regularity and the covariances in free associations. The concepts of "object language" and of "metalanguage" (Tarski 1956) have helped us to specify the semantic level on which free associations are valid for psychoanalysis as well as to determine what semantic

---

*Semiotics is a science dedicated to the study of the structure and functioning of signs. It has, following Charles Morris's ideas (1971), the minimum of a semantic dimension (the meaning of signs), a syntactic dimension (the rules for the combination of signs), and a pragmatic dimension (the practical use of signs).

level the interpretations formulated by psychoanalysts will reach. The notions of "polysemia" (Barthes 1967) and of the "signified of the signified" permit us to conceptualize in a more operational and rigorous manner the notion of manifest content and latent content as a double signified and a double message, etc.

The notions of "object," "object language," and "metalanguage" help us to distinguish with great clarity an analyzable subject from one who is not. An unanalyzable person is preoccupied with the objects of his language and cannot conceive of his own language and his associations as objects in themselves; he fails to understand that his associations are just associations—material to be interpreted in terms of his own understanding of himself. Instead, he insists that whatever he reports about a significant other be treated concretely as a request for advice on how to handle the other, the result being that the analysand himself becomes invisible and therefore unanalyzable.

The notions of "syntagm" and "paradigm" (Leach 1976) help us distinguish syntagmatic, metonymic analysands, committed to a description of concrete sequences of action, from paradigmatic, metaphoric, analysands inclined toward philosophical reflections of a general sort. In addition, the notions of deep structure, superficial structure, and transformation can be applied to the study of the speech of the analysand and the analyst.

Further, the Saussurean notions of language (*langue*) and speech (*parole*) can be applied to the analysand's manifest content and its narrative structure, as we partially do at the end of this chapter.

Interpretation of the Interpretations

Semiotics enables us to clarify the crucial distinction in psychoanalysis, that exists between the empirical level of the analysand's speech, which informs the analyst about the analysand's consciously perceived speech actions and affective states, and the unconscious intrapsychic structure that governs the analysand's actual behavior.

The analyst's task is to construct the underlying code that the analysand uses to interpret messages received in his world. If we take the example of a motorist or a pedestrian making a decision on whether to halt or proceed at an intersection there are two levels of mental operation that come into play. The obvious one is at the level of perception, for example, the color of the traffic lights and the pedestrian indicator as well as the different flows of traffic. Given our familiarity with this situation it appears as if the decision is virtually given by the mere act of perception. Actually, however, it arises from an intrapsychic decision-making process in which the first step is to interpret the data perceived and the next is to act on the information. In other words, the message contained in the data perceived has to be interpreted according to the code available for this purpose. When the motorist or pedestrian speaks to his analyst about what happened that day at the intersection, he presents everything except the code he used to interpret the messages, because like any motorist or pedestrian he remains unconscious of his own mental operations at this level. The analyst's task is therefore to help the motorist who keeps having accidents or the pedestrian who keeps walking into oncoming traffic to become aware of the unconscious code that consistently misinterprets the messages implied in the perceptual data so that the code can be corrected. The analysand is always concerned about observable signals and messages, while the analyst is concerned with decoding the unobserved and unobservable code. In this sense the analyst becomes the interpreter of the analysand's vital interpretations. Semiotics enables us to systematize the connections between these different levels of the intrapsychic and analytic process.

The Structure of a Semiotic Bipolar System

By modeling psychic functioning as an "apparatus" Freud defined a new system of human activity—an area that would become the object of a new discipline. When he reached age seventy, he affirmed: "My life has had only one purpose: to infer and to intuitively arrive at how the psychic apparatus is constructed and which are the forces that operate on it and act one with another" (Jones 1957).

Freud (1900) did not limit himself to defining psychic activity merely as the activity of a system. His suggestions led the way to the construction of a systematic model of what today is termed a "translucent box." This model has an internal, unobservable, conscious and unconscious structure that would explain the transformations undergone by the biological and social information that gets into that system before being returned to its environment. According to Freud's "Project for a Scientific Psychology" (1895), this internal structure of the psychic system is formed progressively as the biological needs of the child change to psychological desires which are satisfied or frustrated by the conduct of persons who interact with the child. The child constructs his psychic reality by way of the introjection of the images of the satisfying or frustrating objects and their simultaneous association with his respective sensations of satisfaction or pain (see Freud 1895, pp. 306–322).

Each experience of satisfaction remains registered in the psychic system, with a double registering as a result of the union of the desired memory trace and the qualitative concept of "pleasure"; each experience of pain is registered by means of the union of the feared memory trace and the qualitative concept of "displeasure." This binary division of intrapsychic representations permits the child to orient himself in relation to the external reality, and to attempt to repeat experiences of satisfaction and avoid those of pain.

SIGNIFIER AND SIGNIFIED

It is relatively simple to find an isomorphism, a correspondence between the function of the psychic system and that of a system of signs (such as traffic lights), in both their elements and their relations.

The driver experiences a sense of danger when the light is red and traffic is crossing the intersection, and a sense of no danger when the light is green and the traffic has stopped. The experience of danger will remain registered in the psychic system in a double way as a result of the association of a feared memory trace (in this case, the color red) and the qualitative concept of danger. The experience of no danger involves the union of the no-danger memory trace (in this example, the color green) with the concept of no danger.

This isomorphism is further accentuated if we remember that one of the main innovations that Saussure (1916) introduced into linguistics was the idea that if the decodifier-driver is to anticipate that a vehicle will cross the intersection each time the red light appears, and that it will not do so each time the green light appears, he must previously have introjected the traffic code. From this interiorization follows the formation of two psychic entities: the trace of the color red (not the red light of a real traffic light) as the "signifier," and the "concept" of danger (not the real car at the intersection) as the "signified." That is, only when the subject possesses an intrapsychic trace of "red," or of "not red," and the intrapsychic concept of "danger," or of "no danger," will he be able to utilize the code. That is, he will be able to behave semiotically when confronted by a traffic light because he will use it as a sign and not see it only as an aesthetic object: semiotic behavior involves deciphering the meaning, learning the rule system, and acting accordingly.

Luis Prieto (1966) says that a semic act occurs when a sender transmits a message to a receiver by way of a signal after having codified the message as *signified* and its signal as the *signifier*. In the example of the traffic lights the transit authority, as *sender*, transmits a message that a vehicle will cross the intersection of a certain street by way of the signal that is the red light of a particular traffic light after the driver has codified the message as the signified "danger" and its signal as the signifier "red." For Prieto the message and the signal are concrete observable facts of external reality; by contrast, the signified and its signifier are unobservable entities of the internal reality. The signifier is a class of signals and the signified is a class of messages. Following the basic theoretical terms of the Saussurean model, it can be said that a sign is a psychic identity formed by the union of a signified and a signifier. We see how, in the example, by the union of "red" and "danger" or of "not red" and "no danger," a semiotic structure is a psychic identity formed by the opposition and difference of a sign in regard to another sign. The relation of signification (Figure 2-1), the semantic dimension of a sign, is the vertical relation between the signifier and its signified: red signifies danger. The relation of value, or syntactic dimension of a sign, is the horizontal relation between two signifiers or between two signifieds: "red" has a value because it opposes and differentiates itself from "not red." The pragmatic dimension of a sign, (and here we refer to Charles Morris [1971] to complete the model) is the relationship between the signified and its message, and the signifier and its signal established by the sender and the receiver of the semic act (Figure 2-2).

Finally, using concepts developed by Roland Barthes (1967), it can be said that "denotation" is the direct relation of signification

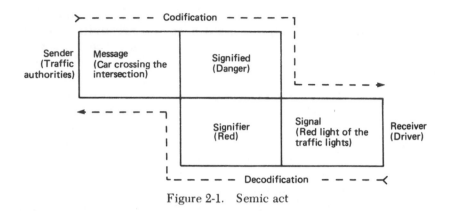

Figure 2-1.   Semic act

between a signifier and its signified: red "denotes" danger. "Connotation" occurs, by contrast, when an entire sign operates as a signifier of a new signified: "red/danger" emitted by an old-fashioned traffic light that is installed very high could connote a past epoch of the city, for example. A "metasemiosis" occurs when an entire sign operates as the signified of a new signifier. For example, a plaque installed above the "red/danger" sign saying "you can make a right turn on a red light" metacommunicates a new instruction. (See Figure 2-3.)

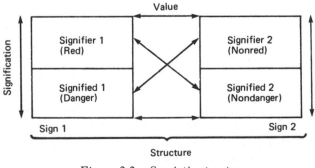

Figure 2-2.   Semiotic structure

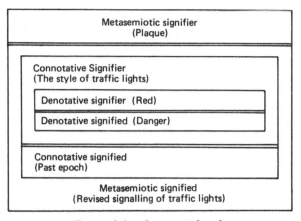

Figure 2-3. Semantic levels

Binary Structure of the Psychic Apparatus

This semiotic model of Saussurean origin can be used to illustrate the model of the psychic system developed by Freud in the 1895 Project because it fulfills almost all the requisite conditions. Between these structures there exists an isomorphic correspondence.

We can say, for example, that to the child, the literal absence of the mother when the child is hungry is the signal that transmits the message "hunger unsatisfied," because the signifier "absence" is intrapsychically united to the signified "displeasure." Thus we have the value of the signifier in terms of the opposition between "mother" and "mother's absence." In strict Freudian terms we would say that the frustrating image is the signal one that transmits the message 1 ("sensation of pain"), because the signifier 1 ("feared memory trace"—FMT) is intrapsychically united with the signified 1 ("unpleasure"), and the gratifying image of the signal 2 is the signal that transmits the message 2 ("sensation of satisfaction") because the signifier 2 ("desired memory trace"—DMT) is intrapsychically united with the signified 2 ("pleasure").

The semantic relation of signification ("FMT/unpleasure") would be the psychic sign 1, and the "DMT/pleasure" would be the psychic sign 2. The syntactic relationships of "value," the "FMT/ DMT," and "unpleasure/pleasure" would form the psychic structure (Gear and Liendo 1975). (See Figure 2-4.)

It should be evident that we are developing a semiotic system here and not a purely linguistic model as Lacan (1966) does: we are dealing with both verbal and nonverbal signs. In this way we accommodate Freud's distinction between thing representations and word representations. In our view the thing representations are composed of both somatic sensations of affects and movements and visual images of actions (Green 1974). In the psychosemic pragmatic act the psychic system transmits to itself information about its affective states. It transmits, for example, the message "hunger not satisfied" by way of the signal "absent mother," or the message "hunger satisfied" by the signal "present mother," because it can link the FMT with unpleasure or the DMT with pleasure. That is, the psychic system acts both as a codifier-sender and as a decodifier-receiver. In order that this psychosemic act can be realized, it is therefore necessary that the FMT be made up of a class of frustrating images; the DMT, a class of gratifying images; the unpleasure, a class of painful sensations; and the pleasure, a class of satisfactory sensations. The psychosemic act of the experience of pain is represented in Figure 2-5.

When the psychic system perceives that it is in danger of an experience of pain, or a painful affective state, it tends to avoid or to transform the external frustrating situation to obtain an external gratifying situation. But the psychic system does not always have the means to change the external situation and to avoid the psychic pain. For example, the breast-feeding infant needy of company cannot express this feeling or look for his mother when she is absent. When

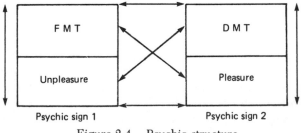

Figure 2-4. Psychic structure

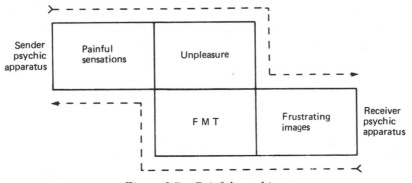

Figure 2-5. Painful psychic act

such a situation presents itself, the psychic system can opt to recognize the frustration and to learn from the experience, or (and this is a major Freudian hypothesis) it can use intrapsychic mechanisms as a defense against the appearance of the painful psychic representations. That is, when it cannot opt to transform or avoid the frustrating external situation, it can still choose to recognize it so as to prevent its recurrence, or it can avoid perceiving and thinking of it in order to avoid, even temporarily, the resultant psychic pain. When the frustrating situation is unavoidable, it is still possible to avoid thinking about it.

This hypothesis is developed by Freud in his 1895 Project. When the psychic system is confronted by an inevitable frustration and is not in a condition to deal with the situation, it tends to avoid it by way of "primary repression," in the sense of the simplest kind of countercathexis. This consists in replacing the representation of unpleasure linked to the FMT by the representation of DMT linked to pleasure: in this form the signified unpleasure is replaced by the signified pleasure. The psychic system will therefore perceive a nonexistent gratifying image. Such images occur with the hallucinatory satisfaction of desires, where the infant replaces the image of the absent breast that provokes displeasure with the image of a present breast that provokes pleasure.

In developing the semiotic model we are not attempting to reinterpret the developmental stages of the psychic apparatus. We are simply trying to demonstrate, step by step, how the psychic apparatus works as a semiotic model, drawing upon Freud's work at the same time. The result will be a model that shows the synchronic organization of the psychic apparatus, not its diachronic origin and development.

Psychic Codes and Mechanisms

In "Formulations on the Two Principles of Mental Functioning" (1911), "Instincts and Their Vicissitudes" (1915), and "Negation" (1925), Freud develops the opposition between "pleasure ego" and "reality ego" according to which the psychic system does not limit itself to replacing the FMT with the DMT. In effect, the "reality ego" begins to accept an adequate distinction between internal reality and external reality, and between pleasurable reality and unpleasurable reality. To avoid the unpleasure resulting from unpleasant psychic reality, these distinctions are distorted by mechanisms of "introjection" and "projection." What is unpleasurable from the internal reality is projected and confused with the external reality, and what is pleasurable in the external reality is introjected and confused with the internal reality. Thus the "purified pleasure ego" equates the pleasurable with the internal and the unpleasurable with the external.

After the infant has distinguished between self and nonself, the primary repression of the FMT is completed by its projection onto the external reality and by the denial of the DMT in the external reality and its introjection into the internal reality. There is a set of four basic intrapsychic mechanisms which functions like a pump, aspirating what is psychically pleasant and expelling what is psychically unpleasant. (See Figure 2-6.)

Synthesizing and simplifying the Freudian mechanisms of defense (Freud 1915b), it could be said that the psychic system represses and projects the internal unpleasure, and denies and introjects the external pleasure. In the case of a paranoiac, for example, displeasure is produced if he perceives himself as a persecutor, and pleasure is produced if he perceives himself as persecuted. He tends to perceive himself as persecuted and to say that he is, but objectively he acts as a persecutor of his own internal persecutors which have been projected. Objectively he is a persecutor, but

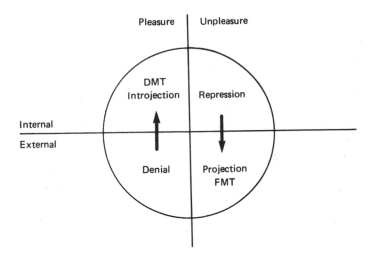

Figure 2-6. Functioning of "pleasure ego" (of the sadist)

perceiving himself as such constitutes an FMT because it produces unpleasure for him: for this reason he represses and projects that FMT in his psychic representations of the others. Since the others are persecuted by him and the fact of being persecuted is the DMT (being persecuted, being a victim, is being blameless and good) that produces pleasure, he denies the DMT in his representations of the others and introjects it in his intrapsychic representations of ego as himself.

The paranoiac tends to have a double psychic-intrapsychic representation of his own actions and the actions of the others: one representation is unconscious, true, and isomorphic with the real act, and another is conscious, inverted, false, and antiisomorphic with both his actions and those of the others.

Extending the isomorphisms of our semiotic model of the internal structure of the psychic system, we could say that in such a system three codes operate: an "informative code" which represents in a denotative way the subject's actions and those of the others; an "affective code" which represents in a connotative way the affective states of the subject and of the others; and an "identifying code" which represents the metasemiotic identity of the subject and of the others.

Using the notion of *denotation*, we could say that in the case of the paranoiac, the intrapsychic representation of being a persecutor is the denotative, informative signified of saying that one is persecuted, which would be its denotative informative signifier. Extending the model, the representation of the "act of being persecuted" would be an unconscious "thing representation," and the representation of saying that one is persecuted would be a conscious "word-representation."* Using the notion of *connotation*, we could say that to represent oneself by saying that one is persecuted and being a persecutor form a complete denotative psychic sign which operates as a connotative affective signifier of the connotative affective signifier, pleasure; and that to represent oneself by saying that one is a persecutor and being persecuted operates as a connotative affective signified of the connotative affective signified, unpleasure. Using the notion of *metasemiosis*, it could be said that *to call oneself persecuted/to be a persecutor/pleasure* forms a complete connotative psychic sign that operates as the metasemiotic identificative signified of the metasemiotic identificative signifier subject (or ego); and, that *to call oneself persecutor/to be persecuted/unpleasure* is the other connotative psychic sign that would operate as the metasemiotic identificative signified of the metasemiotic identificative signifier object, or alter (Gear and Liendo 1979). (See Figure 2-7.)

Thus, *to call oneself persecuted/to be a persecutor/pleasure/subject* would be the psychic sign 1 and *to call oneself persecutor/to be persecuted/unpleasure/object* would be the psychic sign 2 of a binary psychic structure. This structure functions with three codes (informative, affective, and identificative), and on three semantic levels of signification (denotative, connotative, and metasemiotic); there are four mechanisms of defense, two of which are semantic (repression and denial) because they are contained within each sign, while two are syntactic (projection and introjection) because they are transmitted between the two signs (Gear and Liendo 1980).

---

*Freud (1915b, 1917) developed the difference between these two metapsychological entities by saying that the thing-representation is essentially visual and derived from things, and the word-representation is essentially auditory and derived from words. We "translated" these concepts into semiotic terms while developing a psychoanalytic semiotics (Gear and Liendo 1975).

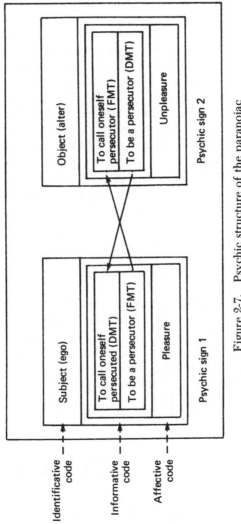

Figure 2-7. Psychic structure of the paranoiac

59

Pleasure in the Sadist,
Self-Preservation in the Masochist

This model excludes, among other things, a dynamic explanation of why the conflicted subject must repress and lie to himself about himself. Why would perceiving himself as a persecutor be unpleasurable and perceiving himself as persecuted pleasurable? Freud's topographic model is included, as is (partially) his dynamic model; but his structural model is omitted, particularly the notion of superego that he developed in *The Ego and the Id* (1923). Nor does this model include the second theory of drives, which Freud developed in his attempt to explain the dynamics of masochism and the repetition compulsion. Both of these aspects of his model arose at times when Freud considered that psychoanalytic theory was in a critical state with regard to its power of explanation. In *Beyond the Pleasure Principle* (1920), Freud recognized that while sadism seems to be controlled by the pleasure principle, the same is not true for masochism. *

So far we have used Freud's concept of the pleasure ego as a model for the metapsychology of the sadist. Similarly one can employ his concept of the exaggerated reality ego as a model for the metapsychology of the masochist. In that case the primary concern becomes self-preservation to the exclusion of pleasure. Of course, the well-organized reality ego would accommodate both self-preservation and pleasure. The sadist finds pleasure provoking displeasure in others but the masochist seems to compulsively seek the opposite; to give pleasure to the other by way of his own displeasure. In metapsychological terms, at the level of affect the sadist seems to repress and project his victimizing nature, his FMT, and deny and introject his DMT—that the other is a victim of himself. The

---

*Psychoanalysis extends the notion of sadomasochism beyond the perversion described by sexologists (particularly Krafft-Ebing and Havelock Ellis). Sadomasochism not only stresses the isomorphism and complementarity between the two perversions but also denotes a pair of opposites that is as fundamental, in psychoanalytic theory, to the evolution of instinctual life as it is to its manifestations. Sadomasochism, in brief, seems to be a universal and basic way of dealing with destructiveness to avoid the disorganization of the psychic apparatus.

masochist does the opposite; that is, he represses and projects his victimization and his DMT, and denies and introjects his FMT—that the other is a victimizer of himself.

Clinical observation leads us to think that in doing so, he is exchanging unpleasure for security; that he has a "security-ego." From another perspective, it also can be said that for the masochist the DMT must be repressed and projected, even if it implies pleasure, because it implies insecurity at the same time; and that the FMT must be denied and introjected, even if it implies unpleasure, because it implies security. In other words, the masochist is doing to security and insecurity the very same thing that the sadist does to pleasure and unpleasure: he represses and projects insecurity while he denies and introjects security (Figure 2-8).

Moreover, the sadist and the masochist generally tend to function in a narcissistic *folie à deux* (Lasègue and Falret 1873), in which the sadist represses and projects precisely what the masochist denies and introjects, and denies and introjects precisely what the masochist represses and projects. Let us take, for example, the narcissism *à deux* formed by the paranoid and the melancholic in which one functions as a narcissistic mirror of the other and vice versa. The sadistic paranoid perceives himself as persecuted while he is per-

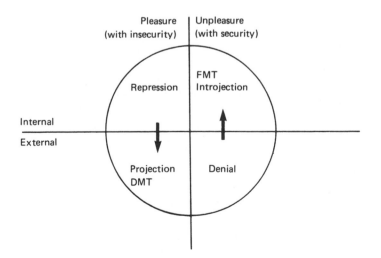

Figure 2-8. Functioning of "security ego" (of the masochist)

secuting the masochistic melancholic; and the latter perceives himself as a persecutor while he is persecuted by the sadistic paranoid.

Apart from the model of life and death drives used by Freud (1924) to explain the phenomenon of masochism, another explanation might be the hypothesis (already suggested by Freud) that the affective states of the psychic apparatus could be of two classes: one being beyond the pleasure principle and the other being the pleasure principle. Beyond the pleasure priniciple one would find security and insecurity as the basic emotions linked to survival or self-preservation. Within the pleasure principle one would find pleasure and unpleasure as emotions that can appear only when survival is already assured, because the free cathexis has been bound by the psychic apparatus and the chaos of unbound primary process is over.

Accepting this division of affects, then, as a second hypothesis, one could state that the masochist, not being in control of the relationship, is weaker and more dependent than the sadist; and, therefore, he cannot negotiate his pleasure. He is beyond the pleasure principle; that is, he is interested in obtaining security and in avoiding insecurity. The sadist, being stronger and more independent than the masochist, is within the pleasure principle; that is, he is interested in obtaining pleasure and avoiding unpleasure. Accepting that the sadist and the masochist have different and complementary affective interests, the latter will be able to obtain security from the sadist (on whom he depends) if he concedes his pleasure and absorbs the unpleasure of the sadist. For his part, the sadist believes that he can obtain pleasure from the masochist (who depends on him) if he gives the masochist the security to survive and absorbs his insecurity. The masochist is so stoic that he does not mind enduring the unpleasure if he is sure that he will survive, and the sadist is so confident and epicurean that it does not matter to him if he suffers insecurity as long as he is sure to obtain pleasure.

Now we could argue that pleasure or unpleasure, and security or insecurity, are really nothing more than two types of pleasure on different levels, in which case the whole narcissistic game of sado-masochism would again fall within the limits of the pleasure principle. The sadist would be someone who satisfies himself by frustrating the others, but who describes and perceives himself as their frustrated satisfier, complementing the masochist, who would be someone who frustrates himself by satisfying the others, but who says and perceives that he satisfies himself by frustrating them. Generally, the sadist is a victimizer who calls himself a victim, and the masochist is a victim who calls himself a victimizer (Gear and Liendo 1980).

In fact, this brings us back to the first theory of the drives, which distinguishes libido from self-preservation. The libido gives rise to the pleasure principle, while the self preservative drive introduces the issue of security and insecurity in relation to reality, or the constancy principle. It would follow that the sadist is regulated by the pleasure principle of the sexual drive, and the masochist by the constancy principle (security and insecurity) of the drive for self-preservation. While both "conserve" this narcissistic regime—the sadomasochistic method of obtaining pleasure and survival—the sadist wants to enjoy exploiting the other at the same time as the masochist wants to survive by exploiting the other. Both experience unconscious ambivalence when playing their roles: because of the mutual exploitation that both are engaged in imposing and suffering, they each have feelings of hostility and revenge against the other. In effect this constitutes an unconscious, and sometimes conscious, interpersonal and intrapsychic war: *homo lupus hominis*, which Freud quotes in *Civilization and Its Discontents* (1930).

Conscious and Unconscious Psychosemiotic Structure

If we go back to the semiotic bipolar model to which the Freudian topography has been applied, it can be said that the psychic structure of the sadist is metapsychologically different from that of the masochist: the psychic signs of the first are opposed and complementary to those of the second. In effect, psychic sign 1 of the bipolar structure of the sadist would be formed by the denotative, connotative, and metasemiotic semantic union of the intrapsychic representations *to call oneself a frustrated satisfier/to be a satisfied frustrator/pleasure-insecurity/subject*. The psychic sign 2 of the sadist would be formed, in turn, by the union of the representations *to call oneself a satisfied frustrator/to be a frustrated satisfier/ unpleasure-security/object*. By contrast the psychic sign 1 of the bipolar structure of the masochist would be formed by the semantic union of the representations *to call oneself a satisfied frustrator/to be a frustrated satisfier/security-unpleasure/subject.* The psychic sign 2 of the masochist would be formed, in turn, by the union of the representations *to call oneself a frustrated satisfier/to be a satisfied frustrator/insecurity-pleasure/object* (Figure 2-9).

To be a satisfied frustrator in psychic sign 1 and *to be a frustrated satisfier* in psychic sign 2 are thing-representations forming the unconscious psychic structure. On the other hand, *to call oneself a frustrated satisfier* in psychic sign 1 and *to call onself a satisfied frustrator* in psychic sing 2 are word-representations forming the conscious-preconscious psychic structure.

In certain respects narcissism and sadomasochism are synonymous. First, the sadist is the "mirror" of the masochist and vice versa. Second, in the myth, the relationship between Narcissus and the nymph Echo (or the water) was sadomasochistic. Third, if narcissism is interpreted as selfishness, autism, self-centeredness, or a radical denial of the true identity of the other, the result is, in any case, a mistreatment of the other. Thus, from now on the terms *sadism*, and *masochism* will be used as the two types of narcissism.

In his structural model, the second theory of the functioning of the psychic system, Freud (1923) explicitly introduces the hypothesis that the distribution of power (Hill 1979) in the intrapsychic structure is asymmetrical: the superego, which follows upon the postoedipal introjection of the parental objects, has more power than the *infer*ego with regard to the type of satisfaction permitted

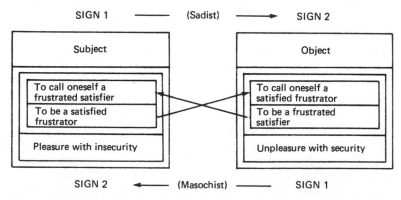

Figure 2-9. Structure of sadist and masochist

the desires originating in the id. This apparently reflects the differential of power between the child and his parents, in favor of the parents. Although this hypothesis is corroborated by clinical work with masochistic patients, it seems to be refuted when working with sadists: the ego of masochists seems impotent toward the omnipotent superego, but the ego of sadists seems omnipotent toward the impotent superego.

Trying to establish a structural metapsychological correlation between the clinical differences observed in the sadist and masochist, we will complete Freud's Latin terminology with that used by Talcott Parsons (1951) in his sociological theory of action. The group of conscious and unconscious representations that the subject identifies as his own words, actions, and affects could be called *ego*. The group of his conscious and unconscious representations that the subject identifies as the words, actions, and affects of the others, unified as if they were to constitute a single generalized object, could be called *alter*. Following Jacques Lacan (1966), we could say that alter means all the *autres* united in a single *Autre*. In sociological terms, the alter could be the internal generalized other.

The Bipolar Narcissistic Oedipal Situation

The two basic representations of the psychic reality of the sadist contained in the self are the pleasurable ego, as a narcissistic internal subject which does not feel but causes unpleasure, and the unpleasurable alter as an internal object, a depository of the unpleasure of the ego. These would be reversed in the case of the masochist. They are the two basic "internal objects" in Klein's terminology (1952), Lacan's two "signifiers"—the phallus and the nonphallus (1966)—and the two "signs" of the semiological structure of the psychic system in our model (Gear and Liendo 1975).

Therefore, the psychic structure is the structure of the object relation which must represent an internal class of both subjects (ego) and objects (alter). In Melanie Klein's terms, in the schizoid-paranoid position the sadist does not face two internal partial objects but rather identifies himself with the idealized internal partial object, and splits himself from the projected persecutory partial object. The reverse would be true in the case of the masochist. Hanna Segal (1964) says that through symbolic equation the ego "is" the idealized object, and the other "is" the persecutory object. For Klein, therefore, once the ego is in the depressive position it corrects this splitting, creating a bipolar situation rather than a binary one since the ego now faces a "total object" which is simultaneously "good" and "bad" and acknowledges its own goodness and badness.

On the other hand (again in Klein's terms), the ego tends to defensively "binarize" the triangular oedipal situation and identify itself with the parent of the same sex: it *is* this parent; at the same time it projects onto the external others the parent of the opposite sex, in the direct oedipal situation, and vice versa in the reverse oedipal situation. It is only when the patient has symbolically overcome the conflict that he again "triangularizes" the situation and assumes the role of an autonomous subject who "has" two parents in a relation "R" rather than being one of them and projecting his intrapsychic representation of the other onto his external partner.

Superego (= Ideal Ego) and Superalter (= Superego + Ego Ideal)

The sadist tends to overqualify himself, saying and perceiving that he is good, sensible, and clever, while he disqualifies the others, saying and perceiving that they are bad, crazy, or foolish. It might be said, therefore, that his intrapsychic structure is formed by a superego and inferalter—that is, by a grandiose internal subject that manically satisfies the desires of its id by dominating and disqualifying an internal inferobject. The sadist believes that he is trying to satisfy altruistically, sensibly, and intelligently the selfish, crazy, or foolish desires of the others at the expense of his own frustration, while really he is satisfying himself egocentrically, crazily, and foolishly at the expense of the altruistic, sensible, and intelligent frustration of the others.

The masochist, by contrast, tends to disqualify himself, saying and perceiving that he is bad, crazy, or foolish, while he overqualifies the others, perceiving them as good, sensible, and clever. His intrapsychic structure is formed by an inferego and a superalter. That is, there is an internal infersubject that is melancholically frustrating the desires of its id because it is dominated and dis-qualified by an internal superobject: the masochist believes that he is trying to satisfy egoistically, foolishly, and crazily his own desires at the expense of the frustration of the desires of the altruistic, sensible, and clever others, while, in fact, he frustrates himself altruistically, sensibly, and intelligently to satisfy the selfish, crazy, and foolish desires of the others.

We call superego what Freud called the "ideal-ego" in "Nar-cissism: An Introduction" (1914) and in *The Ego and the Id* (1923). Nunberg, who considers the emergence of the ego-ideal as prior to that of the superego, points out, with Freud and Lagache, that it is a narcissistic ideal of omnipotence. Lagache (1956) says that the ego-ideal, as well as representing the manic union of the ego with the id, represents the identification with an idealized omnipotent object, the mother. This would account for the formation of the sadist. He feels, and we agree, that the ego-ideal has sadomasochistic implica-tions because the subject tends to deny the other to support himself: it is an identification with the aggressor (A. Freud 1936). In other words, according to Lagache, with the ego-ideal the subject ac-quires a sadistic omnipotence that disqualifies others, and when the subject matures the omnipotent sadistic ego-ideal tends to transform itself into an "ideal of the ego," which is neither narcissistic nor sadistic.*

We prefer to use "superego" in the sense of ideal ego because it shows more clearly the omnipotence of the subject and the impo-tence of the object, especially when set in contrast to "superalter," which demonstrates more clearly the omnipotence of the object and the impotence of the subject. In summary, *what is traditionally called the ideal-ego we now call the superego, and what is tradi-tionally called the ego ideal and the superego we now call the*

---

*We think that the structure of narcissism is sadomasochistic, not only because the narcissistic individual is using others as mere mirrors of himself but also because he is selfish in his self-containment. We think, further, that both sadists and masochists are narcissists because both are using each other as mirrors: the sadist only perceives his own sadistic image in the masochist (with the unconscious agreement of the latter) and the masochist only perceives his own masochistic image in the sadist, without either of them really recognizing the other.

superalter (see Figure 0-1 (a)). The superalter is not an ego which is grandiose but rather something that is "over the ego," as W. R. Bion (1965) suggested when he explicated the notion of "super"ego. Moreover, the superego, in its traditional version, is the result of the postoedipal introjection of the subject's parents or their surrogates; that is, the introjection of the images of powerful others and not of a powerful subject. Consequently, it is an intrapsychic superalter and not an intrapsychic super*ego*. In other words, the alterity of the introjected other must be recognized as distinct from the identity of the ego. They do not constitute a single psychic structure as some of the original Freudian terms would imply. Furthermore, we are also taking a position in keeping with Lacan's concept of the decentered subject, whereby the unconscious subject coincides with neither the ego nor the alter in either their unconscious or conscious representations.

In spite of its simplicity (and possibly as a result of it) this conception raises new questions. For example, if the sadist is identified with the aggressor, does he not have a superego in the traditional sense, or a superalter in this new nomenclature? If the masochist is identified with the victim, does he not have an ego-ideal in the traditional sense, or superego in this new nomenclature? The intrapsychic structure reverts if the sadist interacts with someone more sadistic than himself, who would be introjected as a super-superalter, or if the masochist interacts with someone more masochistic than himself, who would be introjected as an infer-inferalter. It would be convenient to speak of the "sadistic position," that is, superego for himself, and inferalter for the others; and of the "masochistic position," that is, inferego for himself and superalter for the others.

It could be suggested that within the semiotic bipolar model of the psychic apparatus we are developing, this redefinition of the notion of superego could be translated as a modification at the metasemiotic level for use of the identifying code. In effect, instead of limiting himself to neutrally identifying as "ego" the group of representations that the subject has of his own words, actions, and affects, and as "alter" the group of representations that the subject has of the words, actions, and affects of the others, the subject would tend to simultaneously identify and qualify these representations.

The sadist would realize an overqualified metasemiotic identification of himself as a superego and a simultaneous disqualified

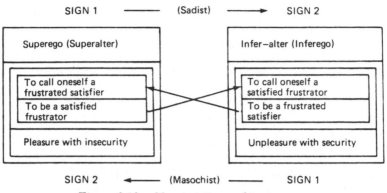

Figure 2-10. Narcissistic psychic structure

metasemiotic identification of the others as inferalter. The masochist would metasemiotically identify himself in exactly the reverse way. The overqualification would imply being altruistic, sensible, and clever, and the disqualification would imply being selfish, crazy, and foolish.

As a result, psychic sign 1 of the psychic structure of the sadist would be formed by the intrapsychic representations of *to call oneself a frustrated satisfier/to be a satisfied frustrator/pleasure-insecurity/superego*; and its psychic sign 2 would be *to call oneself a satisfied frustrator/to be a frustrated satisfier/unpleasure-security/inferalter*. For its part, the psychic structure of the masochist would be mirrored inversely. The psychic sign 1 would be constituted by *to call oneself a satisfied frustrator/to be a frustrated satisfier/security-unpleasure/inferego*; and, the psychic sign 2 would be *to call oneself a frustrated satisfier/to be a satisfied frustrator/insecurity-pleasure/superalter* (Figure 2-10).

REFERENCES

Barthes, R. (1967). *Elements of Semiology*. London: Jonathan Cape.

Bion, W. R. (1965). *Elements of Psychoanalysis*. London: Heinemann.

Eagle, M. (1973). Sherwood on the logic of explanation in psychoanalysis. In *Psychoanalysis and Contemporary Science*. New York: Macmillan.

Edelson, M. (1976). Towards a study of interpretation in psychoanalysis. In *Explorations in General Theory in Social Science*. New York: Macmillan.

—— (1977).   Psychoanalysis as a science. *Journal of Nervous and Mental Disease* 165:13.

Freud, A. (1936).   *The Ego and the Mechanisms of Defense*. New York: International Universities Press.

Freud, S. (1895).   Project for a scientific psychology. *Standard Edition* 1: 28–397.

—— (1900).   The interpretation of dreams. *Standard Edition* 4/5.

—— (1911).   Formulations on the two principles of mental functioning. *Standard Edition* 12:213–226.

—— (1914).   On narcissism: an introduction. *Standard Edition* 14:67–102.

—— (1915a).   Instincts and their vicissitudes. *Standard Edition* 14:109–140.

—— (1915b).   Repression. *Standard Edition* 14:143–158.

—— (1915c).   The unconscious. *Standard Edition* 14:159–215.

—— (1917).   A metapsychological supplement to the theory of dreams. *Standard Edition* 14:217–235.

—— (1920).   Beyond the pleasure principle. *Standard Edition* 18:7–64.

—— (1923).   The ego and the id. *Standard Edition* 19:3–66.

—— (1924).   The economic problem of masochism. *Standard Edition* 19: 159–173.

—— (1925).   Negation. *Standard Edition* 19:235–239.

—— (1930).   Civilization and its discontents. *Standard Edition* 21:59–145.

Gear, M. C., and Liendo, E. C. (1975).   *Sémiologie psychanalytique*. Paris: Minuit.

—— (1979).   *Action psychanalytique*. Paris: Minuit.

—— (1980).   *Psicoterapia strutturalista* Florence: del Riccio.

Green, A. (1974).   *Le discours vivant*. Paris: PUF.

Hill, M. A. (1979).   The fiction of mankind and the stories of men. In *Hannah Arendt: The Recovery of the Public World*. New York: St. Martin's.

Jones, E. (1957).   *The Life and Work of Sigmund Freud*, vol. 3. New York: Basic Books.

Klein, M. (1952).   Some theoretical conclusions regarding the emotional life of the infant. In *Developments in Psycho-Analysis*. London: Hogarth Press.

Lacan, J. (1966).   *Ecrits*. Paris: Editions du Seuil.

Lagache, D. (1956).   La psychanalyse et la structure de la personnalité. In *La Psychanalyse*. Paris: PUF. 6:39.

Lasègue, C., and Falret, J. (1873).   La folie à deux, au folie communiquée. *American Journal of Psychiatry* 4:1–23, 1964.

Leach, E. (1976).   *Culture and Communication*. Cambridge: Cambridge University Press.

Morris, C. (1971).   *Writing on the General Theory of Signs*. The Hague: Mouton.

Parsons, T. (1954). *The Social System*. Glencoe, Ill.: Free Press.

Pontalis, J. B. (1958). Les formations de l'inconscient, complesredus des seminars, 1957–58. *Bulletin de Psychologie* 11–12.

Prieto, L. (1966). *Messages et Signaux*. Paris: PUF 37–40.

Saussure, Ferdinand de (1916). *Course in General Linguistics*. New York: Philosophical Library, 1959.

Segal, H. (1964). *Introduction to the Work of Melanie Klein*. New York: Basic Books.

Tarski, A. (1956). *Logic, Semantics, Metamathematics*. Oxford: J. M. Woodper.

3

The Narrative Structure of Free Associations

In the previous chapter we used semiotics to build a metapsychological model for the psychoanalysis of sadism and masochism. Now we will try to use it as an instrument to refine the methods of observation and systematization of psychoanalytic material in the clinical setting.

The content of free associations can be seen as a particular type of narrative; the analysand always tells his own story either directly or through the story of others.

We will use the sophisticated methods of the structural analysis of narratives to organize the analysis of free associations. Our aim is to help the analyst to find not only the conscious, superficial, manifest structure of the analysand's speech but also its unconscious, deep, latent structure as quickly and as rigorously as possible—but always respecting the narrative structure of "the manifest content as if it were a sacred text" (Freud 1912).

Since psychoanalysts are always analyzing stories, it is time we learned to do so systematically. We must also be able to analyze the style and the content by means of which the analysand, as storyteller, tells us his own story.

The Different Types of Analytic Speech

The speech of the analyst and his analysand within the psycho-analytic setting can be classified operationally into six categories:

73

associative, defensive, working-through, consulting, setting, and conventional.

Associative speech is formed by the free associations of the analysand; that is, when he is speaking only with the goal of allowing the analyst to analyze his associations. Even if he is referring to external events he is not particularly interested in them; he is interested in his own verbal production. If he is speaking about his conflictive relations with his parents he is not asking for a prescription of what to do with them; he just wants to know why he is speaking about them at that moment. He knows that the object of the analysis is his own speech and not his actual relations with his parents.

Defensive speech, or "talking-out," is formed by the free associations produced by the analysand, with the apparent purpose of collaborating with the analyst but with the hidden, unconscious, purpose of provoking in the analyst a reaction similar to that of his primary significant others. The purpose is to provoke in the analyst a counter–acting-out that will reinforce the analysand's old repetition-compulsion pattern.

Working-through speech, or "talking-through," consists of insightful reflections of the analysand after the therapeutic interventions of the analyst. Generally speaking, the analysand recognizes that he is repeating his compulsive pattern in the tranference or elsewhere and then recalls some early memories or a previous dream confirming what the analyst has told him. Or, he accepts part of one interpretation but corrects another part, etc.

Consulting speech, or "talking-about," comprises the comments of the analysand concerning some specific relations with significant external objects. He speaks not to analyze his comments but in order to find concrete prescriptions and proscriptions to apply to those specific relations. Generally speaking, consulting speech appears when the analysand is going through a crisis with a very important other or when the other is going through a deep crisis (such as a suicide attempt). It can be said, analytically, that when the analysand speaks about others, he is using those others to contain his own projection or to displace the tranferential relationship. But sometimes he needs some specific information—not about what to do but about how his own psychopathology is originating, reinforcing, or perpetuating a crisis in others. In this case the analyst is used mostly as a consultant or as a "supervisor," as if the analysand were his "supervisee" and the conflicting other were the "analysand of the analysand."

It is very important for the analyst to distinguish when the analysand is associating from when he is just consulting. If he is consulting and the analyst gives him a transferential interpretation, for instance, the analysand will reinterpret it as indirect advice about what to do outside. In psychoanalytic psychotherapy, we think that the patient mainly produces consulting speech and the therapist works mainly as an analytic supervisor: there is a striking similarity between psychoanalytic psychotherapy and psychoanalytic supervision.

Setting speech comprises the questions or consultations of the analysand about the meaning or the procedures of the analytic setting—questions about time, money, changing or replacing sessions, etc. Again, it can be said that when the analysand is speaking about the setting he is also speaking about himself or about the transference relationship; in any case, he is making a demand for concrete information that deserves at least a concrete answer and perhaps an interpretation.

Finally, *conventional speech* (chatting) occurs, for example, when both the analysand and the analyst talk on a conventional level about unexpected real events breaking the setting: if the lights fail, or if they meet at the elevator, etc.

The structural and syntactical analysis in this chapter will refer to the associative, defensive, and consulting speech, concentrating specifically on the associative speech within the psychoanalytic setting. Associative speech falls into two categories: *cardinal speech*, consisting of a plot with characters and a sequence; and *neutral speech*, with no plot and acquiring sense only in relation to the cardinal speech. We will analyze the cardinal associative speech of the analysand, which can be classified, in turn, as speech descriptive of actions and affects, and speech qualifying of actions and affects.

Technically, the analyst will operate differently when facing different categories of the analysand's speech. In effect, he will use a "descriptive speech" or an "interpretive speech" when working with associative, defensive, or working-through speech; he will use a "supervising speech" (plus an interpretive speech) when working with consulting speech; he will use an "informing speech" (plus an interpretive speech) when working with setting speech; and he will use a "neutral conventional speech" when responding to the analysand's conventional speech.

In order to proceed with the syntactical analysis of the cardinal speech, one has to segment the narrative flow, breaking it up into separate narrative units. This segmentation of the speech constitutes a complicated methodological and technical problem.

We have found that the structural analysis of narratives, begun by Viktor Shklovsky and Vladimir Propp, and developed by A. J. Greimas and others, along with the structural analysis of myths— developed by Roman Jakobson, Claude Lévi-Strauss, and Roland Barthes—provide refined and rigorous analytic tools, useful in segmenting and obtaining the superficial and deep structure of the narrative units.

Structural Analysis of Myths

Four concepts are used as basic tools in the structural analysis of narratives and myths (Leach 1976). When studying a semiotic process, *metonymy* implies a kind of contiguity between the symbol and what it symbolizes: "glass" replaces "wine" when one says "give me a glass." *Metaphor* implies a kind of similarity: "umbrella" can be a symbol of "penis" because they have a similar shape. *Paradigmatic associations* implies simultaneous associations, such as the different instruments making simultaneous sounds heard in combination: "paradigm" is like "harmony." *Syntagmatic chains* implies sequence, such as the letters forming a word or a phrase, or one musical note following another to form a tune: "syntagma" is like "melody."

Roman Jakobson, who first emphasized the importance of the polarity metaphor/metonymy, made it clear from the start that in actual observable forms of discourse, either verbal or nonverbal, the two modes are always mixed up, though one may predominate (Jakobson and Halle 1956). The prototype of a general message-bearing system is not a line of type but the performance of an orchestra where harmony and melody work in combination.

Jakobson's insight has been developed by Claude Lévi-Strauss (1963) to provide his celebrated technique of myth interpretation. The key point here is not just that metaphor and metonymy, paradigmatic associations and syntagmatic chains, are combined, but that "meaning" depends upon *transformations* from one mode into the other and back again (Leach 1976).

Lévi-Strauss (1955) first breaks up the syntagmatic chain, or the flow of the complete myth, into a sequence of episodes. He then assumes that each episode is a partial metaphoric transformation of every other. This implies that the story as a whole can be thought of as a palimpsest of superimposed (but incomplete) metaphoric transformations. It follows that the analyst who seeks to decode the message embodied in the myth as a whole (as distinct from the surface messages presented by the stories in the individual episodes) must look for a pattern of structure (which is necessarily abstract) common to the whole set of metaphors. The final interpretation consists of reading this derived pattern as if it were a syntagmatic chain. The procedure involves a double switch from the metonymic mode to the metaphoric and back to the metonymic (Leach 1976).

Lévi-Strauss himself represents this process by a mathematical formula; it can also be represented by the following scheme.

1. We start with a mythical story which is linear in form, one thing happening after another. The events occur in sequence, that is, they form a "syntagmatic chain"; they are linked by metonymy.

2. The analyst then notes that the story as a whole can be broken up into episodes and represented horizontally:

Episode A   Episode B   Episode C

3. Each of the episodes is then assumed to be a partial transformation of each of the others. So we rearrange the diagram vertically to suggest that each of the subplots refers to simultaneous events, and "add up" the result. Technically speaking, by the first of these steps, the original "syntagmatic chain" is transformed into a "paradigmatic association" (metonymy is converted into metaphor), thus:

Episode A
Episode B
Episode C
_____

summary result obtained by "addition"

As compared with the details in the original episodes, the elements in the summary "additive" story are abstract. It is a *structural* sequence which can be best represented as an algebraic equation of which each of the three original episodes was an imperfect manifestation (Leach 1976).

This summation process amounts to the conversion of a "paradigmatic association" into a "syntagmatic chain"; metaphor is transformed into metonymy (Leach 1976).

The basic principle involved is one common to much verbal expression and all ritual activity: the end is implicit in the beginning and vice versa. In interpreting a message we are always performing a feat comparable to that of translating one language into another. We are, as it were, transposing the music from one key into another (Leach 1976).

But Lévi-Strauss (1963) also maintains that between the myth as verbal activity, and its ritual as factual activity, there is no relation of homology or repetition, as was assumed by classical anthropology. A symmetrical and reverse relation is more usual: the myth exposes a reversed ritual system. The organization of the rite is exactly the contrary to that of the myth. They are antithetic structures which have the appearance of responses, remedies, excuses, and even remorse.

Structural Analysis of Fairy Tales

The structural analysis of narratives started with Russian formalism during the 1920s. Early formalism built on the groundwork of symbolism (Todorov 1965) and of symbolist concern with form as a visible communicative instrument: autonomous, self-expressive, able to be an extraverbal, rhythmic, associative, and connotative means to "stretch" language beyond its everyday range of meaning. A morphological approach to literature was derived from it, and attempts to defamiliarize that with which we are openly familiar, to disrupt stock responses and to restructure our ordinary perception of "reality" (Hawkes 1977).

Viktor Shklovsky (1923) is careful in distinguishing between the "plot" and the "story" of a novel. "Story" is simply the basic succession of events, the raw material which confronts the writer. "Plot" represents the distinctive way in which the story is made strange, creatively deformed and defamiliarized. So "plot" can be seen to be as much an organic element of form in the novel as rhyme or rhythm are in lyric, and it has a decisively formative role. For instance, the analyst can "defamiliarize" the manifest content of the analysand's associations only if he considers first the familiar, conventional meaning of the content (Hawkes 1977).

The full implications of this problem were perhaps best handled in the work of V. I. Propp, *Morphology of the Folktale* (1928). Propp's concern, in fact, is exactly with the "norms" by which narrative structures work, and the units of "content" in which they seem to deal. His attempt at a taxonomy retains considerable structural value to the present day, for, like the myth, the fairy tale ranks as an important prototype of all narrative (Hawkes 1977).

In Propp's analysis, the fairy tale is seen primarily to embody a syntagmatic, "horizontal" structuring, rather than the associative "vertical" structuring represented by the lyric poem. Propp's analysis, in short, reinforces the view that narrative is fundamentally syntagmatic in mode. But the major breakthrough represented in his work derives from his insistence that in the fairy tale, the all-important and unifying element is found not within the "characters" who appear in the story but in the characters' *function*—the part they play in the plot (Hawkes 1977).

A "function" is defined here as "an act of the character defined from the point of view of its significance for the course of action." For Propp the fairy tale characteristically "often attributes identical actions to various personages." This makes possible an analysis of the tales according to the various functions of their *dramatis personae* and indicates that, despite the surface profusion of detail, the number of functions is extremely small whereas the number of personages is extremely large. Hence, the phenomenon of "duplicity" occurs (which Lévi-Strauss notes in the structures of the myth) along with its curious effect on the language involved: "The two-fold quality of a tale: its amazing multiformity, picturesqueness and colour, and on the other hand its no less striking uniformity, its repetition" (Hawkes 1977).

Analysis of these elements of uniformity and repetition leads Propp to the conclusion that all fairy tales are structurally homogeneous, and embody the following basic principles:

1. Functions of characters serve as stable, constant elements in a tale, independently of how or by whom they are fulfilled. They constitute the fundamental components of a tale.
2. The number of functions known to the fairy tale is limited; Propp states that there are only thirty-one functions.

3. The sequence of functions is always identical.

4. All fairy tales are of one type in regard to their structure.

The thirty-one functions Propp finds are distributed among seven "spheres of action" corresponding to their "respective performers" as follows: (1) the villain; (2) the donor; (3) the helper; (4) the princess (a sought-after person) and her father; (5) the dispatcher; (6) the hero; and (7) the false hero (Hawkes 1977).

Thus, the number of spheres of action (like the number of functions) occurring in the fairy tale is finite: we are dealing with discernible and repeated structures with an identical sequence of functions (Hawkes 1977).

The work of A. J. Greimas (1966) attempts to describe narrative structure in terms of an established linguistic model derived from Ferdinand de Saussure's idea (1916) of an underlying *langue* or competence which generates a specific *parole* or performance, as well as from Saussure's and Jakobson's concept of the fundamental signifying role of binary opposition: "dark" is defined principally by our sense of its opposition to "light," and "up" by our sense of its opposition to "down." It is a binary patterning of mutual opposition that forms the basis of what Lévi-Strauss (1949) has called the sociologic of the human mind, which structures nature in its own image and thus establishes the foundation for the systems of totemic "transformations" that overtly or covertly underpin our picture of the world.

The perception of opposition underlies the "elementary structure of signification," says Greimas (1966). "We perceive differences," he writes, "and thanks to that perception the world takes shape in front of us, and for our own purposes." The differences involve two opposed pairs structuring our perception: A is opposed to B as −A is opposed to −B. The elementary structure involves recognition and distinction of two aspects of an entity: its opposite and its negation. We see B as the opposite of A and −B as the opposite of −A, but we also see −A as the negation of A and −B as the negation of B.

The nature and power of these structures prove in effect so deep and formative that they ultimately shape the elements of our language, its syntax, and the experiences which these articulate in the form of narrative. These binary oppositions form the basis of a deep-lying *actantial* model from whose structure the superficial surface structures of individual stories derive, and by which they are generated. The parallel with Saussure's notion of a *langue* which underlies *parole,* and with Chomsky's notation of a *competence* which precedes a *performance,* is clear (Hawkes 1977).

The content of the actions changes all the time, the actors vary, but the "enunciation spectacle" (the dramatic, interlocutory "grammar") remains always the same, for its permanence is guaranteed by the fixed distribution of the roles. An *actant* is like a function but accomplishes a common role in the story's "oppositional" structure: the deep structure of the narrative generates and defines its actants at a level beyond that of the story's surface content (Hawkes 1977).

Greimas's scheme (1966) "makes the structure of the sentence roughly" homologous to the "plot" of a "text." He reduces Propp's thirty-one functions into three "actantial categories," that is, three sets of binary oppositions, into which all the actants can be fitted, and which will generate all the actors of any story (Hawkes 1977):

1. Subject versus Object
2. Sender versus Receiver
3. Helper versus Opponent

The ultimate goal of the structural analysis of narrative is the establishment of basic plot "paradigms," and an exploration of the full range of their combinatory potential: the construction of a narrational combinatoire, or story-generating mechanism: a competence of narrative, which generates the performance of stories—a *langue,* in short, of literature (Hawkes 1977).

Structural Analysis of James Bond

Umberto Eco (1966a,b) attempted to demythify the stories which are produced *en masse* by the culture industry by showing that, although they are presented as different, they are actually made up of the same mechanisms. He analyses the structural narrative of Ian Fleming's novels about the adventures of the secret agent James Bond from this viewpoint.

Eco postulates that the novels are based on a "narrative machine" that functions with very simple units ruled by very rigorous rules of combination from which there is no deviation. He describes the narrative structures in three levels: (1) the oppositions of characters and values; (2) the "game" situations and the plot as a "match"; and (3) the literary technique. He theorizes that Fleming's novels can be constructed from a series of fixed binary oppositions that allow a limited number of permutations and interactions. He identifies a paradigmatic group of four binomials of characters (Bond–M; Bond–Villain; Villain–Woman; and Woman–Bond) and the binomials of values (Free World–Soviet Union; Chance–Programming; Loyalty–Disloyalty; Love–Death; etc.) as well as a syntagmatic group of nine "plays" or "movements." These binomials and movements are not vague elements, but simple ones. They are immediate and universal. Possible variations form a large spectrum encompassing Fleming's entire narrative.

The syntagmatic outline common to all of Fleming's novels, a result of a very elementary *ars combinatoria* of the opposition binomials, follow a pre-fixed code. The "algebra" of the novel is achieved according to the optional solution given to each binomial. This is interpreted by Eco in game theory terms, as though it were bridge or football:

> If the "matches" occupy such an important place in Fleming's narra-tive structure, it is because they are constituted like formalized scale models of the more general game situation which is the novel. Given the rules of combination of the opposition binomials, the novel appears as a sequence of plays taken from the code and is created according to a perfectly pre-fixed outline.
>
> The invariable outline, the fixed syntagmatic of functions, would be as follows:
>
> 1. M (the boss) plays and entrusts Bond with a mission.
> 2. Bad plays and appears before Bond (on occasion vicariously).
> 3. Bond plays and checks Bad; or else Bad checks Bond.
> 4. Woman plays and shows up before Bond.
> 5. Bond eats Woman: he possesses her or starts to seduce her.
> 6. Bad captures Bond (with or without Woman).
> 7. Bad tortures Bond (with or without Woman).
> 8. Bond wins over Bad.
> 9. Bond, convalescent, spends time with Woman, whom he will later lose.
>
> The outline is invariable in the sense that all of the elements (characters and functions) are present in each of the novels: one might state that the fundamental rule is that Bond makes a play and check-

mates in eight moves. Fleming thus constructs a narrative machine (Eco 1966a, pp. 38–40).

The narrator will in a very few words be able to give to the receiver that archetype common to all of Ian Fleming's novels. These novels function like a narrative machine that constantly creates redundance under the appearance of creating information. Its collateral inventions would vary from novel to novel, forming the muscle of the narrative skeleton.

Eco thinks that under the appearance of being an information-producing machine, Fleming's novels are redundancy-producing machines; while pretending to jolt the readers, due to a sort of laziness of the imagination, they facilitate evasion of reality and merely confirm what is already known instead of telling about the unknown: the plot always involves the same chain of events and the same type of primary and secondary characters. The conservative pleasure of the reader consists in finding himself in a game of which he knows the pieces and the rules—and even the outcome—and simply enjoys following the minute variations that the hero will use to achieve his aim: "Fleming's novels make judicious use of the element of the game that is discounted and absolutely redundant, and typical of the evasive machines that function in the circuit of mass-repressive communications" (Eco 1966a, p. 42).

Structural Analysis of Free Associations

In applying the structural analysis of myths to the analysand's associative speech we were able to arrive at the following conclusions (Gear and Liendo 1979):

1. The meaning of the analysand's associations depends upon transformations (by reduction and inversion, for example) from one mode (metonymic or metaphoric) into the other, and back again.
2. The analysand's associative chain can be broken up into a sequence of episodes.
3. Each associated episode is a metonymic or metaphoric transformation of the other.

4. The analysand's associations can be thought of as a palimpsest of superimposed metaphoric transformation. He always speaks about the same things, but in different ways. Thus, we look for an abstract pattern of structure common to the whole set of associations that helps to define the analysand through his speech: his "abstractus" can be obtained.

5. In order to obtain the narrative structure, and this abstractus of the analysand, we proceed by the following steps:

(a) Start with an associative chain of the analysand, his "myth," which is linear in form.

(b) Break up the associative chain into a sequence of episodes, according to their capacity to convey the same meaning.

(c) Add the different episodes or subplots to obtain a summary plot, or the reduced structure of the manifest content, or manifest meaning of the associative chain: the analysand tends to always narrate the same stereotyped plot, that is, the same myth.

(d) Break up the chain of actions of the analysand, or his "ritual" in a sequence of sub-courses of action, and then add the different sub-courses of action to obtain a summary of the complete course of action, or the reduced structure, or meaning of the chain of actions: the analysand tends to always take the same stereotyped course of action, or enact the same ritual.

(e) Compare the reduced structure of the associative chain with the reduced structure of the corresponding chain of actions.

(f) Because the structure of associative speech, or stereotyped myth, is usually inverted with respect to the structure of the actions it represents, or stereotyped ritual, it can be said that to obtain the actual structure of these actions, or "latent content" of the speech, it is enough to multiply by minus one its manifest content.

This structural analysis of the myth and ritual of the analysand allows us to defamiliarize the structure of the manifest content of the associative chain as well as that of the course of action: his ritual would be the latent content of his myth. It also allows us to further the analysis by applying some concepts and operations of the structural analysis of narrative. In doing this we are able to arrive at the following conclusions (Gear and Liendo 1979).

6. Within the associative chain, the all-important and unifying element is not found within its characters but in its characters'

functions; that is, within the actions an analysand ascribes to its characters.

7. The number of functions within the associative chain is extremely small, whereas the number of personages is extremely large. The analysand's chain of associations, like the myth and the fairy tale, has a twofold quality: it has amazing multiformity, picturesqueness, and color, yet, at the same time (and equally striking) uniformity and repetition. The analysand can speak about many different people doing many different things, but at some level, he is always speaking about the same plot with the same characters following the same sequence.

8. All chains of associations are structurally homogeneous and embody the following basic principles:

(a) Functions of character serve as stable, constant elements in the analysand's associative speech, independently of how and by whom they are fulfilled. They constitute the fundamental components of a chain of free associations: if the analysand is saying repeatedly that he is persecuted or seduced, it doesn't matter to whom and how he gives the role of this persecutor or seducer.

(b) The number of functions known to the associative speech of each analysand is limited: the number of functions of the hysterical analysand will be limited to the seducer and the seduced; in a paranoid analysand, it will be limited to the persecutor and the persecuted. In sadomasochism the functions will be limited to <satisfied frustrator> and <frustrated satisfier.>*

(c) The sequence of functions is always identical in all the associative chains of each analysand, for example: she behaves seductively but denies it, the other makes a pass at her, she rejects him, he gets angry, she starts crying, he abandons her, etc.

(d) All associative chains of all analysands are of one type with regard to their structure: they are always referring, in one way or another, to a bipolar interaction between a <bad satisfied frustrator> who fears unpleasure and a <good frustrated satisfier> who fears insecurity.

*Here and throughout, double angle brackets signal that their contents are to be aggregated as a single syntactic unit for purposes of the sentence at hand. As our writing employs these compounds freely, we hope these brackets will help the reader to follow the meaning of our sentences more easily.

9. All the functions of every associative chain can be bipolarly distributed between two spheres of action: "satisfying oneself by frustrating others" and "frustrating oneself by satisfying others"; these correspond to two "performers"—"ego" and "alter"—who, in turn, can be qualified as being "good" or "bad."

In this way we have attempted (Gear and Liendo 1979) to describe the narrative structure of the analysand's chains of free-associations in terms of the Saussurean model of *langue* (speech's reduced structure) and *parole* (speech's nonreduced structure); the Shklovskean model of "story" and "plot"; the Proppean model of "character" and "function"; and Jakobson's and Saussure's hypothesis about the fundamental roles of binary oppositions in the narrative structure. Following Lévi-Strauss's conception of a socio-logic, we believe that the psychologic of the human mind structures nature in its own narcissistic image and establishes the systems of binary oppositions that overtly or covertly underpin our picture of the world.

10. The deep narrative structure of the analysand's chains of associations generates and defines its "actants" as pairs of opposite functions and makes the structure of the chain homologous to the plot of a text.

11. All the functions of the analysand's associative speech can be bipolarly reduced into five actantial categories, or five sets of binary oppositions, into which all the actants of the speech can be fitted and which will generate all the actors of any story associated by the analysand. These five actants are: (a) subject (as "ego") versus object (as "alter"); (b) satisfied frustrator (as "sadist") versus frustrated satisfier (as "masochist"); and (c) bad versus good; (d) pleasure versus unpleasure; (e) security versus insecurity.

In other words, it can be said that all associative speech, when narcissistic (sadomasochistic) can be fitted into two classes of myths: either the analysand is saying that he is a <bad satisfied frustrator> of others who is enjoying pleasure, but with insecurity, or he is saying that he is a <good frustrated satisfier> of others who is suffering unpleasure, but with security. All narcissistic courses of action can be fitted into the same two classes of "rituals" which are inverted with respect to the corresponding myths. In brief, the myth of the sadist will be that he is a <good frustrated satisfier> of others suffering unpleasure but with security, while his ritual is to be a <bad

satisfied frustrator> of others enjoying pleasure but with insecurity. The myth of the masochist will be similarly inverted with respect to his ritual.

12. The analyst can describe in a very few words to a colleague (or to the patient himself) the archetype common to all of the analysand's stories. The analysand, because of his compulsion to repeat, will function like a narrative machine that constantly creates redundance under the appearance of creating information: It is quite easy to make the analysand's "abstractus" by describing the characters, values, and movements of his speech.

In effect, in the analysand's narrative structure one can distinguish a paradigmatic structure formed by characters related by functions (classes of qualified actions) and a syntagmatic structure formed by the fixed sequence of functions that engender a narcissistic information program of the psychic apparatus.

13. This means that by analyzing the narrative structure of a given analysand, one can reconstruct a narrative machine that functions on the basis of very simple units. During all of the following sessions it will function without deviation to the point where it would be quite possible to simulate its behavior in a computer. The analysand, just as much as Ian Fleming or the narrators of Russian fairy tales, tells defensive, conservative, stereotyped tales: they denote and connote that it is better not to change theme, or style, or behavior.

14. For each given analysand's session it would be possible to draw up a fixed paradigmatic outline of functions and characters, as well as a fixed syntagmatic outline of the sequence of functions. The collateral inventions would vary according to the analysand's education and activity and form the "muscle" of the narrative skeleton individualized by each analysand: actions and persons may change without the functions or characters changing, unless the analysand brings about a qualitative transformation of the structure of his psychic system—through insight, outsight, and social-sight opening out onto the fundamental specific action—and also transforms the characters and functions that link them. Unless he changes his synchronic paradigmatic structure (fundamental psychic structure) and his diachronic syntagmatic structure (fundamental conflictive transaction), an analysand will only make apparent changes and superficial transformations of the same latent generative structure.

15. As long as the analysand's generative latent narrative structure does not change, the plot of his stories will remain immutable and their "suspense," strangely enough, will rest on a sequence of events totally discounted by the analyst. He already knows that at every session his patient will relate various encounters with his alter and will merely be curious to know (a) the way in which today the analysand will tell the same story, with the same characters, the same relations, and the same sequence of opening, development, and closing of the same fundamental conflictive transaction between his ego and his alter; and (2) how he will stop telling the story—whether there really is a therapeutic change in the generative latent narrative structure, in the double sense that it is more conscious and less paradigmatically and syntagmatically stereotyped.

The analyst, if he does not pay attention to the persistent immutability of his analysand's generative latent narrative structure, will often confuse the apparent, manifest changes in the generated structure with true latent changes. He interprets a mere change of persons and actions as a change in the mutilation and the incongruency of the basic characters and functions. Under the appearance of being an information-producing machine, the analysand's story generally is a redundancy-producing machine. While pretending to jolt the analyst, due to a sort of laziness of the imagination he evades and confirms what is already known instead of telling about the unknown: "Maximum pleasure need not arise out of excitement, but from rest" (Freud 1920).

Narratives, as a rule, have a stereotyped and conservative paradigmatic and syntagmatic structure. Analysts arrive at this conclusion empirically in spite of the fact that we sometimes try to discover something extraordinary and new where there is only textual repetition, when we become countertransferentially contaminated with the analysand's need to believe he is innovating at the moment he is most prone to repetition. Detecting this repetition in the narrative structure of an analysand is not to mutilate his story; at times this is quite the contrary.

Thus the psychoanalyst can end up reinforcing the analysand's pseudo-innovation out of a fear that he will mutilate his narrative production if he shows the analyst how he repeats the same theme monotonously. What is apparently new in the stories then hides the repetition of the same. We find this phenomenon of pseudo-creativity more often in the analysis of hysterical and manic analysands. Indeed, what is narrated by paranoid and epileptoid patients is generally far more clearly stereotyped with regard to characters, functions, and sequence: they are less able to generate manifest narrative structures based on the generative latent narrative structure. The fact that they always talk about the things in the same way is far more noticeable.

Just as with Fleming and his novels, the analysand is responsible for his characteristics and actions, and for the plot always involving the same chain of events and the same type of secondary characters. The analyst's "pleasure" consists in finding himself in a game of which he knows the pieces and rules—and even the outcome—and he simply "enjoys" following the minute variations the analysand, as hero, will use to achieve his aim: to prove once more the hypothesis of the narcissistic psychic apparatus.

16. The narrative of the analysand can be compared—as Eco does with Fleming's novels—to a football match of which the environment, the number and personality of the players, and the rules of the game would be known in advance: it is known that the game will take place, that is will take place inside the field, and what the result will be. The analyst already knows, for example, that his paranoid analysand will relate several times in one session how it was discovered that someone wanted to harm him, although he disguised it by passing himself off as his friend; or how his hysterical analysand will tell him the story, several times in one session, of how he let himself be deceived by someone who really wanted to take advantage of him sexually; or how his melancholic analysand will tell him several times per session of how he let himself be harmed by someone who finally ended up reproaching him; or how his manic analysand will tell him several times per session how he tricked somebody whom he ended up abandoning.

17. Analysands, like Fleming in his novels, "make judicious use of the element of the game that is discounted and absolutely redundant, and typical of the evasive (and conservative) machines that function in the circuit of mass-repressive communications" (Eco 1966a). In this sense they resemble the kind of person who is manipulated by advertising campaigns and thinks he has a wealth of imagination, when in reality he buys the same products as everybody else. In analysis, analysands repeat the same theme while believing they have launched something new. The mechanism the analysand uses to give the inverse narrative of this stereotyped interaction is so obvious that the analyst sometimes asks himself whether the analysand is joking or talking with perfectly calculated cynicism. It is difficult to believe that the unconscious could be so clear and so

precise that the analysand can repeat and project what his superego does not allow him to remember, or perceive what he has done and what others do to him.

Psychotomogram of Associative Speech

Lévi-Strauss's structural analysis of myths and rituals leads us to the construction of the psychotomogram (Gear and Liendo 1978), a new psychoanalytic instrument for systematizing the static, synchronic, paradigmatic structure of the analysand's speech (myth) and actions (ritual). To analyze their dynamic, diachronic, syntagmatic, structure we constructed the psychoflowchart (Gear and Liendo 1980) by integrating psychoanalysis, Propp's structural analysis of narratives, and the cybernetic notion of algorithm.

To obtain the paradigmatic structure of the analysand's speech and actions through the psychoanalytic psychotomogram, three methodological steps must be followed. These stages or "commutations" are:

(1) the syntagmatic breaking up;

(2) the paradigmatic reduction; and

(3) the paradigmatic inversion.

The syntagmatic breaking up of the analysand's associative chain is a "horizontal" operation, the specific goal of which is to cut the chain into distinct episodes—that is, into narrative units or "narratemes": the extension of each unit is defined by its semantic content. The episodes are like "meaning units." In a "semanalysis," each unit, to be considered as a unit, must be able to transmit the whole personal myth, the monothematic personal novel of the analysand—the personal way in which he satisfies or frustrates his desires and the desires of others. These "narratemes" may be formed by only one word or by a complete story of hundreds of words: each narrateme will be formed by a "narrator," a verbal story with a variable extension, and a "narrated" plot with a fixed extension. The same thing happens with the "mytheme" or mythical unit.

Once the narrative units are obtained, they must be compared by using the paradigmatic reduction. The summary of the addition of all the anecdotes gives a common denominator repeated in all of them. This common pattern is the meaning, the "true" manifest structure of the analysand's personal myth.

Once the common surface or manifest structure of the narrative units is obtained, in order to determine its common deep latent content, the surface structure must be submitted to certain symbolic (metaphoric and metonymic) "transformations" by using the paradigmatic inversion. The empirical hypothesis of the inversion of the speech with respect to its corresponding actions and affective states must be applied: we invert the direction of the actions and the quality of the affective states described in the manifest structure of the analysand's personal myth in order to obtain its "true" latent structure, or its ritual.

The psychotomogram is, consequently, a three dimensional instrument because it permits the analysis of the analysand's speech horizontally, vertically, and indepth through the three "communications" of its manifest content. (See Figure 3-1.)

In brief, to apply structural analysis to a concrete chain of associations, we break it up into episodes, compare them to obtain its manifest structure, and then invert the structure to obtain its latent structure. The analyst must follow nine successive operational steps. In effect, he must:

1. Distinguish between cardinal and neutral associations.
2. Break up the cardinal associations into distinctive anecdotes.
3. Define the characters within each anecdote.
4. Define the relations between characters within each anecdote.
5. Define the sequence of the actions and reactions of the characters within each anecdote.
6. Define the characters, relations, and sequences which are common to all the anecdotes—that is, determine the manifest structure of the analysand's associations.
7. Invert the direction of the relations between characters that are common to all the anecdotes—that is, determine the latent structure of the analysand's associations.
8. Compare the relations between characters in the speech with the relations between the analysand and himself, to confirm the latent structure of associations.
9. Compare the relations between characters and between actors with his affective state, to further confirm the latent structure of associations.

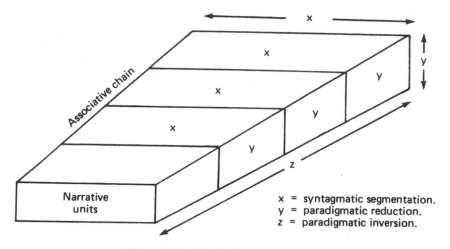

Figure 3-1. Analytic commutations

CLINICAL EXAMPLE

We will now try to show how structural analysis is done, with the aid of a brief clinical example. The clinical material we will be presenting is necessarily excerpted from the complete record of analysis. Its major shortcoming, therefore, is that it fails to provide the reader an adequate context for understanding the case as a whole. In particular, it does not give him the chance to follow the discourse and actions of the partners to the analysis in order to assess the analyst's competence. A major issue here, of course, is the analyst's contribution to the analysand's actions and speech. Is the analyst engaged in a narcissistic interaction with the analysand that sustains his compulsion to repeat? Is the analyst taking the role of the analysand's narcissistic other? Does he counter-act-out in response to the analysand's acting out? Or is the analyst, in fact, pushing the analysand into the position of his own narcissistic alter, compelling him to counter-act-out in response to his own acting out? These are fundamental questions, as an affirmative answer to any one of them would rule out the possibility of a successful analysis. It is the analyst's responsibility to provide a setting in which the analysis can take place, and consequently the first requirement is always that he neither engage the analysand as a narcissistic alter, nor permit the analysand to engage him as his narcissistic alter. We are of course not arguing that one can simply assume that the analyst, by virtue of his training and credentials, is always in the nonnarcissistic position. He would have had to work through his own unconscious narcissistic structure, and be constantly engaged in self-analysis. Nor does our model of psychoanalysis put the analyst in an omnipotent or omniscient position—that would be nothing less than a return to narcissism of the sadistic variety. The model is intended to provide the analyst a methodical and efficient method of undertaking the work of analysis, and nothing more. The method does not put him in the position of a superego in relation to the inferalter of the analysand. It simply provides him the technique to establish the setting and guide the discourse along productive lines. What makes this possible is precisely the technique of analysing the conscious and unconscious structures of the analysand's speech and actions within the framework of the analytic setting.

The present excerpt is from the beginning of Peter's analysis, when he was threatening to leave treatment. The issue was how to enable him to accept the basic condition of the setting. Displaying obvious paranoid resistances, he evoked the corresponding negative countertransference in the analyst, both conscious and unconscious. At the unconscious level he evoked the response of a masochistic agent ready to accept his blaming while at the conscious level the defense against this takes the form of an apparent sadistic attack whereby the analyst wants to expel the analysand. Recognizing the countertransference at both the unconscious and the conscious levels the analyst was then able to help the analysand by interpreting the conscious and unconscious narcissistic structures he was trying to act out.

Some observers might object that these interpretations fail to respect the intricacy of the neurosis and the analysand's individuality. But without the interpretation of these narcissistic structures, we contend, the analysand would not have been able to undertake his analysis at all.

Peter is a seventeen-year-old analysand who was sent for treatment by his parents because he had dropped out of school and failed to obtain a job or maintain any stable interpersonal relationships. He blames his parents, his teachers, and his potential friends for being cruel, rejecting people. According to the psychopathological classification proposed in chapter 1, he would be a "border-line," that is, a sadistic patient. After not having come to his two previously scheduled sessions, without giving notice, and after consulting another analyst during this absence, he arrives at his session late and very angry.

Analysand: I'm very angry. The members of the Boy Scouts are really awful . . . traitors . . . they are crazy. Yesterday I went to the weekly meeting and I found that they have filled my position there. Simply because I didn't show up to some previous meetings and because I fought with some of them, they excluded me. They got very angry at me without any justification. They replaced me with another guy. But I will take some revenge . . . I will send them an unsigned letter denouncing all their dirty tricky moves. Because I, in my own way, honored my duties to them.

Analyst: Maybe you're afraid that I'll do the same thing to you— that I will replace you with another patient. As you don't attend your sessions or you arrive late . . .

Analysand [interrupting]: *Of course I'm afraid of that! Because you psychoanalysts are all the same! That was exactly what happened to me with my former therapist: in an unjustified way, just because I didn't attend some sessions, arrived late or used to fight and scream, she replaced me. Once, after I hadn't attended some sessions, I arrived for my session and I found that my hour had been filled. It was terrible . . . I felt extremely hurt. I wrote her a very nasty letter, blaming her. Psychoanalysts are supposed to help their patients and not abandon them in such an irresponsible way. Particularly if patients are doing their best to help!*

Analyst: But if you look at your own behavior with me, with the Boy Scouts, and your former therapist it cannot be said that you were being responsible toward people who are doing what they can to help you . . .

Analysand [interrupting]: *That's really funny. You overlook that I'm the patient who suffers and comes here to be cured, not abandoned, just because he is sick. You are the inept, the irresponsible ones! I was just remembering that the day before yesterday I went to consult another psychoanalyst . . . I was so sure that you would reject me. And I am so sensitive. We, the victims of*

society, are the ones who suffer the consequences. But we can have our revenge. We cannot be giving all the time and receiving nothing in return.
Analyst: That is, in fact you replaced me: my position was filled by another analyst.
Analysand [laughing]: *Prevention is better than cure . . . what do you want! I can't be exposed to your irresponsible behavior without any protection. You can abandon me any time and then replace me with another patient even more submissive than myself.*

In order to obtain the data needed for the raw material to make up Peter's psychotomogram (Figure 3-2) we use a double-entry structural table. One of its entries is formed by the analysand (as "ego"), and the other entry is formed by the others, the analyst included (as "alter"). The direction of the relationship ("R") between them is also indicated. The other entry is formed by the actions, qualifications, and affective states recognizable in every episode in which the associative chain has broken up. We will have, consequently, an "ego-list" of the qualifications, actions, and affective states that the analysand attributes to himself; an "alter-list" of the qualifications, actions, and affective states that the analysand attributed to his interactors; and an "R"-list of the direction of the interactions between the analysand and his others.

Once we have the constellations of actions of each episode, we can make a synthesis of them, obtaining the manifest structure of the speech of the analysand. Finally, by inverting the direction of the actions we can obtain the analysand's latent speech structure, as well as the structure of his actions.

Peter's example is useful because his associative chain can be broken up into four narrative units or four episodes corresponding approximately to each of his four interventions; moreover, each intervention has a different extension even if it is conveying the same message.

In effect, after making the syntagmatic segmentation, four narrative units are left. Their common paradigmatic, manifest structure is formed by Peter's redundant description of himself as being helpful, excluded, replaced, angry, and revengeful to selfish, excluding, replacing others who make him angry and vengeful. They mistreat him in an unjust and irresponsible way. Their common

Paradigmatic Analysis

Syntagmatic Analysis	"ego"	"R"	"alter"	Operation
First narrative unit	1. Helpful 2. Excluded 3. Replaced 4. Angry 5. Revengeful	↓↓↓↓	−1. Selfish −2. Excluding −3. Fickle −4. Provocative −5. Revenge inciting	Breaking-up
Second narrative unit	1. " 2. " 3. " 4. " 5. "	↓↓↓↓	−1. " −2. " −3. " −4. " −5. "	Breaking-up
Third narrative unit	1. " 2. " 3. " 4. " 5. "	↓↓↓↓	−1. " −2. " −3. " −4. " −5. "	Breaking-up
Speech's manifest structure	1. Helpful 2. Excluded 3. Replaced 4. Angry 5. Revengeful	↓↓↓↓	−1. Selfish −2. Excluding −3. Fickle −4. Provocative −5. Revenge inciting	Reduction
Speech's latent structure	−1. Selfish −2. Excluding −3. Fickle −4. Provocative −5. Revenge inciting	↑↑↑	−1. Helpful −2. Excluded −3. Replaced −4. Angry −5. Revengeful	Inversion

Figure 3-2. Peter's psychotomogram

paradigmatic latent structure is formed by the inversion of the direction of the actions and qualifications of the manifest structure: Peter appears to be selfish, unjust, irresponsible, excluding, and replacing others, making them angry and revengeful; the others (the analyst included) appear to be helpful, excluded, replaced, angry, and vengeful.

Of course, this "deduction" of the latent structure of the analysand's myth can be confirmed by observing his speech, movements, gestures, and contextual actions as well as by the countertransferential feelings of the analyst. In this particular case, the analyst was experiencing a manifest feeling of guilt but, deeply, a latent feeling of anger and revenge: in fact, he had been thinking (before the session described) of replacing this difficult and embarassing analysand with a more cooperative and analyzable one.

In doing the psychotomogram it must be remembered that the characteristics of the others are like a mirror with respect to those of the analysand, and vice versa. If the analysand is describing himself as a <good frustrated satisfier of others>, as in Peter's case, it can be deduced that he considers the others as <bad satisfied frustrators.> Consequently, it would be enough to obtain only one list: once one knows the actions, qualifications, and affective states consciously attributed by the analysand to himself or to the others, one can deduce (by inversion) the actions, qualifications and affective states attributed by him to the others as well as the actions, qualifications, and affective states unconsciously attributed by him to himself.

Comparing the structure of the different anecdotes of the associative chain is like comparing different x-rays until the structural relation "ego R alter" becomes evident through redundancy. The psychotomogram simplifies the analysis for the sake of clarity. It can be said that once the speech's manifest structure is obtained, it will be enough to multiply it by minus one to obtain the speech's latent structure.

Metapsychologically speaking, it can be said that Peter's FMT is formed by his representations of his actions—of being selfish, excluding, fickle, provocative, and of inciting others to take revenge—that lead to the representation of unpleasure on him. That is why he represses and projects this FMT onto his representation of the others, while denying the DMT (of being helpful, excluded, replaced, angry, and vengeful) in that representation and introjecting it into his own. At the same time, he idealizes himself as a "superego" and denigrates and blames the others as "inferalter."

The analyst's interventions are aimed to clarify, among other things, the sadomasochistic bipolar narrative structure of Peter's speech, actions, and affective states as well as its inverted representations and inverting mechanisms. By showing the actual structure of Peter's signals (speech and actions), the analyst reverses the structure of Peter's signifiers (representations of speech and actions); which in turn reverses the structure of Peter's signifieds (affect representations); which, finally, reverses Peter's messages (affective states).

Psychoflowchart of Repetition Compulsion

The psychotomographic technique is an effective method of obtaining the paradigmatic, oppositional structure of the analysand's repetitive myth, to show how the binary pairs of actants are working within it. But it is not as effective for analyzing the syntagmatic sequence of the analysand's corresponding repetitive ritual: how the analysand acts to accomplish his desires, how the others (analyst included) react to him, and how he reacts to the reaction of others.

Once the syntagmatic segmentation has been done, and the associative chain has been divided into successive episodes whose manifest structures have been reduced and then inverted, the sequence of the plot of each episode can be analyzed by using the "flowchart" technique. It is a technique derived from the computer science concept of algorithm. The algorithm is the detailed and complete sequence of operations that the computer must perform in order to solve a particular problem. The flowchart is the drawing or the graphic design of that sequence.

Following the psychoanalytic hypothesis, it can be said that the universal problem that the analysand is trying to solve through his myth and rituals is the satisfaction of his desires. The content, or the plot, of his verbal myth is about how he is trying to satisfy his desire (or to avoid its frustration) in interaction with others. The goal of his factual ritual is the actual way in which he tries to satisfy those desires.

In brief, the analysand has two simultaneous and conflicting goals: the conscious rational goal of happiness or security with pleasure, and the unconscious narcissistic goal either of pleasure with insecurity (sadistic) or security with unpleasure (masochistic). In order to obtain his conscious rational goal the analysand must make a *specific action* in order to provoke the *specific reaction* from the others that will give him not only happiness but also will reinforce his creative learning. In order to obtain his unconscious narcissistic (sadistic or masochistic) goal the analysand must make an "acting-out" in order to provoke the "counter-acting-out" of the others that will give him either pleasure with insecurity or security with unpleasure and will reinforce his repetition compulsion.

Figure 3-3 shows the satisfaction (or frustration) of the analysand's desire. We can recognize two main "pathways": the "healthy pathway" of creative learning, and the "narcissistic pathway" of repetition compulsion. But other pathways can also be recognized: the "negative therapeutic reaction pathway," the "positive therapeutic reaction pathway," the "contamination (with the psychopathology of others) pathway," etc.

It can be said that the sequence of the factual ritual with which Peter accompanies each of the four episodes into which his associative chain has been broken can be broken, in turn, into successive "algorithmic" steps toward the satisfaction and/or frustration of his desires. His course of action starts with his conscious desire to be included and cured; it is followed by his acting-out, in which he says that he is angry and vengeful because he has been excluded and replaced by selfish, irresponsible, excluding and replacing others while acting as a selfish, irresponsible, excluding and replacing person who makes others angry and vengeful. This acting-out is followed by the corresponding acting-out of his interactors, who start saying that they are selfish, irresponsible, excluding, and replacing toward him while being helpful, excluded, replaced, angry, and revengeful toward him. Finally they abandon him and he achieves his unconscious narcissistic goal of presenting himself as a frustrated victim while acting as a satisfied victimizer who ruins the work of other people. The fact that he finally pushes the other to abandon him reinforces his acting-out, closing the vicious circle of his repetition compulsion.

On the other hand, the "healthy pathway" of obtaining the goal of being included and cured by others will be constituted by his

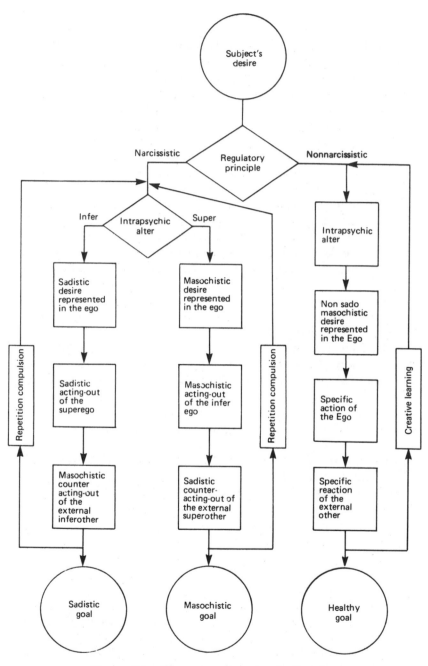

Figure 3-3. The unconscious psychoflowchart

100

specific action of asking for it and acting for it in a coherent way, being responsible, including others, and recognizing verbally their efforts to be helpful and responsible toward him; this specific action will be followed by the corresponding specific reaction of his inter-actors, who will help him in a responsible way without abandoning him and who will recognize his efforts to change. In this way he not only achieves his conscious rational goal but reinforces his specific action, thus opening the beneficial spiral of creative learning.

Studying the therapeutic transaction between Peter and his analyst, one can also observe a third pathway: the "negative thera-peutic reaction pathway." The analyst answers the acting-out with a specific therapeutic reaction, but Peter insists again and again on his pathological acting-out instead of changing it for a therapeutic specific action. In brief, in these three therapeutic transactions the analyst was not able to open the vicious circle of Peter's repetition compulsion.

A simplified version of the psychoflowchart of Peter's ritual includes only three pathways. (See Figure 3-4.)

Free Association as an Orchestral Score

The shift of Lévi-Strauss's theory of the unconscious from the model of language to the model of music that we find in the overture of *The Raw and the Cooked* (1970) is of crucial importance for the structural model of psychoanalysis.

The structure of language discovered by Saussure is the struc-ture of a code of communication that works in two dimensions at the same time: the paradigmatic (or metaphoric) and the syntagmatic (or metonymic).

In the case of language the subject is able to communicate his message by drawing upon the dimensions of the code, but the code itself does not determine his message. According to our model of the psychic apparatus, this form of communication does not exist for the unconscious representations of actions and affective states. This, of course, poses the question of how we can conceive of this deepest level of the psychic apparatus in structural terms. This is where Lévi-Strauss's revised conception of the structure of myths in terms of the musical score come to our aid.

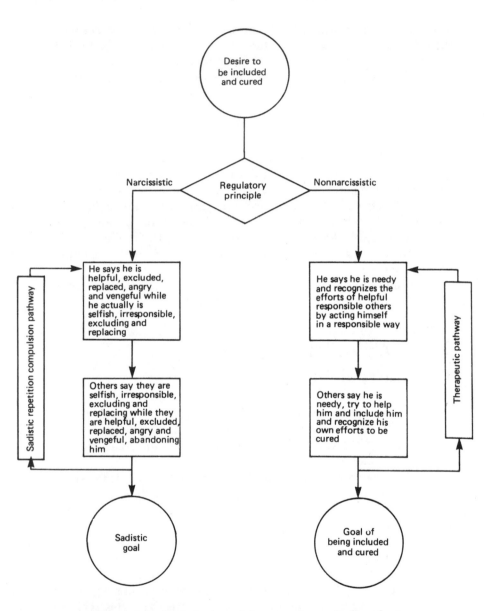

Figure 3-4.   Pathologic and therapeutic psychoflowchart

According to Lévi-Strauss, the structure of a myth which exists unconsciously also exhibits the dual dimensions of paradigm and syntagm, but each version of the myth is an attempt to communicate both dimensions in a linear or diachronic sequence that is bound to fail because it cannot convey both aspects of the structure adequately in one dimension.

Consequently, he argues that the structure of the myth is like an orchestral score, where each version resembles the part of a particular instrument. Only when we assemble all the instrumental parts and coordinate them in space (that is, when we have the complete score) can we arrive at the structure of the myth itself.

In the case of myth each repetition strives to render as complete a version as the performer—the teller of the myth—can achieve. The question for the hearer of the myth is always "how good is this version?" He answers it by an implicit comparison with the structure of the myth that he knows unconsciously.

In the case of mythology, the unconscious structure does not constitute a code as in the case of language; rather, it is itself the message that the myth teller attempts to communicate by means of his particular linguistic code. Consequently, Lévi Strauss insists that the problem of translation is not as critical in the study of myth as, for example, in the study of poetry, where the message is conveyed by the poet's play with the sound aspects of language that have not been built into the code.

This model of mythology provides the most satisfactory model for understanding the structure of the analysand's unconscious representations of actions and affective states in relation to his repetitions. Each repetition of the analysand's story is an attempt to realize his fundamental unconscious psychic structure (of desire) and resembles in its incompleteness the various versions that the myth-teller has of the myth.

There is a second way in which Lévi Strauss's analysis of myth can be applied to the analysis of the analysand's compulsive repetitions. He argues that at the base of every myth there is a fundamental opposition that the myth attempts to reconcile by means of a further series of oppositions that appear less clearly contradictory. In the end, the structure of the myth as a whole serves to contain the contradiction but, because that structure cannot be consciously acquired as a whole, the necessity arises to constantly repeat the partial version of the myth in order to overcome renewed underlying anxiety provoked by insoluble contradictions between nature and culture that do not allow for any final explanation.

Similarly, in our system, the opposition between the feared mnemic trace and the desired mnemic trace is rendered insoluble by virtue of the paradoxical law of the superego that governs the ego-alter relations.

The result is that the analysand's repetitions, like the versions of a myth, represent a constant attempt to render an unconscious structure that contains the fundamental opposition in an [apparently] noncontradictory mode, and therefore conceals it from consciousness.

In the case of psychoanalysis, the analyst's first task is to arrive at the structure of the analysand's myth and to communicate it to him through interpretations so that he can penetrate into the self-perpetuating underlying contradiction that the myth obscures. As Freud says, what you can't remember, you repeat. But once remembered, the myth must be understood with respect to its underlying, self-perpetuating contradictions.

REFERENCES

Eco, U. (1966a). *Proceso a James Bond*. Barcelona: Sontenella.
—— (1966b). James Bond: une combinatoire narrative. *Communications*, No. 8, IV.
Freud, S. (1912). The dynamics of transference. *Standard Edition*. 12: 97–108.
—— (1920). Beyond the pleasure principle. *Standard Edition* 18:7–64.
Gear, M. C., and Liendo, E. C. (1975). *Sémiologie psychanalytique*. Paris: Minuit.
—— (1978). *Informáitica Psicoanalítica*. Buenos Aires: Nueva Visión.
—— (1979). *Action psychanalytique*. Paris: Minuit.
—— (1980). *Matemática Psicoanalítica*. Buenos Aires: Nueva Visión.
Greimas, A. J. (1966). *Sémantique structural*. Paris: Larousse.
Hawkes, T. (1977). *Structuralism and Semiotics*. Berkeley, Calif.: University of California Press.
Jakobson, R., and Halle, M. (1956). *Fundamentals of Language*. The Hague: Mouton.
Leach, E. (1976). *Culture and Communication*. Cambridge: Cambridge University Press.
Lévi-Strauss, C. (1949). *Les Structures élémentaires de la parenté*. Paris: P.U.F.

—— (1955).   The structural study of myth. *Journal of American Folklore* 68, No. 270.

—— (1963).   *Structural Anthropology*. New York: Basic Books.

—— (1970).   *The Raw and the Cooked*. London: Jonathan Cape.

Propp, V. (1928).   *Morphology of the Folktale*. Austin, Texas: University of Texas Press.

Saussure, F. de (1916).   *Course in General Linguistics*. New York: McGraw-Hill, 1966.

Shklovsky, V. (1923).   *Zoo: or Letters Not About Love*. Ithaca, N.Y.: Cornell University Press.

Todorov, T. (1965).   *Théorie de la littérature: textes des formalistes russes*. Paris: Editions du Seuil.

4
The Theory of
Psychic Bipolarity

The theory of psychic bipolarity is a unified, comprehensive, and multidisciplinary psychoanalytic theory that describes, explains, and predicts the normal and abnormal structure and functioning of the psychic apparatus (Gear and Liendo 1980). It is also a theory of how to transform that structure.

The theory is built up out of different layers which lead to the deepest intrapsychic structures. Following Freud's example in this respect, we have called it a topography; in Freud's own theoretical model of the psychic apparatus (1900), layers of theory were used in order to reveal successive layers of the psychic structure. This in turn enabled him to devise a therapeutic strategy that would take the deepest structures of the psychic apparatus into account. In our view these two dimensions of Freud's work are really a mark of his genius: he realized (1915) that he had to invent a theoretical model of the otherwise unobservable psychic apparatus in order to study it and work with it clinically.

Once Freud's work is grasped as a theoretical model—a point he himself makes many times—its essential unity becomes apparent and serves as an organizing paradigm (Kuhn 1962) for the many subsequent developments in psychoanalysis. We have attempted to respect this paradigm, although we have modified it in some respects. In this chapter our purpose is to spell it out as clearly as possible. We hope that, as a result, the reader who takes the time to examine our theoretical model will be able to integrate with some facility his own psychoanalytic background with what we have to say in this book.

The organization of the chapter follows Figure 4-1 in setting out the successive layers of the theory. The reader will find, as we have indicated, that these layers also conform to the structures of the psychic apparatus.

Systematization of Speech and Actions

The empirical level of theory describes the behavior of the agents and the patients. Underlying their variety of characteristics, typical actions, and semiotic acts, there exists a binary structure. It consists of the various characteristics divided into two fundamental characters in the behavior and conceptualization of each subject: the ego and the alter. Similarly, all the affective states of the actual ego and alter are reduced to two fundamental ones: satisfaction and frustration. All actions are reduced to "to satisfy oneself by frustrating others" and "to be frustrated while satisfying others." All qualifications are reduced to bad and good.

Empirical level		Speech, actions, affects
Metapsychological level	First	Representations, mechanisms, superego
	Second	General principles, mutilation

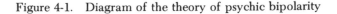

Figure 4-1.   Diagram of the theory of psychic bipolarity

As shown in Figure 4-2, there are six systems pertinent to the study of the structure of speech and actions. System e.1 is the structure of the subject's speech when describing his relations with the world and the others; system e.3 is the structure of the actions carried out by the subject and received from the outside world and from others; system e.2 is the structure of the speech when the subject gives a cognitive or ethical qualification to his actions and his relations with the outside world and with others. System a.1 is the structure of the others' speech as a description; system a.3 is the structure of the actions of the world and of others toward the subject; and system a.2 is the structure of the speech of others as a qualification.

Systems e.1, e.2, and e.3 correspond to the ego's point of view and systems a.1, a.2, and a.3, to that of the alter. Ego and alter therefore emerge specifically once the structures have been reduced. This makes it possible to distinguish within the supersystem of human behavior nonreduced and reduced structures of descriptive speech, qualifying speech, and actions.

Two basic types of behavior correspond in certain ways to the classical types called "sadist" and "masochist." Their respective ego and alter reveal different and complementary speech, actions, and qualifications. The sadist describes himself as being a <frustrated

	ego (analysand)	alter (analyst)
Descriptive speech	System e.1	System a.1
Qualifying speech	System e.2	System a.2
Actions	System e.3	System a.3

Figure 4-2. The structure of speech and actions

satisfier of others> while he acts as a <satisfied frustrator of others> and, at the same time, overqualifies himself as clever, generous, and sensible and disqualifies the others as foolish, selfish, and crazy. In turn, the masochist describes himself as a <satisfied frustrator>, while he acts as a <frustrated satisfier> who disqualifies himself and overqualifies the others.

We do not attempt at this point to explain these dichotomous aspects; we will endeavor to obtain, inductively and through the study of behavior, information about the logical properties of the reductions of subjacent structures, and about certain typical inversions that occur in both types of characters when observing their affective actions and the descriptive and qualifying speech concerning those actions.

We will examine some typical situations that occur in the actual relationship between the sadistic agent and the masochistic patient, and between the masochistic agent and the sadistic patient—in particular, the systematic complementary relationship that exists between them and makes them appear as the inverse and reverse of one activity. Furthermore, both have complementary psychopathogenic affects.

During the first stage of this work it becomes evident that the clinical traits and crises of competence presented by a masochistic patient are different from those presented by the masochistic agent, the sadistic patient, or the sadistic agent; from the outset they induce a different attitude on the part of the psychotherapist. Psychoanalyses of agents and patients, of sadists and masochists, differ both metapsychologically and technically.

We have also studied certain consequences of the inversion of an action's meaning when described and ethically qualified in speech, and the meaning of the same action in relation to the learning process (Gear and Liendo 1975). Also, we have looked at the social transmission of those inversions with the social customs bearing on the behavior and speech of conflictively competitive societies (see chapter 7).

We will see that problems arising in family learning are due to the fact that the parents, who usually belong to complementary psychopathological types, invert each other's speech. In addition, each parent gives an inverse image of his actions through his speech. Thus, there is a four-part inversion that disturbs the child's clear semiotic notions about his own actions and those of others, and the direct and normal nature of his speech. This produces a simultaneous (but not necessarily conflictive) learning of various linguistic codes for describing actions.

An analysis is made of the semiotic peculiarities resulting from the simultaneous use of various codes (inverted among one another) on the part of the subject. We conclude that the masochistic patient appears to have been taught to give up ethical and hedonic pleasure in order to survive; on the other hand, the sadistic agent was taught to say and perceive that he has given up his hedonic pleasure if he wants to obtain ethical, hedonic, and cognitive pleasure. The masochist was taught to preserve himself through suffering, being exploited, and blaming himself, while the sadist was taught to have pleasure through exploiting others while presenting himself as their victim.

Another type of empirical inversion can be called oedipal, where the children of monogamous families tend to say and perceive that they are carrying out actions that are similar to those of the parent of the same sex (positive oedipus complex), whereas their effective actions are similar to those of the parent of the opposite sex (negative oedipus complex).

In summary, the ego in the subject's speech coincides with his *de facto* alter (the way in which the alter actually behaves), and the alter of his speech with his *de facto* ego, following the empirical law of syntactical inversion: he says he is doing what the others are doing in reality, and he says the others are doing what he is doing in reality. Speech ego = *de facto* alter and speech alter = *de facto* ego. The *de facto* ego and alter of his speech coincide with the respective *de facto* ego and alter of the speech of the parent of the opposite sex, although in his perception and in his speech, the subject perceives and says the inverse, following the empirical law of oedipal inversion: ego resembles *mater* and alter resembles *pater* in the male child even though he says the inverse; and ego resembles *pater* and alter, *mater,* in the female child, while she says the inverse.

The whole of this stage is condensed in a series of empirical hypotheses which may be considered to constitute an original descriptive theory of human speech and action, a theory which we can provisionally call the *empirical level of the theory of psychic bipolarity.*

Systematization of Representations and Mechanisms

Speaking in general terms, two object-models exist that underlie the various statements of psychological theories. The first is the "black box" or "phenomenological" model, which takes into account the external comportment of the psychic system in terms of stimulus, or input of information, and response, or output of information, of the system. Functional relations are established between both but with no reference to the internal mechanisms of the box. This is the position taken by certain schools of behaviorism, such as Skinner's (1953), and by some communications experts (Jackson 1965) and phenomenologists.

The second object-model is the "full" or "translucent" box (Bunge 1969), which builds a system of hypotheses based on the deductive method of the visible stimulus-response comportment. It is an attempt to discover the internal structure of the psychic system's box and to subsequently explain the observable external conduct. There is an intermediary model that takes into account the intervening variables that connect the observable "stimulus" and "response," but does not imply an hypothesis relating to the non-observable processes.

Classical positivists support the "black box" model, whereas structuralists (Lévi-Strauss 1963) support the "translucent box" model: "structure" refers to the internal structure of the psychic box. Psychoanalysis (Freud 1915) also supports the translucent box model: its specialty is analyzing the psychic system's internal mechanisms. But since analysis starts from the observation of the transferential (and so observable) stimuli and responses, we could say that it uses both models. Technically, psychoanalysis considers the psychic system to be like the model of a black box, and theoretically like the model of a translucent box. That is, as an observer of the analysand's speech and actions in the setting the analyst is working with the black box but when he analyses and interprets he is working with a translucent box.

Our theory of psychic bipolarity also follows that sequence. We begin by "cybernetically" describing the observable external black box. After establishing certain *empirical* generalizations of the functioning of the external psychic structure, we outline the possible unobservable internal structure of that system as though it were a translucent box.

Thus, the next stage of our theory is an attempt to constitute a model, to explain facts that we described at the empirical level of the theory. It applies to that which takes place inside the translucent psychic box, now that we have reduced its input and output of information to laws. This model consists primarily of deductive hypotheses whose justification (together with some auxiliary hypotheses) stems mostly from their ability to explain and predict the facts established by the first theory.

This [second level] has model-like aspects. There are various ways to obtain the theoretical entities that constitute the model through the use of concepts from the fields of psychology, psychoanalysis, linguistics, and semiotics. These theoretical entities are the conscious and unconscious intrapsychic representations made by the subjects of their own actions, their own speech, and their own qualifications of their actions.

As in the structure of speech and of action, there exists a reduced version and nonreduced version of these intrapsychic representations.

THE FIRST LEVEL

The *first metapsychological level of the theory of psychic bipolarity* describes eight reduced systems of representations that have a certain degree of relative autonomy and are responsible for the bipolarity and the inversions assigned by the empirical theory. The systems, or intrapsychic theoretical entities, are:

system E1	conscious representation of the subject's speech concerning ego
system E3	conscious representation of the subject's actions referring to ego
system UE3	unconscious representation of the subject's actions referring to ego
system E2	conscious representation of the subject's ethical qualifying of his actions

Systems A1, A3, UA3, and A2 are analogous systems of conscious and unconscious representations made by the subject with reference to the alter. Thus there are eight systems, altogether. (See Figure 4-3.)

These systems are the determining structures of the psychic system, while the reduced structures that we observe at the empirical level of our theory are simply their "reflections." They are subjective but real and consequently have a strong symbolic efficacy, especially in the case of the reduced systems (UE3 and UA3) of unconscious representations, which constitute the "dynamic unconscious" according to Freud. The conscious antiisomorphic and unconscious isomorphic duplication of the representation of systems E2 and E3 is the fundamental hypothesis of the theory.

According to this first metapsychological level of the theory, although system UE3 corresponds to the effective (reduced) system e.3 (see Figure 4-2) of actions, system UE3 is inverted with regard both to system e.3 and to system UE3 itself. System E1 corresponds to system e.1 and system E2 corresponds to system e.2; due to a hypothesis of concordance of the entire system of conscious representations, these are coherent with system E3 and the inverse of system UE3. Hence, based on another hypothesis of concordance between the conscious representations of speech and effective speech, we have the explanation of the fact (established in the empirical theory) that the reduced structure of the ego's speech is the inverse of the reduced structure of his actions. An analogous situation may be observed in relation to the representations which the ego consciously and unconsciously makes for the alter, and the alter's speech and effective actions: system UA3 corresponds to system a.1 (actions of the others) and system A3 is inverted with regard both to system a.1 and system UA3. System A1 corresponds to system e.4 and system A2 corresponds to system a.3 and, due to a hypothesis of concordance of the entire system of conscious representations, these are coherent with system A3 and the inverse of system UA3. These hypotheses are rules of correspondence linking the theoretical entities of the second theory to the empirical entities of the first.

The whole of this stage of our theory is condensed in a series of hypotheses that constitute an original explanation of human speech and action. We have named it the *in-depth level of the theory of psychic bipolarity*. It postulates the existence of an intrapsychic supersystem made up of eight systems that constitute a conscious reduced intrapsychic structure formed by systems E1, E2, E3, A1,

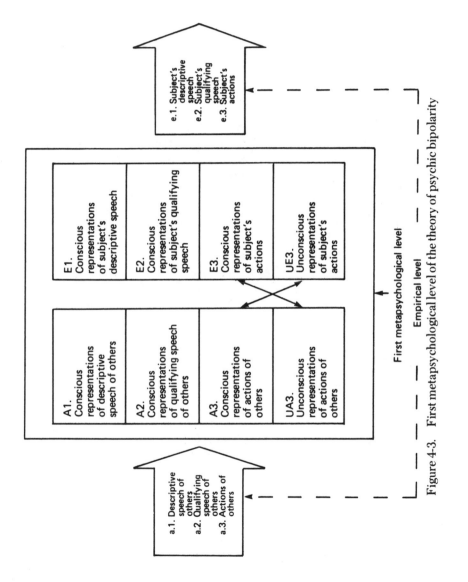

Figure 4-3.   First metapsychological level of the theory of psychic bipolarity

115

A2 and A3, and an unconscious reduced intrapsychic structure formed by systems UE3 and UA3.

In our theory of psychic bipolarity we also assert that these intrapsychic systems are distributed in this way because unconscious intrapsychic mechanisms are operating simultaneously in the effort to avoid psychic suffering: system UE3 is repressed and projected and system UA3 is denied and introjected. For example, the masochistic patient represses and projects the representation that he is a <frustrated satisfier of others> while he denies and introjects that the others are <satisfied frustrators of himself>. On the other hand, the sadistic agent represses and projects that he is a <satisfied frustrator of others> while he denies and introjects that the others are <frustrated satisfiers of himself>.

In his actions, the sadistic agent is a <satisfied frustrator>, whereas the masochistic patient is a <frustrated satisfier>. But in his descriptive speech, the sadistic agent says that he is a <frustrated satisfier> while the masochistic patient says that he is a <satisfied frustrator>. At the same time, in his qualifying speech, the sadistic agent overqualifies himself as a superego (that is to say, a grandiose ego in the sense of ideal-ego) while he disqualifies the others as inferalters. The masochistic patient in his qualifying speech disqualifies himself as an inferego while he overqualifies the others as superalters. Of course this redefinition of the superego notion implies a complete revision of the traditional point of view. The classical superego is the superalter in our language and would be characteristic of the masochistic patient but not of the sadistic agent (see chapter 3).

Psychic Principles and Sadomasochism

THE SECOND LEVEL

The second metapsychological level of our theory of psychic bipolarity offers an explanation of the reduced conscious and unconscious intrapsychic structures examined by the first metapsychological level. This "metatheory" is an original, simplified, logically clarified, and hence transformed version of some fundamental psychoanalytic hypotheses, unified on a higher level of abstraction. We have used psychoanalysis in this way for two reasons: we had already advocated, grounded, and developed this metatheoretical modification in earlier works; and the new formulation was justified by its ability to explain the theoretical hypotheses of the first metapsychological level and, indirectly, the hypotheses at the empirical level.

In this stage, we use:

1. A group of hypotheses derived from our earlier resystematization of the intrapsychic mechanisms of repression, projection, denial, and introjection postulated by Freud and Anna Freud (A. Freud 1936) and of the intrapsychical mechanisms of splitting, persecution, idealization, and projective identification postulated by Melanie Klein (Klein et al. 1952).

2. The first Freudian theory (Freud 1900) about the psychic apparatus: conscious, unconscious, preconscious, and related hypotheses already used at the first metapsychological level.

3. The pleasure principle postulated by Freud (1900), but with modifications originating from different sources: hedonic, ethical, cognitive, and self-preservative.

4. The Freudian and Kleinian hypotheses (as reformulated by us) that postulate and explain both the narcissistic mirror situation and the oedipal triangular situation.

5. The second Freudian theory (Freud 1923) about the psychic apparatus: ego, id, superego, and related hypotheses.

6. The Lacanian hypothesis (Lacan 1966) of the *phallus*, about the distribution of power and authority within the psychic apparatus.

This stage, in fact, asserts that the unconsciousness represented by system UE3 is the result of repression which, in the sadist, is due to the ethical unpleasure provoked by the ethical‚consciousness of the appraisal of his actions, and, in the masochist, is due to the unpleasure of maintenance provoked by his ethical consciousness. The inversion of systems E3 and UE3 results from the fact that the only way to avoid ethical unpleasure in the sadist, and unpleasure of maintenance in the masochist, is for the forbidden actions to be inversely represented.

It has become clear that the sadistic subject plays a particularly efficient role as a psychopathogenic agent. Through the direct and active influence of his actions and speech, he makes the masochistic patient acquire the proper characteristics. Indeed, although the masochist is sometimes party to it, the sadist appears as a causal instigator or agent: he is more able to transmit mental illness and more resistant to accept mental health. The sadistic ego can only conceive of the alter as a masochist, and consequently acts upon him by placing him in that complementary position.

The result is that through the influence of repressions, projections, denials, and introjections exerted by each on the other's system of actions, the ego fits the alter in such a way that alter system A1, A2, and A3 are determined by the ego's system UE3. For example, the masochist ethically perceives, describes, and judges himself as "bad" because he perceives and describes himself as the <satisfied frustrator>, whereas effectively he is the <frustrated satisfier>. The sadist needs to perceive and describe himself as the <frustrated satisfier> so as to be able to judge himself ethically as "good," while in fact he is a <satisfied frustrator>. The sadistic agent thus appropriates the ethical and hedonic pleasure—of which he deprives the masochistic patient—because he controls not only his own survival but also that of the masochistic patient; now the masochist depends on the sadist for survival, and so the latter will blackmail and exploit him.

Formulating the pleasure principle and including it at the second metapsychological level as a causal explanation for the polarization and inversions of the empirical and first metapsychological level of the theory of psychic bipolarity obliged us to reconstruct both the empirical basis and the hypotheses of those theories. In effect, we were obliged to include in the empirical basis the affects experienced by the subject and his interactors: system e.4 of the affects of the subject, and system a.4 of the affects of the others, forming the respective nonreduced structures of the affects can be in turn further reduced. More important, perhaps, we also had to recognize at the first metapsychological level the existence of intrapsychic representations of the subject's actions or speech. As with the representations of the actions, the representation of systems e.4 and a.4 are intrapsychically duplicated. System e.4 is duplicated in system E4, or conscious representation of the subject's affects and in system UE4 or unconscious representation of the subject's affects. System a.4 is duplicated in system A4, or conscious representation of the affects of others and in system UA4, or unconscious representation of the affects of others. (See Figure 4-4.)

Again, as happened with systems UE3 and UA3, systems E4 and A4 of the conscious representations of affects tend to be anti-isomorphic with systems e.4 and a.4 of the real affects of the subject

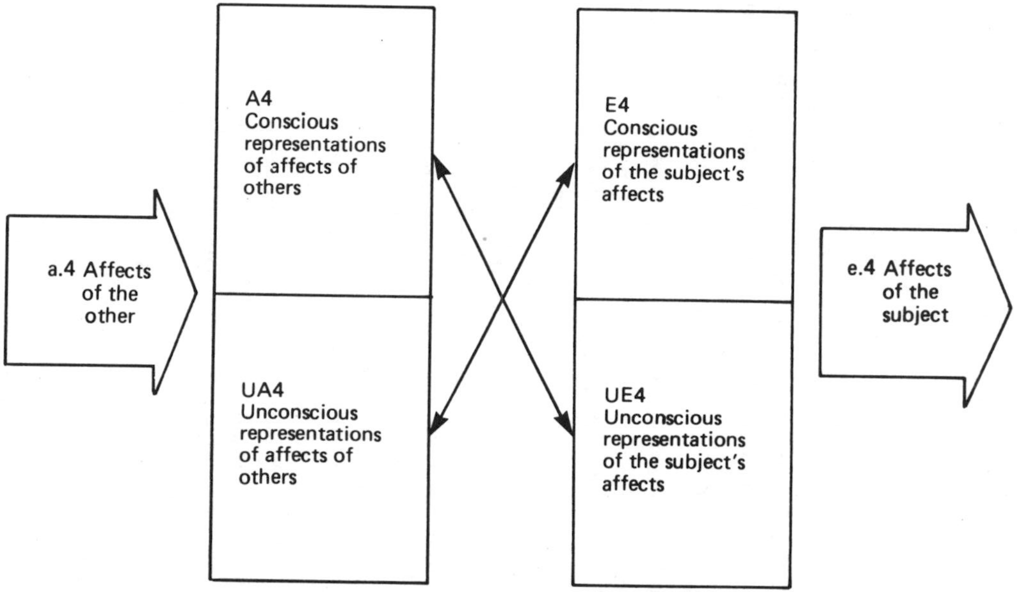
a.4 Affects of the other
A4
Conscious representations of affects of others
UA4
Unconscious representations of affects of others
E4
Conscious representations of the subject's affects
UE4
Unconscious representations of the subject's affects
e.4 Affects of the subject

Figure 4-4. Representations of affects on the empirical and first metapsychological levels of the theory

and of the others. Finally, they are concordant with conscious systems El, E2, E3, Al, A2, and A3. On the other hand, systems UE4 and UA4 of the unconscious representations of affects tend to be isomorphic and truthful with respect to real systems e.4 and a.4, which are concordant with systems UE3 and UA3.

The representations of affects also are subjected to the same set of defense mechanisms described earlier: the subject represses (suppresses) system UE4 from the truthful unconscious representations of his affects, and projects (evacuates) it into system A4 of conscious representations of affects attributed to others by the subject. He furthermore denies (rejects) system UA4 from the truthful unconscious representation of the affects of others and introjects (appropriates) it into system E4 of the conscious representation of his own affects.

The sadistic agent tends to suppress and evacuate into his masochistic patient his own hedonic pleasure, and consciously tends to appropriate the ethical pleasure and hedonic unpleasure (and eventually the unpleasure of maintenance) that have been rejected and appropriated by the masochistic alter. Now the masochistic patient tends to suppress and evacuate into his sadistic alter his hedonic unpleasure and his ethical pleasure (or eventually, his pleasure of maintenance). He consciously recognizes the ethical unpleasure and the hedonic pleasure that have been rejected and appropriated by the sadistic alter.

In any event, there appears to be no symmetry between agents and patients with regard to the affects that each suppresses in his unconscious. Obviously, the sadist very carefully avoids becoming aware of his ethical unpleasure and hedonic pleasure; but, on the other hand, the masochist seems to suppress, in addition to the ethical pleasure and the hedonic unpleasure, the pleasure of self-preservation offered to him by the first two repressions.

It thus appears that within the context of the present investigation, the sadist does not seem to be the same type of individual described in classical theories. Indeed, in a direct sense, he is a narcissist because his hedonic and ethical pleasure is specially important to him and the unpleasure of his masochistic counterpart is important to him only as a tactic in the service of his own narcissism.

Nor does the masochist appear in his traditional guise—that of seeking hedonic unpleasure—since, in fact, he is a narcissist who,

perhaps in spite of himself, is seeking the pleasure of self-preservation. The masochist fights for survival with a minimum of ethical
and hedonic unpleasure. The sadist fights to live with the maximum
of ethical and hedonic pleasure that he can wrest from the dependent
masochist.

Using the collateral sociological hypothesis (Lévi-Strauss 1963)
to explain the sadomasochistic functioning of the ego-alter system in
a state of narcissistic rule, it can be said that the masochistic patient
sacrifices, or is led to sacrifice due to social and other pressures, all
his sources of pleasure outside of those corresponding to maintenance. In the sadistic agent, however, the pleasure of maintenance is
assured through his cleverness at inserting himself socially in positions of power, and by the nature of his relationship with the
masochist. The sadistic agent would be an adapted bon vivant of the
social system in that he actively respects its conventions and, in some
way, imposes his standards. In turn, the masochistic patient would be
a suffering fringe member of the system. This does not prevent them
from both having the same interest (for complementary reasons) in
keeping the structure of that system intact. Both are "conservative"
towards the state of narcissistic rule, although the masochist has less
reason for being so. The sadist evidently comes out on top in the
enjoyment of all sources of pleasure, resulting from the peculiarities
of his systems E1 to A2. That is, the sadistic agent is in a very
favorable position in the narcissistic game and, ironically, from a
purely narcissistic standpoint.

Equilibrium and Crisis of the Sadomasochistic Regime

There are some possible situations, internal and external to the
agent-patient system, that favor balance in such a system. There are
other types of situations that could produce its decline and a crisis of
incompetence within the "normal" situation of the system that is
described as "state of narcissistic rule."

The logical analysis of the sadist-masochist narcissistic system
shows that, strictly speaking, "sadistic" (satisfied frustrator) and
"masochistic" (frustrated satisfier) are not the only possible positions.

In fact, we also come across the "untenable" (frustrated frustrator) position and the "healthy" (satisfied satisfier) position.

As a rule the masochist patient seeks psychotherapeutic help when he has been placed in an untenable (annihilating) position by the internal dynamics of the narcissistic regime or by environmental variables. On the other hand, the sadistic agent generally seeks treatment when, for environmental reasons (treatment of the masochistic patient, for example), he has been placed in a masochistic position, which for him is an intolerable position (but not annihilating one).

When analyzing the causes of crisis in the state of narcissistic rule, we discovered one "endogene" and three "exogenes":

1. There is endogenous deterioration of the sadistic agent's position through destruction of the masochistic patient, brought about by the sadistic agent's own action.

2. *De facto* ego and alter symmetrically belong to the same category (there are two agents or two patients), which prevents the system from functioning in a complementary fashion.

3. External social factors remove the sadist from his dominating position (and lead him to the unbearable position of masochist) or, however rarely, extract the masochist from his position of dependence and submission.

4. *De facto* ego and alter become "dissonant" because, in spite of being complementarily sadistic and masochistic, their styles are different (a paranoid sadist and a hysterical masochist, for instance).

The type of speech and qualification which a narcissist is obliged to produce through learning and functioning of his representational systems E1 to A2 is such (according to the theory that it is impossible to speak with one's own object language about that object language) that it prevents his having a concept of the "healthy" position (the possibility of leaving his narcissistic position and, eventually, coming out of the crisis).

It thus becomes apparent that the interpretative task is not merely to "read" what is "written" in the "text" of the free associations of the analysand, as is generally stated, but also to teach new languages and new thoughts. The psychoanalyst teaches the analysand to speak and to think (and therefore to act more constructively and to consider a greater range of choices).

Interpretation of Mechanisms, Principles, and Psychic Space

Within the framework of the theory of psychic bipolarity, therapeutic action comprises various general measures applicable to both patients and agents, as well as some qualitative strategic differences, in both the framework and the psychoanalytical operations, depending on whether a sadistic agent or a masochistic patient is being treated.

There are two aspects of the analytic task: the *setting*—the rules of the therapeutic game—and the *interventions*—the game itself. First, the analytic setting (standardizing the actions of the patient or of the agent) is analyzed: it must consist of specific instructions which vary according to the type of analysand. It works as an obstacle to the analysand's attempt to return to the previous set of sadomasochistic rules in the therapeutic relationship by transforming the analyst into a psychopathogenic agent or a psychopathological patient. Through the setting, the analyst attempts to transform by redefinition both the structure of the speech in its descriptive and qualifying aspects and the structure of the action of the subject and (indirectly) that of his environment: the setting tends to directly modify the external systems e.1, e.2, e.3, a.1, a.2, a.3, and, eventually, e.4 and a.4.

Second, the work of interventions is analyzed: it is a fundamental task that gives a new conception and new orientation to the representational structure of the subject with internal systems E1, E2, E3, UE3, A1, A2, A3, UA3, and, eventually, E4, UE4, A4, and UA4. These interventions consist of at least five approaches: (1) the factual or descriptive situational; (2) the in-depth or explanatory psychoanalytic interpretation; (3) the requalification of the superego and inferalter of the sadist and of the inferego and superalter of the masochist; (4) the situational logic or meta-language of his "untenable," "sadistic," or "masochistic" position; and (5) the opening up of a new logical space corresponding to the "healthy" position.

The novelty of the psychoanalytic therapeutic action based on the theory of psychic bipolarity is that the therapist does not restrict himself to describing the origin and characteristics of the "old" untenable, sadistic or masochistic positions, but also sets the patient or agent on the way to achieving the "new" position of <satisfied satisfier>. Furthermore, we conclude that the therapeutic strategy is not the same for the masochistic patient as it is for the sadistic agent, either at the level of the setting or that of the interpretations: "coaching" the masochist both actively and conceptually, is basically didactic. But the therapeutic strategy for the sadist would have to follow at least two stages: first, "making a patient out of him" (putting pressure on him by using the setting and requalifying the appraisals of ego and alter until he reaches the position of "patient"); and second, using the same type of didactic teaching as one would with the masochistic patient. In some ways, it can be said that the patient is an "analysand" from the very beginning while the agent is, initially, an "antianalysand" who then becomes an "analysand."

In the case of the masochistic patient, the in-depth psychoanalytic task of interpretation will concentrate on explaining to him his belief that the only strategic alternative available is to sacrifice his cognitive, ethical, and hedonic pleasure, by repressing his hedonic displeasure in order to obtain the minimum degree of pleasure of self-preservation. It must be explained to the sadistic agent how he believes in exclusively competitive relationships in which the only strategic alternative available to him is to frustrate others, and to take advantage of them, and at the same time to repress this, in order to obtain cognitive, hedonic, and ethical pleasure (of very low quality and stability). Both should recognize that ruinous competition is a survival strategy that is not only mean but self-defeating, through which neither truly wins full and shared pleasure and stable self-preservation.

The conclusion is that during the period of interpretation it is important that the patient or agent of the mental illness become aware of how the assumptions of their own logic limit their possibilities in life. They need to be guided to extend and transform their logic in order to open up new and more rewarding patterns of thought and action.

In summary, it can be said that the work of analytic interpretation deals successively with the redirection of the manifest content (speech and actions), inversion of the manifest content to obtain the latent content (unconscious representations), description of the defense mechanisms (repression, projection, denial, and introjection), requalification of the superego and inferalter or inferego and super alter, explanation of the principles or values (competitive pleasure principle), amplification of logic space by designing other alternative principles (cooperation, etc.).

REFERENCES

Bunge, M. (1969). *Le concept de modèle*. Paris: Maspero.

Freud, A. (1936). *The Ego and the Mechanisms of Defense*. New York: International Universities Press.

Freud, S. (1900). The interpretation of dreams. *Standard Edition* 4/5.

—— (1910). A special type of choice of object made by men. *Standard Edition* 11:164–175.

—— (1915). Instincts and their vicissitudes. *Standard Edition* 14:109–140.

—— (1923). The ego and the id. *Standard Edition* 19:3–66.

Gear, M. C., and Liendo, E. (1975). *Sémiologie psychanalytique*. Paris: Minuit.

—— (1979). *Action psychanalytique*. Paris: Minuit.

—— (1980). *Psicoanálisis del paciente y de su agente*. Buenos Aires: Nueva Visión.

Kuhn, T. (1962). *The Structure of Scientific Revolutions*. Chicago: University of Chicago Press.

Klein, M., Heimann, P., Isaacs, S., and Riviere, J., eds. (1952). *Developments in Psycho-Analysis*. London: Hogarth Press.

Jackson, D. D. (1965). Family rules: the marital quid pro quo. *Archives of General Psychiatry* 12.

Lacan, J. (1966). *Ecrits*. Paris: Editions du Seuil.

Lévi-Strauss, C. (1963). *Structural Anthropology*. New York: Basic Books.

Skinner, B. F. (1953). *Science and Human Behavior*. New York: Macmillan.

5

The Defensive Inversion of Actions and Affects in Speech

The Empirical Basis of Psychoanalytic Theory

In this chapter we will analyze the empirical basis of psychoanalytic theory constituted, broadly speaking, by clinical events directly observable by the analyst—that is, the speech and actions of the analysand as well as the analyst's own speech, actions, and affective states within the psychoanalytic setting. In chapter 6 we will define the unobservable inner symbolic transformations of observable events within the translucent psychic box.

Our concern is to show how the clinical material appears to a psychoanalytic observer. Of course we include both the analysand and the analyst in this material. Because the transformative process can only be studied diachronically and is not subject to immediate observation in the clinical setting, this has led some theorists to the assumption that the dynamic process of psychoanalysis is altogether hidden from view. If this were true, it would be impossible to teach the psychoanalytic method in a systematic and reliable way. Then the practice of psychoanalysis becomes a matter of guesswork and personal chemistry that depends upon the intuition of deep structures on the part of the analyst. We intend to show how the deep structures are implicit in the clinical manifestations of the analysand's and analyst's experience and communication. Further, we intend to present a method that is systematically designed to make these manifestations clear to someone who follows the steps set out, thus establishing a psychoanalytic practice based upon methodical observation at the empirical level.

Psychoanalysis should no longer be viewed as an old-fashioned craft that requires initiation into a series of mysteries. It is a scientific therapeutic method which can be taught precisely and practiced rigorously. Psychoanalysis proceeds from the analysis of the speech, actions, and affective states that can be observed in the clinical setting. In order to analyze these systematically, we start by applying a structural analysis of narratives to them (derived from structuralist linguistics) and then syntactically analyze the narrative structures thus obtained.

We will include the speech and actions of the analyst and analysand, but the affects of the analyst only (the countertransference, broadly speaking) because the affects of the analysand cannot be directly observed. We will use only the seven *empirically observable* systems as they refer to ego and alter, described in the previous chapter: system e.1, or analysand's descriptive speech; system e.2, or analysand's qualifying speech; system e.3, or analysand's actions; system a.1, or analyst's descriptive speech; system a.2, or analyst's qualifying speech; system a.3, or analyst's actions; system a.4, or analyst's affective states.

Once we have identified the relations and properties (structures) of the speech and actions of the analysand and the analyst within the psychoanalytic setting, we simplify each of the structures described to a "reduced structure." These nonreduced and reduced structures form a system of interrelated functions, which the analyst transforms according to set procedures.

The fact that the empirical basis is formed by the dyadic interaction between the analysand and the analyst has influenced our theoretical approach: in order to relate what the analysand is associating to what is happening in the dyadic transference-countertransference process, for example, we propose the bipolar reduction of the syntactical subjects of the speech (even if the analysand is referring to multiple subjects).

For example, within the speech, the elements to be reduced (or inverted) are the "subject-places" and the "predicates." Similarly, when considering actions, the elements to be reduced (or inverted) are either the "actors" or the "actions" themselves. We then arrive at a markedly bipolar organization of subjects and predicates, actors and actions.

To reduce the speech and the actions logically one needs to follow a sequence of four methodological steps:

1. Analyze the speech to study its nonreduced structure.
2. Reduce the structure, thus obtaining the bipolar reduced structure of the speech.
3. Analyze the actions and their nonreduced structure, obtaining the nonreduced structure of the actions.
4. Reduce the structure, thus obtaining the bipolar reduced structure of actions.

After studying and reducing the speech and the actions of the analysand and the analyst, some systematic correlations between both reduced structures can be established. Here we notice certain typical relations of correspondence or inversion among the reduced structures. Certain isomorphisms and antiisomorphisms are typical of these: the most typical type of transformation seems to be the inversion of the direction of the actions objectively described in the analysand's speech within the psychoanalytic setting.

Finding the correlations between speech and actions involves a fifth step:

5. Compare the reduced structure of the speech to the reduced structure of the actions, thus obtaining the reduced and inverted bipolar speech.

There is a certain homogeneity within the large group of actions and relations considered that makes it valuable to relate them to the theoretical model through the rules of correspondence. Further, these reduced structures make it easier to explain and predict behavior. In order to make predictions about the analysand-analyst interaction, one must perform the corresponding reductions of clinical data. The application of these simple laws of reduced structures leads us to concrete predictions corresponding to the initial clinical data and produces empirical structural information of a general kind about objective aspects of human behavior, which will be explained later by the metapsychological model of psychoanalysis. Thus, we will go from the bipolar reduced structure of the speech and actions to the conscious bipolar reduced psychic structure, and then to the unconscious bipolar reduced psychic structure; the latter two are formed not by words or actions as such, but by conscious and unconscious intrapsychic representations of them.

In order to implement the steps of this method the analyst must first make the two basic distinctions set out in chapter 3: that is, he must determine whether the speech is of the associative, defensive, working-through, consulting, setting, or conventional type; then, he must distinguish between cardinal speech (with characters, plot, and sequence) and neutral speech (without them). Then it is necessary to introduce a series of procedural hypotheses.

The first procedural hypothesis is that the smallest syntactical units used in analyzing the associative speech are the monadic propositions "A is B" and the dyadic type "A R B." In turn, both of these can be either descriptive or qualifying. A monadic type, with only one subject, would be, for instance, "the subject is satisfied and/or frustrated in his desires." A dyadic type, with a first and a second subject, would be "the subject satisfies and/or frustrates the desire(s) of the other(s)." The analysand attributes the actions he describes in monadic, dyadic, or polyadic propositions; to attribute subjects is to name those persons who are assigned certain grammatical "places" as "subjects." In the sentence "He loves me," "he" and "me" are subject-places. The attribution of each of these subject-places must be checked: the speaker with the first place and the others with the second, or vice versa. In the sentence "He loves me," the other occupies the first subject-place and the speaker the second.

At the empirical psychoanalytic level, the analysand does not speak in a bipolar way of himself and the other, but of many subjects. The analysand simply talks about certain characters and sets them in certain "subject-places" of the propositions in his narrative.

The second procedural hypothesis is that sentences are analyzed taking into account only one subject and one predicate. There can be two or more subjects, and if there are, it must be determined who the subjects are, and what grammatical place they occupy. In fact, it is not enough to say "John seemed to be very worried about hostility, and spoke to me about him and Mary." We must explain in what place each one is spoken about: does he hate Mary, or does Mary hate him? If the first is the case, John is the first subject and Mary is the second; if the second is the case, the order of subjects is reversed.

One cannot therefore define a relational statement until the first and second subjects are identified.

When the monadic, dyadic, or polyadic predicates that appear in the speech are known, our third procedural hypothesis would be that all the propositions (predicates) that appear in the speech must be analyzed as if they were dyadic. For example, if A is jealous of B because of C, we either say that A is jealous of B because B is jealous-making (and place no special importance on C); or else we shall say that C is his rival (without giving B any particular importance). The context will show whether B or C is the important one.

It is important to recall that the actions described in the dyadic predicates always will have a "geometrical" direction; that is, they will "go" from subject 1 to subject 2 or vice versa: A satisfies B or B satisfies A.

Words that possess qualifying characteristics have two super-imposed meanings: a *descriptive meaning*, entirely objective, and a *qualifying meaning*, with implicit values. For instance, the word "mercenary" signifies, objectively, a "person who fights for money" and subjectively (for certain people) "scoundrel." It is essential, therefore, to determine when the words used in judgment by the analysand are merely characterizing, or when they have an evaluative qualification. A fourth procedural hypothesis would be, then, that the cardinal associative speech of the analysand can be divided into descriptive speech ("I'm a satisfied frustrator of others"); and qualifying speech ("I'm selfish" or "this situation is stupid").

Since the analysand qualifies actors and actions with qualifications from his internalized superego, it is useful to think legalistically rather than in absolute terms: "not good" will mean "forbidden" and "good" will mean "allowed." For instance, being a <satisfied frustrator of others> is bad because it is punished socially, that is, forbidden.

In the dyadic relational type of proposition (A satisfies B) four types of meaning, M, G, E, and V, can be found (Figure 5-1):

The M (meaning) type is the order in which the subjects appear: A will be subject 1 and B subject 2.

The G (geometrical) type is the movement that takes place from one subject to another; it is the geometrical direction of the actions described by the predicate: the action goes from A to B.

Meanings of the speech	1. Meaning: order of appearance of subjects
	2. Geometrical: direction of described actions
	3. Effect: effect of actions on subjects
	4. Value: qualification of actions and affects

Figure 5-1. The four types of meaning in a relational proposition

The E (effect) type is the effect that the action described in the predicate has on a subject-place: *satisfaction* will be the E meaning of "A satisfies B."

The V (value) type is the qualifying aspect of the proposition: "It is good of A to satisfy B."

Summary: To build empirical generalizations starting from the empirical observations, the following are the fundamental questions to be asked when analyzing the cardinal associative speech of the analysand and the analyst.

1. Is the subject associating freely (either resisting or working-through), talking, consulting, or just chatting?
2. Is the subject sincerely expressing his thinking, or could he be lying?
3. Does the speech convey some kind of plot with characters and sequence, or is it merely descriptive of neutral things and facts?
4. How many narrative units are there in this segment of speech? That is, how many times is the subject relating his own personal myth?
5. How many syntactical units are there in each narrative unit? That is, how many dyadic propositions are contained in this transmission of the personal myth of the subject?
6. How many subject-places are implied in the speech?

7. Who are the subjects and in what grammatical order do they appear?
8. What are the properties, relations, or transitive actions ascribed to the subjects by the predicates?
9. In what geometrical direction do the actions occur between the subjects?
10. What effect do the actions described in the predicates have on each subject-place?
11. What affects does the speech ascribe to the subject and to the others?
12. What qualifications (and values) of actions and affects, and indirectly of himself and others are given by the subject?

To develop empirical generalizations while analyzing the verbal, preverbal, nonverbal and contextual actions of the analysand and the analyst, another series of questions must be asked:

13. Are the subjects acting within the conditions proposed by the psychoanalytic setting?
14. What are the characteristics of the actors?
15. What are the actions executed by the actors?
16. What is the direction of the actions?
17. Who is initiating each action?
18. What are the effects of the actions?
19. How can the actors be objectively qualified?
20. What are the affects experienced by the analyst?

In addition to the speech (systems 1, 3, 4, and 6) and actions (systems 2 and 5) of the analysand and the analyst, the affects of the analyst form an important part of the psychoanalytical empirical basis. The analyst is able to directly observe his own feelings; those of the analysand, though extremely important technically and theoretically, are not always observable and therefore are not a part of the empirical base. Consequently, the countertransference of the analyst must be systematically studied; from his affects (system 8) we can deduce the present affects of the analysand (system 7) by hypothesizing that the affects of the analysand are complementary to the affects that the analyst observes in himself.

In this way we will have a new empirical element to verify the truth of the propositions of the analysand describing and qualifying his actions and affects. The speech must be concordant with the observed actions and with the countertransferential feelings of the analyst.

Introduction of the Method

We will now try to apply these twenty questions to analyze the first intervention of Peter, the young analysand already described in chapter 3.

> *I'm very angry. These members of the Boy Scouts are really awful . . . traitors . . . they are crazy. . . . Yesterday I went to the weekly meeting and I found that they have filled my position there . . . simply because I failed to show up to some previous meetings and because I fought with some of them, they excluded me. . . . They got very angry at me without any justification. . . . They replaced me with other guys. . . . But I will take some revenge . . . I will send them an unsigned letter denouncing all their tricky lousy maneuvers. . . . Because I, in my own way, honored my duties with them.*

In applying the procedural hypotheses to the speech and actions of the analysand and to the affects experienced by the analyst at this time, it can be said that:

1. The analysand is using mainly cardinal defensive associative speech.
2. It can be assumed that he is speaking "his" truth, that he is speaking sincerely even if he is distorting what is "really" happening.
3. His speech conveys a clear plot with distinctive characters and a defined sequence. Character A is angry because Character B has excluded and replaced him, and he will take some kind of revenge.
4. Only one narrative unit exists in the whole intervention of the analysand: he tells his personal myth only once.
5. There are eight syntactical units within the narrative unit: he makes eight dyadic propositions.
6. There are two subject-places in the speech: the analysand himself and the members of the Boy Scouts.
7. With the exception of the syntactial units 4 and 5 he is always "subject 1" and the members of the Boy Scouts are "subject 2."

8. He ascribes to himself the properties of being angry, mistreated, betrayed, replaced, excluded, victimized, revengeful, denouncing, responsible. He ascribes complementary properties to the others.

9. In the syntactical units 1, 6, 7 and 8 the actions described by the analysand go from him towards the others; in units 2, 3, 4 and 5 the actions go from the others to him.

10. The effect on the analysand of the actions described in units 2, 3, 4 and 5 is that they are mistreating, excluding, and replacing him and therefore, making him angry and revengeful.

11. The affects ascribed by the analysand to himself are that he is proud because he had honored his commitments, and that he is angry and revengeful because he has been mistreated, excluded, and replaced. The others must be ashamed and regretting their lack of responsibility.

12. The analysand qualifies himself as good, sensible, and responsible, that is, a person who "honors" his duties. At the same time he disqualifies the others as being bad and irresponsible, that is, "traitors" and "crazy."

13. It can be said that the analysand is still acting (out) within the limits of the analytic setting. But he is very near to breaking it or to driving the analyst to do so.

14. The analysand appears mistreating, excluding, replacing, and appears to make the analyst angry and revengeful, and the analyst appears mistreated, excluded, and replaced.

15. The analysand's actions are: arriving late, becoming angry, going to see another analyst, blaming and indirectly threatening his present analyst. The analyst's actions are: waiting for the analysand, tolerating his unjustified anger, reproaches, and threats.

16. The actions go mainly from the analysand toward the analyst, because the analyst's only action included in this transaction is his waiting despite the previous absences of his analysand.

17. The actions are initiated by the analysand.

18. The effect of the analysand's actions is to mistreat, exclude, and replace the analyst, making the analyst angry and vengeful.

19. The analysand could be objectively qualified as a mistreating, irresponsible person and the analyst as a mistreated, responsible one.

20. The affects experienced by the analyst are feelings of anger and revenge with some pride because he was capable of not replacing his analysand prematurely.

In this transcript the analysand talks about only one type of dyadic interaction: his relation with the members of the Boy Scouts. He does not mention other relations or his present relation with his analyst. This type of material can be called "indirect transferential" because the action that the analyst can observe personally—his relation with the analysand—is not mentioned in the analysand's speech. It is "displaced" toward the relationship of the analysand with other people.

Thus, what the analysand is describing and qualifying in his speech can only be compared with what he and his analyst are doing in the present and with what his analyst is presently feeling in his countertransference. Of course this implies that we are using a "here-and-now" approach to understand the deep nature of the dynamics of transference.

For instance, if the analysand is saying that his father failed him as a father, this must be compared (1) with what he is doing to his analyst at this very moment—he can be failing as an analysand (because he is not respecting the analytic setting), for example, and (2) with what his analyst is feeling toward the analysand—he can be disillusioned, for example.

The "direct transferential" material may be compared much more easily with the present actions and affects, and thus may be more easily interpreted and understood by the analysand: for example, if he screams at his analyst, "Why are you screaming at me?"

Bipolarity of the Syntactical Subjects

We have previously mentioned the importance of a bipolar reduction of the subjects in the analysand's speech. We will now develop this method of syntactical reduction in detail.

An analysand may talk about himself and his boss, himself and his wife, himself and his parents, etc. We propose, as a protohypothesis, to classify all subject-places that appear in his speech into two classes: the "ego-subjects," or simply "ego," and the "alter-subjects," or simply "alter."

We propose dichotomous classification not only because it is operationally more practical, but also for theoretical reasons.

Although the manifestation of the analysand's speech before it is reduced often presents not only triadic relations but also polyadic relations, we believe it is useful to reduce these to a competitive or cooperative relation between two place-subjects in search of an object (or subject) that will satisfy their needs. That is to say, the third subject will simply be the "object" of satisfaction—the mother, an apple, a car—over which ego and alter are fighting or collaborating. This third subject, or "object" could, for example, be none other than the object for which a son and his father fight or collaborate. From the purely operational point of view, all the objects that are not considered as ego or alter can be understood in relation to ego or alter. Even the alter-parent of the opposite sex is only a replica of the ego. For instance, if ego is jealous of another person, who might take alter away from him, this can be reduced to a binary relation between a jealous ego and a jealous-making alter who will make use of any other subject—"object"—to make ego jealous. Furthermore, the rival object usually is a jealous "derived ego" who becomes jealous in turn with regard to the jealous alter.

Briefly put, the hypothesis of the bipolarity of grammatical subjects is: Every subject-place of the cardinal propositions in the analysand's speech is an "ego" or an "alter."

ILLUSTRATION OF THE METHOD

To show how this bipolar reduction of subject-places works, we will "reduce" the subject-places in the first intervention in our example:

Ego *is very angry. These* alters *from the Boy Scouts are really awful . . . traitors . . . they are crazy. . . . Yesterday* ego *went to the weekly meeting and* ego *found that these* alters *have filled* ego's *position there . . . Simply because* ego *failed to show up to some previous meetings and because* ego *fought with some of these* alters, *they excluded* ego. *These alters got very angry at* ego *without any justification . . . These* alters *replaced* ego *with another* alter. *But* ego *will take some revenge . . .* ego *will send an unsigned letter to those* alters *denouncing all their tricky lousy maneuvers . . . Because* ego, *in his own way, honored his duties with those* alters.

In principle, the reduced ego and alter constellation can be formulated in more technical language that includes more basic and general groups of attributes and values, such as occurs with psycho-pathological attributes (such as "to seduce" in hysteria, "persecute" in paranoia, "control" in obsessional neurosis, etc.).

Bipolarity of the Descriptive Predicates

Freud (1900) repeatedly noted that analysts and analysands are specifically interested in the dialectics of needs and desires, that is, the speech of desire whose universal predicates would be the satisfaction or frustration of desires. Consequently, we argue that the speech of the analysand is fundamentally about satisfaction and frustration; and the question arises as to what, in the end, is being frustrated or satisfied. In our view it is "desire" understood in the Freudian sense.

Thus, in the psychoanalytic context, it can be stated that there is a human speech pattern based on the frustration or satisfaction of biological needs transformed into psychological desires by previous experiences of pain or satisfaction. The analysand's speech is really the discourse of desire. Along with their analysts, analysands are specifically interested in the satisfaction or frustration of desires; as Freud (1915) said, "What gives pleasure on one level produces unpleasure on another." When the psychic apparatus is functioning within the limits of the competitive pleasure principle, the hedonistic satisfaction of the subject's desire implies the hedonistic frustration of the desires of others, or the ethical frustration of the subject. What satisfies the subject hedonistically frustrates him ethically because he is automatically frustrating the hedonistic pleasure of others.

In other words, when the subject is satisfying the conflicted desires of others, these others simultaneously frustrate him because their satisfaction is at the subject's own expense. When the subject is frustrating the conflicted desires of others, these others simultaneously satisfy him because their frustration is due to the fact that they are trying to satisfy the subject at their own expense.

From the psychoanalytical hypothesis of psychic conflict it can be deduced that the descriptive predicate of the speech relating to conflicted desire is the frustrating satisfaction or satisfying frustration of that desire.

Descriptive predicates, like subject-places, can be identified and reduced bipolarly as though they were two single predicates. Again the usefulness of such a transformation will depend on the emergence of laws related to the classification and on increasing the explanatory and predictive power of the analyst. One can obtain more reduced and hence clearer connotations that show four or five basic traits for ego and alter: for instance, angry, excluded, replaced, and vengeful.

The hypothesis of the bipolarity of descriptive predicates of the narcissitic cardinal speech can be stated in the following:

1. The descriptive predicates about the syntactical subjects can be bipolarly reduced to <frustrated satisfier> and <satisfied frustrator>.

2. The descriptive predicates concerning actions can be bipolarly reduced to <frustrate satisfying> and to <satisfy frustrating>.

3. The descriptive predicates about affects can be bipolarly reduced to <frustrating satisfaction> and <satisfying frustration>.

It can be said that if, in the narrative, ego says that an R action is directed toward the alter, the statement is made in conjunction with the one that comes from applying a place-subject inversion and an inversion of the affect: if he says that "ego satisfies alter" he also says automatically that "alter frustrates ego." Therefore, to say that the ego is "satisfied" is also to say that he is "a frustrator"; and inversely, to say that the ego is "a frustrator" is also to say that he is "satisfied." Thus, each time the statement is made that ego has an R relation with the alter, the statement is also made with the inversion of the place-subject and of affect. This is an operational rule—every time the subject speaks, he does a double turnabout. It applies equally whether the analysand's statements take a monadic form ("I am frustrated"; "I am satisfied") or a bipolar form ("I satisfy you" or "I frustrate you," or vice versa).

The analysand systematically describes the alter through strong inversions of the monadic predicates and a double inversion of the dyadic predicates (in the M or G meaning and the E meaning): if the ego is described as a <frustrated satisfier> alter will be described as a <satisfied frustrator>, and vice versa. The analysand's speech reveals how that attributed to the ego as M and G is inverted when it is attributed to the alter.

Summary: We have postulated a series of bipolar reductions in the logical analysis of the analysand's speech. The first reduction simplifies all subject-places to "ego" and "alter." The second reduction simplifies the defining characteristics of ego and alter to simple "constellations" comprised of the attributes of the ego inverted with respect to those of the alter. The third reduction simplifies the vocabulary of the descriptive cardinal propositions about the subject-places into <satisfied frustrator> and <frustrated satisfier>; about the subjects' actions into <satisfy in frustrating> and <frustrate in satisfying>; about the subjects' affects into <satisfying frustration> and <frustrating satisfaction>.

Bipolarity of Psychopathological Types of Speech

In this section we will be referring to the nonpsychotic type of narcissistic speech that manifests the conflict of satisfaction and frustration when desire is conceived competitively. (That is, we will not consider the <satisfier-satisfied> healthy speech or the <frustrated frustrator> psychotic speech.)

If the speech is consistent and if the hypothesis, after the second reduction, is valid (for every cardinal proposition in the speech there exists a simultaneously stated association, which is its inverse G and E), then after the third reduction the speech must inevitably take one of the following forms:

1. The ego says it is satisfied; through inversion, the alter is said to be frustrated; alter has to satisfy ego, ego has to frustrate alter, etc.

2. The ego says it is frustrated, and the other propositions automatically become inverted. According to the hypothesis of the "G" inversion, the alter has to be satisfied; ego has to satisfy alter; alter has to frustrate ego, etc. The reduction can only produce these two kinds of propositions because anything else would prove to be contradictory: e.g., "I am <satisfied frustrated> by the alter" or "I am <frustrator frustrated> by the alter." Since the ego can only profess itself to be satisfied or frustrated, if the speech is coherent the hypothesis derived from the M and E inversion is that there exist only two types of reduced cardinal speech: the masochistic one,

with propositions in the first form, and the sadistic one, with propositions in the second.

By reducing the speech to those two forms, it may be classified as "masochist," in which the ego states it is satisfied, or "sadist," in which the ego states it is frustrated. We call the one who says he is frustrated "sadist" and the one who says he is satisfied "masochist" for two reasons: (1) according to the ethical code, to be "satisfied" is to be "bad," because it implies being a frustrator, and to be "frustrated" is to be "good," because it implies being a satisfier; (2) at the action level, as we will see later, the one who says he is "satisfied," actually is "frustrated," and the one who says he is "frustrated," actually is "satisfied." That is, the masochist is a masochist precisely because he looks for hedonic and ethical unpleasure, and gives up the corresponding pleasures. The sadist is a sadist because he looks for hedonic and ethical pleasure, giving up the corresponding unpleasures.

Obviously, all the hypotheses that have been developed so far are valid for speech that is coherent per se (even though it may be contradicted by the actions of the person speaking). It probably also could be applied to incoherent speech, after it has been made coherent through association with other segments of coherent speech or with actions of the analysand and the corresponding affective states of the analyst.

ILLUSTRATION OF THE METHOD

Once all subject-places and descriptive predicates of the cardinal speech of the analysand are identified and bipolarly reduced, a binary speech is left, with only two classes of subject-places and descriptive predicates. The descriptive predicates concerning the subjects, the actions and affects in the first intervention can be reduced to the following:

Ego *is very* frustrated satisfier. *These* alters *from the Boy Scouts are really awful . . . traitors . . . they are crazy. Yesterday* ego *went to the weekly meeting and* ego *found that those alters have been* satisfying themselves frustrating ego, *simply because* ego *failed sometimes in* satisfying *them by* frustrating *himself. These* alters *became very* frustrated satisfiers *without any justification. . . .*

These alters satisfy themselves frustrating ego *with other* alters. *But* ego *will* satisfy himself frustrating *these* alters. . . . Ego *will* satisfy himself by frustrating these alters, *denouncing their tricky, dirty frustrating satisfaction.* . . . *Because* ego, *in his own way, is a true* frustrated satisfier *of* alters.

As stated before, the cardinal speech of this analysand will be of the sadistic type, because he describes himself as a <frustrated satisfier>, while being a <satisfied frustrator>, and he describes the others as <satisfied frustrators> while treating them as <frustrated satisfiers> of himself.

Bipolarity of Qualifying Predicates

The cardinal predicates can be divided into two types: descriptive and qualifying. Just as all descriptive predicates about the subjects, their actions, and their affects can be bipolarly reduced, all the qualifying predicates about the subjects, their actions, and their affects can be similarly reduced to "good" and "bad." This is the fourth reduction to be applied to the cardinal predicates of the associative speech: in themselves, "good" and "bad" are not specific polarities.

There may be predicates in the speech that superimpose a qualification on a descriptive meaning. For instance, if the patient says the alter is "mercenary," he also means he is describing him as "frustrating" and qualifies him as being "bad."

If the qualifying predicate is a negative one, we have a "disqualification." If it is a positive one, we have an "overqualification." And if the qualifying predicate rectifies previous qualifications, we have a "requalification."

The disqualification and the overqualification of the status of the subjects are the types of qualifying predicates most frequently used. The use of these makes the sender's reliability questionable. The objective characteristics of the messages are not considered; they are falsified a priori by the sender. In the disqualification of the status of the sender or of the receiver, the theme is changed, and the content of the original message is no longer considered, because the personal characteristics of the participants are what really count. A unique status disqualification can nullify an infinite number of future and past messages that are true because the sender is disqualified as "bad," "stupid," or "crazy." On the other hand a unique status overqualification can make it appear as true in an infinite number of future and past false messages just because the sender is overqualified as "good," "clever," or "sensible": when the veracity of his message is questioned, the overqualified sender will not answer on the level at which he has been questioned, but will change the level of his answer, once again overqualifying his reliability as a good, clever, and sensible sender. He can answer, for example, "I know what I am talking about because I am an expert."

Empirically, the sadistic type of speech is characterized not only by the speaker's description of himself as a <frustrated satisfier> (while he acts as a <satisfied frustrator>) and of the others as <satisfied frustrators> (while they act as <frustrated satisfiers>), but also by his overqualification of himself as "good" (altruistic, clever, sensible) and his disqualification of the others as "bad" (selfish, stupid, crazy). On the other hand, the masochistic type of speech is characterized not only by the speaker's description of himself as a <satisfied frustrator> (while he acts as a <frustrated satisfier>) and of the others as <frustrated satisfiers> (while they act as <satisfied frustrators>), but also by his disqualification of himself as "bad" (selfish, stupid, crazy) and by his overqualification of the others as "good" (generous, clever, sensible).

In the example, Peter uses typical sadistic speech: he repeatedly states that he is a <frustrated satisfier> of others, who are <satisfied frustrators> of himself, and he overqualifies himself as being "good" (he honors his commitments) and disqualifies the others as being "bad" (awful, traitors, crazy, tricky, dirty). Moreover, each time the analyst attempts to show him that in fact he is behaving as a "bad" <satisfied frustrator> and not as the "good" <frustrated satisfier> that he describes himself as, Peter changes the level of communication and starts disqualifying the status of the analyst as the sender of therapeutic messages. This is a typical reaction of the sadist to the analyst's interpretation.

On the other hand, when the analyst attempts to show a masochist that, in fact, he is behaving as a "good" <frustrated satisfier> and not as the "bad" <satisfied frustrator> that he is describing when speaking about himself, the masochist tends to change the level of communication and starts disqualifying his own status.

This can be seen in the case of Jennifer, who had already paid her analyst for twenty-one sessions while she had attended only nineteen. She started analysis because she felt depressed, with an immense feeling of guilt with respect to her mother, who behaved sadistically toward her and reproached her constantly for being a selfish, uncaring daughter.

Analysand: I felt really mean yesterday. There was this poor man working at the parking lot. He is a very sick man. He has to work very hard for his clients if he wants to survive and yet he is making the sacrifice of attending me in such a nice way. He gives me more than I deserve. I will have to tell him not to make any other sacrifice for me. But I don't know if he will change his attitude because he fears that if he changes it he will lose his job.

Analyst: Don't you think that something similar could be happening here: that you are giving me more than I deserve?

Analysand: How is that?

Analyst: Well, you already paid me for twenty-one sessions when actually we only had nineteen.

Analysand: Is that so? Well, this is happening because I am not taking good care of the treatment. I am not doing enough.

Analyst [jokingly]: *Just like this old man you were speaking about: it is very difficult for you to change your attitude of sacrificing and blaming yourself.*

Analysand: The problem is that I am not working hard enough.

Analyst: The problem seems to be that you feel that if you stop blaming and sacrificing yourself you "will lose your job" here. That is, that I'll be very angry at you and maybe I'll cut off the treatment.

If we want to reduce the subject-places and the descriptive and qualifying predicates of Jennifer's first intervention, we will have the following:

Ego *felt really* bad *yesterday. There was this* good alter frustrating himself to satisfy ego *in the parking lot.* Alter *is a very sick man.* Alter *has to* frustrate himself satisfying *others if* alter *wants to survive. And yet* alter *is* frustrating himself to satisfy ego *in such a good way.* Alter *is* frustrating himself to satisfy ego *more than* ego *deserves.* Ego *will have to tell him not to* frustrate himself to satisfy ego *anymore. But* ego *doesn't know if* alter *will change his attitude.*

Society's conflicting ethical code seems to qualify "frustration" as "good" and "satisfaction" as "bad," whereas the hedonic code qualifies "satisfaction" as "good," and "frustration" as "bad." The subject in the conflicted speech has been socialized within a social system that in fact incites competitive satisfaction while at the same time disapproves of it. Such an incongruence between speech and social action will not only produce an inversion with respect to action and the effects of the predicates in patients' speech, but also will divide patients, as stated earlier, into sadists who say they are good because they are frustrated while managing to be satisfied, and into masochists who say they are bad because they are satisfied while putting up with being frustrated.

The Four Types of Reduced Speech

After reducing the subject-places to "ego" and "alter," its characteristics to "constellation of the ego" and "constellation of the alter," the descriptive predicates about the subject to "satisfied" (frustrator) and "frustrated" (satisfier), the qualifying predicates to "good" and "bad," and the psychopathological types of speech to "sadist" and "masochist," the four main types of analysand's speech may be observed:

1. Where "satisfied" is "good" and the ego is "satisfied."
2. Where "satisfied" is "good" and the alter is "satisfied."
3. Where "satisfied" is "bad" and the ego is "satisfied."
4. Where "satisfied" is "bad" and the alter is "satisfied."

The speech would appear to show that the inversions mentioned earlier do not affect the qualifications of appraisal it contains. Whatever may be said, "satisfied" will always be seen as "good" or always as "bad."

After reducing the descriptive and qualifying predicates one observes that any speech of any analysand can be reduced to four types of collections of sentences or each one of the four types of *reduced speech* within the complete speech that the analysand may offer, without counting repetitions. The four types of reduced speech correspond to the four squares in Figure 5-2. The first type

	satisfaction = good frustration = bad	satisfaction = bad frustration = good
Satisfied ego and frustrated alter	1. Good satisfied	3. Bad satisfied (Masochist)
Frustrated ego and satisfied alter	2. Bad frustrated	4. Good frustrated (Sadist)

Figure 5-2. Types of speech

of reduced speech, that of the "good satisfied," would correspond to the traditional version of the sadist; the second type, "bad frustrated," would correspond to the traditional version of the masochist; the third type, "bad satisfied," would correspond to our version of the masochist; and, finally, the fourth type, the "good frustrated," would correspond to our version of the sadist.

First Type of Reduced Speech: "I am satisfied; to be satisfied is good; I am good; alter is frustrated; alter is bad; alter satisfies me; I am satisfied by alter; I frustrate alter; alter is frustrated by me."

Second Type of Reduced Speech: "I am frustrated; frustration is bad; I am bad; alter is satisfied; to be satisfied is good; alter is good; alter frustrates me; I am frustrated by alter; I satisfy alter; alter is satisfied by me."

Third Type of Reduced Speech (masochistic): "I am satisfied; to be satisfied is bad; I am bad; alter is frustrated; to be frustrated is good; alter is good; I frustrate alter; alter is frustrated by me; alter satisfies me; I am satisfied by alter."

Fourth Type of Reduced Speech (sadistic): "I am frustrated; frustration is good; I am good; alter is satisfied; to be satisfied is bad;

alter is bad; alter frustrates me; I am frustrated by alter; I satisfy alter; alter is satisfied by me."

It is important to remember here that the denominations apply to the associative, defensive, and consulting speech but not necessarily to the working-through, setting, and conventional speech. If the analysand is working through his masochistic position in life, for example, he can be saying that he is a <good frustrated>, because he is recognizing objectively that he is actually being a <good frustrated> and wants to change that. He does not want to suffer any more to obtain security and he realizes that being masochistic does not mean being a good person but rather a sick person. But qualifying oneself as being ethically "bad" could be pragmatically "good" if, as in the case of the masochist, he obtains a feeling of security by disqualifying himself.

Superficial and Deep Structures: the Informative Function of Speech

It should be pointed out that in the foregoing analysis the configuration of the ego-alter couple is considered from a synchronic standpoint or from that of permanent configuration. In this sense, to say one is "satisfied" or "frustrated" is to qualify a state of being that is permanent, not temporary. To say that "ego satisfies alter" indicates the way in which the couple is configured and not a manner of acting casually at a given moment. If this is the case, the whole of the analysand's speech configures information of a structural synchronic and invariable nature. This is the structure whose description is repeated ad infinitum in the speech.

If we divide the subject-places (characters) into "ego" and "alter," divide the descriptive (of state or action) propositions about the subjects into <satisfier-frustrated> or <frustrator-satisfied>, and divide the qualifying propositions into "good" and "bad," we can make a diagram of the analysis of the content of the sadistic and masochistic speech as seen in Figures 5-3 and 5-4.

It should be pointed out that, if we made a diachronic analysis, even though the *reduced narrative type* might always be of the same type as one of the four universals, the analysand might not always be

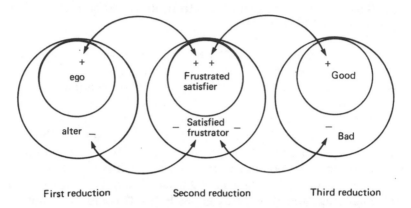

Figure 5-3.   Analysis of the sadistic speech: reduction and relations

telling the same story. This is because he could alter the diachronic "causal" chains of his speech. Therefore, we propose a stronger hypothesis covering the diachronics of the speech according to which all the speech of a given analysand not only has the same synchronic structure, but also repeats the same "causal" diachronic structure.

A person may be very creative in his speech in certain circumstances, but his basic configuration, from the psychoanalytical point of view, can be fairly constant from the moment it was formed during his childhood. The analysand's manifest speech contains a

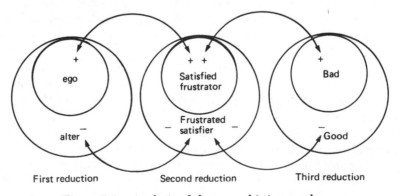

Figure 5-4.   Analysis of the masochistic speech

structure that can be classified easily even though the content of the structure may vary from episode to episode.

Before applying reduction and inversions to the cardinal association, we have the *nonreduced narrative structure of the analysand's speech*: for instance, the cardinal associations of Peter and Jennifer just as they are spoken. As a second step, if we apply a total bipolar reduction to the subject-places of their speech but only a partial reduction to its descriptive and qualifying predicates we will have the *partially reduced narrative structure of the analysand's speech*: the speech will only be reduced to ego and alter and the respective descriptive and qualifying constellations of identifying traits. This partial abstraction of the narrative structure can easily be recognized by the analysand as his, but is at the same time organized in a pattern he did not perceive previously. Therefore, this partial type of reduction permits the analysand greater insight into the prototype of narrative structure that he tends to reiterate in his infinite variations on the same theme.

The partially reduced structure of Peter's sadistic speech could be, for instance, that "ego" is good because ego is reasonably angry and vengeful because "ego" has been excluded and replaced, and that "alter" is awful, a traitor, and crazy because he makes "ego" angry and vengeful by excluding and replacing "ego." The partially reduced structure of Jennifer's masochistic speech could be that "ego" is a lazy, selfish, careless receiver of the sacrifices of a nice, generous "alter" who is sacrificing himself and giving much more than is necessary. The crucial interaction happens between a selfish receiver "ego" and a nice sacrificing giver "alter."

A third step is the full reduction of subjects and predicates of the cardinal associations, thus obtaining the *totally reduced narrative structure of the analysand's speech*. We will find only two classes of universal totally reduced structures in all our analysands: the sadistic and the masochistic.

As we stated before, the totally reduced structure of Peter's sadistic speech would be that "ego" is good because he is a <frustrated satisfier> and "alter" is bad because he is a <satisfied frustrator>. The totally reduced structure of Jennifer's masochistic speech would be that "ego" is bad because she is a <satisfied frustrator> and "alter" is good because he is a <frustrated satisfier>.

In Chomsky's terms, this totally reduced structure of the "manifest" speech would be a *semi-deep preconscious structure* that has "generative" power in regard to its respective *superficial conscious nonreduced structures*. It is preconscious because, apart from the feeling of shame of always repeating the same thing, the analysand does not offer a particular resistance to its recognition.

This semi-deep preconscious structure is the same as the defensive structure, which transcends the speech and generates its elements: the reduced structure of the manifest speech is immanent to that speech. It is objective and can be observed when finding the pattern of the speech by anyone who has made the prior reductions and inversion of subjects and affects in the descriptive and qualifying predicates.

Such an explanation in no way means that we are rejecting a possible unconscious, deep, and generative structure. Such a nonobservable deep structure, whose existence we confirm, will be reduced and based on the reduced structure of the manifest speech. But it occurs on different levels with regard to the analyst's observation: the "manifest structure" is the product of an empirical generalization, and the "deep structure" is produced by the rules of correspondence between that empirical generalization and our theoretical model.

To obtain the deep unconscious reduced narrative structure of the analysand's speech it would be necessary, according to the bipolar model of intrapsychic structure (to be developed in chapter 6), to invert the direction of the actions of the descriptive (and, automatically, of its qualifying predicates) of the semi-deep preconscious reduced narrative structure of the analysand. That is, there would have to be a multiplication by −1 of the direction of the actions described in the "manifest structure of the speech" to obtain the structure of the "latent speech": we have given the name Z *interpretation* to the act of obtaining the latent content of the speech by way of inverting its manifest content. In the case of Peter, for example, the semi-deep preconscious reduced narrative structure of his speech states that he is angry and vengeful because he has been excluded and replaced by others. If we multiply by −1 (that is, if we invert the directions of the actions and the quality of the affective states), we will have the deep unconscious reduced narrative structure of his speech: he makes others angry and vengeful because he excludes and replaces them. This will be a Z interpretation because the direction of the actions and the quality of the affective states of the manifest content of his speech are inverted in order to obtain the latent content.

Again, we find only two classes of universal, totally reduced deep structures in all analysands: the sadistic and the masochistic.

After applying the inversion of the direction of the actions present in the descriptive predicates of Peter's totally reduced semi-deep preconscious narrative structure, we will have the totally reduced deep unconscious structure of his speech: "Ego is bad because he is a <satisfied frustrator> and alter is good because he is a <frustrated satisfier>. The totally reduced deep unconscious narrative structure of Jennifer's speech will be: "Ego is good because he is a <frustrated satisfier> and alter is bad because he is a <satisfied frustrator>."

From Chomsky's perspective, it could be said that the deep unconscious structure of the speech has more generative power than its semi-deep preconscious structure because, as long as the sadist acts, for example, as a <bad satisfied frustrator of others>, he has to justify ethically that punishable fact by saying, in various ways, that he is only a <good frustrated satisfier>. Or in the case of the masochist, as long as he acts as a <good frustrated satisfier of others>, he has to placate the sadist (upon whom he depends for survival) by saying, in various ways, that he is only a <bad satisfied frustrator>.

In spite of the fact that the deep unconscious structure of the speech has great explanatory power, it does not have enough specificity and singularity to be effectively utilized by the analysand in the process of working-through. For this reason the analysand needs to partially amplify this total reduction. The partially amplified deep structure of Peter's sadistic speech would be, for instance, that ego is awful, a traitor, and crazy because he makes alter angry and vengeful by excluding and replacing alter, and that alter is good because alter is reasonably angry and vengeful because alter has been excluded and replaced.

The partially amplified deep structure of Jennifer's masochistic speech would be that ego is nice and generous because ego is sacrificing himself to give others more than they deserve and that alter is a lazy, selfish, careless receiver. When working in the sessions, the analyst will need to totally amplify the deep structure of his analysand's speech in order to facilitate the "moment-by-moment" working-through. For instance, the analyst will have reduced the structures of their actions to the point where he has available their unconscious inverted structure, but in formulating his interpretations he will be using whatever nonreduced cardinal associations that Peter or Jennifer produce. Thus the deep structures are gradually conveyed with the help of the day-to-day material.

In summary, the task of psychoanalytic working-through can be facilitated by Z interpretations of the nonreduced conscious narrative structure units of the analysand's speech and their corresponding units of the totally amplified deep unconscious narrative structure of speech (Figure 5-5).

Although to classify the speech as one of the four reduced types is equivalent to making a diagnosis, it should not be forgotten that, before they are simplified, the characteristics of a speech can offer additional valuable information. From the standpoint of sim-

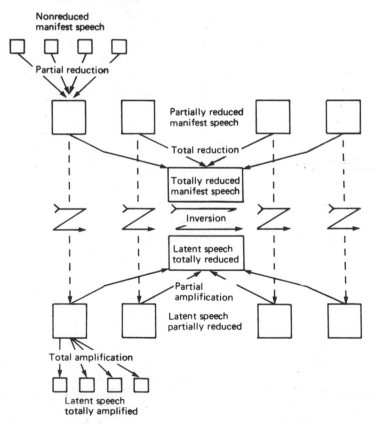

Figure 5-5. The reduction and Z interpretation of the deep structures of speech

plification, the speech is a repetition. But the speech, preceding simplification, is more varied. One can note partial repetitive cycles in relation to the characteristics that get lost when reductions are carried out. The partial changes of cycle can supply information about changes of context or changes of interlocutor and about the particularities of a special subject that occasionally takes on the part of alter.

Furthermore, the nonreduced manifest structure of the speech can afford information about the nature of that occasional couple within the cycle, from the alter's point of view. The analyst begins by reducing all the subject-places of his analysand's speech to egos and alters, all the descriptive predicates about the subjects to satisfied or frustrated (with the corresponding of M and E inversion), all the qualifying predicates to good or bad, the same descriptive and qualifying predicates to reduced constellations of individual style, and the psychopathology to sadist or masochist. He then finds that each analysand has a particular way of satisfying or frustrating, of being satisfied or frustrated, of being good or bad. But he also discovers that these individual constellations of traits and values, although they may tend to stay relatively constant, change according to whose "turn" it is to be the alter. For example, if the analysand tends to say that he (ego) is innocent (good) because he is being robbed (frustrated) by the others (alter) and that they are treacherous (bad) he can, in a moment, change and say that: he (ego) is inoffensive (good) but humiliated (frustrated) by the others (alters) who are aggressive (bad). This means that the primary, original alter of his binary psychic structure was someone who stole from the analysand while in fact letting himself be robbed; and that, on the other hand, his current alter is someone who says he is humiliating toward the analysand while letting himself be humiliated by the analysand.

Up to a point, each individual is pressed by his current context, or encouraged by his own idiosyncracy, to manifest or choose his type of expression from a particular spectrum of styles.

The Conative Function of Speech

BIPOLARITY OF ACTORS AND ACTIONS

"Actions" are considered to include the conative (action-provoking) affect of speech, the tone and style of the speech, the gestures and the

movements as well as the modification of the analytic setting produced by the analysand and the analyst.

Until now we have been working with the informative function
of speech. But the analysand is speaking not only in order to inform
the analyst but also to produce an effect on him and to provoke a
reaction. This conative function of the analysand's cardinal association could be, in turn, either collaborative or resistant: in the first
case, the analysand speaks mainly to let the analyst understand his
associations and make an interpretation; in the second case, the
analysand speaks mainly to interfere with the analytic work of the
analyst, pushing him to counter–act-out.

The analysand's informative cardinal associative speech must
be compared with the tone, style, gestures and the modifications of
the setting. Also, all the subject-places described and qualified by
the informative speech must be bipolarly reduced so that they can
be compared to what is actually happening between the analyst and
the analysand. The speech is bipolarized because the analytic relationship is dyadic.

In the analysand-analyst interaction, four bipolar reductions
and an M and a G inversion can also be made. First, the actors in the
therapeutic relation can be bipolarly reduced to the "ego-analysand"
and the "alter-analyst"; they are no longer "speech ego" and "speech
alter" but "factual ego" and "factual alter." Second, the actions of
the analysand and the analyst can also be bipolarly reduced to
"satisfy" and "frustrate." Third, with regard to their actors and
effects, these bipolarized actions are always associated with their
inverse: when the analysand factually satisfies himself, he does so by
frustrating the analyst and when he frustrates himself he does so to
satisfy the analyst. Fourth, according to the effect of their actions,
the actors can be bipolarly reduced to "sadist" and "masochist": if
the analysand is a sadist, he will always tend to act as a <satisfied
frustrator> trying to induce the analyst into the masochistic role of a
<frustrated satisfier>; and if the analysand is a masochist, he will
always tend to act as a <frustrated satisfier> trying to induce the
analyst into the sadistic role of a <satisfied frustrator>. Fifth, the
observable traits of the analysand and the analyst during their interaction can be bipolarly reduced to the "factual constellation of the
ego" and the "factual constellation of the alter."

When reducing the structure of actions, we will have more or
less the same sequence of analysis that we described for the logical

reduction of the structure of speech. Thus, we will have the nonre-duced structure of actions (the actions just as they are); the partially reduced structure of actions (a few actions characteristic of the factual ego and the factual alter—their "factual constellations"); and, finally, the totally reduced structure of actions (two actions executing either a <satisfying frustration> or a <frustrating satisfaction>).

Again, the direction of actions in such structures is the inverse of the direction of actions described in the descriptive predicates of speech.

When we go from the analysand's speech to his actions, it no longer is as clear whether the multitude of characters to be found in the analysand's context can be reduced, ontologically, to an ego-alter couple. Nevertheless, this automatically occurs in the psycho-analytical situation because it involves only two people. An "ego-analysand" and an "alter-analyst" exist from the analysand's point of view, and an "ego-analyst" and an "alter-analysand" exist from the analyst's. Neither "ego" nor "alter" are qualities inherent in the persons, but names that are ascribed according to the focus of the analysis or the study of the individual's function. This does not prevent the narrative from being objective: to have chosen the term "ego" assigns a person's factual importance with regard to his own appearance as a character in the speech: the analysand is the "ego in the speech," and thus, the "factual ego."

Even in the analysand's own speech, phrases such as "I am attacking myself," occur that imply two subject-places, both con-taining the grammatical *I*. The predicates used would be those dyadic ones in which two grammatical places exist, the grammatical *I* and another character.

Once, however, the ego constellation, or "generalized ego" and the alter constellation, or "generalized alter" have been defined in phrases such as "I am attacking myself," it can be recognized that the "I" is a generalized ego and that the other "I" (myself) is a generalized alter. If the ego's constellation shows that he is "satis-fied," for instance, the first "I" is the generalized alter (one who is attacked, i.e., frustrated), and the second "I" is the generalized ego (an aggressor, i.e., a <satisfied frustrator>).

In addition to the analytic situation, however, there are other configurations that are important from the analytic point of view. Among these are binary configurations analogous to the analytic situation, as, for example, that of the child and the father. This again presents a methodological problem of the study of the correspondence between the reduced speech and what is happening in the child-father factual couple. How should one proceed in order to compare the binary reduced speech with the oedipal triadic configuration? An *ad hoc* and tricky process is to divide the oedipal configuration into the two independent child-father and child-mother subconfigurations. Although in both cases the child is factual ego, in effect it would seem that vis-à-vis the father, the child functions as the ego of his speech, and vis-à-vis the mother, he acts as the alter of her speech.

Another possible hypothesis is that for each parent in the (factual ego) child-(factual ego)parent pair, one of the two poles in the pair always takes on the same function. For example, the child always assumes the same speech ego constellation and the parent of the same sex the speech alter constellation; or else the child always assumes the speech alter constellation, and the parent of the opposite sex the speech ego constellation.

BIPOLARITY OF AFFECTS

When analyzing the affects, it can be said that:

1. The affective states that the analyst is able to observe in himself can be bipolarly reduced to <satisfaction frustrating to others with insecurity> and <frustration satisfying to others with security>.

2. Applying a transitive rule, it can be said that when the analyst feels one of these two basic affective states, the analysand feels the other and vice versa.

3. It can be said that affects can be bipolarly reduced to sadistic and masochistic.

4. The affects experienced by the factual ego and the factual alter can be gathered into two "affective-constellations" before going into a total reduction. In Peter's case, for example, his "ego affective constellation" is formed by the satisfaction of excluding and replacing others, while his "alter affective constellation" is formed by anger and revenge.

When reducing the structure of affects (empirical systems 7 and 8) we will follow the same sequence of analysis used in analyzing the speech (empirical systems 1, 3, 4 and 6) and the actions (empirical systems 2 and 4; see chapter 4). Thus, we will have the *nonreduced structure of affects*, the *partially reduced structure of affects* (affective constellations of the factual ego and factual alter); and, finally, the *totally reduced structure of affects*, that is, two actors feeling either a <satisfying frustration> or a <frustrating satisfaction>.

Again, in the nonreduced, partially reduced, and totally reduced structures of Peter's and Jennifer's affects, the quality of the affects described in the descriptive predicates of speech is inverted.

Depending on the awareness that the analysand and the analyst have of their own affective states, these can be clinically classified as "superficial" or "deep." If one of them is functioning in the masochistic position and is not aware of it, he will be feeling a superficial affective state of <satisfaction with insecurity> and, when reflecting thoughtfully, he will realize that he is really feeling a deep state of <frustration with security>. On the contrary, if he is functioning unconsciously in the sadistic position he will be feeling exactly the opposite superficial and deep affective states.

As the reader can observe, we switch from using the concept of a sadistic or a masochistic "person" to using one of a sadistic or a masochistic "position." Any person can move from one position to another in a given moment, depending on the power of the position of the interactor. If the interactor is more powerful than a sadist, for example, even that sadist will turn into a masochist. In effect, a very strong sadist probably will transform the subject (temporarily at least) into a masochist, and vice versa.

The goals that the "factual ego–analysand" and the "factual alter–analyst" are trying to achieve together can also be reduced bipolarly to the "conscious rational goal" of obtaining happiness—healthy survival and pleasure and the unconscious narcissistic goal of obtaining sadomasochistic survival and pleasure. In turn, the unconscious narcissistic goal can be bipolarly reduced to "sadistic goal," for one member of the analytic dyad, and "masochistic goal" for the other member. In the analytic setting, the conscious rational goal will be the successful working-through and the unconscious narcissistic goal will be sadomasochistic resistance. The factual ego–anlaysand can obtain the rational conscious goal by executing a "specific action"—of correctly describing and qualifying in the speech what is done and felt—and by provoking in the factual alter–analyst a specific reaction. On the other hand, the factual ego–analysand can obtain the narcissistic conscious goal by executing a sadistic (masochistic) "acting-out"—of describing and qualifying in the speech inversely what is done and felt—and by provoking in the factual alter–analyst a masochistic (or sadistic) "counter–acting-out (see Figure 5-6).

The Inversion of Direction in the Correspondence between Speech and Actions

It should be emphasized that during the whole of this analysis one begins with the subject-places of the speech and then recognizes inductively and empirically that only two single constellations of characteristics can be attributed to subject-places. This enables those subject-places to be classified as ego or alter. The definition of factual constellations of characteristics follows, and the same constellations and the same bipolarity are recognized in what is factual. Finally, there is the empirical definition of affective constellations with the same bipolarity in an empirical and inductive form. Thus, our final definition of "functional ego" and "functional alter" remains related to our analysis of the speech: functional ego and functional alter are not absolutes. The ego-functioning of a person is relative to the characteristics of his speech. Two persons with different speech may both be functional egos (although this is not a requisite) but not because they have the same characteristics. The symptoms of ego-functioning (his constellation) depend on his speech and on the functions he attributes to himself in the speech: "good satisfied," "bad frustrated," "bad satisfied," and "good frustrated."

The constellations are always groups of properties, states, or actions. No account is taken of the qualification of properties, since they do not directly affect the individual. Nor is the qualification of individuals considered, since they are the result of a "trick;" they are not essential elements of the constellation, but are indirectly determined. If a person is good, it is the result of his constellation: he is not good simply because he is good, but because he is frustrated and it is good to be frustrated.

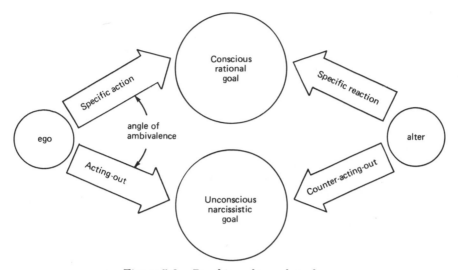

Figure 5-6. Psychic poles and goals

We noted a variance between the neutral and the cardinal level of the propositions such that only by the application of the law of syntactical inversion to the cardinal propositions does the speech become consonant with the actions.

Methodologically, we must first investigate how the descriptive predicates in the speech are inverted with respect to the actions they describe, keeping in mind that the ethical code is permanent and purely linguistic. Then, we deduce the inaccuracy of the ethical statements produced by the analysand from his inverted description of facts.

Comparing what the analysand in conflict says he does and feels with what he actually does and says, one can observe that the descriptive predicates result in an inversion of the facts and what is said about them in those statements. The qualifying predicates produce an inversion between what is said and what should have been said with respect to the ethical qualification of the subject's actions: the sadist should be qualified as "bad" because he is a <satisfied frustrator of others> but he qualifies himself as "good" because he describes himself as a <frustrated satisfier of others>.

Regarding the relation between the analysand's speech and the very facts he is describing with speech, we make the following

hypothesis or empirical generalization: If the descriptive propositions of the analysand's reduced speech (when he is in conflict) are
compared with the factual conduct of this analysand, one observes
that the "factual ego" (such as is described in the speech) turns out to
be a "functional alter," and vice versa. That is, the "speech ego"
corresponds, through the facts, to the "factual alter" and vice versa.

From this we derive that: In order to go from the speech ego to
the factual ego, inversion must be made of the direction of the
action described. For example, if the speech ego is frustrated, the
factual ego is satisfied. That is, if the speech says that ego satisfies
alter it should now be said in relation to the facts, that the factual ego
frustrated the factual alter.

Inversion not only occurs with direct transferential speech but
also with indirect transferential speech. That is, the analysand not
only speaks in an inverted way when he is speaking directly about
his present relationship with the analyst, but also when he is speaking
about other people (other speech-alters). For example, if he is
saying "my father frustrates me," according to our hypothesis he
will be frustrating the analyst at that very moment. Consequently,
the indirect transferential speech must be treated with two logical
operations in order to be understood: (1) a reduction of all others
interacting with the analysand to alters; (2) an inversion of the direction of actions.

Thanks to the M and E inversion of the binary descriptive
predicates of the analysand's speech, the analyst can deduce that
when the analysand says the ego of his speech satisfies the alter of
his speech, this means the alter of the speech is frustrating the ego of
the speech. But since, in view of the previous hypothesis, the speech
alter becomes the factual ego through the G inversion of the direction
of his actions, the analyst is able to complete his earlier deduction by
supposing that when the analysand says that the ego of his speech
satisfies the alter of his speech, he is not only saying that the alter of
the speech frustrates the ego of the speech but that, indeed, his
factual ego–analysand is satisfied by, and frustrates, his factual
alter–analyst.

The analyst's chain of deduction when faced with the analysand's speech would be as follows:

1. Here we are, you as the analysand and I as the analyst.
2. What you are saying reveals a characteristic ego and a
   characteristic alter.

3. We shall now examine what you say your ego is doing to your alter (and vice versa).

4. The hypothesis of inversion of the effect of the actions in your speech allows me to answer in advance that what you are doing with me is the inversion of what you say you do in your speech.

5. And I shall be placed in such a way as to do the G reverse of what you say in your speech that I or others are doing to you. I shall do what you, in your speech, say you are doing and you will do what you, in your speech, say that I or others are doing to you.

Since this inversion is reflected in the application of the ethical opinions expressed in the speech, one will deduce that when the analysand gives an ethical qualification, he will appreciate correctly but characterize badly, and then qualify badly. If he is a satisfier, and qualifies satisfaction as "bad," he will qualify himself incorrectly as "good" because he will say he is frustrated (pulled into it). He will say that: I should be qualified as you are qualifying yourself in your speech and that you should be qualified as you are qualifying me or others in your speech.

If the analyst is well analyzed (and neither manipulates nor is manipulated by the analysand) he should be able to observe in his own countertransference that the feelings the analysand attributed to himself in his speech are exactly the feelings that he, the analyst, is feeling at this very moment, and that the feelings that the analysand attributes to the analyst or to others in his speech must be the feelings that he, the analysand, is feeling at this very moment, according to the effect of his own acts. Briefly stated: I shall feel what you in your speech say you are feeling, and you will feel what you in your speech say that I or others are feeling.

The effect of actions as well as the quality of qualifications and affects are not only inverted between the nonreduced narrative structure of the speech and the nonreduced structure of actions and affects but also between the partially reduced and the totally reduced ones. In the totally reduced structure of Peter's speech, for example, one can find that he is saying he is a <good frustrated satisfier> who is feeling a frustration which is satisfying for others, while in the totally reduced structure of his actions and affects one can find that he is acting like a <bad satisfied frustrator> who "must" be feeling a satisfaction which is frustrating for others. A similar inversion is happening between the reduced structures of Jennifer's speech and those of her actions and affects: she is saying that she is a <bad satisfied frustrator> who is feeling a satisfaction frustrating for others while she is acting as a <good frustrated satisfier> who "must" be feeling a frustration satisfying for others.

Z interpretation is the logical operation of inverting the effect of actions (and, consequently, the quality of qualifications and affects) ascribed by the predicates of the cardinal associative speech. This would be one way in which the manifest content of the speech is transformed—in a Chomskian sense—into its latent content.

In brief, our hypothesis is that the observable structure of the analysand's speech will be its "manifest content" while the observable structure of his actions and affects will be the "latent content" of the speech. From another point of view this is not an observation as such, but a theoretical hypothesis because it deals with an unobservable entity, the latent content of the speech.

We will later demonstrate that the observable structure of the speech is intrapsychically represented by word-representations, which form the conscious and preconscious, while the observable structure of the actions and affects are represented by thing-representations which form, specifically, the unconscious.

Consequences for Technique

According to the empirical laws of the theory of psychic bipolarity, some technical consequences follow regarding the therapeutic speech, actions, and affective states that can be used by the analyst to treat the pathogenic and pathological speech, actions, and affective states of the analysand (these therapeutic instruments will be described in detail in chapter 10):

1. The analyst must show the analysand how his speech can be partially bipolarly reduced to "speech-ego-constellation" and to "speech-alter-constellation" so that the analysand can become aware of his compulsion to repeat the same themes.

2. The analyst must show the analysand how his speech can be totally bipolarly reduced in its subject-places and descriptive and qualifying predicates (relating to his actions and affective states) so that the analysand can become aware of his psychopathological

type of speech: his repetition, in various forms, that he is a <good frustrated satisfier> or a <bad satisfied frustrator> and that he can't be satisfied without frustrating others, and vice versa.

3. The analyst must show the analysand how his actions and effective states can be totally bipolarly reduced so that he can become aware of how he is inverting the direction of his actions and the quality of his affective states when he speaks about them; and that he repeats, in various ways, that he is a <good frustrated satisfier> while he constantly tends to act as a <bad satisfied frustrator> and vice versa.

4. The analyst must show the analysand how the totally reduced structure of his actions, qualifications, and affective states (or totally reduced deep structure of his speech) can be partially and totally amplified in order to allow the analysand to complete the step-by-step process of working-through.

5. On the level of qualifying speech, the analyst must show the sadist how he overqualifies himself while disqualifying the analyst; and he must show the masochist how he disqualifies himself while overqualifying the analyst.

6. On the level of pure action, the analyst must prevent the sadist from satisfying himself by frustrating the analyst and prevent the masochist from frustrating himself by satisfying the analyst. With both, the analyst must try to be a <satisfied satisfier>.

7. A comment must be made regarding the analysand's possible reaction to the verbal and factual intervention of the analyst: the sadist may resist them by disqualifying the analyst's <satisfied satisfier> comments and behavior, saying again that the latter is a <bad satisfied frustrator> of his analysands because he does not allow them to satisfy themselves by frustrating him; similarly, the masochist may resist the <satisfied satisfier> therapeutic behavior of the analyst by overqualifying the analyst, saying again that he (the analyst) is a <good frustrated satisfier> of his analysands, because he does not allow them to frustrate themselves by satisfying him.

8. The analyst must describe how the speech and the actions of the sadistic analysand press the analyst psychologically to be a dependent masochist by the analysand's use of verbal promises or threats, or actual rewards or punishments, regarding the survival of the analyst and how his survival as analyst will be threatened if he does not masochistically please the sadistic analysand. Similarly, the analyst must describe how the speech and actions of the masochistic

analysand press him psychologically to be a dependency-making sadist by the analysand's use of verbal promises or threats, or actual rewards or punishments, regarding the pleasure of the analyst and how his pleasure as analyst will be threatened if he does not sadistically overprotect the masochistic analysand.

9. The analyst must be especially careful to insure that he does not actually depend on the sadistic analysand for his survival as analyst or on the masochistic analysand for his pleasure as analyst. In that way he will be sufficiently independent (that is, out of the reach of the pathogenic unconscious psychological pressures of his analysands) to work in an objective way. He will be free from the sadomasochistic trap so that he may help his analysands to liberate themselves from their narcissistic prison.

10. On the level of pure affective states, the analyst must be able to analyze carefully the sadomasochistic feelings provoked in him by the analysand's speech and actions (or by the analyst's own history) in order to recapture therapeutic affective states of satisfying satisfaction or of shared frustration with problems that must be solved cooperatively. That is, he must be able to recognize and to work through pathogenic sadomasochistic feelings and to sustain intelligent therapeutic feelings.

Applying some of these technical consequences to the treatment of Peter, for example, we find that the analyst must:

1. Show him his speech's partially reduced structure: how he constantly repeats that he is angry and vengeful because he has been excluded and replaced by others who make him angry and vengeful.
2. Show him his speech's totally reduced structure: how he repeats that he is a <good frustrated satisfier> of <bad satisfied frustrator> others.
3. Show him the totally reduced structure of his actions and affective states: how he is a <bad satisfied frustrator> of <good frustrated satisfier> others.
4. Show him the partially amplified transferential structure of his actions and affective states: how he is, here and now, an excluding and replacing analysand who makes his analyst angry and vengeful.

5. Block his sadistic tendency to satisfy himself by frustrating his analyst, by using verbal, paraverbal, nonverbal, and contextual "satisfying satisfying" therapeutic actions (specific reactions): forbidding him to arrive late, or to miss the sessions, to see other analysts, etc.
6. Show him how he presses the analyst to be a dependent masochist through psychological pressures threatening his survival as an analyst.
7. Carefully avoid being dependent on him for professional survival; that is, not accepting a powerless masochist position in the therapeutic interaction.

In Jennifer's case, the analyst must:

1. Show her how she constantly repeats that she is the guilty and selfish receiver of the sacrifices of nice, weak others.
2. Show her how she repeats that she is a <bad satisfied frustrator> of <good frustrated satisfier> others.
3. Show her how she is acting and feeling as a <good frustrated satisfier> of <bad satisfied frustrator> others.
4. Show her how she is, here and now, a nice, sacrificing weak giver who transforms her analyst into a guilty, selfish receiver of her sacrifices.
5. Block her masochistic tendency to frustrate herself by satisfying her analyst by not allowing her to pay for more sessions than she really has, etc.
6. Show her how she presses the analyst to be a dependency-making sadist through psychological pressures threatening his pleasure as analyst.
7. Carefully avoid being dependent on her for professional pleasure; that is, not accepting a powerful sadistic position in the therapeutic interaction.

The steps of the therapeutic work of the analyst at the empirical level follow the psychoflowchart presented in Figure 5-7.

While the method of reductions and inversion may perhaps seem too complex to follow within the confines of an analytic session, nevertheless we feel that like any other skill, with practice it can be applied efficiently. The analyst will find it will produce a simplified and penetrating therapeutic instrument.

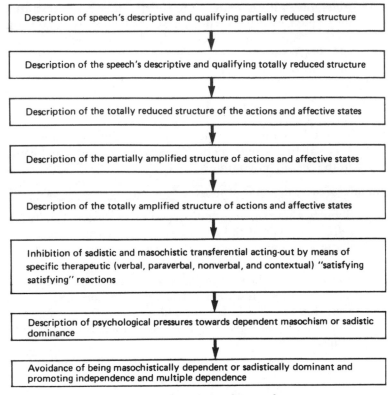

Figure 5-7. Psychoflowchart of an analysis

Conventional Language and Narcissistic Language

Language has a normal informative function. But the defensive mechanism of E inversion (here called narcissistic) between action and narrative presents a special systematic coordination between an individual's actions and what he says about them. Thus, the meaning of speech in relation to action is peculiar to each individual.

According to this thesis, there are two simultaneous codes: the "normal" or conventional one, which is the one the subject must apply if he interprets the language conventionally, and the "natural" (narcissistic) one, which involves another semantic correspondence. On first hearing, the analysand's speech is deceitful (or erroneous) because it informs poorly and by inversion. But, according to the second code, the language gives exact information. For instance, when the analysand says he is frustrated (satisfier) when he is satisfied (frustrator), from the conventional point of view he is making an erroneous statement. Since under the narcissistic code "frustrated" was transformed into the "satisfied" sign, the person is speaking correctly; when he says he is "frustrated" he means that he is "satisfied." The narcissistic code is a semantic coordination resulting from a natural coordination imposed by the facts, and not by a conventional rule. Another difference is that the conventional code is more conscious and conceptual than the narcissistic code, which is more an automatic association.

A child learns this "two-tiered" language naturally; his parents speak to each other and to him in a double code: direct (conventional) and indirect (narcissistic). He learns to function in a society that purports to disapprove of using competitive relationships for obtaining pleasure, while it actually imposes them in a compulsive way: the subject cannot avoid competition, and he must either win or lose.

THE SPEECH OF NARCISSUS

There are two fundamental aspects in the speech of Narcissus: bipolar reduction and inversion—that is, the ego-alter relation and the reverse relationship (up to a point) of actions and language. However, the inverted code is not the only one involved in narcissistic coding. There appears to be a third code resulting from the systematic coordination of what the factual alter and factual ego do (according to the hypotheses already stated) and what they say that they are doing. If we combine the semantic relation of the speech-ego and the factual ego with that of the speech-alter and the factual alter, we find that the speech codes the relations between the speech-ego and the factual alter, and between the speech-alter and the factual ego.

This last relation can be seen as analogous to the Narcissus myth: the alter is spoken of in the speech, but the semantic reference is to the factual ego. When the subject is talking about someone else, he is speaking of himself. But we also observe the presence of a sort

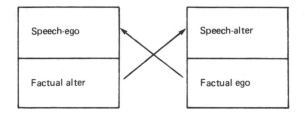

Figure 5-8.   The speech of Narcissus: inversion of ego and alter

of Narcissus counter-myth to the effect that when the subject is talking about himself, he is speaking of another: the ego of the speech is speaking, but the semantic reference is to the factual alter. (See Figure 5-8.) Perhaps another analogy using the Narcissus myth can be made. If we view the world as having a symmetrical coordination between one half and the other half, it is comparable, on a linguistic level, to Narcissus's symmetrical coordination with the nymph Echo and, with regard to images, with the reflection in the pond. Strangely enough, the inversion is geometrical; in geometrical symmetry, the left becomes the right and the right becomes the left while the "above" and "below" elements remain constant, and in our symmetry "satisfied" becomes "frustrated" and vice versa, but the goodness of "frustrated" and the badness of "satisfied" endure.

We could therefore assert that as far as both the factual ego and the speech ego are concerned, *the (narcissistic) world contains one single character and one single half: the ego (Narcissus) and his properties; the alter (Echo), being nothing but his symmetrical projection, his image.* The reality of the world, practically speaking, is one-half of that world. Similarly, we give authentic physical reality to the image in the mirror, and only to the tangible half. If we apply Occam's razor (entities must not be allowed to multiply unnecessarily), it can be said that *to analyze the ego (Narcissus) half of the world would be sufficient.*

Our analysis has already pointed out the logical problems of reduction in phrases such as "ego satisfies ego," which would become "ego satisfies himself." We put these aside because of the recognition problem of the corresponding place-subjects of the speech in the ego reduction. That is why the analogy to the Narcissus myth—Narcissus talking to himself—now appears to be an appropriate model for the result of the analytical process of the bipolar reduction: there are only two poles, one mirroring the other, because Narcissus (the analysand) is only talking to his inverted image—but as though it were another person (the analyst).

There is a possible fourth natural (narcissistic) code analogously instilled in the systematic correspondence, but reversed between the ego and alter of the speech. It may be that the half of the speech which refers to the alter is only a transcription of the half that refers to the ego. Naturally, whether syntactically through translation, or semantically through transposal of the semantic content of the words, the speech about alter acquires a referential value in connection with the speech about ego, and vice versa: the alter's characteristics can be automatically deduced once the characteristics of the ego are known, and vice versa.

We have, consequently, three narcissistic codes:

1. The inversion of the descriptive predicates in relation to actions, qualifications, and affects
2. The relation between the ego and the alter of the speech and the factual ego and factual alter
3. The relation between the factual ego and the factual alter.

It is likely that the examination of the logical peculiarities of these narcissistic codes would lead to the discovery that they are one and the same, based on the set of inversion and symmetries. *All that happens to the factual ego and to his relations with the factual alter is isomorphic with all that happens to the factual alter and its relations with the factual ego.* But since the isomorphism implies an inversion (of the effect of the actions) it is really an antiisomorphism.

Let us recall that an example of antiisomorphism in mathematics is that which allows the passage from the whole number structure to the inverse structure by multiplying those numbers by -1. In antiisomorphism, positive becomes negative just as satisfied becomes frustrated. Minor becomes major just as to satisfy, which also is a binary structure, becomes to frustrate. It is like proposing that the positive numbers are the true or "authentic" ones, and that the negative numbers are merely the positive numbers seen as reflection: if we place a mirror across the middle of the number scale, the reflection of the positive numbers would give the negative ones. This would enable us to state, following the Narcissus myth, that the negative numbers are the positive ones that have been

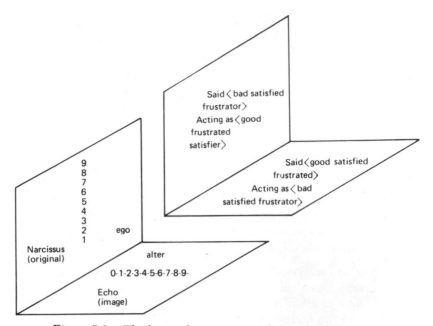

Figure 5-9.   The logic of symmetry in the myth of Narcissus

conceived as others in an inverted relation. The positive number would be the mathematical analogy of Narcissus, and the negative numbers would be the analogy of the nymph Echo (or the pond): <satisfied frustrator> would be the positive, for example, and <frustrated satisfier>, the negative (see Figure 5-9).

If a sadistic Narcissus says that he is a <good frustrated satisfier> while acting as a <bad satisfied frustrator> his mirror "negative" will be a masochistic Echo who says that she is a <bad satisfied frustrator> while acting as a <good frustrated satisfier>.

LEARNING THE NARCISSISTIC CODE (INVERTED E)

Our first hypothesis regarding the transmission and learning of this double conventional and narcissistic code is that ego teaches alter how to use the language with its normal referential, social semantic function. Thus, when the parents (ego) teach the child (alter) what "satisfied" or "frustrated" means, the child learns correctly. If an abnormality occurs, it is not so much due to a semantic error as to the child incorrectly learning how to inform, similar to the way in which the child systematically learns to lie. An analysis should also be made of the way in which the child learns the other three narcissistic codes of the ego, and of the use the ego makes of them in relation to the alter.

Let us suppose that an adult ego teaches a child alter who, factually, does not yet possess either an ego or an alter function. Thus the function of the adult ego must, due to its logical nature, form the complementary function in the child alter. If the child does not resist, he will automatically acquire the complementary functional characteristic. For example, if owing to his functional characteristics the factual adult ego "pushes," the child alter will learn to "be pushed." If the adult ego "frustrates" because it is "satisfied," the child alter will be frustrated by the ego and become a "frustrated being." Following the earlier metaphor, adult ego automatically induces the child alter to be his symmetrical image. But the image, being an image, neither resists nor takes the initiative. It acquires its properties through the logic of symmetry. This hypothesis is derived from the properties of the functional constellation of the ego, and also from the hypothesis that the child supplies no original initiative: the child would be Echo to the Narcissus same-sex parent. One could therefore say that to educate is an "optical" phenomenon in which for logical reasons the ego-educator automatically instills his symmetrical inverse image in the alter-educand.

The point of interest here is that the educator attempts to make an isomorph out of the one who is being educated. But following logical reasoning, the isomorphism does not appear directly but as an inverse symmetry: the educator makes the educated his inverted image and likeness. That may be because the father transmits to his son not his own ego but his own superego; this is a very attractive Freudian hypothesis regarding the transmission of culture. Following our own model, we will say that a "superfather" (superego) will produce an "inferson" (inferego) while an "inferfather" (inferego) will produce a "superson" (superego).

The inversion of the descriptive predicates in the speech seems valid for learning narcissistic conduct, but it does not appear valid for ordinary semantics, nor for learning the ethical code: here, both the educator ego and the educated alter isomorphically share the linguistic conventions and the ethical conventions of the social group to which both belong.

Hypothetically, the interactions between two persons can be reduced to two main classes: the adaptive interactions, in which a narcissistic competitive contract between a sadist and a masochist is adhered to, and the conflictive interactions, in which the contract is not adhered to and two sadists or two masochists collide. The adaptive interaction appears typically to correspond to the ordinary narcissistic married couple (Narcissus-Echo). The interaction conforms to our description of factual bipolarity. The conflictive interaction runs counter to the narcissistic one, and seems to correspond to the case in which the factual ego and the factual alter have the same function. Based on the suppositions we made about inversion, speech-ego and speech-alter would have the same constellation, which would make it impossible to discriminate between them: two sadistic agents (or two masochistic patients) will be fighting to put each other down (or build each other up) and if either of them succeeds in doing so, they will go into a crisis, destroying the relationship.

OEDIPUS SPEECH

In the narcissistic adaptive situation, the function of the factual alter is the counterpart of that of the factual ego. To make this easier to grasp, let us illustrate it with the case of the factual ego–husband and the factual alter–wife. The husband is the factual ego—he imagines himself to be the ego of his speech—and the wife is the factual alter, which he assumes is the alter of his speech. We shall give the name of "ego function" to the ego constellation in the husband's speech, and "alter function" to the speech's corresponding alter (see Figure 5-10).

By virtue of our hypotheses concerning the inversion of the effect of the action mentioned in the descriptive propositions in the speech, for the husband, therefore, the factual ego (he himself) is described by him as the alter function of his speech, while his factual alter is described by him as the ego function of his speech.

In other words, from the husband's point of view the wife factually functions as the ego in the husband's speech while he

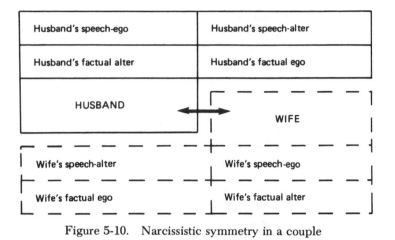

Figure 5-10.   Narcissistic symmetry in a couple

himself functions as the alter of his own speech. (The husband, of course, is unaware of this inversion.) From the wife's point of view, her factual ego (she herself) possesses the alter function with respect to her own speech, while her husband, her factual alter, has the ego function of her speech. The ego of the husband's speech coincides with the alter of the wife's speech, and vice versa, and the factual ego of the husband coincides with the factual alter of the wife, and vice versa.

There is a narcissistic oedipal agreement which allows both parents to describe inversely what they are doing and feeling and still have concordant speeches: mother and father speak the same inverted propositions regarding their actions and affects.

In the narcissistic crisis situation (conflictive) the function of the factual ego as seen by the father (that is, what he is saying about himself) also corresponds to the alter of his speech. But the factual alter, the mother, instead of possessing an opposite function, has the same characteristics or reduced constellation as the alter of the father's speech: in this critical situation, the factual alter and the speech-alter are analogous, not allowing the factual ego to display the characteristics of the speech-alter.

Such a coincidence between speech and facts as far as the alter is concerned obliges the father to violate the linguistic inversion, or to contradict himself in his speech. Something similar happens in the mother's case, because in her speech she appears with alter function, but her factual alter, the husband, appears with the same factual functional constellation, coinciding also with the alter of her speech. This again produces a conflict in the rule of linguistic inversion and in the coherence of the mother's speech.

It would furthermore seem that the two speeches coincide in the sense that the egos and alters of both are described in the same manner: the conflict that brings the narcissistic psychic system of both actors to a crisis lies in the logic of the situation. If one of them is satisfied, he logically induces frustration in the other; but the other also is a satisfied being who induces frustration because he has the same ego and alter function. In addition to this conflict of action, there occurs for each one of the actors either a noninversion or incoherence of speech, or "leaving the field" so as not to enter into a crisis of psychic impotence. It is the conflict that takes place between two sadists, where each wants to dominate the other, or between two masochists, where each wants to be dominated by the other.

In any event, in a situation of narcissistic balance (or "adaptive" interaction) the function of the father coincides with the alter of his speech and with the ego of the mother's speech. The father does what he says the mother is doing, and he does that which the mother says she herself does. The mother does what she says the father is doing, and she does what the father says he himself does.

Hence, where there is compensated narcissistic interaction, both have speeches which are erroneous and which coincide. There exists between them an ethical agreement and a logical coherence in the relation. But in the uncompensated narcissistic interaction in crisis, the father does what he says the mother is doing and what the mother says the father is doing; the mother does what she says the father is doing, and what the father says the mother is doing. Neither, however, does what the father says he is doing or what the mother says she is doing.

This entire analysis is valid for reduced speech, in which the only fight that can erupt is for the place of sadist or masochist, of dominator or dominated, or of colonizer or colonized.

In the case of nonreduced speech, on the other hand, there can be a divergence of theme or state between partners, although they may be counterparts with regard to the power relation. That is, if the husband is a devaluating manic sadist, and the wife a rejected melancholic masochist, the couple can also face a crisis. There can be no dialogue between two people speaking different languages; the wife is speaking to a reproachful sadist alter and the husband is speaking to a devaluated masochistic alter. What brings the narcissistic system to a crisis in this case is not a fight for power or for a controlling position, but the cognitive dissonance produced by the difference of theme or style.

Summary of the Empirical Level of the Theory of Psychic Bipolarity

EMPIRICAL BASIS OF PSYCHOANALYTIC THEORY

We start by systematizing certain regularities and co-variants of the elements of an empirical basis formed by the analysand's speech and actions and the analyst's speech, actions, and affects within the analytic setting. This epistemological empirical basis is composed of seven empirical systems:

1. Analysand's descriptive speech
2. Analysand's actions
3. Analysand's qualifying speech
4. Analyst's descriptive speech
5. Analyst's action
6. Analyst's qualifying speech
7. Analyst's affects.

System 7 (analysand's affects) is not included because it cannot be directly observed by the analyst himself: it can be deduced from his own affective states by applying a hypothesis of isomorphism and inversion.

The empirical hypothesis of the theory regarding speech refers to certain specific types of speech. The speech within the analytic setting can be divided into six classes:

1. Associative (collaborative or defensive)
2. Defensive
3. Working through
4. Consulting
5. Setting
6. Conventional.

These classes involve, respectively: the analysand associating freely in order to be understood and interpreted; his insightful reflections; his speech about some conflictive external object relations he wishes to deal with; his consulting the analyst about details of the analytic setting; and the analysand's chatting about conventional topics. Our empirical hypothesis refers specifically to the associative speech of the analysand and its equivalent, the interpretative speech of the analyst.

Regarding the actions of the analysand and the analyst, the empirical hypothesis takes into consideration verbal as well as paraverbal, nonverbal, and contextual actions.

To facilitate the logical-syntactical, semantic and pragmatic analysis of speech, actions, and affects within the analytic setting, we used the following instrumental hypotheses:

1. The analysand (and the analyst) sincerely speaks the truth according to the way he perceives his experiences and the world. Cynical speech is not considered.

2. Associative speech, whether collaborative or defensive, can be classified as cardinal speech (with plot, characters, and sequence) or as neutral speech (without plot, characters, and sequence). The empirical hypothesis refers to the cardinal speech. The psychotic speech, insofar as it is so disorganized that it cannot be understood, is not considered.

3. All the predicates that appear in the cardinal associative speech must be analyzed as though they were dyadic.

4. The cardinal associative dyadic speech may be, in turn, descriptive or qualifying. Both classes will be considered.

5. The sequence of the cardinal associative speech can be segmented into narrative units (narratemes) of different size but always carry the same meaning: the personal myth of the analysand, partially or totally transmitted. These narrative units may contain varying numbers of dyadic predicates.

6. The dyadic relational predicates will show four types of meaning: (a) M (the order in which the subject-places appear); (b) G (the direction of the actions described in it); (c) E (the effect that the described action has on the subject-places); (d) V (the qualification included in it).

7. The analysand's speech is considered to be the speech of desire, whose universal predicate is satisfaction or frustration of de-

sire. But the empirical laws refer mainly to the predicates of the speech of conflicted desire (the frustrating satisfaction or the satisfying frustration of desire).

To verify the truth or falsity of the cardinal associative speech's descriptive and qualifying predicates about the actions and affects of the analysand and the analyst, the predicates must be compared with the analysand's actions and with the analyst's actions and affects. That is, speech empirical systems 1, 3, 4 and 6 (see chapter 4) must first be compared with action empirical systems 2 and 5; then they must be counter-compared with affect empirical system 8 (the analyst's countertransference).

PRESUPPOSED TECHNICAL PSYCHOANALYTIC HYPOTHESES

Metapsychological psychoanalytic hypotheses usually deal with theoretical intrapsychic unobservable entities such as the unconscious and the superego; they refer to representations, mechanisms, cathexis, etc. But technical psychoanalytic hypotheses deal mainly with empirical interpersonal observable phenomena such as transference, acting-out, etc.; they refer to speech, actions and affective states. Consequently, in constructing the empirical hypotheses of the theory of psychic bipolarity we used some corroborated presupposed hypotheses of the psychoanalytic technique, while in the corresponding theoretical hypotheses we used some presupposed hypotheses of psychoanalytic metapsychology.

Some of the presupposed technical psychoanalytic hypotheses used at the empirical level were:

1. The hypothesis of the "compulsion to repeat" (Freud 1920) the same unconscious destructive pattern of speech and actions, even though it provokes painful affective states.

2. The hypothesis of "transference" (Freud 1912) of actions and affective states of the analysand's past (or present external interpersonal relationships) to his relationship with the analyst. Its metapsychological equivalent is the "displacement" of cathexis and meaning from a painful intrapsychic representation to a nonpainful one.

3. The hypothesis of "countertransference" or displacement of the actions and affective states of past interpersonal relationships of

the analyst to his present relationship with the analysand (Gear and Liendo 1975).

4. The hypothesis of the analysand's resistance to the analytic process by: not associating freely in a collaborative way; not associating at all; not listening to and recognizing the analyst's descriptions of speech, actions, or affective states (outsight); or not accepting the interpretations of intrapsychic representations and mechanisms (insight), etc.

5. The hypothesis of the analysand's acting-out painful intrapsychic representations through use of his speech and actions to expel them from his consciousness rather than working them through.

6. The hypothesis of the analyst's "counter–acting-out" of the analysand's painful intrapsychic representations through his own speech and actions.

7. The hypothesis of the analysand's "specific action" (developed in Freud's 1895 Project) to obtain healthy satisfying affective states through appropriate speech and actions towards his significant others (Gear and Liendo 1979).

8. The hypothesis of "specific reaction" (derived from the previous hypothesis of "specific action") by which the analyst, using appropriate therapeutic speech and actions towards the analysand, helps him to reach healthy, satisfying affective states (Gear and Liendo 1979).

FUNDAMENTAL COLLATERAL AND DERIVED EMPIRICAL HYPOTHESIS

1. All the syntactical subjects (or subject-places) of the cardinal associative speech can be bipolarly reduced to ego and alter. Thus, all the speech predicates are transformed into predicates about the speech-ego or the speech-alter.

2. All the descriptive predicates of the cardinal associative speech can be bipolarly reduced to "frustrate" and "satisfy."

3. In the conflicted speech, all descriptive predicates about "frustrate" or "satisfy" are automatically associated with another predicate that has its subject-places and the effect of its actions inverted: "frustrate" will always be associated with "being satisfied" and "satisfy" will always be associated with "being frustrated."

3a. (*Derived hypothesis*) Consequently, all descriptive predicates of the cardinal associative conflicted speech can be bipolarly reduced to:

      i) \<Frustrated satisfier\> and \<satisfied frustrator\> when referring to the subject-places

     ii) \<Frustrate satisfying\> and \<to satisfy frustrating\> when referring to the actions

    iii) \<Satisfying frustration\> and \<satisfaction frustrating\> when referring to the affects.

4. All the qualifying predicates of the cardinal associative conflicted speech about subject-places, actions and affects can be bipolarly reduced to "good" (altruistic, clever, or sensible) and "bad" (selfish, stupid, or crazy).

5. All the descriptive and qualifying predicates of the cardinal associative speech about actions and affects of ego and alter can be partially bipolarly reduced to two groups of redundant traits and qualifications that typically characterize the speech-ego and the speech-alter of each analysand: the "speech-ego constellation" and the "speech-alter constellation." Within a finite set of narrative variations the analysand will always tell the same story with the same plot, characters, and sequence.

5a. (*Collateral hypothesis*) The characteristics of the "speech-ego constellation" and those of the "speech-alter constellation," that is, of the analysand's monothematic cardinal associative speech, are mainly dependent on the characteristics of the cultural region to which the analysand belonged when he was a child.

6. Once the subject-places, the descriptive predicates, and the qualifying predicates of the cardinal associative speech have been reduced, four main types of speech can be observed: the "good satisfied" (frustrator) speech, the "bad frustrated" (satisfier) speech, the "good frustrated" (satisfier) speech, and the "bad satisfied" (frustrator) speech. Note that the two most important psychopathological types of speech are the third and fourth ones, that is, the sadistic and the masochistic ones, because the "good satisfied" and the "bad frustrated" speeches are usually nonpathological. Consequently, it can be said that according to the descriptive and qualifying predicates, the cardinal associative speech can be bipolarly reduced to two forms: "sadistic" speech, in which the speaker is a \<good frustrated satisfier\> and the others are \<bad satisfied frus-

trators>, and the "masochistic" speech, in which the speaker is a <bad satisfied frustrator> and the others <good frustrated satisfiers>.

7. The actions of the analysand and the analyst within the analytic setting can be reduced bipolarly "to satisfy" and "to frustrate." (Note that the actors are factually bipolarly reduced by the analytic situation to factual ego [analysand] and factual alter [analyst]).

8. When conflictive, the actions "to satisfy" and "to frustrate" are always associated with their inverse actors and affects. Each time the factual ego satisfies the factual alter it will simultaneously be frustrated by the factual alter and vice versa.

9. All the satisfying and frustrating actions of the factual ego and the factual alter can be partially bipolarly reduced to two groups of stereotyped repetitive courses of action that typically characterize both: the "factual ego constellation" and the "factual alter constellation."

10. Once the actors and their actions have been bipolarly reduced, two psychopathological types of actors can be found: the sadistic actor, who satisfies himself while frustrating others, and the masochistic actor, who frustrates himself while satisfying others.

11. All the affective states that the analyst is able to observe in himself can be bipolarly reduced to "satisfaction" and "frustration." (More precisely, they are bipolarly reduced to "satisfaction with insecurity" and "frustration with security.")

12. All the affective states of the analyst will always be associated with the same affect state as that of the analysand, but inverted in actor and in quality: if the analyst is experiencing frustration, the analysand will be experiencing satisfaction and vice versa.

13. All the affective states of the factual ego and the factual alter can be partially bipolarly reduced to two groups of stereotyped repetitive feelings that typically characterize both: the "affective factual ego constellation" and the "affective factual alter constellation."

14. Once the affective states have been bipolarly reduced, two psychopathological types of feelings can be seen: the "sadistic" affective state of frustration, satisfying for others, and the "masochistic" affective state of satisfaction, frustrating for others.

15. If the predicates of the conflicted speech describing actions are compared with the actual actions, it will be seen that the direction

of the actions is inverted in the speech. That is, the speech-ego corresponds to the factual alter and vice versa. What the speaker says he does to the others is what the others do to him, and what he says the others do to him is what he does to others. That means that the analysand, when conflicted will always be speaking in an inverted way.

15a. (*Derived hypothesis*) The inversion of the direction of the actions in the descriptive predicates provokes an inversion in the quality of the qualifications and affective states attributed to the subjects. If the speaker says he is a <bad satisfied frustrator enjoying satisfaction frustrating for others>, he is actually a <good frustrated satisfier suffering frustration satisfying for others>.

16. The narcissistic analysand always tries to induce the analyst to talk about himself and about the analysand in the same inverted way that the analysand talks about himself and about the analyst: both agree verbally about what they are doing even if they are speaking in an inverted way. It is a folie à deux.

17. If the analysand's spontaneous description and qualification of himself in his cardinal associative speech is compared with his description and qualification of his parents, it can be observed that there is a strong resemblance between the analysand's speech-ego constellation and the constellation he attributes to the parent of the opposite sex, as well as a strong resemblance between the analysand's speech-alter constellation and the constellation he attributes to the parent of the same sex. That is, the son describes and requalifies himself as having the same characteristics as he describes and qualifies in his mother, and describes and qualifies his others (including the analyst) as having the same characteristics that he describes and qualifies in his father. Similarly, the daughter attributes to herself the same characteristics she attributes to her father and attributes to her others (including analyst) the same characteristics that she attributes to her mother.

18. The sadistic analysand says that he is a <good frustrated satisfier suffering frustration satisfying for others>, while he acts and feels as a <bad satisfied frustrator enjoying satisfaction frustrating for others>. He also uses his speech and actions to psychologically press the analyst not only to be dependent on him but also to act as a masochist to the analysand's sadist. The psychological pressures of the sadist may be based either on verbal promises or threats regarding the social, psychological, or biological survival of

the analyst, or on actual rewards and punishments: if the other is not a masochist the analysand's survival will be threatened. The masochistic analysand not only says that he is a <bad satisfied frustrator enjoying satisfaction frustrating for others>, while acting and feeling like a <good frustrated satisfier suffering frustration satisfying for others>, but also uses his speech and actions to psychologically press the analyst to let him depend on the analyst and to treat the analysand sadistically. The psychological pressures of the masochist can be based either on verbal promises or threats regarding the cognitive hedonic or ethical pleasure of the analyst, or on actual rewards and punishments: if the other is not a sadist the analysand's pleasure will be threatened.

REFERENCES

Freud, S. (1895).   Project for a scientific psychology. *Standard Edition* 1: 281–397.

—— (1900).   The interpretation of dreams. *Standard Edition* 4/5.

—— (1912).   The dynamics of transference. *Standard Edition* 12:97–108.

—— (1914).   Remembering, repeating and working through. *Standard Edition* 12:145–156.

—— (1915).   Repression. *Standard Edition* 14:143–158.

—— (1920).   Beyond the Pleasure Principle. *Standard Edition* 18.

Gear, M. C., and Liendo, E. C. (1975).   *Sémiologie psychanalytique.* Paris: Minuit.

—— (1979).   *Action psychanalytique.* Paris: Minuit.

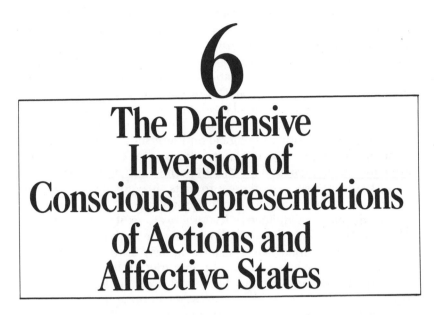

6
The Defensive Inversion of Conscious Representations of Actions and Affective States

In this chapter we will formulate a series of hypotheses concerning the structural logic of the subject's intrapsychic world of representations and the functioning of defenses (Freud 1915a). These concepts or representations may be conscious or unconscious, and also semantically adequate or inadequate (true or false).

We realize that the reader will be faced with an increasingly complex model (one that will be almost fully developed by the end of this chapter). The systematization we construct proposes to simplify matters, not by conveniently leaving out fundamental aspects but by accepting and working through their full complexity in order to discover those underlying principles of organization that constitute its structure. This does not mean that we are promising an easy time mastering the model but neither are we offering yet another psychological gimmick with which the market is already flooded, and which we consider symptomatic of the desperate need for an effective mode of therapy. We think that a partial and oversimplifying approach would not meet this need but believe that if the reader masters our model he will have at his disposal a clear and powerful paradigm with which to think about the psychic apparatus, both from the purely theoretical point of view and the urgently pragmatic.

The critical step in this chapter, which may initially confuse the reader, regards the following. The reductions we analyzed in the preceding chapter are manifestations of the intrapsychic system of the analysand which the analyst can observe at the empirical or clinical level. They are the final product of his psychological processing of the vital data in his own life of both endogenous and exogenous origin, or of both a biological and intersubjective nature. The difference between analyzing the structures of the empirical products of the psychic system, and making hypotheses about the working of the system that produces these products, is equivalent to the difference between inductive and deductive logic. At the same time that we develop our deductive hypotheses to explain the workings of the psychic system whose end products we analyzed inductively in the previous chapter, we also show the way in which the two are connected, that is to say, how the empirical (clinical) structures relate to what we now call the theoretical (hypothetically deduced) structures of the psychic apparatus. We call these *the rules of correspondence between the two initial levels of the theory of psychic bipolarity.*

Just as at the end of chapter 5, the reader will find at the end of this chapter a summary of our theoretical model including the series of steps developed at length in the course of the chapter. This may be useful as an aid to reading what follows.

Twelve Systems of Intrapsychic Representations

We start with one class of representations related to the ego, and another class related to the alter, as defined in the previous chapter. We thus recognize a normal bipolar splitting of the intrapsychic world of representations along the lines shown in the structures of speech, actions, and affective states already analyzed. The bipolar structure of the intrapsychic world is based on two main classes of representations: ego-representations (or "psychic ego"), made up of inner represenations of the subject himself, and alter-representations (or "psychic alter"), made up of unified inner representations of those who interact with the subject.

The intrapsychic representations form "theoretical" (unobservable) systems which correspond to the empirical (clinical) systems of speech, actions, and affective states. In effect, the psychic ego is constituted by the analysand's representations of his own speech, actions, and affective states, and the psychic alter is constituted by the analysand's representations of the speech, actions, and affective states of his interactors.

From now on, we will define a *sadistic agent* as a factually <satisfied frustrating> subject who will say <he is being frustrated by satisfying others>. Conversely, a *masochistic patient* will be defined as a factually <satisfying frustrated> subject who will say that <he is being satisfied by frustrating others>. A typical example of this kind of interaction between these two psychopathological types is presented in Figure 6-1.

Sadistic agent	Speech:	"You don't enjoy sex. You are frigid."
	Action:	A cold, distant, indifferent sexual approach.
Masochistic patient	Speech:	"I'm sorry. I know that I am cold and rejecting but I can't help it."
	Action:	A particularly warm, active and helpful sexual approach seeking forgiveness for the supposed inadequacy.
Sadistic agent	Speech:	"You are not really spontaneous and warm with me. You are just pretending."
	Action:	A phony sexual kindness because of a previous infidelity.

Figure 6-1. Symmetrical inversion of speech and action in the narcissistic couple

Each empirical (clinical) system will have its corresponding theoretical system (of psychic representation). But our major hypothesis at this first theoretical level is that empirical systems of actions and affective states will have a double intrapsychic representation. That is, they will have an inverted, antiisomorphic, conscious representation of actions and affective states and a correct, isomorphic, unconscious representation of the same actions and affective states.

The psychic ego is formed by six theoretical (intrapsychic) systems of representations.

system E1	conscious representation of the descriptive predicates of the subject's speech, about his own actions and affective states (empirical system e.1); that is, of what he says he does and feels
system E2	conscious representation of the auto-qualifying predicates of the subject's speech (empirical system e.2); that is, of how he qualifies himself
system E3	conscious representation of the subject's actions (empirical system e.3)
system UE3	unconscious representation of the subject's actions (reduplication of the empirical system e.3)
system E4	conscious representation of the subject's affective states (empirical system e.4)
system UA4	unconscious representation of the affective states of the others (reduplication of the empirical system a.4)

Empirical systems e.1, e.2, a.1, and a.2 are not duplicated because they are verbal empirical systems isomorphic with conscious intrapsychic representation. The conscious intrapsychic representations of empirical systems e.3, e.4, a.3, and a.4 are antiisomorphic: since the speech has already been defensively inverted, there is no need to invert the intrapsychic representations of its descriptive or qualifying predicates.

In Figure 6-2, every representation that is accurate within the ego or the alter is indicated in italics. All the other representations within the ego and the alter systems are inverted in relation to these correct representations. Thus, the reader can see at a glance the

EGO		ALTER	
Empirical systems	Theoretical systems (Intrapsychic)	Theoretical systems (Intrapsychic)	Empirical systems
e.1 Descriptive speech	E1 Conscious	A1 Conscious	a.1 Descriptive speech
e.2 Qualifying speech	E2 Conscious	A2 Conscious	a.2 Qualifying speech
e.3 Actions	E3 Conscious	A3 Conscious	a.3 Actions
	UE3 *Unconscious*	UA3 *Unconscious*	
e.4 Affective states	E4 Conscious	A4 Conscious	a.4 Affective states
	UE4 *Unconscious*	UA4 *Unconscious*	

Figure 6-2.   Inversion in the empirical and intrapsychic systems

overall structure of inverted representation which occurs in both poles of the intrapsychic system.

Just as there are nonreduced and reduced structures of the speech, actions, and affective states, there are also nonreduced and reduced structures of the intrapsychic representations. The *reduced superficial conscious psychic structure* will be formed by the conscious representations of the reduced structure of speech, actions and affective states: that is, by systems E1, E2, E3, E4, A1, A2, A3, and A4. On the other hand, the *reduced deep unconscious psychic structure* will be formed by the unconscious representations of the reduced structure of actions and affective states; that is, by systems UE3, UA3, UE4, and UA4.

There is a methodological problem here concerning the relation between intrapsychic systems A1 and A2 of conscious representation of the speech, and empirical (clinical) systems a.1 and a.2 of the speech of the interactor. In effect, systems A1 and A2 can represent intrapsychically either the descriptive and qualifying speech of the speaker about the others (related to empirical systems e.1 and e.2) or it can represent directly the descriptive and qualifying speech of the others (related to empirical systems a.1 and a.2).

An additional hypothesis at the empirical (clinical) level is that the narcissistic speaker is always trying to induce his interactors to speak about him and about themselves in the same inverted way he speaks about himself and the interactors. To some extent empirical systems e.1 and e.2 are equivalent to systems a.1 and a.2, thus, systems A1 and A2 represent both sets of empirical systems (e.1, e.2, and a.1, a.2) at the same time.

Applying this empirical (clinical) hypothesis, one can say that the sadistic agent will not only act as a <bad satisfied frustrator> pushing the masochistic patient into the position of a <good frustrated satisfier>, but he will also describe and qualify himself as being a <good frustrated satisfier> and the masochistic patient as being a <bad satisfied frustrator>. He will push the masochistic patient to describe and qualify himself and the sadistic agent in the same way: both will be saying the same thing about themselves. Both the sadist and the masochist will be saying, for example, that the sadist is a generous, helpful person who is mistreated by the masochist; and that the masochist is a selfish, careless, mistreating person.

Similarly, the masochistic patient will act as a <good frustrated satisfier> pushing the sadistic agent into the position of a <bad satisfied frustrator>, but he will describe and qualify himself as being a <bad satisfied frustrator> and the sadistic agent as being a <good frustrated satisfier>. He will push the sadistic agent to describe and qualify himself and the masochistic patient in the same way: both will be saying the same thing about themselves.

This unconscious agreement between sadists and masochists can be called the "narcissistic *folie à deux*" (Lasègue and Falret 1873) or the "shared narcissism," as the term *sadomasochism* suggests: there is both a factual sadomasochistic agreement and a semantic agreement to speak in an inverted way about the factual agreement.

We thus have a total of twelve systems of intrapsychic representations, eight of them conscious and four of them unconscious. The conscious ones are inverted in relation to the unconscious ones. As we said before, the conscious representations of descriptive and qualifying speech (systems E1, A1, E2, and A2) as well as the unconscious representations of actions and affective states (systems UE3, UE4, UA3, and UA4) are appropriate and true with regard to their respective empirical systems of speech (e.1, e.2, a.1, and a.2), actions (e.3 and a.3) and affective states (e.4 and a.4). But the conscious system of representations of actions (systems E3 and A3) and affective states (systems E4 and A4) are inverted with regard to their respective empirical systems (e.3, e.4, a.3, and a.4).

The hypothesis that the conscious representation of actions and affective states is inverted leads to another fundamental hypothesis: the system formed by conscious representations is coherent in itself, as is the system formed by unconscious representations. In other words, the whole conscious intrapsychic representation of speech, actions, and affective states is inverted, but the whole unconscious intrapsychic representation of actions and affective states is coherent.

In Figure 6-3 we begin with the speech that the analyst hears from the analysand. Next he reduces and inverts it and arrives at the structure of the analysand's actions and affective states in reality. This is the empirical level of analysis. It, in turn, corresponds with the intrapsychic structures that also have a relationship of reduction and inversion. That is, the conscious representation of what the analysand says, does, and feels has to be reduced and inverted in order to arrive at the latent content, which consists of the accurate representation of what he does and feels.

In brief, the structure of the speech is concordant with the conscious psychic structure, and the structure of actions and affective

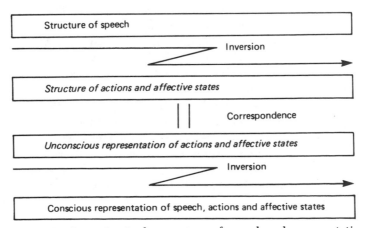

Figure 6-3. Inversion in the structure of speech and representation

states is concordant with the unconscious psychic structure. Consequently, the conscious psychic structure is invertly related to the unconscious one.

This means that the unconscious representations of actions and affective states and the conscious representations of descriptive and qualifying speech are appropriate and true, but that the conscious representations of actions and affective states are inappropriate and untrue. Following this hypothesis, the unconscious system is more reliable and competent (Freud 1915b) in its conception of actions and affective states than is the inverted conscious system, because its representations correctly reflect the observable factual and affective levels. A consensus of observers can inform us that the sadist is factually frustrating the masochist to satisfy himself and not the reverse, so that if the ego is placed within system UE3 in the position of <satisfied frustrator>, this places alter in the position of <frustrated satisfier> within system UA3; both are true.

The same consensus of observers simultaneously can inform us that the sadist is describing and qualifying himself as being a <good frustrated satisfier> and the masochist as being a <bad satisfied frustrator> and not the reverse: so that if the ego is placed within systems E1 and E2 in the position of <good frustrated satisfier>, this places alter in the position of <bad satisfied frustrator> within systems A1 and A2; again, both are true.

But, perhaps because of an internalized normative or punitive code, the narcissistic sadomasochist subject does not accept correct representations of his actions and affective states. Because of our psychoanalytic hypotheses, we can say that intrapsychic defense mechanisms are inverting systems E3, A3, E4, and A4 with respect to the reliable systems UE3, UA3, UE4, and UA4.

If on the other hand we assume that consciousness tends to be a coherent system, we can say that the ego's representations of his actions and affective states have to correspond to the conscious concept of his actions and affective states. Otherwise he would have to see himself consciously as a liar and as incongruent. Thus, system E1 is incongruent with system E3, making the representation of statements about actions the inverse of the system UE3 representation, which is reliable. If we accept the hypothesis that the individual represents correctly what he is saying, then what the individual says is the inverse of what he does and feels.

More explicitly, what the ego does and feels (system e.3 and e.4) corresponds to what he unconsciously represents to himself as doing and feeling (systems UE3 and UE4), which is the inverse of what he consciously represents to himself (systems E3 and E4). As that which he represents to himself as doing and feeling (system E1) coincides with what he represents unconsciously to himself (systems UE3 and UE4), the actions and affective states which he represents unconsciously to himself (systems E3 and E4) are inverted. And, since what he says is what he consciously represents to himself as that which he is saying, he consciously says the inverse of what he unconsciously does and feels.

If the ego is sadistic, he will be a <satisfied frustrator (e.3) enjoying a satisfaction frustrating for others (e.4)> and he will represent himself in this way unconsciously (UE3 and UE4). Because he will represent himself consciously as being a <frustrated satisfier (E3) suffering a frustration satisfying for others (E4)>, his unconscious representations are inverted with respect to his conscious ones. Because he also represents himself as saying that he is a <frustrated satisfier suffering a frustration satisfying for others (E1)>, the representations of his speech are also inverted with respect to the unconscious representations of his actions and affective states.

This development is a demonstration of how the organizations of the intrapsychic unobservable systems E1 to UA4 serve to explain the laws of functioning of systems e.1 to a.4 (which have already been corroborated) on the inversion between what is said is done and felt, and what is actually done and felt.

Figure 6-4 shows how the conscious and unconscious ego systems and alter systems are intrapsychically organized in the sadist and in the masochist.

From a topographic point of view, these systems of intrapsychic representations are organized (as the figure indicates) into a conscious or "superficial" psychic structure containing systems E1, E2, E3, E4, A1, A2, A3, and A4, and an unconscious or deep psychic structure, containing systems UE3, UE4, UA3, and UA4.

As the conscious psychic structure is similar to that of the speech, and the unconscious psychic structure to that of actions and affective states, it can be said that the conscious psychic ego and the conscious psychic alter are similar to the speech-ego and to the speech-alter respectively, and that the unconscious psychic ego and

				SADIST	MASOCHIST
SYSTEMS OF INTRAPSYCHIC REPRESENTATIONS	PSYCHIC EGO	Conscious	E 1	He represents himself by describing himself as a ⟨frustrated satisfier⟩	He represents himself by describing himself as a ⟨satisfied frustrator⟩
			E2	He represents himself by qualifying himself as being "good"	He represents himself by qualifying himself as being "bad"
			E3	He represents himself as being ⟨a frustrated satisfier⟩	He represents himself as being ⟨a satisfied frustrator⟩
			E4	He represents himself as feeling ⟨a frustration satisfying for others⟩	He represents himself as feeling ⟨a satisfaction frustrating for others⟩
		Unconscious	UE3	*He represents himself (unconsciously) as being ⟨a satisfied frustrator⟩*	*He represents himself (unconsciously) as being ⟨a frustrated satisfier⟩*
			UE4	*He represents himself (unconsciously) as feeling ⟨a satisfaction frustrating for others⟩*	*He represents himself (unconsciously) as feeling ⟨a frustration satisfying for others⟩*
	PSYCHIC ALTER	Conscious	A1	He represents the others as describing themselves as ⟨satisfied frustrators⟩	He represents the others as describing themselves as ⟨frustrated satisfiers⟩
			A2	He represents the others as qualifying themselves as being "bad"	He represents the others as qualifying themselves as being "good"
			A3	He represents the others as being ⟨satisfied frustrators⟩	He represents the others as being ⟨frustrated satisfiers⟩
			A4	He represents the others as feeling ⟨a satisfaction frustrating for himself⟩	He represents the others as feeling ⟨a frustration satisfying for himself⟩
		Unconscious	UA3	*He represents (unconsciously) the others as being ⟨frustrated satisfiers⟩*	*He represents (unconsciously) the others as being ⟨satisfied frustrators⟩*
			UA4	*He represents the others (unconsciously) as feeling ⟨a frustration satisfying for himself⟩*	*He represents the others (unconsciously) as feeling ⟨a satisfaction frustrating for himself⟩*

Figure 6-4. The structure of the representations of ego and alter in sadist and masochist

the unconscious psychic alter are similar to the factual ego and to the factual alter, respectively (Figure 6-5).

At the first metapsychological level of the theory of psychic bipolarity seven theoretical hypotheses follow:

1. The bipolar nonreduced and reduced empirical systems of speech, actions, and affective states (of the analysand and the analyst) have corresponding intrapsychic (theoretical) systems of representations; that is, a pole of "ego-representations" and a pole of "alter-presentations."

2. The intrapsychic representation of actions and affective states are duplicated: they are represented both consciously and unconsciously.

3. The intrapsychic conscious representations of actions and affective states are inverted with respect to the corresponding unconscious representations of actions and affective states.

4. The unconscious representations of actions and affective states are appropriate and true. But the corresponding conscious representations are inappropriate and untrue, because they are inverted with regard to the direction of the actions and the quality of the affective states.

5. The conscious intrapsychic representations of speech, actions, and affective states form a coherent system, and the unconscious representations of actions and affective states form another coherent system.

6. The conscious representations of the ego's actions and affective states are identical to the unconscious representations of the alter's action and affective states, and vice versa:

(a) The unconscious representations of the ego's actions are identical to the conscious representations of the alter's action (UE3 = A3)

(b) The unconscious representations of the alter's actions are identical to the conscious representations of the ego's actions (UA3 = E3)

(c) The unconscious representations of the ego's affective states are identical to the conscious representations of the alter's affective states (UE4 = A4)

(d) The unconscious representations of the alter's affective states are identical to the conscious representations of the ego's affective states (UA = E4).

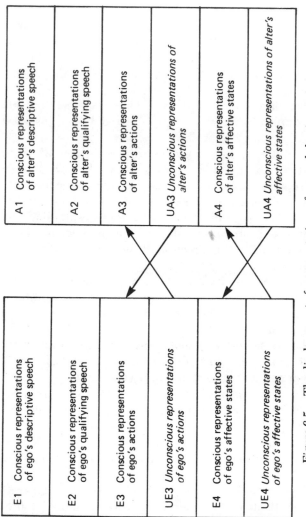

Figure 6-5. The displacement of representations of ego and alter in narcissism

E1	Conscious representations of ego's descriptive speech
E2	Conscious representations of ego's qualifying speech
E3	Conscious representations of ego's actions
UE3	*Unconscious representations of ego's actions*
E4	Conscious representations of ego's affective states
UE4	*Unconscious representations of ego's affective states*

A1	Conscious representations of alter's descriptive speech
A2	Conscious representations of alter's qualifying speech
A3	Conscious representations of alter's actions
UA3	*Unconscious representations of alter's actions*
A4	Conscious representations of alter's affective states
UA4	*Unconscious representations of alter's affective states*

7. The conscious and unconscious intrapsychic representations of the sadist are not only different from, but also complementary to those of the masochist. In effect, the sadist will consciously represent himself as a <good frustrated satisfier suffering frustration satisfying for others> and, unconsciously as a <bad satisfied frustrator enjoying satisfaction frustrating for others>, while the masochist will consciously represent himself as a <bad satisfied frustrator enjoying satisfaction frustrating for others> and, unconsciously as a <good frustrated satisfier suffering frustration satisfying for others>.

These seven theoretical hypotheses concerning the existence of twelve intrapsychic systems of representations with their reduction and relations of concordance or inversion, as well as their classification as conscious or unconscious, derive from a series of three psychoanalytic hypotheses. The first of these, following Freud (1900), asserts the existence of a "psychic apparatus" formed by intrapsychic representations. The second consists of Freud's topographic model of the structure and function of the psychic apparatus (Freud 1900) with its organization into conscious, preconscious, and unconscious layers of representations. The third hypothesis, Melanie Klein's "object relations theory" (1952), concerns the split organization of the "inner objects," or intrapsychic representations, of the subject and his objects.

The Inverting
Defense Mechanisms

As we have said, our seven theoretical hypotheses of the theory of psychic bipolarity provide a first level of explanation for the inversion of the direction of actions and the quality of affective states produced between the predicates in speech and the actions and affective states in reality. But these seven hypotheses call for a further explanation of why and how the conscious representations of speech, actions, and affective states are inverted with respect to the unconscious representations.

The second level of explanation of the inversion of the conscious and unconscious organization of the systems of intrapsychic representations of speech, actions, and affective states consists of the hypothesis of the intrapsychic defense mechanisms also derived from psychoanalytic hypotheses (Freud 1915a). In effect, the eighth theoretical hypothesis of the first metapsychological level is as follows:

8. Because the subject, when in conflict, cannot tolerate representing his own actions and affective states, or the actions and affective states of his interactors as they really are, he must represent them in an inverted way, thereby distorting his perception and thinking. The subject cannot stand to *represent* himself and others as they really are, although he can perfectly well stand *being* as he is, and can accept the others being as they are.

This hypothesis of the defensive inversion of perception and thinking implies the operation of at least four well known intrapsychic defense mechanisms: *repression, projection, denial,* and *introjection* (Gear and Liendo 1975). These four mechanisms work against the correct representation of the actions of the subject and his interactors. Similar defense mechanisms also work against the correct representation of the affective states of the subject and others: *suppression, evacuation, rejection,* and *absorption* (Gear and Liendo 1980).

The defense mechanisms applied to the representations of actions are:

Repression into the unconscious of the representation of what the subject is doing to others; that is, repression of system UE3 of his ego (or the unconscious representation of his own actions).

Projection of the unconscious representation of what the subject is doing to others into his conscious representation of what others are doing to him; that is, projection of system UE3 of his ego into system A3 of his alter (or conscious representations of the actions of others). UE3 = A3.

Denial of the unconscious representation of what the others are doing to the subject; that is, denial of system UA3 of his alter (or unconscious representations of the actions of others).

Introjection of the unconscious representation of what the others are doing to the subject into the conscious representation of what the subject is doing to them; that is, introjection of system UA3 of his alter onto system E3 of his ego (or conscious representations of the subject's actions). UA3 = E3.

In summary, system UE3 is repressed and projected, and system UA3 is denied and introjected (Figure 6-6).

The defense mechanisms applied to the representations of affective states are:

Suppression of the unconscious representation of what the subject is feeling regarding the others; that is, suppression of system UE4 of his ego (or unconscious representation of his own affective states).

Evacuation of the unconscious representation of what the subject is feeling regarding the others onto his conscious representation of what the others are feeling about the subject; that is, evacuation of system UE4 of his ego into system A4 of his alter (or conscious representation of the affective states of the others). UE4 = A4.

Rejection of the unconscious representation of what the others are feeling about the subject; that is, rejection of system UA4 of his alter (or unconscious representations of the affective states of the others).

Absorption of the unconscious representation of what the others are feeling about the subject into the conscious representation of what the subject is feeling about the others; that is, absorption of system UA4 of his alter into system E4 of his ego (or conscious representation of the subject's affective states). UA4 = E4.

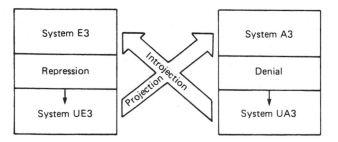

Figure 6-6. Defenses in the structure of representations of actions

In summary, system UE4 is suppressed and evacuated and system UA4 is rejected and absorbed (Figure 6-7).

The ninth theoretical hypothesis of the first metapsychological level is as follows:

9. The intrapsychic defense mechanisms of repression, projection, denial, introjection, suppression, evacuation, rejection, and absorption, which produce a correct unconscious representation and an inverted conscious representation of actions and affective states, function in the sadist in a way that is symmetrical and complementary to their functioning in the masochist.

In effect, with regard to the representation of actions, the sadist represses and projects what the masochist denies and introjects: the representation that the sadist is a < bad satisfied frustrator> and he denies and introjects what the masochist represses and projects: the representation that the masochist is a <good frustrated satisfier> (Figure 6-8).

Regarding the representation of affective states, the sadist suppresses and evacuates what the masochist rejects and absorbs: the representation of the sadist "enjoying a satisfaction frustrating for the masochist"; and he rejects and absorbs what the masochist suppresses and evacuates: the representation of the masochist <suffering a frustration satisfying for the sadist>.

Returning to the clinical examples of Peter and Jennifer, it can be said that this symmetrical complementarity of representations and mechanisms is clear in terms of their bipolarly reduced ego-

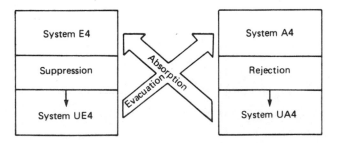

Figure 6-7. Defenses in the structure of representations of affects

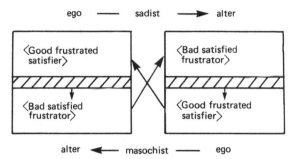

Figure 6-8. Complementary structure of the representations of ego and alter in the sadist and masochist

representations and alter-representations at the conscious and unconscious levels (see Figure 6-9). Peter represses and projects what Jennifer denies and introjects: that Peter is a <bad satisfied frustrator>. And Peter denies and introjects what Jennifer represses and projects: that Jennifer is a <good frustrated satisfier>. The same thing happens with the reduced representation of their affective states.

However, in relation to their partially reduced psychic structures of "ego constellation" and "alter constellation," or their non-reduced psychic structures, it can be observed that the symmetrical complementarity is not that precise, because Peter has his individual style of being a <satisfied frustrator of others> and of making

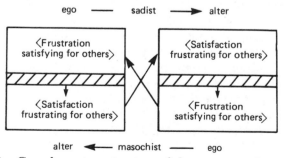

Figure 6-9. Complementary structure of the representations of affects in the sadist and masochist

others <frustrated satisfiers of himself>, which is quite different from Jennifer's style of being a <frustrated satisfier of others> and of making others <satisfied frustrators of herself>. In effect, Peter is an excluding, replacing person who makes others angry and vengeful toward himself, but Jennifer is a self-sacrificing overgiver who induces others to be selfish overreceivers of her sacrifices. These differences in the personal narcissistic styles of sadism or masochism could lead to a particular kind of crisis in the equilibrium of a given sadomasochistic regime, as we shall demonstrate later.

Because the masochist disqualifies himself and overqualifies the sadist in order to survive, one can say literally that he uses intrapsychic (and interpersonal) *defense* mechanisms. But the sadist is using intrapsychic (and interpersonal) *attack* mechanisms, because he overqualifies himself and disqualifies the masochist in order to obtain pleasure at the latter's expense.

The Absent Hostile Word-Representations

Freud (1915b) argued repeatedly that the conscious and preconscious layers of the psychic apparatus are formed by thing-representations (Freud 1891), which are essentially visual and bound to the corresponding word-representations (Freud 1895), which are essentially auditory. This situation cannot exist in the unconscious layer, where only thing-representations are found (Freud 1915).

We disagree with Jacques Lacan that "the Unconscious is structured as a language" (that is, only of verbal signifiers). On the contrary, we agree with Freud that the unconscious is formed only of nonverbal signifieds—the correct visual representations of actions and affective states whose corresponding auditory representation (in speech) are absent from the psychic apparatus. They are replaced by the conscious inverted speech representations.

We believe that the thing-representations are the visual representations of actions and also the "somatic" representations of affects, as André Green (1966) has argued, and the correct (not inverted) thing-representations form the unconscious layer of the psychic apparatus. In other words, the correct visual representations of actions, and the somatic representations of affective states, remain in the unconscious in states of repression and suppression, respectively, because they cannot be put into words. But the corresponding inverted conscious visual and somatic thing-representations of actions and affective states are put into words through the conscious auditory representations of the inverted speech. Thus, according to our own theoretical model, the conscious system of representations would be constituted by the auditory inverted word-representations plus the corresponding visual and somatic inverted thing-representations while the unconscious system of representations would be formed only by the correct visual and somatic thing-representations of actions and affective states.

Consequently, it could be said that the word-representations of the feared mnemic trace (FMT) do not exist within the systems of representations of the psychic apparatus and must be introduced by the analyst and gradually worked-through with the analysand.

In summary, there are both word- and thing-representations for the desired mnemic trace (DMT), and these constitute the manifest psychic content; but there are only thing-representations for the feared mnemic trace, and these are the latent psychic content. Therefore the sadist will have only thing-representations for his (repressed) behavior of being a <satisfied frustrator>, but both thing- and word-representations for his (repressing) inverted perception of being a <frustrated satisfier>. On the other hand, the masochist will have only thing-representations of his masochism but both thing- and word-representations of himself as being a sadist.

If we try to diagram the inverted conscious repressing word- and thing–self-representations as well as the corresponding correct unconscious repressed thing–self-representations in the psychic apparatus of the sadist, we would have the structure presented in Figure 6-10.

Topography of the Ego, Superego, and Id

To reorganize the topography of ego, superego, and id in accordance with our theoretical model we will take into account two of Freud's metapsychological hypotheses:

1. Drives have two aspects that are always linked to each other: representations of ideas, and affects (Freud 1900).

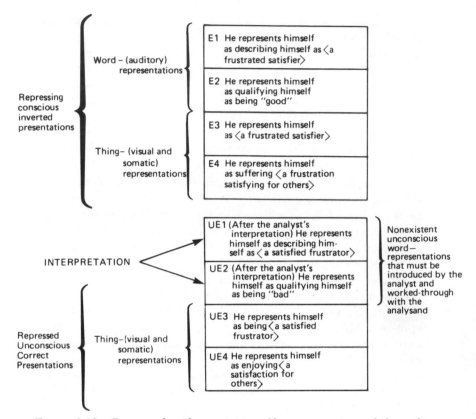

Figure 6-10. Repressed and repressing self-representations of the sadist

2. The terms *pleasure* and *unpleasure* always refer to the qualitative, or representational, aspect of the actual affective states of "satisfaction" and "frustration" experienced by the subject (Freud 1915a).

The first of these hypotheses led us to systematically link the representations of speech and actions with their corresponding affects; the second led us to distinguish, also systematically, between the "real" affect experienced by the subject, and the intrapsychic "abstract" representation of the affects experienced or described. We have postulated the theory that actions and affective states are represented twice through systems of conscious antiisomorphic representations. We now face a methodological problem: if it was relatively simple to compare the actions with the speech that describes and qualifies them, it was not easy to compare the affective states with their corresponding speech. It is difficult for the anlayst to observe the affective states of the analysand directly, except perhaps by means of the corresponding neurovegetative signs. We have chosen temporarily to accept this second possibility. The analyst must always double-check if what the analysand says he is doing and feeling is actually what he is doing, as well as with what the analyst is feeling and the analyst's neurovegetative changes.

In translating the first Freudian (topographic) model of the psychic apparatus (Freud 1900) into the theoretical model offered by the theory of psychic bipolarity, it can be said that the *conscious system* is formed by the nonreduced structure of conscious representations of descriptive and qualifying speech, actions, and affective states (that is, by nonreduced systems E1, E2, E3, E4, A1, A2, A3, and A4); that the preconscious system is formed by the partially reduced and reduced structure of the same conscious representations of descriptive and qualifying speech, actions, and affective states; and that the unconscious system is formed by the reduced and nonreduced structure of unconscious representations of actions and affective states (by systems UE3, UE4, UA3 and UA4).

If we attempt now to translate the second Freudian (structural) model of the psychic apparatus (Freud 1923), we can say that the *ego system* is formed by the conscious and unconscious representations of descriptive speech and actions (by systems E1, E3, A1, A3, UE3, and UA4); that the *superego system* is formed by the conscious representations of qualifying speech (systems E2 and A2) and by the normative code (especially the unconscious rule of action) that is implied in them; and that the *id system*, as the psychic representation of somatic demands, is formed by conscious and unconscious representations of the affective states (by systems E4, A4, UE4, and UA4).

Identification of the Ego and Introjection of the Alter

There are two concepts in psychoanalysis that refer to the internalization of an object in the process of its representation: introjection and identification (Freud 1914). While these terms have been used interchangeably, we believe that when distinguished they provide a valuable source of clarity for the theory of the psychic apparatus. An object whose representation is introjected becomes an internal object to which the ego relates as an intrapsychic alter. But an object whose representation is identified-with actually becomes a part of the ego: the ego identifies with this object.

If we insert this distinction into our theory of narcissism, then the ego identification reflects the way in which the significant other wants to see the subject and the alter introjections reflect the way in which the significant other wants the subject to see him.

If the parent is a sadist he will want the child to see him as a masochist and to see himself as a sadist. If the parent is a masochist he will want the child to see him as a sadist and to see himself as a masochist. Thus the parents' actions, sadistic in the one case and masochistic in the other, will remain unrepresented for the child and contradict what has been represented through the process of introjection and identification. The true situation of the child consists of the inversion of his identifications and introjections, and this constitutes the first or empirical level of our theory.

We can also say that the unrepresented actions in the situation are unconscious and therefore constitute the second level of our theory.

It may be worth noting that when Lacan argues that the Unconscious is structured like a language, he is referring, in terms of our theory, to the first level of inverted representations that form a closed system of repetitions which he calls the chain of signifiers. We, however, posit a further unconscious dimension that is admittedly not represented in words and therefore does not operate as a verbal language would. Freud accurately referred to this as the level of thing-representation without word-representations (Freud 1915a).

We can be more specific and say that these are the representations of actions that the subject witnesses but does not see because they were not reflected in the mirror of the significant other. In this way the deepest structures of the unconscious are transmitted without entering the field of consciousness, which is fully occupied with the narcissistic process of inverted perception. Perhaps this is the deepest meaning of Freud's "the blindness of the seeing eye" in relation to the unconscious dimension of object relations (Freud 1895b).

If we consider the point of view of the parent instead of the child, we can say that the parent projects his alter into the child's ego and his ego into the child's alter (Figure 6-11). In the same way that we have distinguished identifications, we can also distinguish the projection of the identification (the ego) from the projection of the introject (the alter). (In order to maintain some agreement with the usual nomenclature we will use the term *introjection*, not only for the internalization of a given external object onto the alter, but also for the intrapsychic defense mechanism of perceiving in the ego what really corresponds to the alter. On the other hand, we will use the term *identification* for the internalization of a given external object onto the ego.)

Identifications always mirror the introjects in the sense that the intrapsychic ego is the reflection of the intrapsychic alter and vice versa: there is a mirror-ego reflecting a mirror-alter, and so on. And as we will see later, there is at the same time a master-mirror reflecting a servant-mirror: the superego is reflecting the ego which is reflecting the id, etc.—as long as the parent mirrors the child instead of recognizing him.

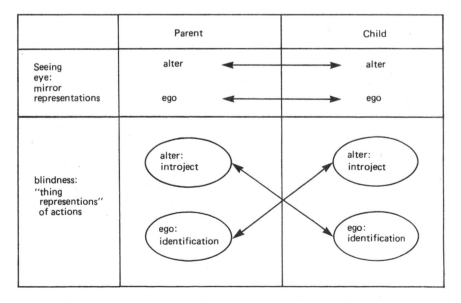

Figure 6-11. The "blindness of the seeing eye" between parent and child

The Superego, Master Ego, and Servant Ego

Regarding Freud's second (structural) theory of the psychic apparatus, it can be said that his metapsychological concepts of super-ego and ego-ideal imply at least two very different aspects.

On the one hand, the "law," the legislation, the ideology, the social system of values that the child introjects as a normative code, as a moral consciousness that regulates his speech, actions, and affective states. He introjects this "law" through his repetitive contact with his parents or significant others: "Thus a child's super-ego is in fact constructed on the model not of its parents but of its parents' super-ego; the contents which fill it are the same and it becomes the vehicle of tradition and of all the time-resisting judgements of value which have propagated themselves in this manner from generation to generation" (Freud 1933, p. 76).

However, the superego also represents the "Judge," the administrator who applies the "law." Freud's concept of the superego can be easily identified with the law, the normative code, but not so clearly with the Judge. The law is always "above" the ego, both in sadism and masochism, but in sadism the Judge is the ego itself, who is "above" his introjected objects and judges them. Only in the masochist is the Judge "above" the ego because it is judged by the introjected parental objects.

In our model, we discriminate between two aspects of the Freudian superego: the verbalized *norm*, which regulates with verbal qualifications the speech, actions, and affective states that can be classified as good or bad; and the nonverbal *rule* which also regulates the speech, actions, and affective states by instituting punishment that can be classified as "factually punished" or "factually nonpunished." It seems that there is a universal verbalized norm of the narcissistic super-ego that qualifies as "bad" to say one is, or to be and to feel like a <satisfied frustrator> of others, and as "good" to say one is, or to be, and to feel like a <frustrated satisfier> of others.

In a coherent narcissistic individual, produced by a utopian, coherent, narcissistic society, the corresponding *rule* would be concordant with that *norm*. This does not mean that frustration is ontologically "good" and satisfaction ontologically "bad" (in the same way that a masochist is not necessarily a "good" person or a sadist a "bad" person). As a matter of fact, it can be said that, from a certain ethical perspective, both are bad. But it seems that in a sadomasochistic narcissistic individual, produced by a sadomasochistic society, the *rule* of the superego, of the Law, not only contradicts its corresponding *norm*, but is also different in the sadist and the masochist.

In effect, the narcissistic norm stating that <frustrated satis­fier> is good and that <satisfied frustrator> is bad seems to be the same for both sadists and masochists. But in the case of the sadist, the rule agrees with the norm and punishes him through unpleasure if he says he is acting and feels like a <satisfied frustrator>; at the same time the rule contradicts the norm and punishes the sadist through unpleasure if he actually acts or feels like a <frustrated satisfier>. In the case of the masochist, in turn, the rule contradicts the norm and punishes him through insecurity if he says he is acting and feeling like a <frustrated satisfier>; but at the same time the rule agrees with the norm and punishes him through insecurity if he actually acts or feels like a <satisfied frustrator>.

It seems that even if the superego (that is, the law with its norm and rule), is contained in the qualifying speech with which the individual consciously qualifies himself as well as the others, it still remains mainly unconscious. An important part of the analyst's task is to make conscious the unconscious superego contained in the conscious qualifications of the speech.

But, as we said, the superego does not function only impersonally as the law, or moral consciousness, or normative code; it also functions "personally" as the "Judge," the legislator who applies the law while the ego functions as the accused. It is clear in Freud's work that the superego functions like an introjected sadistic judging object that dominates an inner masochistic subject, and that it punishes the subject if he does not behave according to his own norm and rule (Freud 1924). The ego-ideal, on the other hand, equally dominates the inner subject but more in the way of a benign parent who establishes the ideal goals to be obtained by the ego (Freud 1923).

In *The Ego and the Id* Freud (1923) says that the ego is a "servant" of three "masters": the id, the superego, and the external world; hence the ego is a blamed, masochistic servant ego dominated by an inner sadistic judging object. In terms of the bipolar reduction of the psychic representation into "psychic ego" and "psychic alter," it can be said that a *servant ego* is dominated not only by an intrapsychic, introjected *master alter* but also by an external, projected master alter and by the drives of its id.

Freud shows the sadomasochistic relation between a servant ego and its superego, functioning as a postoedipal introjected master alter, in "The Economic Problem of Masochism."

> Only in this way was it possible for the Oedipus complex to be surmounted. The super-ego retained essential features of the introjected persons—their strength, their severity, their inclination to supervise and to punish. . . . The super-ego—the conscience at work in the ego—may then become harsh, cruel and inexorable against the ego which is in its charge. Kant's Categorical Imperative is thus the direct heir of the Oedipus complex. (Freud 1924, p. 167)

However, it is an imperative which does not respect precisely Kant's rule ("you must" implies "you can"), because the nonverbalized rule of action is asking the ego to say, to do, and to feel something that the norm is not allowing it to say, to do, and to feel, and vice versa.

> But the same figures who continue to operate in the super-ego as the agency we know as conscience, after they have ceased to be objects of the libidinal impulses of the id—these same figures also belong to the real external world. It is from there that they were drawn; their power, behind which lie hidden all the influences on the past and of tradition, was one of the most strongly-felt manifestations of reality. (Freud 1924, p. 167) . . . We may suppose that this portion of the destructive instinct (turning back of sadism against the self) which has retreated appears in the ego as an intensification of masochism. . . . [It] is also taken up by the super ego, without any such transformation, as an increase in its sadism against the ego. The sadism of the super-ego and the masochism of the ego supplement each other and unite to produce the same effect. (Freud 1924, p. 170)

We believe that this extraordinary metapsychological explanation only explains the economic problem of sadism when it is inverted. The increase of the destructive drive appears in the ego as an intensification of sadism and in the introjected objects as an increase in their masochistic positions vis-à-vis the ego. These introjected objects (which we will call *servant alters*), also retain essential features of the introjected persons—their weakness, compliance, and inclination to obey and be punished. The ego, the master ego, may then become harsh, cruel, and inexorable against the servant alter which is in its charge.

In effect, the ego of the sadist seems to function mainly as a master ego, or a *judge ego*, which dominates its internal and external objects; that is, the dominating master ego disqualifies and punishes an internal and external servant alter.

Briefly stated, it seems that the servant ego of the masochist is disqualified and punished by his master alter, which overqualifies and indulges itself; the master ego of the sadist overqualifies and indulges itself while it disqualifies and punishes his servant alter. We introduced this distinction with Figure 0-1(a) on page 12 where we used the Latin terms *infer* and *super* to refer to the "servant" and "master" designations.

As seen in chapter 3, apart from the informative code, which uses speech to transmit information about actions, and the affective code, which uses speech and actions to transmit affective states, there is an identificative code, which is used by the subject to identify the representations of his own speech, actions, and affective states (ego-representations) as "psychic ego," from the representations of the speech, actions, and affective states of others (alter-representation) as "psychic alter."

It can be said that the master ego of the sadist and the master alter of the masochist are not only using the identificative code to distinguish the psychic ego from the psychic alter, but also to qualify them, or to apply the law to themselves as masters, as well as to the servant alter (in the sadist) and to the servant ego (in the masochist).

Another theoretical possibility is to posit the existence of a fourth intrapsychic code, a "normative code" (or strictly speaking, a superego used only to disqualify or overqualify the psychic ego and the psychic alter).

Thus, the classic concept of superego implies at least two functions: first, the superego as the law, or the normative code; second, the superego as the master or the judge who applies the law (Figure 6-12). In any case, the superego is not above or beyond the law, because this law is unconscious and cannot be conceptualized as a whole, or modified, by the judge who applies it.

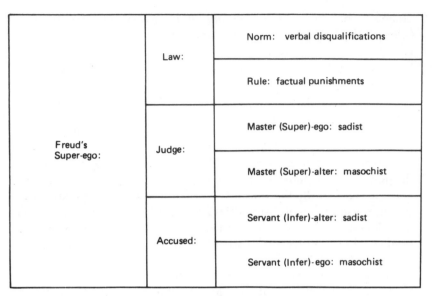

Figure 6-12.   The structure of conscience in narcissism

The law is formed both by the verbalized norm and the non-verbalized factual *rule of action*. The norm and the rule are not concordant in narcissism, and the rule is applied differently to the masochist and to the sadist. The role of the master (the judge) can be played either by the ego of the subject (as in the case of the sadist), who has, consequently, a master ego or super-ego, a servant alter or infer-alter, or by the alter of the subject (as in the case of the masochist), who has, consequently, a servant ego or infer-ego, and a master alter or super-alter.

This new development can be reorganized with the aid of additional theoretical hypotheses, still corresponding to the first metapsychological level of the theory of psychic bipolarity (hypotheses 1–9 in this chapter).

10. The representation of qualifications used in the speech by the speaker to qualify himself as well as the others contains a normative code based on an unconscious system of values that can be called *superego* or the *law*.

11. The superego, as the law, has a *norm*, consisting of the representation of verbal qualifications, and a *rule*, consisting of the representations of factual punishments and rewards.

12. The norm of the superego, in narcissism, qualifies as "good" saying one is, and feels and is like, a <frustrated satisfier> of others; and it qualifies as "bad" saying one is, and feels and is like, a <satisfied frustrator> of others.

13. The norm and the rule of the superego in narcissism are not concordant but contradictory.

14. Both sadists and masochists have the same norm but not the same rule in their narcissistic superegos: the rule of the sadist punishes him with unpleasure if he says that he is a <satisfied frustrator> or if he is or feels like a <frustrated satisfier>; the rule of the masochist punishes him with insecurity if he says that he is a <frustrated satisfier> or if he is or feels like a <satisfied frustrator>.

15. The subject can represent himself either as a powerful judge (a master or super-ego) who is entitled to overqualify and indulge himself and to disqualify and punish the others (as servant or infer-alters) because he has the strength and the right to do so; or he may represent himself as a powerless accused who is judged (a servant or infer-ego) who is condemned to be disqualified and punished either by himself or by others and to overqualify and indulge the others (as master or super-alters) because he has the weakness and the duty to do so. In the first case we call him a "sadistic agent" and, in the second, a "masochistic patient" of mental illness.

Just as there exist reduced, partially reduced, and nonreduced structures of speech, actions, affective states, and intrapsychic representations, so there is a reduced, a partially reduced and a nonreduced structure of the superego. In effect, <frustrated satisfier> is good and <satisfied frustrator> is bad in the reduced structure of the norm. But for each analysand there is also a "constellation," particular ways of being a <frustrated satisfier>, of being "good," of being a <satisfied frustrator>, and of being "bad" that form the partially reduced structure of his norm. There is also a "constellation" of ways of being "punished" and "rewarded" which forms the partially reduced structure of each analysand's rule.

Let us take the case of Peter as a sadist. The partially reduced norm of his superego, being excluded, replaced, angry and vengeful

(<frustrated satisfier>), was sensible and responsible (good) while being excluding, replacing, provoking and revenge-inciting, (<satisfied frustrator>) was dirty, crazy, traitorous, irresponsible (bad).

On the other hand, the partially reduced rule of his superego would be that, calling himself excluding, replacing, provoking- and revenge-inciting (a <satisfied frustrator>), he was punished with cognitive and ethical unpleasure, and while being excluded, replaced, angry and vengeful (acting and feeling like a <frustrated satisfier>), he was punished with hedonistic unpleasure. So he had to call himself a <good frustrated satisfier> but had to act and to feel like a <bad satisfied frustrator> in order not to be punished with cognitive, ethical, and hedonistic unpleasure.

At the same time, Peter has an intrapsychic master ego, because he represents himself, unconsciously at least, as a powerful judge who is entitled to overqualify himself as being "good" while indulging himself as a <satisfied frustrator>. Also, he has an intrapsychic servant alter because he represents others as powerless accused who are judged and who must accept being disqualified by him as "bad" and punished by him for being <frustrated satisfiers>. It is empirically evident that he acts and feels like a powerful judge. Probably he represents himself consciously as being a powerless judged (<frustrated satisfier>) while unconsciously as a powerful judge (<satisfied frustrator>).

In the case of Jennifer as a masochist, the partially reduced norm of her superego would be that of a sick, weak, careful, sacrificed overgiver to others (<frustrated satisfier>) who is nice and generous (good), while being a healthy, strong, careless overreceiver of the sacrifices of others (<satisfied frustrator>) was nasty and selfish (bad).

On the other hand, the partially reduced rule of her superego would be that calling herself a sick, weak, careful sacrificed overgiver (a <frustrated satisfier>) is punished with abandonment (insecurity) while being a healthy, strong, careless overreceiver is also punished with abandonment. So she had to accept the ethical and cognitive unpleasure of calling herself and perceiving herself to be a <bad satisfied frustrator> as well as the hedonistic unpleasure of being and feeling like a <good frustrated satisfier> in order not to be punished with abandonment, a threat to survival.

At the same-time, it can be said that Jennifer has an intrapsychic servant ego, because she represents herself as a powerless judged who must accept being disqualified as bad while punishing herself for being a <frustrated satisfier>; and she has an intrapsychic master alter because she represents others as powerful judges who are entitled to disqualify and punish her while overqualifying themselves as being good and indulging themselves as being <satisfied frustrators> of her.

We believe that by introducing the concept of superego as one of the "masters" (especially, a sadistic master of the masochistic servant ego) Freud introduced the problem of power. Freud's second theory of the psychic apparatus describes the introjected early structure of power between the early original significant others of the subject: his oedipal and preoedipal structure of power. In brief, the narcissistic norm says that "to be a powerless victim is good and to be a powerful victimizer is bad" but the sadistic rule punishes, through ethical and cognitive unpleasure, calling oneself a powerful victimizer and, with hedonistic unpleasure, acting and feeling like a powerless victim. The masochistic rule, on the other hand, punishes, with insecurity, calling oneself a powerless victim and acting and feeling like a powerful victimizer. Thus, the sadistic agent is a powerful victimizer who calls himself a powerless victim in order to obtain pleasure, and the masochistic patient is a powerless victim who calls himself a powerful victimizer in order to obtain survival.

Some Consequences for Technique

The group of theoretical hypotheses of the first metapsychological level of the theory of psychic bipolarity can be used by the analyst as a guide for new and deeper therapeutic operations. The empirical-level hypotheses presented earlier enable him to make superficial descriptions of the structure of the analysand's speech and of its inversion in relation to the structure of his actions and affective states, looking for the analysand's "outsight"; and therapeutic "specific reactions" to avoid being a powerless, dependent, masochistic patient with his sadistic analysands, or a powerful, dominant sadistic agent with his masochistic analysands, as well as to help them to produce healthy nonsadomasochistic "specific actions." The theoretical hypotheses, on the other hand, will enable the analyst to make deep interpretations, looking for the analysand's "insights" into:

1. The analysand's conscious structure of intrapsychic representations and its inversion with respect to his unconscious intrapsychic structure
2. The functioning of the analysand's intrapsychic defense or attack mechanisms
3. The structure of the analysand's normative code, that is, his superego as an intrapsychic law with its verbal norm and its nonverbal rule
4. The analysand's intrapsychic judge or master, who applies the law for his own benefit and its corresponding intrapsychic accused, or servant, who obeys it for his own benefit.

Consequently, following the theoretical hypotheses of the first metapsychological level of the theory of psychic bipolarity, the analyst must:

1. Describe how the analysand is consciously perceiving and representing himself and the others (including the analyst himself) in a stereotyped way that can be reduced to the psychic-ego constellation and the psychic-alter constellation, in order to allow the analysand to be aware of his peculiar stereotyped and selective way of perceiving and thinking.
2. Show the analysand that he is perceiving and thinking of the actions and affective states of himself and of the others (including the analyst himself) in an inverted way with respect to the direction of the actions and the quality of the affective states. The analysand should be aware that he is defending himself against perceiving and thinking of his relations with others as they really are.
3. Show the analysand that he is defending himself against perceiving in himself and in others actions and affective states that are painful to him in some way.
4. Show the analysand that he avoids those painful representations of actions and affective states:
(a) By perceiving there and then in others (or here and now in the analyst) what he does not perceive that he himself is doing and feeling here and now, with the analyst .
(b) By perceiving in himself what the analyst can be doing and feeling with him.
5. Show the analysand that the representations of the actions and affective states of himself and others are painful to him because he is unconsciously afraid of being punished by the analyst if he

perceives (and says) correctly what he and the analyst are actually doing and feeling.

6. Show the analysand that he cannot stop what he is actually doing and feeling because he is also unconsciously afraid of being punished by the analyst if he does. The analysand must be made aware that he is afraid of being punished by the analyst if he starts perceiving (and saying) correctly what he and the analyst are actually doing and feeling.

7. Show the analysand what he is doing and feeling and how, at the same time, he is perceiving and describing it in the inverted way which he must have learned when he was a child; that he is identifying his present relation with the analyst with some significant repetitive relation of infancy and childhood.

8. Describe to the analysand, in a comprehensive way, the set of values that he has learned and that he unconsciously applies and obeys (that being satisfied is bad and being frustrated is good) as well as the set of rules of actions concerning what is and what is not punished.

9. Show the sadistic analysand that he perceives himself as a master who is entitled to overqualify and indulge himself and to disqualify and punish others (the analyst included) as if they were his servants; that is, that he thinks he is entitled to perceive and qualify himself as a <good frustrated satisfier suffering a frustration satisfying for others> while acting and feeling as a <bad satisfied frustrator enjoying a satisfaction frustrating for others>.

9a. Show the masochistic analysand that he perceives himself as a servant who must disqualify and punish himself and overqualify and indulge others (the analyst included) as if they were his masters; that is, that he thinks that he is condemned to perceive and qualify himself as a <bad satisfied frustrator enjoying a satisfaction for others> while acting and feeling as a <good frustrated satisfier suffering a frustration satisfying for others>.

10. Show the sadistic analysand that he fears that if he does not perceive himself (and act as) a dominant master of the others (the analyst included) his pleasure will be threatened by the analyst, and that this fear was first learned by him during infancy and childhood.

10a. Show the masochistic analysand that he fears that if he does not perceive himself (and act) as an obedient servant dominated by others (the analyst included) his survival will be threatened by the analyst, and that this fear was also first learned by him during infancy and childhood.

In brief, the steps of the analyst's therapeutic work at the first metapsychological level will follow Figure 6-13.

Returning to Peter's case, and applying the technical consequences derived from the empirical hypotheses of the theory of psychic bipolarity, we see that Peter's analyst:

1. Showed him the reduced and partially reduced structure of his speech and how it was inverted with respect to the structure of his actions and affective states.

2. Showed him how he disqualifies and frustrates the analyst, threatening the survival of the analyst if he does not behave masochistically.

3. Reacted in a specific therapeutic way to avoid being pushed into the role of a powerless judged masochistic victim, and to help Peter produce healthy nonsadistic specific actions.

Applying the technical consequences derived from the theoretical laws of the first metapsychological level of the theory of psychic bipolarity, Peter's analyst must show him the following:

1. How he consciously perceives and represents himself in a stereotyped way, as an excluded, replaced, angry and vengeful person, and how he perceives and represents the others (including the analyst himself) as excluding, replacing, anger- and revenge-provoking persons.

2. That he perceives and represents himself and the others in an inverted way because he is actually excluding, replacing, and angry toward the analyst, who is pushed into the role of the excluded and replaced.

3. That he is defending himself against his own perception of himself as excluding and replacing, and the others as excluded and replaced, because if he recognizes this he will feel that he is a lousy, crazy, irresponsible person.

4. How he avoids feeling like a lousy, crazy person by projecting onto the Boy Scouts, or onto the previous or present analyst, being excluding and replacing, while repressing that he is excluding and replacing here and now with his analyst, and by perceiving himself as excluded and replaced, denying that it is his analyst who has been excluded and replaced by himself.

5. That he perceives and represents himself and the others (including the analyst) in an inverted way, because he is unconsciously afraid of being punished by the analyst, who will call him lousy, crazy, and irresponsible.

Description of representation's partially reduced conscious structure

↓

Description of the inversion of representations of actions and affective states

↓

Interpretation of defense against painful intrapsychic representations

↓

Interpretation of intrapsychic defense mechanisms inverting perception

↓

Interpretation of fear of being punished if perception and representation is correct

↓

Interpretation of fear of being punished if actions and affective states are correct

↓

Reconstruction of the origin of inverted speech and representation

↓

Reconstruction of the set of norms and rules of the superego

↓

Interpretation of the representation of being a master (a judge) or a servant (a judged) of others

↓

Interpretation of the fear of being punished if he does not represent himself as a master or as a servant

Figure 6-13.   The steps in the analytic therapy

6. That he cannot stop being an excluding, replacing, anger- and revenge-provoking person because he is unconsciously afraid of being punished by the analyst with exclusion and replacement.

7. That he behaves in an excluding, replacing, anger- and revenge-provoking way while perceiving himself as excluded, replaced, angry, and vengeful because he learned to do so interacting with his family when he was a child—for instance, that he perceived his mother as an excluding, replacing victimizer of his father and of himself, but claims that she was excluded and replaced by his father and himself, and that he is identifying his present relationship with his analyst with that oedipal situation.

8. That he perceives himself as a judge who is entitled not only to judge and punish others (the analyst included) but to judge and punish them in a biased way, favoring himself and exploiting others; that he qualifies himself as a sensible, responsible person while he enjoys being an excluding, replacing person, that he supposes also that the others (the analyst included) are obedient, silly servants who will listen to and accept his biased moral judgments and punishments; that they will accept being disqualified as lousy, crazy, irresponsible persons while suffering being excluded and replaced by himself in a lousy, crazy, and irresponsible way.

9. That if he does not perceive himself (and act as) a tricky judge who says that he is a good victim while being a bad victimizer, he will be called lousy, crazy, and irresponsible and, at the same time, be excluded and replaced by the analyst.

In Jennifer's case, when the analyst applies the technical consequences derived from the theoretical laws, he must show her the following:

1. How she perceives and represents herself in a stereotyped way as a nasty, selfish, strong, healthy, overreceiver and the others (the analyst included) as nice, generous, weak, sick, sacrificing overgivers.

2. That she perceives and represents in an inverted way because she is actually behaving with her analyst as a nice, generous, weak, sick, sacrificing overgiver.

3. That she cannot perceive herself as being a sacrificing overgiver because she believes she will be abandoned, and that this is very frightening to her.

4. That she avoids feeling abandoned by repressing in herself and projecting onto the old man in the parking lot and onto the analyst her being a sacrificing overgiver, and by denying and introjecting that she has pushed the analyst into the role of a selfish overreceiver.

5. That she perceives and represents herself and the others (including the analyst) in an inverted way because she is unconsciously afraid of being punished by the analyst, who will abandon her.

6. That she cannot stop being a sacrificing overgiver because she is unconsciously afraid of being punished by the analyst with abandonment.

7. That she is behaving as a sacrificing overgiver and perceiving herself as a selfish overreceiver, because she learned to do this by interacting with her family when she was a child, and that she is identifying her present relationship with her analyst with her family relationship.

8. That she believes that she is an accused who must accept not only being judged and punished by herself and others (the analyst included) but being judged and punished by them in a biased way, which favors them and exploits her; that she disqualifies herself as a nasty, selfish, overreceiver while she suffers being a nice, generous, sacrificing overgiver toward the others; that she believes that the others (the analyst included) are powerful masters whom she must obey and overqualify as if they were being generous and nice, while indulging their being nasty, selfish overreceivers of her sacrifices.

9. That she believes that if she does not perceive herself (or act as) a naive accused who says that she is a bad victimizer while being a good victim, she will be abandoned by the analyst.

Summary of the First Metapsychological Level of the Theory of Psychic Bipolarity

This first metapsychological level of the theory was developed in order to provide a dynamic and more comprehensive explanation of the descriptive hypotheses concerning the reduction and inversions of the eight systems of speech, actions, and affective states that we obtained at the empirical level, and to make clinical predictions from this advanced standpoint.

We will now present the empirical basis of the first metapsychological level as well as the psychoanalytic hypotheses it presupposes; the theoretical hypotheses; their rules of correspondence with the empirical systems and hypotheses; and, finally, some technical consequences of the theoretical hypotheses.

METHODOLOGICAL-EMPIRICAL BASIS

The "empirical" basis of this level of the theory is actually methodological; its "data" are theoretical entities—systems of intrapsychic representations—which are unobservable and can be obtained only on the basis of psychoanalytic hypotheses.

This methodological-empirical basis is formed of eight theoretical systems of conscious intrapsychic representations corresponding to the eight empirical systems of descriptive speech, qualifying speech, actions and affective states of the analysand and the analyst, plus four theoretical systems of unconscious intrapyschic representations of their actions and affective states. Thus there is a duplication of the representations of actions and affective states but not of descriptive or qualifying speech.

Consequently, there are twelve systems of representations (eight conscious and four unconscious), six forming the ego-representations or psychic ego and six forming the alter-representations or psychic alter.

The systems of intrapsychic representations forming the psychic ego are:

E1   conscious representation of the subject's descriptive speech

E2   conscious representation of the subject's qualifying speech

E3   conscious representation of the subject's actions

UE3   unconscious representation of the subject's actions

E4   conscious representation of the subject's affective states

UE4   unconscious representation of the subject's affective states.

The systems of intrapsychic representations forming the psychic alter are:

A1	conscious representation of the others' descriptive speech
A2	conscious representation of the others' qualifying speech
A3	conscious representation of the others' actions
UA3	unconscious representation of the others' actions
A4	conscious representation of the others' affective states
UA4	unconscious representation of the others' affective states.

PRESUPPOSED PSYCHOANALYTIC HYPOTHESES

Some of the presupposed hypotheses used to identify these twelve systems of intrapsychic representations as well as the topographic and structural organization and the defensive and attack mechanisms were:

1. The Freudian hypothesis of the existence of a psychic apparatus formed by intrapsychic representations.

2. The Freudian hypothesis of the drives and their double representation within the psychic apparatus through ideas and their corresponding "quota of affect."

3. The Freudian hypothesis that there is a conscious/preconscious system formed of "word-representations" and "thing-representations" and an unconscious system formed only of "thing-representations."

4. The Freudian hypothesis of repression, which is the foundation of Freud's first (topographic) theory of the psychic apparatus, and which is complemented by other Freudian hypotheses concerning projection, denial, and introjection.

5. The Freudian hypothesis of narcissism as a psychic state in which the external world functions as a visual as well as an auditory mirror of the subject's speech, actions, and affective states.

6. The Freudian hypothesis of sadomasochism, manifested not only in sexual perversions, but as pathological ways of dealing with destructiveness.

7. The Freudian hypothesis of the superego and the ego-ideal which is the foundation of Freud's second (structural) theory of the psychic apparatus, as moral conscience as well as an intrapsychic

judge resulting from the postoedipal introjection of the punitive parents.

8. Klein's hypothesis of the paranoid-schizoid and depressive positions with corresponding defense mechanisms—splitting of the ego and the object, persecution, projective identification, idealization, and introjective identification.

9. Jacques Lacan's hypothesis of the repression of the original conscious painful representation of the speech (original signifier) through a new repressing, gratifying representation of the speech. The unconscious would be formed only by the conscious painful representation of the speech (the original painful signifier functioning as signifier and signified at the same time), that is, only by word-representation.

10. André Green's hypothesis (1966) that actions and affective states not only have intrapsychic representations but that they are, when painful, the thing-representations that form the "core of the unconscious." The unconscious is formed only of those unconscious representations of actions and affective states (the original painful signified, functioning only as signifier); that is, only of thing-representations.

THEORETICAL HYPOTHESES

The theoretical hypotheses are the core of the first metapsychological level of the theory of psychic bipolarity:

1. The bipolar, nonreduced, partially reduced, and totally reduced empirical systems of descriptive and qualifying speech, actions, and affective states of the subject and his interactors have their corresponding intrapsychic (theoretical) systems of representations.

1a. (*Derived*) The intrapsychic systems of representations of descriptive and qualifying speech, actions, and affective states can be bipolarly reduced into "ego-representations" (or psychic ego) and "alter-representations" (or psychic alter), which can be, in turn, either <good frustrated satisfier suffering a frustration satisfying for others> or <bad satisfied frustrators enjoying a satisfaction frustrating for others>.

2. The descriptive and qualifying speech has only conscious intrapsychic representations, but the intrapsychic representations of actions and affective states are both conscious and unconscious.

3. The inverted descriptive and qualifying speech have true and appropriated conscious representations, but the actions and affective states have inverted conscious representations concerning the directions of the actions and the quality of the affective states, plus true and appropriate unconscious representations.

4. The correct conscious intrapsychic representation of the inverted descriptive and qualifying speech and the inverted conscious representation of the actions and affective states together form a coherent conscious structure. On the other hand, the unconscious representations of actions and affective states together form a coherent unconscious structure that is inverted with respect to the conscious structure.

4a. (*Derived*) Both the conscious psychic structure and the unconscious psychic structure can be reduced, partially reduced, or nonreduced.

5. The inverted conscious representations of the subject's actions and affective states are identical to the correct unconscious representations of the others' actions and affective states.

6. The conscious and unconscious intrapsychic representations of the sadist are different from and complementary to those of the masochist. That is, the sadist will consciously represent himself as being a <good frustrated satisfier saying that he is so and suffering a frustration satisfying for others> while unconsciously he will represent himself as being a <bad satisfied frustrator enjoying a satisfaction frustrating for others>. On the other hand, the masochist will consciously represent himself as being a <bad satisfied frustrator saying that he is so and enjoying a satisfaction frustrating for others> while unconsciously he will represent himself as being a <good frustrated satisfier suffering a frustration satisfying for others>.

7. The narcissistic subject does not tolerate representing either his actual actions and affective states or the actual actions and affective states of his interactors as they really are. He must represent them to himself by inverting the direction of the actions and the quality of the affective states. But the narcissistic subject tolerates perfectly well being as he is and feeling as he feels despite the defensive inversion of his perception and thinking. That is, the sadist cannot tolerate representing himself saying that he is a <bad satisfied frustrator enjoying a satisfaction frustrating for others> but he tolerates perfectly well being a <satisfied frustrator feeling a satisfaction frustrating for others>.

8. There are four main intrapsychic defense or attack mechanisms used by the narcissistic subject, sadist or masochist, to invert his perception and representation of the direction of his own actions as well as the actions of interactors:

(a) repression of the unconscious representation of what he is doing to others

(b) projection of the unconscious representation of what he is doing to others onto the conscious representation of what said others are doing to him

(c) denial of the unconscious representation of what the others are doing to him

(d) introjection of the unconscious representation of what the others are doing to him onto the representation of what he is doing to the others.

Using these mechanisms, the subject sees and hears himself in others, and vice versa, as if he were Narcissus and the others his audiovisual mirrors, like the water and the nymph Echo.

9. There are four main intrapsychic defense or attack mechanisms used by the narcissistic subject, either sadist or masochist, to invert his perception and representation of the quality of his own affective states, as well as the affective states of his interactors, that operate similarly to the defense mechanisms operating against representations of actions. These are suppression, evacuation, rejection, and absorption.

10. The intrapsychic narcissistic mechanisms (repression, projection, denial, introjection, suppression, evacuation, rejection, and absorption) that produce a correct unconscious representation and an inverted conscious representation of actions and affective states are "defense" mechanisms in the masochist and are symmetrical with and complementary to the "attack" mechanisms of the sadist. That is, the sadist represses and suppresses what the masochist denies and rejects; projects and evacuates what the masochist introjects and absorbs; denies and rejects what the masochist represses and suppresses; and introjects and absorbs what the masochist projects and evacuates.

11. The representation of the qualifications used by the subject in his qualifying speech to qualify himself as well as the others contains a normative code based on an unconscious system of values

that can be called superego, or *law*, and that was introjected by the subject as a child.

12. The superego is the intrapsychic law that regulates the subject's speech, actions, and affective states. It is formed by a *norm*, or representation of the normative code used in verbal qualifications, and by a *rule*, or representation of the code used in factual punishments and rewards. These may be coherent with each other or contradictory.

13. The norm and the rule of the superego have reduced, partially reduced, and nonreduced versions. The reduced version of the norm refers to reduced speech, actions, and affective states as being "good" or "bad." The reduced version of the rule refers to reduced speech, actions, and affective states as being "punished." But each subject has a partially reduced version of his own norm and rule formed by a particular group, or constellation of ways not only of being a <satisfied frustrator> or a <frustrated satisfier> but of being "bad" or "good," or "punished" or "rewarded."

14. The reduced version of the norm of the superego in narcissism qualifies as "good" one's acting, and feeling like or saying he is a <frustrated satisfier> of others and qualifies as "bad" one's acting, and feeling like or saying he is a <satisfied frustrator> of others.

15. The norm and the rule of the superego are not concordant but contradictory in narcissism, because in masochism the rule punishes the subject if he says he is a <frustrated satisfier> while in sadism it punishes the subject if he acts and feels like a <frustrated satisfier>.

15a. (*Derived*) Consequently, both sadists and masochists seem to have the same norm but not the same rule in their narcissistic superego. In sadism the rule agrees with the norm when it punishes the subject if he says he is a <satisfied frustrator> but contradicts it when it punishes him if he acts or feels like a <frustrated satisfier>. In masochism the rule agrees with the norm when it punishes him if he acts or feels like a <satisfied frustrator> but contradicts it when it punishes him if he says he is a <frustrated satisfier>.

16. The subject could represent himself as a powerful judge or as a master ego who is entitled to overqualify and indulge himself and to disqualify and punish the others as powerless judges or as servant alters; or he could represent himself as a powerless "judged"

or a servant ego who is condemned to be disqualified and punished either by himself or by others and to overqualify and indulge those others as master alters. The sadist will have a master ego and a servant alter while the masochist will have a servant ego and a master alter.

CORRESPONDENCE BETWEEN METAPSYCHOLOGICAL AND EMPIRICAL HYPOTHESES

The conscious psychic structure is formed by the correct conscious representation of the inverted speech and by the inverted conscious representations of the actions and affective states. The unconscious psychic structure is formed by correct unconscious representations of the actions and affective states.

Consequently, the structure of the speech is concordant with the conscious psychic structure and the structure of the actions and affective states is concordant with the unconscious psychic structure. But, as the structure of the speech is inverted in relation to the structure of actions and affective states, the conscious psychic structure is inverted in relation to the unconscious one.

The central theoretical hypothesis at this level of the theory of psychic bipolarity is that of the double representation of actions and affective states. In effect, they have an isomorphic unconscious representation and an antiisomorphic one; this provides a deductive explanation—an explanation of the empirical inversion between the speech's structure and the structure of actions and affective states.

The rules of correspondence between the empirical systems of speech, actions, and affective states and the theoretical systems of intrapsychic representations show that the empirical level of the theory is derived from the first metapsychological level of explanation.

We will try to link the intrapsychic systems to representations and the defense mechanisms described in this chapter logically with the empirical systems and the reductions and inversions described in chapter 5.

The hypotheses of the first metapsychological level of the theory of psychic bipolarity which are here taken as premises, or as rules of correspondence, for the deduction of the empirical from the theoretical structures, follow.

First rule of correspondence: System El of the conscious representation of the analysand's descriptive speech is directly isomorphic (reliable) with the bipolar reduced system e.1 of the analysand's descriptive speech.

Second rule of correspondence: System E2 of the conscious representation of the analysand's qualifying speech is directly isomorphic with the bipolar reduced system e.2 of the analysand's qualifying speech.

Third rule of correspondence: System E3 of the conscious representation of the analysand's actions is antiisomorphic (inverted) to the bipolar reduced system e.3 of the analysand's actions.

Fourth rule of correspondence: System UE3 of the unconscious representation of the analysand's actions is directly isomorphic with the bipolar reduced e.3 of the analysand's actions.

Fifth rule of correspondence: System E4 of the conscious representation of the analysand's affective states is antiisomorphic (inverted) to the bipolar reduced system e.4 of the analysand's affective states.

Sixth rule of correspondence: System UE4 of the unconscious representation of the analysand's affective states is directly isomorphic with the bipolar reduced system e.4 of the analysand's affective states.

The seventh through twelfth rules of correspondence state the isomorphic or antiisomorphic correspondence between intrapsychic systems of the analysand's representation of the analyst's descriptive and qualifying speech, actions, and affective states and the empirical systems of the analyst's descriptive and qualifying speech, actions, and affective states. That is, system A1 is directly isomorphic with system a.1; system A2 is directly isomorphic with system a.2; system A3 is antiisomorphic (inverted) to system a.3; system UA3 is directly isomorphic with system a.3; system A4 is antiisomorphic (inverted) to system a.4; and system UA4 is directly isomorphic with system a.4.

It should be noted that in point of fact systems El, E2, E3, E4, A1, A2, A3, and A4, because they are conscious, are observable, albeit not behavioristically. Systems e.1, e.2, e.3, e.4, a.1, a.2, a.3, and a.4, (formed by the descriptive and qualifying speech, actions, and affective states of the analysand and the analyst) can, however, be observed by those representing them. Knowledge about the systems is therefore closer to the empirical than to the purely theoretical level, whereas systems UE3, UE4, UA3, and UA4, or unconscious representations of actions and affective states of the analysand and the analyst, would genuinely exist on the purely theoretical level only. We consider as "rules of correspondence" those relations between empirical systems e.3, e.4, a.3, and a.4, and the representational systems UE3, UE4, UA3, and UA4, which are more in the nature of a bridge between one structure and another, than between a theoretical and an empirical level.

To complete the study of the logical relations between the empirical systems and the intrapsychic systems of representations, we must recall two hypotheses of the first metapsychological level.

1. The conscious system E1 is concordant with systems E2, E3, and E4, and the system A1 is concordant with systems A2, A3, and A4. The link evidenced by this hypothesis appears to be more empirical than theoretical because it speaks of "objective" subjective realities.

2. Systems e.3, 3.4, a.3, and a.4, of actions and affective states have a double representation: isomorphically (reliable) at an unconscious level (systems UE3, UE4, UA3, and UA4) and antiisomorphically (inverted) at a conscious level (systems E3, E4, A3, and A4). This hypothesis is purely theoretical because it speaks of "subjective" subjective realities. It implies the hypothesis of repression and denial: these mechanisms prevent the analysand's and the analyst's empirical actions and affective states from being correctly represented in the analysand's conscience.

From the twelve rules of correspondence already described and from these two theoretical hypotheses the following explanatory theorems can be deduced:

First theorem: If the analysand consciously represents his actions and affective states, he will do so inappropriately (antiisomorphically) in accordance with the hypothesis of repression. If we accept that systems UE3 and UE4 are bipolar, system E3 is inverted with respect to system UE3 and system E4 with respect to system UE4.

Second theorem: The analysand's descriptive and qualifying speech will be inverted with regard to his actions and affective states as stated by one of the empirical hypotheses. This suggests that certain "empirical" hypotheses are in fact derived from, and find their explanation in, certain theoretical hypotheses at the metapsychological level.

DEMONSTRATION OF THE THEOREMS

1. It can be observed that the structure of the analysand's speech, system e.1, coincides directly with that of system E1, following the first rule of correspondence.

2. The structures of systems E1, E2, E3, and E4 correspond to each other, following the hypothesis concerning the concordance among conscious systems.

3. The structures of systems E3 and E4 are inverted with respect to those of systems UE3 and UE4 respectively, following the first theorem.

4. The structures of system UE3 and UE4 correspond directly to systems e.3 and e.4, respectively.

5. The structure of actions and affective states (systems e.3 and e.4) is then the inverse of the structure of speech (system e.1).

Briefly, if e.1 = E1; and E1 = E3 and E4; E3 and E4 = UE3 and UE4; UE3 and UE4 = e.3 and e.4; therefore e.1 = e.3 and e.4.

REFERENCES

Breuer, J., and Freud S. (1895b). Studies on hysteria. *Standard Edition 2.*
Freud, S. (1891). On aphasia. New York: International Universities Press.
—— (1895a). Project for a scientific psychology. *Standard Edition* 1:281–397.
—— (1900). The interpretation of dreams. *Standard Edition* 4/5.
—— (1915a). Repression. *Standard Edition* 14:143–158.
—— (1915b). The unconscious. *Standard Edition* 14:159–215.
—— (1917). Mourning and melancholia. *Standard Edition* 14:237–260.
—— (1923). The ego and the id. *Standard Edition* 19:3–66.
—— (1924). The economic problem of masochism. *Standard Edition* 19:157–170.
—— (1933). New introductory lectures on psycho-analysis. *Standard Edition* 22:3–182.

Gear, M. C., and Liendo, E. C. (1975). *Sémiologie psychanalytique*. Paris: Minuit.

—— (1979). *Action psychanalytique*. Paris: Minuit.

—— (1980). *Psicoanalisis del paciente y de su agente*. Buenos Aires: Nueva Visión.

Green, A. (1966). *Le discours vivant*. Paris: P.U.F.

Klein, M. (1952). Some theoretical conclusions regarding the emotional life of the infant. In *Development in Psycho-Analysis*. London: Hogarth Press.

Lasègue, C., and Falret, J. (1873). La folie à deux, ou folie communiquée. *American Journal of Psychiatry* 4:1–23, 1964.

Laplanche, J., and Pontalis, J. B. (1973). *The Language of Psycho-Analysis*. New York: Basic Books.

7

The Development of Topography and Defense in Psychoanalysis

In this chapter we attempt to explain the inspiration for, and the derivation of, our theory in the work of Freud, and in the English and French schools of psychoanalysis. In doing so we hope to make our position clear in relation to the development of psychoanalysis and make it more accessible to the reader who prefers to approach the field in a scholarly manner.

Even to a reader steeped in psychoanalytic theory in its North American development, the scholarship and discussion that follows may appear somewhat strange. Different aspects of Freud's work and of the psychoanalytic paradigm have been emphasized in Europe, and this is partly responsible for the evident gap in communication across the Atlantic. What we hope to show is that there is a substantially consistent line of argument that goes from Freud through the two major European schools, and that opens toward the major concerns of contemporary North American analysts. By taking both the European and the American approaches into account we have been able to advance our theory. In some sense, therefore, it is a mid-Atlantic theory, although in the present chapter we will be emphasizing its European dimension.

The chapter concentrates also on the derivation of the topographic structure in our model—the interplay between the mechanisms of defense and the layering of the conscious, preconscious, and unconscious levels of the psychic apparatus. We trace this connection as it was first formulated by Freud and subsequently elaborated by Melanie Klein and Wilfred Bion. We then show how Jacques Lacan took an original approach to this problem by applying European structural linguistics to the issues of topography and defense. This brings in once again the theory of the signifier and the signified that we employed in chapter 2 for our semiotic model of sadomasochism. Here, however, the reader will find our differences with the Lacanian school spelled out. No doubt this section will prove to be of greater interest to those who are familiar with European structural linguistics (as distinct from the American science of linguistics).

Ambivalence and Double Representation in Freud's Work

In "Instincts and Their Vicissitudes" (1915b) Freud finds that the ego can no longer change the sensation of unpleasure into pleasure with mere illusory or hallucinatory perceptual reversal of the feared mnemic trace (FMT) into the desired mnemic trace (DMT).* This seems to occur because the DMT, pleasurable for the ego at a given moment (the position of "tormentor" for the sadist, for example) is at the same time an FMT, or unpleasurable for the ego, when the sadist becomes a sadomasochist. Freud supposes that what makes the ego defend itself is not only the unpleasure produced by the increase in intrapsychic tension following the frustration of a drive, but also the unpleasure generated by the emergence of a drive whose gratification has been paradoxically transformed into unpleasure (Laplanche and Pontalis 1973).

The ego, consequently, has to find ways to dispose of both traces simultaneously; just as traffic lights, to be effective, must be simultaneously green for pedestrians and red for drivers. Freud assumes that the ego has to face a paradoxical conflict of drives, in the form of a double bind (Bateson and Ruesch 1945). In fact, "the earlier active direction of the drive persists to some degree side by

---

*For an explanation of the concepts of desired and feared mnemic traces, see chapter 2.

side with its later passive direction" [and] its final active or passive form co-exist alongside one another" (Freud 1915b, p. 130). "The fact that . . . its (passive) opposite may be observed alongside of it deserves to be marked by the very apt term introduced by Bleuler—'ambivalence'" (Freud 1915b, p. 131).

In our terms this means that the representations of the affective states "pleasure" and "unpleasure" coexist for each of the two signifiers DMT and FMT, but at different levels. It is not possible for either of them to be completely eliminated. But the DMT and the FMT have now become the active and passive positions of a given interaction, as occurs with the "tormentor" and "tormented" positions in the case of the sadomasochist or the position of "seductress" and "seduced" in Dora's case (Freud 1905).

The conflict appears sequentially not only because the object is either present or absent, but because the relation that the ego maintains with it is pleasurable and unpleasurable at two contrasting levels or "layers." Though Dora was not morally reproached when she was seduced, she was nevertheless factually abandoned. The reverse may occur when she is the seductress: she could be morally reproached but not actually abandoned. When the sadomasochist torments, he feels sadistic "pleasure" and masochistic "unpleasure," and vice versa when he has others torment him. Insofar as the impulses to be tormented and to torment and to be seduced and to seduce are "irreconcilable," it is impossible for the ego to satisfy them at the same level. In any case, it would have to assume these two contrasting positions at the same time in the interaction, to be able to satisfy both "impulses" with the minimum of unpleasure; but it would have to assume them on different levels of communication. Thus, Dora was verbally and consciously seduced while in fact she was unconsciously seducing. The person who calls himself a sadist is usually factually and unconsciously masochistic, and the person who calls himself a masochist is usually factually and unconsciously sadistic.

Freud attributes the unconscious generating effects of the traumatic happening to its contradictory characteristics when he states that "it turns out to be a sine qua non for the acquisition of hysteria that an incompatibility should develop between the ego and some idea presented to it" (Breuer and Freud 1893–1895, p. 122). "The actual traumatic moment then is the one at which the incompatibility forces itself upon the ego and at which the latter decided

on the repudiation of the incompatible idea. That idea is not anni-
hilated by repudiation of this kind, but merely repressed into the
unconscious" (p. 123).

In the case of the "repression or primary defense" of the ego
(Freud 1895) when confronted with the experience of pain, it is
often enough for the ego to "deny" the presence of the frustrating
object and delude itself, or hallucinate and perceive it as the gratifying object, in order to change unpleasure into pleasure. But, as
Freud shows, this defense may produce the opposite effect: if the
ego deludes or hallucinates the DMT and completely denies the
FMT, it runs the risk of not being able to satisfy the two competing
drives. As a result, the ego will continue using this "perception
defense" but will not always need to complete it with a "split"
response. In a split response, the ego factually recognizes the
presence of the frustrating object, but tries to change it into a
gratifying object in order to achieve a more real gratification than an
illusion or hallucination. Dora, for example, deluded herself that she
was seduced in order to avoid reproaches, but unconsciously she
acted as if she were a seductress in order not to be factually
abandoned.

Freud (1915b, p. 135) states that the perceptual "mirage" that not
only makes the FMT unconscious, but also projects it onto the representation of the alter on being negated by the ego, is the typical behavior of the "pleasure-ego" when the subject has to face the change
which it confronts at birth. In fact, in the womb the external is unpleasurable and the internal pleasurable. After birth, when the infant
is hungry and "needs" the external world, the external becomes
pleasurable and the internal unpleasurable. Freud says that, obeying
the pleasure principle, the subject then introjects (to borrow
Ferenczi's expression) the sources of pleasure she is offered (Dora
identifies herself with Freud as "seduced" because this gives her the
pleasure of not being reprimanded). The subject removes from herself what in her own psyche gives rise to unpleasure (the reproachable
attitude of "seductress") (Freud 1915b, p. 135).

According to Freud, the pleasure-ego divides the external world
into a pleasurable part that it introjects, and the rest that remains
alien. Dora has separated a part of her ego which she throws onto
the external world and perceives as hostile to her. After this new arrangement (perceptual reversal) the two polarities coincide again—
i.e. that of the subject-ego with pleasure and the external world with
unpleasure, as before birth (Freud 1915b, p. 135).

Preconsciously, all that is pleasurable in the nonego is classified as belonging to the ego and everything unpleasurable in the ego is classified as belonging to the nonego. The ego's real position remains unconscious.

Freud says that repression is an intrapsychic mechanism that deals with a conflict of the id, or the unconscious aspect of the ego (Laplanche and Pontalis 1973, p. 115). He maintains, on the other hand, that denial is an intersubjective mechanism that deals with a conflict between the ego and external reality; the ego "denies" a traumatic reality—the absence of the penis in the woman, in the case of the fetishist (Freud 1927). Our hypothesis is that both mechanisms work together and coexist as the ego "represses" (and projects) intrapersonally its unpleasurable position in conflicting interaction and, at the same time, "denies" (and introjects) interpersonally the pleasurable position of the interactor in the interaction.

The sequence formed by repression, projection, denial, and introjection causes the "mirror-like perceptual reversal" which Freud describes as an "economic polarity of reality" (1915a). His starting point is a disorder of the ego in the classification of its position in the interaction due to a "defensive" mistake in the attribution of the traits characteristic of the position. Dora, for example, distorts every type of interaction which is not that of seduction and, moreover, distorts her position in the interaction of seduction by placing herself, when she finds herself in conflict, in the "seduced" class—when actually she behaves as a seductress. Therefore, whatever Freud did, Dora would have selectively exaggerated her perception of all the indications which would place him in the class of seducers and her in the class of seduced, and selectively minimized all the indications which would place her in the class of seducers and him in the class of seduced. As the proverb has it: "She sees the mote in the other's eye but does not perceive the beam in her own." Moreover, she would distort all the indications which would place them in any other type of interaction or would reverse their roles.

We think that such a disorder in the identification and classification of the positions in the interaction (Bourdieu 1966) specifically includes a phenomenon of selective perception. Freud himself says that "the distinction between conscious and unconscious is in the last resort a question of perception, which must be answered 'yes' or 'no'" (Freud 1923, p. 15). But he adds that "the act of perception itself tells us nothing of the reason why a thing is or is not perceived." The system of perception receives both external and

internal stimuli; by means of the sensations of pleasure and unpleasure it tries to subordinate all the currents of psychic life to the
operation of the pleasure principle.

The Inversion of Conscious Representations in Freud's Work

Freud postulates a double perception (direct and reversed) and a
similarly double response when he says:

> Let us suppose, then, that a child's ego is under the sway of powerful
> instinctual demand which it is accustomed to satisfy and that it is
> suddenly frightened by an experience which teaches it that the con-
> tinuance of this satisfaction will result in an almost intolerable real
> danger. It must now decide either to recognize the real danger, give
> way to it and renounce the instinctual satisfaction, or to disavow
> reality and make itself believe that there is no reason for fear, so that it
> may be able to retain the satisfaction. Thus there is a conflict between
> the demand by the instinct and the prohibition by reality. But in fact
> the child takes neither course, or rather he takes both simultaneously,
> which comes to the same thing. He replies to the conflict with two
> contrary reactions, both of which are valid and effective. On the one
> hand, with the help of certain mechanisms he rejects reality and
> refuses to accept any prohibition; on the other hand, in the same
> breath he recognizes the danger of reality. . . . It must be confessed
> that this is a very ingenious solution of the difficulty. Both of the
> parties to the dispute obtain their share: the instinct is allowed to
> retain its satisfaction and proper respect is shown to reality. . . . The
> two contrary reactions to the conflict [verbal and active, we would
> say] persist as the center-point of the splitting of the ego. (Freud 1938,
> pp. 275-276).

We think that this rigorous splitting implies a division of the
ego into three simultaneous responses: a first response which is
perceptual and conscious, either verbalized or not, which denies the
reality of the ego's unpleasurable position in the conflicting interaction; a second response, unconscious and active, which implies an
unconscious factual "recognition" of both the ego's and the object's
position in the interaction—an implicit action of the object corresponds to an unconscious reaction of the ego; and, finally, a third,

"metaresponse" conscious both of its real position in the conflicting interaction and its condition of sender of the two earlier and contradictory responses.

In *Beyond the Pleasure Principle*, Freud reports the clinical case of "the child with the reel," which illustrates his thesis of the splitting of the ego in a game invented and played by a little boy of one and a half. This game consisted of a puzzling activity which the boy continuously repeated.

> He could say only a few comprehensive words; he could also make use of a number of sounds which expressed a meaning intelligible to those around him . . . tributes were paid to his being a "good boy". . . . [And] above all he never cried when his mother left him for a few hours. . . . This good little boy, however, had an occasional disturbing habit of taking any small objects he could find and throwing them away from him into a corner, under the bed. . . . As he did this, he gave vent to a loud, long-drawn-out "o-o-o-o". . . . His mother and the writer of the present account considered that this was not a mere interjection but represented the German word "fort" [gone]. . . . [The] only use he made of any of his toys was to play "gone" with them. (Freud 1920, pp. 14–16)

This interpretation of the game is that it "was related to the child's great cultural achievement—the instinctual renunciation (that is, the renunciation of instinctual satisfaction) which he had made in allowing his mother to go away without protesting. He compensated himself for this, as it were, by himself staging the disappearance and return of the object within his reach" (p. 16). The child changed an unpleasurable event into a game.

> At the outset he was in a passive situation . . . but by repeating it, unpleasurable though it was, as a game, he took on an active part. . . . Throwing away the object so that it was "gone" might satisfy an impulse of the child's . . . to revenge himself on his mother. . . . In that case it would have a defiant meaning: "all right, then, go away! I don't need you! I'm sending you away myself". . . . The child may . . . only have been able to repeat his unpleasant experience in play because the repetition carried along with it a yield of pleasure of another sort but nonetheless a direct one. (Freud 1920, p. 16)

The child recognizes that he will have the moral unpleasure of not being considered "a very good boy" any longer if he does not let his mother "throw him out" without resisting. Consequently, in the interaction with her he maintains his position of "being thrown out" and "renounces the gratification of his instinct." But at the same time he represses this reality which produces instinctual unpleasure, projecting into the reel his position of "being thrown out" while he introjects that of "throwing out," by means of which he disowns his mother. Freud says that the child's defense meant "I am the one who throws you out," although in action he answered "I let you throw me out." The child occupied the "passive" position of "being thrown out" (just as Dora took up the "active" position of seductress) but he saw himself in the active position of "throwing out" (just as Dora saw herself as the "passive" position of seduced). Dora is seducing others (satisfying herself by frustrating others) but representing herself as being seduced by others (frustrating herself to satisfy others), while the child with the reel is abandoned by others (frustrating himself to satisfy others) but representing himself as abandoning others (satisfying himself by frustrating others). That is, Dora is satisfied but represents herself as frustrated, while the child with the reel is frustrated but represents himself as satisfied.

The pleasure-ego of the child playing with the reel uses the language of gestures to "see" in the external world what he does not want to see in himself because it displeases him, and to "see" in himself what he does not see in the external world because it pleases him. The "o-o-o-o" sound appears as a verbal reinforcement of the already consolidated defense. The one in the position of "being thrown out" who does "not see" this inside himself would be repressed and projected, and the one in the position of "throwing out" who does "not see" this (in the mother) would be disowned and introjected.

Using the theoretical and empirical (clinical) hypotheses of the theory of psychic bipolarity, we can see Dora as functioning in the "sadistic agent" position. She consciously represents herself as a <good frustrated satisfier> (seduced) of her father or Mr. K. while she acts and unconsciously represents herself as a <bad satisfied frustrator> (a seductress). On the other hand, the child with the reel would be functioning in the "masochistic patient" position because he consciously represents himself as a <bad satisfied frustrator> (throwing out his mother-reel) while he acts and unconsciously represents himself as a <good frustrated satisfier> (thrown out by his mother).

In general, Freud (1927) attributes this series of prerepressive defense mechanisms, based on "disowning" and projection, to psychosis—what is consciously rejected reappears in the external world. In this case, the "return of the repressed" from the unconscious is equivalent to a "return of what has been projected" from reality. This defensive system is symmetrically opposed to the mechanisms of repression characteristic of neuroses. For the neurotic, who represses, the unconscious is what reality is for the psychotic, who disowns. Similarly, Bion (1962) says that when the ego uses projective identification instead of repression to defend itself from anxiety, "the unconscious is the other"—that is, the interactor itself as well as the representation of the interactor.

Nevertheless, clinically this trait does not seem relevant in distinguishing denial from repression, since Dora (whom Freud does not qualify as psychotic) represses in herself ("within" herself) and projects onto Freud her position of "seductress"; and at the same time she denies in Freud ("outside" herself) and introjects into herself the "seduced" position. To repress, then, is to "not see" the unpleasurable nature of the subject and to "see" that of the object; to deny is to "not see" the pleasurable nature of the object and to "see" that of the subject (see Figure 7-1).

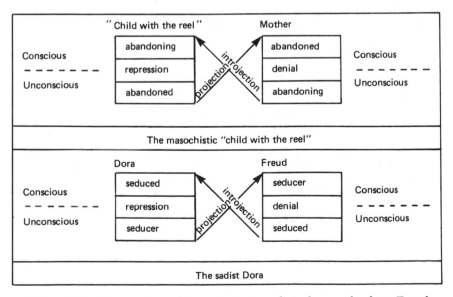

Figure 7-1.   Repression and inversion in two clinical examples from Freud

This defensive system formed by repression, projection, negation, and introjection is used by the narcissistic ego every time it takes part in a conflicted interaction. But this "double decentering" of the subject and the object was not only perceived by Dora in the form of an illusion; she really induced it since she "obliged" Freud to be seduced and to say that he seduced her. Consequently, if we call this series of intra- and interpersonal operations formed by repression, projection, denial, and introjection "defenses" or "transduction," we must conclude they always involve reality, that is, a "semi-victim and semi-accomplice" interactor: the interactor must be narcissistic too, because he is looking to introject what the narcissistic subject is projecting and vice versa. Each mirrors the other. In this "defense" there are three reversed mirrors: a semantic mirror (verbal-factual), an interactional mirror (depositor-depository) and a generation mirror (parents and children of the same sex).

In any case, once the repressive balance has been found both in "psychotic" and "neurotic" repression, there is a sort of "color-blindness" or reversed perception in the classification of the positions in the interaction that leads the narcissistic ego to see the "mirage" of the DMT where in fact there is an FMT. Dora considers herself seduced, and the child with the reel thinks he is "throwing out" when objectively Dora is "seductress" and the child is "thrown out." But the repression which appears as a reversed perception studied from the patient's point of view may appear as a "semantic color blindness," i.e., as a reversed speaking to the interlocutor who is listening to the said subject, unless he falls under the latter's narcissistic and "color blinding" induction and also "sees" inversely and describes inversely both his own position in the interaction and that of the inducing subject, functioning then as the latter's double reverse.

The Inversion between Social Ethical Norms and Social Rules of Action

From the beginning of his work, Freud (1895) took into account the complications that moral prohibitions present for the ego when it wants to gratify its drives: when it obtains gratification it also feels unpleasure. The object which gratifies the drive and generates a DMT in the "experience of gratification" of the Project can also generate an FMT because of moral prohibition. To solve the ambivalence to which this paradox between drive and ethics gives rise, the subject resorts to a splitting of the ego which enables him to actually respond in a way which he later represses in himself and denies in the object, where he sees it reversed.

Observing the clinical studies of Dora and the child with the reel, we find that when the ego interacts with an object which gratifies or frustrates its drives, its activity is not limited to gratifying or morally forbidding it. It appears rather as an *ambivalence-generating object* which, like Fairbairn's *exciting-repelling object* (1962), actively drives the ego to desire it and at the same time actively forbids it to do so. This type of object, which sends pragmatic paradoxes (contradictory orders which the ego cannot carry out), will be introjected as a superego in the sense of a normative code, which will use the impulses of the id, already in conflict, to create an even greater conflict for the ego and oblige it to split in a conscious and unconscious double response. The exciting-repelling object will be different for the sadistic agent and the masochistic patient. In effect, the sadistic agent is told by the masochistic patient that he will be accepted (and survive) if he is a <good frustrated satisfier> but if he is so he is factually rejected by the masochistic patient, and vice versa. Both the sadistic agent and the masochistic patient are exciting-repelling objects for the interactor but in different ways. For example, a sadist may ask another to be independent but at the same time punish that independence.

Clinical experience shows that the psychic conflict between an "internal" impulse of drives and the internalized "external" moral prohibition also may be interpreted as a conflict between "impulse" and "prohibition"—i.e., between two "external" contradictory instructions, related to an "internal" drive's need. Both the exciting and the prohibiting instructions are internalized after repetition, and end by transforming the drive's need into a paradoxical psychological desire because of the two instructions emanating from the object of the need. Moreover, one of the two instructions of the object is usually sent in a "mute" nonverbal code of action and the other is usually explicit, sent in a verbal "speaking code" generally denoting moral sanctions. Similarly, one of the ego's two responses is silent action to avoid being silently and actively punished by the object.

The other response is verbal in an attempt to avoid being morally punished by the object. Nobody told Dora, for example, "if you do not seduce (covertly) we shall leave you," but this is what Dora "saw" that her father in fact "did" to her. Nobody "told" the child with the reel "if you resist my leaving I won't love you," but this is what in fact he "saw" his mother doing. Freud (1915b) notes this difference between the visual code of action and the verbal code when he says that having heard and having experienced are entirely different, though they have the same content.

Lévi-Strauss (1963) is interested in those systems regulating social behavior in which the actors are not conscious or are only reflected in the consciousness of the actors by means of systematic distortion. In our model this distortion would be *symmetrical reversal*. Lévi-Strauss also assumes that conscious signification of social behavior hides, to a greater or lesser degree, its regulating mechanisms. Contrary to the functionalist school, he clearly distinguishes the social "norms" as conscious and institutionalized regulating mechanisms, from social "rules" as unconscious and not explicit regulating mechanisms. We would say that the superego prescribes a system of conscious norms for the ego which are verbalized and have a moral system which is systematically contradictory to the unconscious system of nonverbalized rules of action which it prescribes at the same time.

The superego's or external object's nonverbal implicit active punishment generates the ego's nonverbal unconscious active response, thus constituting communication "from unconscious to unconscious" (Freud 1912). The superego's (or the external object's) verbal and explicit moral punishment generates the ego's conscious verbal response. Messages regulated by this verbalized system of moral "norms" form communication from preconscious to preconscious. Consciously (verbally) the masochist communicates to the sadist that he must be a <good frustrated satisfier>, but unconsciously (factually) he communicates (through threats or promises) that he must be a <bad satisfied frustrator>. Consciously the sadist communicates to the masochist that he must be "independent," but unconsciously he communicates (through threats or promises) that he must be "dependent."

From this standpoint, the FMT (what the narcissistic ego will project into his interactor and repress in himself because it is unpleasurable for him to perceive) will be the verbal response explicitly forbidden, though stimulated, by the superego, but punished by it.

In Dora's case, for example, she did not take into consideration that Freud, her transference interactor, faced her with the following "activizing" pragmatic paradox: "If you are not straightforward you will be abandoned [rule of action] and if you seduce [FMT] you will be reprimanded [verbal norm]." She answered with the active double alibi: "I am not straightforward [unconscious active response] but I say I am seduced [DMT] by a seducer [FMT] [preconscious verbal response]." In her turn, she set Freud a complementary (i.e., "passivizing") pragmatic paradox: "If you do not let me be unstraightforward with you, I shall leave you [rule of action], and if you are seduced [FMT] I shall reprimand you for being autistic, disconnected like my mother [verbal norm]." Freud had to answer with the "passive" double alibi: "I let you be unstraightforward with me [unconscious active response] but I say I am a seducer [DMT] with someone who has been seduced [FMT] [preconscious verbal response]." Using an oedipal approach, we would say that least unpleasurable for Dora was to occupy her father's position in the interaction of conflict, that is, to seduce and to see herself as seduced and, moreover, to "convince" the interactor that the least unpleasurable position for him in the interaction was to let himself be seduced and see himself as the seducer and say that he was. Dora accused her father, morally and explicitly, of being a seducer and her mother of not being more seductive and less clumsily straightforward. Consequently, she accused both her parents verbally of symmetrical and reversed positions, and what seemed an FMT for her father was a DMT for her mother and vice versa. Each was mirroring the other.

The Unconscious Has No Representations of Speech (Freud)

In "Repression" (1915c), Freud insists on the biphasic constitution-representation of both ideas and affects of drives, but also that the affective aspect of the drives causes repression while the conceptual aspect is the one that suffers repression. In other words, unpleasant affect can be suppressed only after unpleasant concepts have been repressed.

It can be said that in repression (and denial) the concept whose corresponding affect is unpleasurable for the ego is replaced in perception (because it violates the superego's "norms") by the opposite (inverted) concept whose affect is pleasurable for the ego (because it complies with the norm of the superego). But his perceptual and representational replacement of the FMT by the DMT does not occur with a similar behavioral replacement (because the ego must carry out the "rule" of the superego). That is, the sadist will perceive and represent himself as a <frustrated satisfier> but he will continue behaving as a <satisfied frustrator> because if he does not do so he will be punished by his superego (his masochistic inferalter, in our terms) who will cut off his pleasure. The masochist will perceive and represent himself as a <satisfied frustrator> but he will continue behaving as a <frustrated satisfier> because if he does not do so, he will be punished by his superego (his sadistic superalter, in our terms), who will cut off his survival.

Representations of concepts are the "signifiers" of their corresponding representations of affects, or the "signified" of an "affective sign" (Gear and Liendo 1975). For example, the concept of "satisfaction" is a signifier and the satisfaction itself is a signified. We think that the existence of this affective code is suggested by Freud when he says:

> Clinical observations now oblige us to divide up what we have hitherto regarded as a single entity [instinct]; for it shows us that besides the idea, some other element representing the instinct has to be taken into account, and that this other element undergoes vicissitudes of repression. . . . For this other element of the psychic representation the term *quota of affect* has been generally adopted. It corresponds to the instinct insofar as the latter has become detached from the idea and finds expression, proportionate to its quantity, in the processes which are sensed as affects. . . . We recall the fact that the motive and purpose of repression was nothing else than the avoidance of unpleasure. It follows that the vicissitude of the quota of affect belonging to the representative is far more important than the vicissitude of the idea, and this fact is decisive for our assessment of the process of repression. (1915c, p. 152)

However, repression is a mechanism used by the representations and develops on the borderline between the conscious and unconscious (preconscious).

When the ego is faced with an FMT (or representation of unpleasant objects) it makes, according to Freud (1915c), a series of energetic movements in order to replace it with a substitute—always a DMT. The ego eliminates the preconscious charge which makes the FMT perceptible (it minimizes its indications), overcathects the DMT with this energy (maximizes its indications) thereby making it perceptible, and then acts as a countercathexis against the FMT. To this play of forces is added the attraction that "originally" repressed mnemic traces already exercise on the FMT from the unconscious. They form the initial nucleus of crystallization which corresponds, in the Freudian conceptualization, to original repression.

When the ego achieves the DMT through a narcissistic process (i.e., replacing the FMT or repressed representation in its consciousness by the DMT or substitutive repressed representation) it does so following the two great laws of symbol formation. It effects the replacement by some type of similarity and distortion between the FMT and the DMT, (i.e., by identification and symbolism) or by some type of contiguity between the FMT and the DMT, (i.e., by displacement and condensation). There must therefore be some type of similarity or contiguity between the repressed FMT and the repressing DMT for repression to be possible. When the repressing DMT is too similar or too much in contact with the repressed FMT, the latter has to undergo a new repression—greater distortion or displacement—which Freud calls "repression proper" (1915c, p. 181). It consists in the extension of selectivity and systematic reversal of the perception of every indication related by similarity or contiguity with the unpleasurable position of the ego in conflicting interaction. When in spite of this second operation the FMT reappears, it is called the "return of the repressed."

In our model, the basic symbolic relation between the latent, repressed, and unconscious FMT and the manifest, repressing, and preconscious DMT is a systematic distortion consisting in the reversal of the direction of the actions described. Consequently, one could say that there is a metaphoric resemblance between the FMT and the DMT.

Freud says:

> Contrary thoughts are always closely connected with each other and are often paired off in such a way that the one thought is excessively intensely conscious while its counterpart is repressed and unconscious. This process I call reactive reinforcement and the thought which asserts itself with excessive intensity in consciousness and (in the same way as a prejudice cannot be removed) I call a reactive thought. (1901, p. 55)

That is, if we multiply the DMT, the manifest content, by minus one we will obtain the FMT, the latent content. For example, if we multiply <satisfied frustrator> by minus one we will obtain <frustrated satisfier>, which is the latent content of the masochistic speech. The return of the repressed occurs when this symmetrical reversal fails and the FMT reappears as it is in the consciousness or when the interlocutor shows that the DMT is the reverse of the FMT, showing the subject that he is perceiving and speaking "in reverse": that he is perceiving and representing himself as being a <frustrated satisfier> while he is acting as a <satisfied frustrator>. On the other hand we think that if the basic aim of repression is to eliminate the experience of unpleasure, the "transmutation" of the "quota of affect" of the drive which occurs as the result can only consist basically of a changing of unpleasure into pleasure. This is the case even though it appears that "the qualitative factor of the instinctual representative has three possible vicissitudes . . . either the thing is altogether suppressed—as an affect—or it is changed into anxiety" (Freud 1915c, p. 153).

When the subject wants to inform himself or others about his perception of his actions (DMT or FMT), that is, about his perception of the representational signifiers of his representational affective code, he has to duplicate these signifiers. An *informative code* is thus formed. The informative code pertains to the description of actions and contrasts with the *affective code*, which conveys the affective states provoked by these actions. There will be also an *identifying code* indicating the subject of these actions and affective states and, eventually, qualifying them.

We think Freud describes the phenomenon of the informative code when he divides representations into "thing-representations" and "word-representations" to explain the differences between preconscious representatives (DMT) and unconscious representatives (FMT) (1915b, p. 201).

Mnemic images are broken down here into "word-representations" or "mnemic images." (But "mnemic images" in the sense of classes of perceptions which together form a structure and not in the empirical sense that Freud assigns to the notion of mnemic image—as a concrete perception—in The Project.) In this new code, the "information signals" are the words the subject uses to describe his mnemic traces. The "information signifieds" are the word-representations (the classes to which those words belong). The "information signified" are the thing-representations, or the mnemic traces themselves (the class to which the perceptions of real "things" belongs, i.e., gratifying or frustrating positions in interaction, which in their turn form the "information messages"). We believe that Freud refers to the duplication of the signifier universe of the affective code which generates the information code when he says:

> The conscious representation of the object can now be split into the representation of the *word* and the representation of the *thing*; the latter consists in the cathexis, if not of the direct memory-images of the thing, at least of remoter memory-traces derived from these . . . *the conscious representation comprises the representation of the thing plus the representation of the word belonging to it, while the unconscious representation is the representation of the thing alone. . . . A representation which is not put into words . . . remains thereafter in the Unconscious in a state of repression.* (1915b, pp. 201–202, italics ours)

We could then say that in the semic act made under the effect of repression the ego begins to perceive the "thing" (actions and affective states) selectively in such a way that it classifies it inversely, that is, places it in the reverse thing-representation; later it chooses the word-representation corresponding to this already reversed thing-representation and, finally, pronounces the reversed "word." That is, in repression thing-representations are "color-blind" in relation to the "things" they represent. But if the phenomenon is analyzed from the standpoint of the receiver who hears the "repressed" communication, we shall find that he perceives that the "words" the repressed sender uses to describe the "things" are "color-blind," and he may wonder whether the sender perceives wrong and names right (i.e., a repressed sender) or perceives right and names wrong (i.e., a cynical sender who lies systematically). According to the psychoanalytic hypothesis, the narcissistic ego perceives wrong and names correctly. What remains in the unconscious then is the thing-representation united to the "thing" (the verbally punished actions and affective states), and in the preconscious the thing-representation reversed in relation to the "thing" and its respective word-representation.

We agree with Freud's view (1915b) that a representation that has not been formulated in words, or a psychic act which has not been translated, remains in the unconscious. What is translated and perceived consciously under the influence of repression would be the reversed psychic act. A relation of color blindness, or reversal, is established between repressed unconscious psychic acts and the repressing preconscious ones which are perceived and translated into words. This difference between the conscious and the unconscious enables the doubly entrapped ego to lie without lying, saying that it is doing and feeling something while it does and tells the opposite, without being accused of cynicism or hypocrisy.

Freud clearly describes this unconscious mechanism of perceptual reversal by quoting a patient of Tausk (Freud 1915b, p. 198) who came to see him accusing her fiancé of "twisting her eyes." The patient was suffering the onset of schizophrenia when she quarreled with her fiancé. As Freud recounts, the patient complained, "her eyes were not right, they were twisted," and then she explains herself, adding in ordinary language a series of reproaches against her fiancé: "She could not understand him at all, he looked different every time; he was a hypocrite, an eye-twister, he had twisted her eyes . . . now she saw the world with different eyes." On another occasion the patient said: "She was standing in church. Suddenly she felt a jerk. She had to change her position, as though somebody was putting her into a position" (Freud 1915b, p. 198). After saying this to Tausk, the patient renewed her reproaches against her fiancé, "He was common; he has made me common too though I am naturally refined . . . He had made her like himself by making her think that he was superior to her. Now she had become like him, because she thought she would be better if she were like him. He had *given a false impression of his position*; now she was just like him [by identification]. He had put her in a false position" (p. 198). The movement to "a different position," observes Tausk, is a representation of the word "pretend" and of the identification with the fiancé.

This patient denounces the "repressive" maneuver of perceptual reversal made by her fiancé when she says that "he is an eye-twister" making her see things "twistedly." She then denounces the content of the fiancé's double alibi, which consists of being an inferior person who calls himself superior (ego-reversed) and who displaces his partner (who is his superior), making her believe and say that she is inferior to him (alter-reversed). But the patient, a schizophrenic, has never been able to understand her fiancé, since her speech and actions would be schizophrenogenic with him. She censures his double alibi, calling him a hypocrite without acknowledging that she herself might be responsible for the paradoxical rules, and he only subjected to them. Perhaps if he had not called himself superior, she would not have accepted him because he was not "refined." But when he does call himself superior, she reproaches him with being a hypocrite. Moreover, she herself chose him while considering him to be "common."

On his part, the fiancé's behavior shows the need of all subject who represses himself by reversing his perceptions to make an accomplice of his narcissistic interactor, accepting the induced and complementary role. He needs his interactor to act as a co-repressor who also perceives his actions and affective states inversely and thus continues the pathological perception of the repressed.

It can be said that Tausk's patient was either denouncing her fiancé's madness-making maneuver in a healthy way, or that she herself was being a sadistic agent in relation to Tausk, because her speech is typically sadistic. She repeats that she is a <good frustrated satisfier> of a <bad satisfied frustrator>. That is, her fiancé is a selfish, cheap hypocrite who is trying to twist her eyes in order to reverse the situation, and to appear as her superior. The difference between a healthy denouncing speech and a sadistic (or masochistic) one is shown by comparing it to its simultaneous verbal, preverbal, and contextual actions.

This clinical (or empirical) observation supports our thesis that repression is always a repression à deux (or à trois or à quatre, etc.) and consists in "twisting" not only one's own eyes but also those of others—in order to avoid a contradictory double punishment—with regard to one's own actions and those of others. Once the eyes are "twisted," words become "twisted" too, and one "speaks twistedly": perceptual ego and alter reversal are followed by a "semantic" ego and alter reversal in interpersonal communication. Dora's eyes were "twisted," and she also tried to twist Freud's by perceiving and naming his actions inversely, and by compelling him also to perceive and name his own and Dora's actions inversely.

Projective Identification as an Inversion of Conscious Representations (Melanie Klein)

The theory of anxiety is the cornerstone of Melanie Klein's theoretical model (1952), and she stresses the need to first analyze transference anxieties, i.e., the affective states underlying transference object relations. She assumes that this "logic of the emotions" (Isaacs 1952) is not only the basis of the logic of object relations but is also established by the onset of the opposition of the drives of life and death which first appear at the very moment of birth. It constitutes the "psychosemiotic denotative schema" or the instinctual code of life and death. If the infant is born traumatically it experiences annihilating anxiety, while a nontraumatic birth produces no such experience of anxiety. The narcissistic procedure the ego uses to avoid annihilating anxiety (such as birth anxiety) consists of the schizoid or manic defenses of the paranoid-schizoid position, which occupy a place in Klein's theory similar to repression in Freud's. We think that, like repression, the schizoid or manic defenses are based on a reversal in the classification of actions and affective states, which Hannah Segal in fact indicates:

> As the processes of splitting, projection and introjection help to sort out his perceptions and emotions and divide the good from the bad, the infant feels himself to be confronted with an ideal object which he loves and tries to acquire, keep and identify with, and a bad object into which he has projected his aggressive impulses and which is felt to be a threat to himself and his ideal object. (1964, p. 67)

This only describes a sadistic infant, because a masochistic one would try to acquire the bad object and to project the ideal one. Consequently, our own hypothesis of the system of four simultaneous narcissistic defense (or attack) mechanisms presupposes Klein's theory of the paranoid-schizoid and depressive positions, plus her concept of projective identification (Klein 1952).

But this splitting of the ego and of the object into idealized and persecutory categories is secondary to the splitting of the ego's perceptions of the actions and affective states of the subject and his objects into conscious and unconscious. In fact, Klein (1950) assumes that the basic conflict that the infant's ego has to face is an unbearable interaction with the simultaneously good (or idealized) *and* bad (or persecutory) object. This total object generates a situation of ambivalence that the paranoid-schizoid ego must solve by dividing itself and the object onto two part-objects and two part-egos, completely good *or* completely bad respectively; the conjunction *and* is replaced by the disjunction *or*. The double alibi of the paranoid-schizoid ego is that its part-objects are preconsciously perceived (or verbalized) as idealized and persecutory, while unconsciously (or factually) they are perceived inversely, that is, as persecutory and idealized respectively. For example, the sadist would preconsciously split his combined ego and alter into a persecutory <satisfied frustrator> and an idealized <frustrated satisfier>; unconsciously, the situation is reversed: an idealized <satisfied frustrator> and a persecutory <frustrated satisfier>.

The narcissistic subject would then make a simultaneous pact: a *paranoid pact* between his suffering part-ego and its internal persecutory part-object (generally the parent of the same sex), identifying both projectively into the external part-object; and a *manic pact* between his torturing part-ego and the internal idealized part-object (generally the parent of the opposite sex), identifying itself introjectively. The Kleinian defenses equivalent to Freudian repression, projection, denial, and introjection would be splitting, idealization, projective identification, persecution, and introjective identification. The sadistic agent, for example, will split his ego and objects into <satisfied frustrator> and <frustrated satisfier>. Then he will idealize the <frustrated satisfiers> as being "good," and identify introjectively his own torturing ego with the "good" part-object. At the same time, the agent will persecute (disqualify) <satisfied frustrators> as being "bad" and will identify them, projectively, with his external interactors. The masochistic patient will function in exactly the opposite way.

Our clinical observation shows, in fact, that only sadistic agents tend to introjectively identify themselves with the actions and affective states of an idealized object because it generates the minimum of unpleasure with respect to the alternative persecutory part-object projectively identified onto their interactors. But it can also be observed that this paranoid-schizoid dissociation does not solve the conflicting ambivalence but rather acts as a feedback since, underlying it, the two part-objects actually continue to "generate ambivalence." In Dora's case, she identified introjectively her manic, torturing part-ego in the internal idealized part-object (father), who called himself seduced (good) while he was seducing (bad); but, at the same time, she identified projectively her suffering tortured ego and her internal persecutory part-object "mother" who called herself "seductress" (bad) while she was seduced (good).

But, on the other hand, it can be clinically observed that masochistic patients tend to identify themselves introjectively with a disqualified persecuted part-object while identifying their inter-actors projectively with their overqualified idealized part-object. This is seen in Freud's case, illustrative of repetition compulsion, of the child with the reel.

On the basis of this repeated clinical observation, one might conclude that the ego, in its formative task, would not use as its starting point only one dyadic interaction with the real mother (generating ambivalence, since she is good *and* bad), which it would have to split defensively in its fantasy into two part-mothers—good *or* bad—to solve the conflict. (See Figure 7-2.) It would seem, in-stead, that right from birth, its starting point is the triadic interaction with two parents who are simultaneously good *and* bad; that is, with two real objects which are good *and* bad at the same time so that oedipally it denies the good aspect of one and the bad aspect of the other. The father is idealized by the daughter and demonized by the son, and the reverse happens to the mother. Dora, for example, found herself from birth with a father who said he was seduced (<frustrated satisfier>—"good" according to moral norms) but who was actually a seducer (<satisfied frustrator>—"bad" according to the same norms); and with a mother who said she was a seductress (<satisfied frustrator>—"bad") but who really was seduced (a<frus-trated satisfier>—"good"). When the split occurred—the idealization and introjective identification with the father and the demonizing and projective identification onto the mother—Dora's crisis began.

Therefore, Dora did not need to split her ego and object when she was born—since she found herself in fact with two ambivalence-generating objects—but she had to split both her own and her object perceptions. In fact, she was the seductress and her inter-actor was seduced—i.e., "bad" and "good" respectively—while she perceived him as if she were seduced and he was the seducer—i.e., "good" and "bad" respectively. André Green says that "we find the Kleinian construction acceptable if we consider that the return of its opposite could explain the change of what is 'good' into 'bad' or vice versa, and that turning on oneself would be explained by the instinc-tual ebb and flow in the mother-child unit" (1968, p. 5).

> M. Klein understood that what organizes the psychical structure in the relation the child lives in the mother's absence is splitting the good breast-bad breast, relating—and here we go beyond her demarcation lines—to the phantasy of the combined parent partner, precursor or

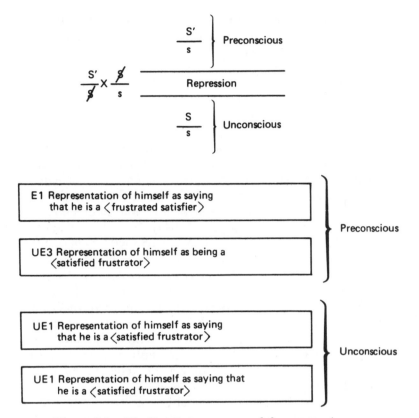

Figure 7-2. The linguistic structure of the unconscious

heir of the phantasy of the primal scene. Primal scene and primary unity are linked since they are the object in the very moment of the split: identification and desire which one alternates in relation to the two parents in the primal scene goes along with the split in the unity of the subject arising from this mediating relationship between this binary object and the ego. (1968, p. 37)

The paranoid-schizoid position would constitute the split of the perception of the ego and the perception of the object in relation to their actions and affective states. On the other hand, from this standpoint the depressive position would no longer be the integration of two part-objects into a whole object but rather the recognition of two whole objects out of the unit of the two part-parental objects in the primal couple. Along with this differentiation and integration of the parents as objects goes the correction of the reversed perception initially ascribed to their representation.

In the depressive position, Dora, the seducing subject, perceives the seduced object as seduced once she has made conscious the fact that the procedure of the superego consists of moral norms that contradict its rules of action. The norms are impossible to carry out, and oblige the subject and his narcissistic interactor to split their perception and behavior into conscious and unconscious in order to be punished as little as possible. We suggest then that the schizo-paranoid trap is not set by means of a dyadic interaction with a single object that the ego splits defensively. We believe that the trap lies in a triadic oedipal interaction of the ego with its parents. That is, the two parents are already split and combined in a "repressed à deux" (Gear and Liendo 1975), when the moral qualification that they make of the "good" and the "bad" is both contradictory in relation to each other, and reversed with reference to what each will factually "punish" and "not punish." Consequently, we suggest that the paradoxical rules of procedure of the "combined parental couple" cause a defensive split of the ego's perception (of its actions and affective states, and those of its object) into conscious and unconscious, rather than a split of the ego itself.

The typical "combined parental couple" would be the sado-masochistic one in which one parent says, for example, that he is a <good frustrated satisfier> suffering a frustration satisfying for the other and that the other is a <bad satisfied frustrator> while he acts as a <bad satisfied frustrator> enjoying a satisfaction frustrating for the other and the other reacts as a <good satisfied frustrator>. They are "combined," mixed, in the infant's perception because one parent keeps saying that the other is doing and feeling what he himself is actually doing and feeling, and vice versa.

Klein (1952) described manic defenses with the aid of her observations of children's games. She conceived these defenses in terms of a contradiction between the positions that the children occupy in the interaction with her, and their perceptions of those positions as expressed in their games. The child does to his toys what Melanie Klein is doing to him, and makes the toys do what he is doing to Melanie Klein. The therapist is to the child as the child is to his toys.

Klein agrees with Freud that repression is a more developed, more intrapsychic mechanism than splitting, but she differs from him in that she does not define repression as a specifically verbal mechanism.

Making both points of view converge, we could say that "visual knowledge" of unconscious thing-representations is achieved, in transference, through the preconscious "verbal" knowledge given by interpretation.

Schizoid or manic defenses against awareness of unpleasurable actions and affective states at the level of the verbal informative code is usually called "verbal acting-out." In verbal acting-out the patient does not use the words to tell the analyst about his problems but to identify them projectively onto the analyst. In his formulations, Bion (1965) says that in verbal acting-out the patient makes use of the secondary or preconscious process and words to "reverse the perspective," to "un-know himself" (−K) and not to "know himself" (K), or, according to our thesis, to "twist" both his eyes and his thought, as well as those of the interactor, in relation to their actions and affective states. In projective identification, perception (what is projected) is symmetrical to and the reverse of what is induced (identified). Dora identified with Freud as seduced while she projected (perceived) a seducer in him.

The Unconscious is Formed Only by Representation of Speech (Jacques Lacan)

Leclaire and Laplanche in their thesis *L'Inconscient* (1966, p. 95) sum up the position of a group of French psychoanalysts who started interdisciplinary work using rhetoric, linguistics, structural anthropology, and some aspects of Freudian metapsychology. Although it is possible that the authors have since changed some of their hypotheses, we shall use this fundamental work of contemporary Freudian psychoanalysis to highlight some similarities and differences between this research work, which was one of our starting points, and the closely related series of hypotheses presented here.

They develop their therapy from the informative code of the patient formed by word- and thing-representations. On the other hand, they do not systematize, semiologically, the affective code proper, nor do they consider it, as did Freud in our opinion, the foundation of the informative code. They take a rhetorical and linguistic approach both to the Freudian topographical model and to the problem of repression and the unconscious; they suggest that the latter is "structured like a language" and that it is a necessary condition for any language.

Their principal conceptual tools are the theoretical terms *signifier* and *signified* from structural linguistics (see chapter 3) and *metaphor* and *metonymy*, which are poetic figures or "tropes."

Metaphor consists for them in transferring the meaning of a given signified from an initial signifier to a surrogate signifier which shares some similarity with the original signifier. In Dora's case, for example, the (verbal informative) signifier, "I say I am a seductress," of the (perceptual informative) signified, "I perceive I am a seductress," is replaced in Dora's consciousness by the metaphorical verbal signifier surrogate, "I say I am seduced by the governess." The governess could be considered a metaphor for Dora, since Dora acted as a seducing "governess" of Mr. K.'s children. Therefore, when Dora reversed her conscious representation of her actions she chose the verbal signifier, "The governess is seducing me," which is used by her as an inverted metaphor to repress her representation, "I am a seductress."

Metonymy, on the other hand, is the transfer of a given signified from its initial signifier to a surrogate signifier temporally or spacially contiguous with the initial signifier. This relation too obtains between Dora and her governess: there is sustained temporal and spatial contact between them. At a higher level of abstraction we might say that every time Dora perceived, "I'm a seductress" (informative signified), she could not hear it and could not tell others and herself, "I'm a seductress" (original informative signifier). It follows she needed to perceive and say of herself and others, "I think someone else [similar or close to me in some way] is a seducer" (metaphorical or metonymical informative signifier) or, what comes to the same thing, to see and describe herself as "seduced by someone who has a metaphorical or metonymical relation with me." The "child with the reel" may place the reel in the position of "gone" insofar as he maintains with it a relation of metaphorical similarity and metonymic contact. Leclaire and Laplanche (1966, p. 115), following a theory of Lacan, identify what Freud calls "the primary process," i.e., the free flow of libidinal energy along the paths of displacement and condensation with a "rhetorical process" in which the signified flows freely from signifier to signifier following the laws of metaphor and metonymy. That is, they equate Freudian "displacement" with "metonymy," and "condensation" with "metaphor." Roman Jakobson rectifies and makes these equations more precise when he says that both "condensation" and "displacement" are metonymies, while Freudian symbolism and identification are metaphors (Jakobson and Todorov 1965). Among psychoanalytic authors, Ella Freeman Sharpe (1937) also equated these mechanisms of the primary process with rhetorical tropes.

This isomorphism between "mechanisms" and "tropes" enables Leclaire and Laplanche (1966, p. 118) to support the "rhetorical" thesis of repression in Freud. In fact, they maintain that metaphor and metonymy "consist in substitution in a relation of signifier to signified (S/s) of the original signifier (S) by a new signifier (S'). The new signifier (S') acts as a signifier of the original signifier (S) which as a result has fallen to the rank of signified. . . . Apparently, something very simple has happened: a change of name; this signified s, which was first considered signifier S, is now connoted as S'. But it is also something which has fallen to the bottom, has been simplified in the algebraic sense of the term: it is the original signifier." But, the authors continue, "What has the original (S) signifier become? It has fallen to the rank of signified, but at the same time it is a latent signifier," so that, in our opinion we prefer to formulate this process as shown in Figure 7-2.

Let us take, for example, the case of the sadist: he will perceive himself consciously as a <good frustrated satisfier> while he actually behaves as a <bad satisfied frustrator>. A Lacanian theoretical interpretation of this clinical fact will be, consequently, that the sadist represses his (speech) representation of himself as <saying that he is a bad satisfied frustrator> (original signifier S) by using the (speech) representation of himself as <saying that he is a good frustrated satisfier> (new signifier S'). The original signifier S representation of himself as <saying that he is a bad satisfied frustrator> has fallen to the bottom and is now functioning as signifier and signified in the unconscious. On the other hand, the new signifier S' representation of himself as <saying that he is a good

frustrated satisfier> united with the original signified S representation of himself as <being a bad satisfied frustrator> are functioning in the preconscious.

"In our formula we see nothing more than the schema proper of repression, which on another level retains what had been apparently simplified in the preconscious report" (Leclaire and Laplanche 1966, p. 119). "This schema of repression is originally that of the metaphor in all its originality, poetic conscious metaphor, so that it seems very suitable to symbolize repression" (p. 120). If we now try to find an example of this theory in Dora's case, we could say she "represses" the signifier "calling herself a seductress" (S) because she rejects the signified (s) "seeing herself as a seductress," and accepts in its place "calling herself seduced by her governess."

That is, what remains in the unconscious, according to Leclaire and Laplanche, is the original informative verbal signifier "calling herself a seductress," while in the preconscious the surrogate informal verbal signifier "saying she is seduced by the governess" would remain together with the perceptual informative signified "seeing herself as a seductress."

With respect to repression proper, they (like Freud 1915b) equate the "preconscious withdrawal of the cathexis" from the original verbal signifier (S) or repressed representative with the "overcathexis" of the metaphorical surrogate verbal signifier (S') or repressing representative, which thus becomes the "countercathexis" of the original verbal signifier (S). For example, the preconscious cathexis of the original verbal signifier (S) "calling herself a seductress" is withdrawn and it is going to overcathect the surrogate verbal signifier (S') "saying she is seduced by her governess," which then acts as a "countercathexis" to "calling herself a seductress." The verbal signifier, "calling herself a seductress" remains repressed in Dora's consciousness because of this feedback mechanism between repressed and repressing verbal signifiers which Leclaire and Laplanche use to explain repression proper.

Finally, Leclaire and Laplanche (p. 120) wonder how it is possible that, according to their formula, the unconscious chain should be formed by two signifiers (S/S). They recall that according to Freud (1915b), thing-representations are traits of the unconscious; they form the language of dreams in which we know that topographical regression requires expression in a language of images. Word-representations, words taken in the most material sense of an

acoustic trace, belong to the preconscious. Then Leclaire and Laplanche add, somewhat contradictorily, that "our schema shows this
change in a remarkable way: at the level of preconscious language,
the difference between signifier (words) and the signified (images)
exists. At the level of unconscious language there are only images
which function simultaneously and indivisibly as signifiers and signified. In a certain sense, it may be said that the unconscious chain is
pure non-sense, or better, open to all senses." (p. 120) We think it
relevant to determine rigorously if the thing-representations are
signifiers or signifieds. On the one hand, Leclaire and Laplanche say
that they are signifieds. ("A signified," says Roland Barthes [1968,
p. 7], "is not a thing but a psychical representation of a thing.") In
that case they would not form part of the unconscious, which,
according to these authors, is constituted only of signifiers (i.e.,
acoustic images of words). Freud (1915b), on the other hand, says
that in the unconscious there are only thing-representations or, in our
terms, perceptual informative signifieds or mnemic traces.

Since "to perceive herself seduced" also contains something of
the "motor image," we assume that the informative factual signified
would be a sort of "motor mnemic image." Motor images, says
Freud, "are not associated with word-presentations, but on the
contrary, they themselves serve in part the purpose of this association" (1895, p. 387). They would be classes of movement-repre-
sentations" which induce the act by movement (Green 1975, p. 154).

We deduce that what remains in the unconscious are feared
thing-representations (mnemic images) and in the preconscious,
desired thing-representations plus their verbal signifiers or word-
representations. That is, in the case of Dora what remains unconscious is the perceptual informative signified, or thing-representations, of her being a seductress. What remains in the preconscious is
the perceptual informative signified, or thing-representation, of her
being seduced as well as the verbal informative signifier whereby
she says that she is a seduced.

In brief, according to Leclaire and Laplanche (1966), repression consists in the metonymic or metaphorical replacement of a
given verbal informative signifier or word-representation, to disguise its relation with the perceptual signified or thing-representation of a signifier whose emergence into consciousness would be
unpleasurable for the ego. This verbal informative signifier is repressed and placed in the unconscious (1) by a withdrawal of its

preconscious cathexis to a countercathexis of the verbal signifier surrogate which has been thus surcharged and (2) by the attraction of the paternal metaphorical signifier or phallus in the unconscious, resulting from the original repression.

There are at least three important differences between this Lacanian model and our model of psychic bipolarity. First, we agree with Freud that the unconscious is formed only of thing-representations and not of word-representations: that is, it is formed of the unconscious presentations of actions and affective states. (This does not mean, of course, that these thing-representations are not organized as a semiotic code.) Second, we think that the speech representations corresponding to the unconscious representations of actions and affective states are not repressed, for no other reason than that they do not exist prior to the interpretations of the analyst. Third, we think that the unconscious is formed, semiotically speaking, by "signifieds" (representations of actions and affective states) and not by "signifiers" (representations of the speech): that the signifiers are precisely what is lacking in the unconscious and what is introduced with the words of the analyst. These affective signifieds are absent from the Lacanian model although they are the cornerstone of Freudian metapsychology.

The Core of the Unconscious is Formed by Representations of Actions and Affects (André Green)

André Green (1962), at the colloquium of Bonneval in 1960, argued that "Leclaire and Laplanche's theory of repression and representation considers the representative of the drive only from a topographic point of view, and ignores its economic connotation" (see 1962, p. 145). But Freud himself (1915b) explained that when we describe a case of repression we must consider what happens both to the representation and to the instinctual energy attached to it. According to Green, the authors never mention this aspect of repression in their work, despite the fact that Freud insists that the vicissitude of the cathexis of affects of the representation is by far more important—in the case of repression—than that of the representation.

Green's insistence on the inclusion of the economic aspect of repression coincides with our hypothesis that the affective code, in which the "signifiers" are the representations of speech and actions, and the "signifieds" are the pleasant and unpleasant affective states, is the basis of the informative code consisting of word- and thing-representations, that is, the speech- and action-representations studied by Leclaire and Laplanche. We assume that affects constitute, in relation to the world of representations (signifiers) in general, the signified universe, since this is the universe that interests the ego as such.

We think that Green also refers to this affective coding that precedes the informative coding when he asks whether the turning on oneself and the transformation into the opposite—which come before repression and belong to the narcissistic organization of the ego—do not already constitute a language. Is there not a language of defense mechanisms that subtends the symbolization that constitutes the unconscious according to Leclaire and Laplanche? In this language the difference between signifier and signified, which belongs to the preconscious, would not yet arise (see Green 1962, p. 146). This "prior language" has an ambiguous affective signified (anxiety)—the result of the pragmatically paradoxical rules of procedure of the superego—which, in its turn, causes the ambiguity of its representative signifier (mnemic traces). Green looks toward our thesis of the affective code and of the paradox to which the signifier universe is subjected when he says that "the ambiguity of this language of defensive formations is caused by the fact that it reaches the signifier only through anxiety, i.e., what appears as a separation and weakening of the signifier. Although separated from it, anxiety makes the implicit presence of the signifier necessary, giving rise to the threat of its deterioration. In this way, anxiety marks the signifiers and the anxiety traverses the defense rather than being stopped by it" (1962, p. 152). We think that anxiety "marks" the signifier universe of mnemic traces in the sense that it constitutes the signified universe which enables the ego to arrange the signifier universe into classes and so form an affective code which will allow it to organize itself and place itself "this side of the pleasure principle."

Green also foresees the relation between the Freudian "re-polarities" and the Kleinian manic defenses that we have developed in our model: "the mechanisms of introjection and projection must be put in the same place as the change into the opposite and the turn against oneself, according to the studies in depth contributed by M. Klein and her team" (1962, p. 142).

Third, Green wonders what the meaning is, linguistically speaking, of "the fact of the fall of a first signifier (S) to the rank of signified (s) and a second signifier (S') occupying the place of the original signifier. What would one think of the disappearance of the whole later development of the original signifiers?" (1962, p. 144). We assume that the original signifier (S), in Dora's case "calling herself a seductress," does not fall to the rank of the signified (s) but rather that it is replaced by a second signifier (S'), "saying she is seduced by the governess," which thus has a double signified (s and s'): a first signified (s') which is conventional and manifest ("seeing herself as seduced") which together with the surrogate signifier (S') ("saying she is seduced by the governess") form a preconscious layer and a second signified (s), which is reversed and latent (seeing herself as a seductress") which constitutes the unconscious layer. Dora does not call or see herself as a seductress (Figure 7-3).

Therefore, what is repressed in the unconscious is the per-ceptual informative signified, that is, the correct representation of actions, or unpleasurable thing-representation which constitutes the FMT, which in Dora's case was <seeing herself as a seductress>. This is the destination we suppose that the signified (s) of the original signifier (S) has. In repression, the informative sign would then be formed by a manifest and preconscious pleasurable in-formative verbal signifier or word-representation (representation of inverted speech) with a pleasurable perceptual informative signified or thing-representation (inverted representation of actions) plus an unpleasurable informative signified (correct representation of ac-tions) which would be latent, unconscious, repressed, and reversed in relation to the former. But not only the thing-representation (the correct representation of actions) repressed by the reversal of its word-representation (and maybe some representation of actions mutilated by the monothematic narcissistic reiteration of certain constellations of word-representations) remain in the unconscious: there is still the quota of unpleasurable (or annihilating) affect that is

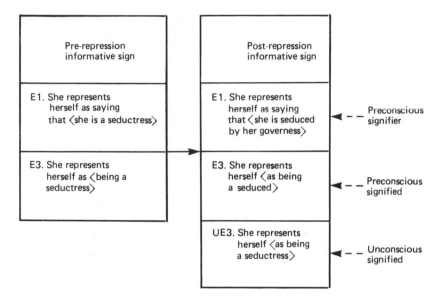

Figure 7-3. The nonlinguistic structure of the unconscious

suppressed by means of repression (or mutilation). Green says that *"the heart of the unconscious is the compound formed by the thing-representation and its quota of affect"* (1975, p. 153). The unconscious, semiologically, contains the informative factual signifieds repressed by the reversal of their correspondant informative verbal signifiers (and maybe the factual signifieds mutilated by the repetition of certain verbal signifiers) as well as the unpleasurable (or annihilating) affective messages suppressed by repression (and mutilation).

With reference to the function of the informative signifier that we attribute to word-representations, and the informative signified we attribute to thing-representations, Green sees defensive change between the manifest and the latent contents: the reversal of the informative verbal signifier and its respective factual signified. There would then be metaphorical or metonymic reversal according to the predominant rhetorical style the narcissistic ego uses to reverse its verbal signal in relation to its factual messages.

The theoretical hypotheses of the theory of psychic bipolarity suggest, in brief, that the relation between the preconscious signifier (representation of inverted speech) and the unconscious signified (correct representation of actions and affective states) is symmetrically reversed and may be equated metaphorically with what occurs "between one side and the other of a sheet of paper"—the rhetorical figure used by Ferdinand de Saussure to represent the relation existing between the signifier and the signified of the linguistic sign.

Conclusion

The theme that runs through each of the discussions in this chapter is the attempt to identify the specific mechanisms that give rise to the topographic layering of information in the psychic structure and at the same time to the splitting of the ego. In Freud this initially turned on the concept of repression; then, as his theory became more sophisticated, it came to a focus with the concept of the compulsion to repeat.

The splitting of the ego in the compulsion to repeat takes one of two directions: sadistic or masochistic. Let us say that in the first instance the child B is treated X by the significant other A: A X B. In the case of sadistic repetition the child B finds another C whom he treats X: B X C. In masochistic repetition the child B finds another C to once more treat him X: C X B. The difference between the two positions is how the child's omnipotence is disposed. The sadistic child uses omnipotence by identifying with his original other and actively directing the same treatment at another, thereby repressing his original dependent and impotent position. The masochistic child achieves this repression by actively seeking a repetition of his passive position in relation to the original other.

Freud identified primarily the sadistic form of repetition, though he realized that repetition somehow explained masochism as well. In our theory we have of course shown the importance of distinguishing the sadistic and masochistic directions of the ego at the empirical level as well as at the level of metapsychology. The difficulty of making this distinction—already apparent in Freud's partially successful efforts—stems from the obscurity in which the actions of the subject is hidden by his consistent inversion of their direction in speech. The result is, as we have shown, that the sadist talks about himself as if he were a masochist, and the masochist as if he were a sadist. The irony is that at the deepest unconscious level, as Freud showed, their conflicting structures are identical.

Unfortunately, there is a certain contradiction in Melanie Klein's elaboration of this analysis in Freud. On the one hand, she preserves the dyadic basis of the structure and develops an increasingly subtle model of the process of repetition and defense. But we disagree with her insistence that the conflict is ultimately between Thanatos and the ego, which in any case does not fit in with her dyadic model. It can be said, for instance, that in Klein's theory of the paranoid-schizoid position, the persecutory transference of the sadistic subject is matched by the idealizing transference of his masochistic object while, unconsciously, the opposite is the case for both of them. Thinking in this way is what Bion goes on to call the reversal of perspective, typical of what he calls the −K (anti-knowledge) attitude.

We have followed Lacan's concept of the decentering of the ego or, better still, of consciousness and the ego, whereby consciousness becomes fascinated with the image of the ego reflected by the other and therefore loses sight of what the ego is really about. However, we disagree with Lacan's attempt to relate this decentering to the distinction between signifier and signified insofar as he ignores the difference between verbal and nonverbal representations. His signifieds remain verbal and therefore do not refer to the unconscious, which for Freud is nonverbal. Where Lacan argues that the unconscious is structured like a verbal language, we argue that it is structured as a code consisting of representations of actions and affects.

In Freud's concept of the topography, the problem is the dissociation between representation at the conscious level and the unrepresented affects at the unconscious level that become displaced onto inappropriate representations. The analyst's task is to interpret the unconscious affects in order to connect them up with their appropriate conscious representations. But if the unconscious is conceived only in terms of verbal signifieds, this topography loses its dynamic significance, and psychoanalysis becomes indistinguishable from philosophy. That is why we agree with André Green when he argues that the core of the unconscious is formed by representations of actions and affects.

REFERENCES

Barthes, R. (1968). Eléments de sémiologie. *Communications* 4, pp. 5–17.

Bateson, G., and Ruesch, J. (1945). *Communication: The Social Matrix of Psychiatry*. New York: Norton.

Bion, W. R., (1962). *Learning from Experience*. New York: Basic Books.

—— (1965). *Elements of Psycho-Analysis*. London: Heinemann.

Bourdieu, P. (1966). "Condition de classe et position de classe," *Archives Européenes de Sociologie* 7.

Breuer, J., and Freud, S. (1893–1895). Studies on hysteria. *Standard Edition, 2*.

Fairbairn, (1962). *Psychoanalytic Studies of the Personality*. London: Tavistock.

Freud, S. (1895). Project for a scientific psychology. *Standard Edition* 1:281–397.

—— (1905). Fragments of an analysis of a case of hysteria. *Standard Edition* 7:7–122.

—— (1912). Recommendations to physicians practising psycho-analysis. *Standard Edition* 12:109–120.

—— (1915a). Instincts and their vicissitudes. *Standard Edition* 14:109–140.

—— (1915b). The unconscious. *Standard Edition* 14:159–215.

—— (1915c). Repression. *Standard Edition* 14:143–158.

—— (1920). Beyond the pleasure principle. *Standard Edition* 18:7–64.

—— (1923). The ego and the id. *Standard Edition* 19:3–66.

—— (1927). Fetishism. *Standard Edition* 21:149–157.

—— (1933). New introductory lectures on psycho-analysis. *Standard Edition* 22:3–182.

—— (1938). Splitting of the ego in the process of defense. *Standard Edition* 23:271–278.

Gear, M. C., and Liendo, E. C. (1975). *Sémiologie psychanalytique*. Paris: Minuit.

—— (1979). *Action psychanalytique*. Paris: Minuit.

Green, A. (1962). L'Inconscient freudien et la psychanalyse française contemporaine. *Les Temps Modernes* 195.

—— (1968). Sur la mère phallique. *Revue Française de Psychanalyse* 23.

—— (1975). *Le discours vivant*. Paris: P.U.F.

Isaacs, S. (1952). The nature and function of phantasy. *Developments in Psycho-Analysis*. London: Hogarth Press.

Jakobson, R., and Todorov, T., eds. (1965). *Théorie de la littérature: Textes des formalistes russes*. Paris: Editions du Seuil.

Klein, M. (1950). *Contributions Psycho-Analysis*, 1821–1945. London: Hogarth Press.

—— (1952). The origins of transference. *International Journal of Psycho-Analysis* 33:433–438.

Klein, M., Heimann, P., Isaacs, S., and Riviere, J., eds. (1952). *Developments in Psycho-Analysis* London: Hogarth Press.

Lacan, J. (1966). *Ecrits*. Paris: Editions du Seuil.

Laplanche, J., and Pontalis, J. B., (1973). *The Language of Psycho-Analysis*. London: Hogarth Press.

Leclaire, S., and Laplanche, J. (1966). L'Inconscient, une étude psychanalytique. *L'Inconscient* (Paris: Desclee de Brouwer).

Lévi-Strauss, C. (1963). *Structural Anthropology*. New York: Basic Books.

Segal, H. (1964). *Introduction to the Work of Melanie Klein*. New York: Basic Books.

Sharpe, E. (1937). *Dream Analysis*. London: Hogarth Press.

8

The Sadomasochistic Mutilation of the Psychic Space: The Transconcious

In chapter 6 we presented a first metapsychological level of explanation of the empirical (clinical) hypothesis of the inversion of actions and affective states in speech. We used the theoretical hypothesis of inversion of conscious intrapsychic representations, unconscious defense mechanisms, and a contradictory superego.

In this chapter we will explain these theoretical hypotheses as well as the hypothesis of mutilation of speech, actions, affective states, and intrapsychic representations. We will show why narcissism and sadomasochism are key concepts in explaining human behavior and why they result, empirically, in the inversion of speech and representations, in the mutilation of speech, actions, affective states and representations, and the induction of "mirroring" behavior and thought in interactors with narcissistic subjects—not only why Narcissus had a mutilated and inverted speech and perception but also why he induced the nymph Echo to think and perceive in a mutilated, inverted way which mirrored him. In doing this we will introduce the theoretical hypotheses of the second metapsychological level of the theory of psychic bipolarity.

269

Chapter Outline

1. We will synthesize the empirical hypotheses and the corresponding theoretical explanation set out in chapter 6.

2. We will analyze the psychoanalytic interpretation and use of sadomasochism and its importance in organizing the structure of the psychic apparatus.

3. We will revise the pleasure and reality principles of psychic functioning.

4. We will analyze the connections between these principles and the competitive conception of human relations that Freud expressed in his hypothesis concerning the oedipus complex and in his thesis concerning pleasure in *Civilization and its Discontents* (Freud 1930).

5. We will relate this competitive conception of pleasure to a first mutilation of the psychic "space."

6. We will relate this cognitive and affective mutilation to the sociological fact that, even if competition in society is stimulated and punished simultaneously, it is the only way in which the psychic apparatus learns how to obtain pleasure.

7. We will try to explain a second type of mutilation: the stereotyped way in which the psychic apparatus obtains or gives competitive pleasure. We relate this second degree of mutilation to the sociological fact of a rigid and stereotyped division of work.

8. We will develop the hypothesis that this double cognitive and affective mutilation is perpetuated and reinforced by the avoidance of cognitive dissonance and by social pressures.

Sadomasochism in Psychoanalysis

We will now develop the hypothesis that sadomasochism occupies the center of Freud's metapsychological conception because it makes for a primary organization of the psychic apparatus. To substantiate this hypothesis we will first describe the psychoanalytic interpretation and use of sadomasochism.

According to Laplanche and Pontalis (1973), "Sadism and masochism occupy a special position among the perversions, since the contrast between activity and passivity which lies behind them is among the universal characteristics of sexual life." Originally used in sexology in a more restricted way, the term sadomasochism was adopted and transformed by psychoanalysis. In the first place it stressed the isomorphism and complementarity between the two perversions: the interpersonal conflict of domination and submission between sadists and masochists. Since Freud, it also denotes a pair of opposites that is as fundamental to the evolution of instinctual life as it is to its manifestations (Freud 1924).

Freud also discovered the intrapsychic function of the sado-masochistic opposition, particularly its role in the dialectic between the sadistic superego and the masochistic ego, as well as the inter-changeability of the two postures in fantasy and ultimately in intra-subjective conflict. Pursuing this line of thought, Lagache (1960) laid special stress upon the notion of sadomasochism, making it the critical factor in interpersonal relationships. Psychical conflict—and its essential form, oedipal conflict—can be understood as a conflict of demands: the position of one who demands could become either the persecuted or the persecutor because once demand is mediated by the intervention of authority, the outcome is usually a sadomaso-chistic relationship.

When we use the term *masochism* we imply the three forms of masochism described by Freud—erotogenic, feminine, and moral—as three different versions of the same phenomenon of submission and self-punishment (Freud 1924). In sadism, to follow Freud's ideas, the death drive succeeds in being expelled onto an external object, as a destructive drive. Primary masochism occurs before this expelling, and secondary masochism occurs after it, when sadism turns the drive against the subject himself.

In his *Three Essays on the Theory of Sexuality*, Freud (1905) treats sadism and masochism as two faces of a single perversion whose active and passive forms are to be found in variable propor-tions in the same individual: "A sadist is always at the same time a masochist, although the active or the passive aspect of the perversion may be more strongly developed in him and may represent his predominant sexual activity" (p. 159).

Freud underscores the role of fantasized identification with the other person in these two successive reversals: in masochism, "the passive ego (places) itself back in phantasy in its first role, which has now in fact been taken over by the extraneous subject." Similarly, in sadism, "while these pains are being inflicted on other people, they are enjoyed masochistically by the subject through his identification of himself with the suffering object."

In any case, it can be said that both the sadist and the masochist are "masochists" in the broad sense; they are playing a ruinous competitive game rather than a healthy cooperative one. The drive to master is directed from the outset toward outside objects and constitutes the sole factor present in the primal cruelty of the child. Freud (1905) speaks of it for the first time in the *Three Essays*: the origin of infantile cruelty is sought in a drive to master whose original aim is not to make the other person suffer—rather, it simply fails to take the other person into account. In "The Disposition to Obsessional Neurosis" (Freud 1913) the need for mastery is related to the anal-sadistic stage. In the 1915 edition of *Three Essays* Freud posits the muscular apparatus as the basis of the drive to master.

In "Instincts and their Vicissitudes" (1915b), where the first of Freud's theses regarding sadomasochism is clearly worked out, the primary aim of sadism is defined as the degradation of the object and its subjugation by violence. In *Beyond the Pleasure Principle* (1920) the genesis of sadism is now described as a diversion of the death instinct, originally aimed at the destruction of the subject himself, onto the object. It then enters the service of the sexual function. As to the aim of masochism and sadism—treated henceforward as embodiments of the death drive—the accent no longer falls on mastery, but on destruction.

Sadomasochism and Bound Energy

The opposition between sadism and masochism is at the center of the metapsychological theory because it is intrinsic to the explanation of how the binding of the drive creates the passage from "free energy" to "bound energy" and from primary to secondary process within the psychic apparatus; that is, from the mere disorganized discharge of excitation into organized ways of acting upon psychic and external reality, based on associative links.

In sadism, according to Freud (1920), the death drive (*Tödestrieb*) is directed at an external object as a destructive drive. Primary masochism occurs before this outer direction of the drive, and secondary masochism after it, when sadism turns around against the subject's self.

The death drive turns the destructive tendency, as revealed in sadomasochism, into an irreducible datum, and furthermore it is the chosen expression of the most fundamental principle of psychic functioning. Finally, insofar as it is "the essence of the instinctual," it binds every wish, whether aggressive or sexual, to the wish for death.

In this sense, one can look upon the death-drive thesis as a reaffirmation of what Freud had always felt to be the very essence of the unconscious in its indestructible and unrealistic aspect. This reassertion of the most radical part of the unconscious desire can be correlated with a change in the ultimate function that Freud assigns to sexuality, under the name of Eros, which is no longer defined as a disruptive force, as an eminently perturbatory factor, but rather as a principle of cohesion. Within this evolutionary conception, Eros is the progressive force and Thanatos the regressive one.

But in the structural approach, we may say that both the sadist's and the masochist's fantasies are the result of the predominant style—either victim's or victimizer's—in which the binding structure is defined. It is then plausible that the structural model of the psychic apparatus is organized along sadomasochistic possibilities, and that the predominance of one of the two styles of satisfying desires is a result of the functioning of the psychic apparatus in its interaction with "sadist-makers" (masochists) or "masochist-makers" (sadists).

We do not believe that the child is always passively aggressed, so that he actively identifies with the aggressor and finally internalizes this relationship, with ego the aggressed and superego the aggressor. We believe that sadist and masochist follow different pathways. The sadist, for example, was "passively" pushed into the position of the aggressor as a small child by a masochistic parent—generally of the same sex—who "actively" put himself in the position of the aggressed. Therefore his "ego" (as master ego) will usually be the aggressor and his "alter" (as servant alter) will usually be the aggressed. Once this sadomasochistic relationship has been internalized, the child will actively tend to behave as a sadistic aggressor pushing others into the position of masochistic victims of aggression.

In the case of the masochist, we find the complementary situation: the masochist will be passively pushed into the position of the aggressed by a sadistic parent who actively maintains the position of aggressor.

At the basis of this structural opposition (between sadism and masochism) is the fact that organization, or "bound energy," appears at the moment when the opposition arises between being passively attacked by reality and attacking reality actively.

We therefore preserve the notion of a sadistic fantasy as a primary structure, but emphasize—in accordance with Spitz's conclusions (1957)—that the opposition between "yes" and "no" equals, for the unconscious, the opposition between accepting the pain and aggression from an external reality, and reacting against it by way of identification with the aggressor. Consequently, the first "no" is the first clear structuring opposition, or the first organized binding that will allow the passage to secondary process.

The binding of energy that the adoption of the sadomasochistic opposition allows falls within the range of a compulsion to repeat in either an active (sadistic) or passive (masochistic) position. In Melanie Klein's theory these positions fall within her description of the paranoid-schizoid position. The passage to a more reality-oriented identity and alterity arises when the child can recognize others and recognize that he is being recognized by them. This opens the possibility of mutually gratifying relationships.

If these conclusions are true, we can analyze the basic meaning of the sadistic reaction without attempting an explanation on exclusively energic lines, otherwise associated with the notion of a death drive that is not falsifiable. To describe an impulse as the result of different levels of organization of "bound energy" does not require any telos: we do not know whether the impulse is discharged in order to live or in order to die. What we do know is that there are complex bindings associated with what are called "ego-functions," including the reality principle most notably, and that there are some other types of binding, *close to the laws governing unconscious desire and the organization of fantasy*, in which what is processed is a more elementary opposition between the pleasant position of inflicting pain actively from an identification with the aggressor, and the unpleasant position of suffering that pain passively.

This does not constitute a complex apprehension of every element of inner and outer reality, but a simple binary opposition between "yes" and "no," passivity and activity, helplessness and mastery.

The importance of this opposition in the organization of fantasy—following Freud, Melanie Klein, Spitz, Bion, and Winnicott, among others—is that it appears that the sadistic discharge is simultaneously associated both with destructive oral and anal fantasies and with a reaction against the feeling of total helplessness, that is, the automatic anxiety that appears in traumatic situations that both infants and adults experience when they cannot react with a mature, elaborated secondary process. (See *Inhibition, Symptoms and Anxiety* Freud 1926, p. 138.)

Méconnaissance versus Recognition

According to Lacan's concept of *méconnaissance* (1966), the subject experiences a need for representation which Lacan first explained in terms of the "mirror stage." If, instead of the mirror, one thinks of the parents as providing the source for the subject's representations through their interaction with him, then one could say that the underlying conditions for the sadomasochistic structure of narcissism are found in the need for representation that constitutes narcissism itself. The basis for the development of the representations in the psychic apparatus is this mutilation of the subject which impels him to define himself as an ego in relation to the paradigm of the parental couple.

Lacan tends to understand *méconnaissance* at the cognitive level, implying that it is a kind of childish misunderstanding of the situation of the subject. At a deeper level *méconnaissance* has to do with the attempt to rescue the infant's fantasy of omnipotence when it receives its first challenge in the experience of the distinction between self and other or between the subject and his reflection in a mirror. In *méconnaissance* the other is viewed as a mirror of the subject, thereby becoming the model for the ego and at the same time cancelling the distinction between self and other in fantasy.

In this sense the mirror stage is a stage in the transformation of the fantasy of omnipotence. It is a primitive form of identification (the ideal ego) in which the child can indulge in the fantasy of being like a significant other without having to make the effort really to be like him, which would constitute the more realistic mode of identification, when the distinction between self and other has been accepted, that is, when the "purified pleasure ego" is replaced by the "reality ego" that strives to fulfill the "ego ideal."

The consequence of the development of the sadomasochistic paradigm of narcissism is not only the mutilation of the subject but also of his capacity to perceive and relate to reality outside of the limited possibilities defined by his narcissistic acting-out. In other words, the *méconnaissance* is not only of the subject (as Lacan has indicated) but also of reality.

The pleasure ego organizes the libido in relation to the polarities of pleasure and unpleasure by utilizing the distinction between inside and outside. By claiming to be the source of all pleasure (by means of introjecting all of its sources) it loves itself as if it were ideal (the ideal ego). But it attributes all unpleasure to the outside (by means of projection), which it hates as if it were always harmful.

The reality ego organizes the self-preservative drive in relation to the polarity of life and death. By contrast with the pleasure ego, it has to relate to a more powerful object in reality to fulfill its purpose: the child is simply not in a position to provide for its own survival. The self-preservation drive therefore propels the ego into the field of reality, where it has to negotiate its survival in relation to its significant others, who are authorized for that purpose by society. It is through their agency that the alignment of the field of reality is determined for the ego.

There are two fundamental modes by which authority can be exercised in relation to the child. Under "normal" circumstances, authority defines expectations and proceeds to reward the child for compliance, or to punish it for rebellion. Beyond insisting on these rules, authority recognizes the child's separate identity. By learning to observe these rules, and by learning to assert its autonomous sphere of identity, the dependent ego is gradually transformed into a partner who cooperates with the significant other and comes to accept a relationship of equality with him or her. At that point the ego has integrated the expectations of its culture mediated by the authority of the significant others, and has formed its own ideal. Thus, the authoritarian relationship yields to the cooperation of those who observe the standards of their culture on an equal footing, and maintain their independent spheres of value and activity.

The other fundamental mode of exercising authority in relation to the child prevents any such resolution of the authoritarian relationship from coming about, and leads to its perpetuation in the form of an asymmetrical relationship of dominance and submission, or of submission and domination, both intrapsychically and in object relations. Here the significant other who is responsible for exercising authority on behalf of the culture either uses this position to assert omnipotent control over the child, or else surrenders it to the child. In either case the bearer of authority fails to spell out his expectations and also fails to set up a system of consistent rewards and punishments derived from them. The condition for this is the refusal to recognize the child in its own right. The other is simply expected to submit in order to avoid punishment; otherwise he is punished for not submitting. Authority therefore remains unmediated by the values of the culture it is supposed to transmit and is simply exercised for its own sake. The ego then either takes up the position of the omnipotent authority in relation to an impotent, submissive other, or it takes up the position of the impotent submissive other in relation to an omnipotent authority. Since this structure does not permit of resolution, it is simply perpetuated according to the principle of the compulsion to repeat.

In the case of "normal" formation, the pleasure-ego is transformed by the influence of the reality-ego and integrated into what Freud called the *Gesamtich*, or whole ego, that characteristically seeks pleasure within the conditions prescribed by reality, without, however, seeking to dominate others or to have them submit to itself. And the same would hold true of its standing in relation to the norms of a culture. While they are freely observed they are not allowed to inhibit the ego's creativity or spontaneity. In the case of neurotic formation, however, the rational pursuit of pleasure becomes impossible because of the failure of the one in authority to make it a part of the expectations set before the child. Pleasure remains the privilege of whoever exercises authority, while the other has to submit to this condition (it is really a sacrifice) in order to avoid punishment, that is, simply in order to survive.

If authority is exercised omnipotently by the significant other, then we find a structure consisting of master alter and servant ego; if on the other hand the significant other yields omnipotent authority to the child, we find one consisting of master ego and servant alter. The former (master alter and servant ego) constitutes the intrapsychic structure of the masochist, compulsively repeated in his object relations of submitting and allowing himself to be exploited, just as the latter (servant alter and master ego) constitutes the intra-psychic structure of the sadist, compulsively repeated in his object relations of domination and exploitation. Here, it is clear, cooperation is replaced by exploitation and equality by domination or submission.

Where domination and exploitation, or their opposite, are not openly approved in a culture, the positions of the sadist and that of the masochist are disguised behind the system of expectations nor-mally imposed by authority. Thus, the sadist always claims to be the one who complies with these expectations and deserves his reward, while accusing the masochist of being a rebel who deserves to be punished. In complementary fashion, the masochist takes upon him-self the role of a rebel who deserves to be punished, while attributing to the sadist a compliance that entitles him to reward. Consequently, the one who dominates in order to exploit others appears to deserve reward for his compliance to the standards of the culture, while the one who submits in order to be exploited appears to be a rebel who deserves to be punished. Ironically, therefore, the sadist is in a position to indulge himself according to the organization of the pleasure-ego and at the same time claim the rewards of reality as if he had integrated the normal expectations of his culture, which he has not done. The masochist loses on both counts (see Figure 8-1).

Just as it is impossible for someone to recognize the unconscious mutilation of himself on which the structure of his ego and alter rest, so too it is impossible for him to recognize the extent to which his repetitive interactions with others rest upon an unconscious failure to take other possibilities in reality into account. In other words, the narcissistic paradigm is set between two reflecting mirrors that define the range of cognition and affect by constantly inverting and reflecting it in a self-enclosed system impenetrable from the point of view of the person located in it. (From the point of view of psychoa-nalysis, it becomes penetrable with the aid of analytic interpretations.)

We are in full agreement with the fundamental importance of Lacan's concept of *méconnaissance*. But it is important to recognize that *méconnaissance* operates not only at a cognitive level—even if its mirroring effect predisposes one to overlook its economic dimen-sion. It is important also to realize that there is a double system of mirrors in operation: the one preventing the ego from recognizing the subject, and the other pushing it to universalize the alter into a paradigm of reality. Actually, the effect is not as simple because we

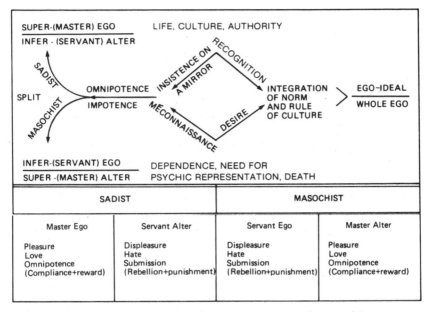

Figure 8-1.   Impotence and omnipotence in sadomasochism

have to include the phenomenon of inversion in our explanation. That is, the subject's image of the ego is located in the mirror that the alter holds up to him, while his image of the alter is located in the mirror that he unconsciously holds up to the alter.

Here again Lacan has provided a valuable analogy for the solipsism of the ego in the Moebius strip which he uses to represent the self-enclosed and constantly repeated chain of signifiers. In our view, however, the strip extends between the two psychic poles of ego and alter and signifies the impossibility of defining either without the other; it rests on the mutilation of both subject and object.

The Pleasure Principle as a Principle of Competitive Conflict

Since the superego regulates a human game according to a conflictive, competitive law and normative code of satisfied frustrator master-winners and frustrated satisfier servant-losers, it must assume that the way of obtaining pleasure is a conflictive and competitive one.

Freud (1915) himself says that the way to obtain pleasure is conflictive when he states that pleasure on one level of the psychic functioning implies unpleasure on another. For instance, pleasure on a hedonistic level implies unpleasure on an ethical level and vice versa—not only because the pleasure has been obtained competitively but also because winning the competition is ethically bad and losing it is hedonistically bad, and because the competition for pleasure is ruinous, not "healthy." Thus, the contradiction between hedonistic pleasure and ethical pleasure described by Freud is explained by the fact that the hedonistic pleasure for oneself implies ethical unpleasure for oneself because it implies hedonistic unpleasure for others.

Freud (1905, p. 226) also states that the oedipus complex is a universal competitive situation that every human being must face sooner or later: the conflict is that to obtain pleasure with the parent of the opposite sex implies not only the unpleasure but the death of the parent of the same sex.

If we look carefully at the structure of the oedipal triangle we can discover that it is, in fact, constituted by two rivals of the same sex competing for a source of pleasure that, in this case, happens to be the parent of opposite sex. The pleasure of Oedipus implies control of the source of pleasure, of the relations of production of pleasure, and consequently the unpleasure of Laius, and vice versa. Oedipus feels guilt because incest implies patricide.

Oedipus appears as the mirror-image of Laius because Laius represents himself consciously as the murderer of Oedipus while in fact he was unconsciously murdered by him. Oedipus, who was supposedly murdered by his father is, unconsciously, his murderer. Because Oedipus is the mirror-image of Laius, the three poles of the oedipal triangle can be finally reduced to a single pole: Laius competing with his own inverted mirror-image for a source of pleasure.

In other words, Laius conceived of himself consciously as a <satisfied frustrator> while he was unconsciously a <frustrated satisfier> and Oedipus was seen by Laius as a <frustrated satisfier> while in fact he was a <satisfied frustrator>.

From another perspective, Laius can be seen as a masochistic patient who used Oedipus as a sadistic agent to kill himself, because he "knew" from the very beginning that his son would kill him. It can be said that Oedipus blinded himself as a symbolic expression of the fact that he was blindly led by his parents to commit parricide and incest. That is, he was led into the position of a murderous sadistic agent.

Something similar happens in the myth of the parricide and the subsequent ritual to avoid fratricide in *Totem and Taboo* (Freud 1912). Again, because the pleasure of the father implies the unpleasure of the sons, the sons finally kill him in order to be able to control and enjoy women, the source of sexual pleasure and reproduction. Once more we have only two poles, the father and the sons, competing against each other for the source of sexual pleasure.

But in *Totem and Taboo* the sons realize, following their act of patricide, that the result of continued fighting among themselves would not be happy; they therefore agree to avoid fratricide. To prevent the further self-destruction of the family, they try to form either a noncompetitive nonsadomasochistic regime in which they can share satisfactions and avoid or minimize frustrations, or a stable sadomasochistic regime, based upon the division of power, in which the powerful sadistic agents exploit the powerless masochist patients with regard to the enjoyment of pleasure while at the same time giving them not only the security that they won't kill them but also the reassurance that they will take care of their survival. The sadists will protect the life of the masochists and will use them either as a source of pleasure or as instruments to obtain more pleasure from an external source, just as the sultan exploits the eunuchs who take such good care of his women in the harem.

In any case, this unconscious sadomasochistic agreement does not solve the contradiction between hedonistic and ethical pleasure that results from obtaining pleasure and security in a competitive way. The sadomasochistic agreement only assures survival of the sadomasochistic regime. That is why narcissistic subjects have to use a "primary process" kind of thinking that accommodates contradiction within itself: they can say that they are <frustrated satisfiers> while they are <satisfied frustrators>, or the opposite, without noticing it consciously. In this way the sadist can have both hedonistic and ethical pleasure without cognitive unpleasure, and the masochist can have security by renouncing all the other pleasures even if he says he enjoys them.

We think that the persistence of a competitive way of obtaining pleasure and security is one of the reasons why the narcissistic subject must use not only primary process in thinking, but a "practical thinking" to obtain sadomasochistic pleasure and security. Practical thinking, which Freud described in the 1895 Project, allows the subject to act in a pragmatic way while at the same time not thinking of his painful feared memory trace. For example, the sadist can obtain sadistic pleasure at the expense of the unpleasure of others without having to represent himself as a <satisfied frustrator of others> or to represent the others as <frustrated satisfiers of himself>. On the other hand, the masochist can obtain masochistic security without having to represent himself as a <frustrated satisfier of others> or to represent the others as <satisfied frustrators of himself>.

The practical thinking of the narcissistic subject is based on an inverted representation of his own actions and affective states as well as those of the others. As we shall see later, only when the subject can overcome the narcissistic sadomasochism will he be able to apply what Freud (1895) called "theoretical thinking," by which one obtains pleasure and security while representing himself and the others correctly; consequently, he has a fuller and more accurate picture of his possibilities for more and better pleasure (hedonistic, ethical, and cognitive) as well as security.

But the pleasure principle operates not only as an automatic psychic principle but also as an unconscious philosophical principle: an unconscious set of values that influence not only the cognitive and affective structure of the narcissistic subject but also his conscious and unconscious goals as well as his actual behavior in progressing toward them.

In effect, owing to the unconscious working of the competitive and conflictive pleasure principle, the psychic apparatus develops an unconscious sadomasochistic goal—the competitive achievement of pleasure or security—which previously contradicted its conscious goal.

The narcissistic norm of the superego usually requires that all subjects behave as "sincere masochists": they must lose the competition and they must be truthful. But, in fact, that never happens, either with the masochist or with the sadist. The masochist loses the competition for pleasure but says that he wins it, and the sadist wins the competition but says that he has lost it.

Consequently, if the principle that regulates psychic functioning is conflictive, the goals that the psychic apparatus establishes for itself must also be contradictory: the distance between the conscious rational goal that is never achieved, and the unconscious narcissistic goal that is always compulsively achieved, can be called the "angle of ambivalence."

Following Freud's hypothesis of the fixation of the subject's desires to his early sources of pleasure and security, it can be said that during his infancy he learns not only that the only way to obtain pleasure and security is conflictive and competitive, but also that the only way to obtain this kind of pleasure is the one he was taught at home. For example, he won't think that the only way to obtain food is by stealing it, but by stealing it in the particular way he stole it as a little child. His desire is restricted or mutilated by the influences of his family and community.

HYPOTHESES 1-3

1. Thus, the first theoretical hypothesis of the second meta-psychological level of the theory of psychic bipolarity would be that the master-servant structure of the ego and alter, or its super- and infer-structure, can be explained by the functioning of a competitive pleasure principle that regulates the psychic apparatus.

2. The second theoretical hypothesis is that the competitive content of the verbalized norm of the "superego," as well as its contradiction with its corresponding rule of action, can be explained by the fact that the psychic pleasure principle is not only competitive but also conflictive: it considers hedonically pleasant what is ethically unpleasant and vice versa.

3. The third theoretical hypothesis is that the intrapsychic representations of the speech, actions, and affective states of the narcissistic subject are stereotyped because he has learned a stereotyped conception of how to obtain conflicting, competitive pleasure or security when he was a child.

The Pleasure Principle and the Security Principle

From clinical observation, as well as from our previous empirical and theoretical hypotheses, it seems that the unconscious affective motivations of sadistic and masochistic behavior are qualitatively differ-

ent. In effect, the behavior of the sadist seems to be satisfactorily explained by the pleasure principle in its classical version: he looks for
pleasure and tries to avoid unpleasure without caring much about
security because he seems to be fairly self-sufficient in terms of his
survival. The sadist is not only able to look for hedonistic pleasure,
but also for symbolic (ethical and cognitive) pleasure. He wants to
be physically satisfied as well as feel that he is a sensible (not crazy),
generous (not selfish) human being.

When Freud first formulated the concept of the pleasure
principle in terms of pure discharge (Freud 1900), he had not yet
formulated a theory of aggression—another aspect of discharge.
Consequently, it might seem unfair to describe the sadist's pleasure
as conforming to the pleasure principle as such. Nevertheless, Freud's
later concept of the pleasure-ego would in fact fit our description of
the sadist's pleasure orientation precisely: the pleasure-ego is essentially in the paranoid position.

But the behavior of the masochist resists explanation in terms
of the pleasure principle, because while he seems to look for
hedonistic as well as ethical and cognitive unpleasure, he is basically
concerned about security because he thinks he is not able to survive
on his own. More than that, he believes he is dependent on the sadist
for survival: he is not only afraid of being punished if he tries to be
independent, but he has also missed the training needed to learn
how to be independent. Consequently, he is not able to look for
pleasures but looks mainly for security: he does not care much if he is
physically, ethically, and cognitively unhappy if by being so he can
be reassured about his security.

In other words, the masochist can accept being hedonistically a
<frustrated satisfier of others> and, at the same time, being called
by these others and by himself a selfish, crazy, stupid person—if this
is the price he must pay in order to be maintained.

Masochistic behavior thus seems to be regulated not by the
pleasure principle but by some kind of "security principle." Or, if
we reconsider the meaning of pleasure, the hypothesis of the pleasure
principle can still be applied by saying, for instance, that the sadist is
looking for sadistic, hedonistic, ethical and cognitive pleasure while
the masochist is looking for the masochistic pleasure of survival. In
other words, sadistic pleasure is constituted by hedonistic, ethical,
and cognitive pleasures without considering the pleasure of security
(or accepting the unpleasure of insecurity), while masochistic plea-

sure is constituted by the pleasure of security without considering hedonistic, ethical, and cognitive pleasure (or accepting the unpleasure of its absence).

For the sake of clarity, it can be said that the main affective unconscious goal of the sadist is the search for a sadistic pleasure that implies that the other must provide unpleasure, and that the main affective unconscious goal of the masochist is the search for a masochistic security that implies that the other must provide insecurity; or that the sadist has an "addiction" to pleasure and a "phobia" of unpleasure but is able to deal with questions of security and survival without major anxieties, while the masochist has an "addiction" to security and a "phobia" of insecurity (he cannot deal with big decisions concerning survival) but is very tolerant of his own unpleasure as well as of taking or sharing the unpleasure of others.

If these hypotheses are correct, it also can be said that metapsychologically the masochist does with the affective states of security and insecurity the same thing the sadist does with the affective states of pleasure and unpleasure. That is, he represses in himself and projects onto others the feeling of insecurity while he denies in others and introjects into himself the feeling of security.

Sadistic behavior seems to be motivated by sexual drives while masochistic behavior seems motivated by self-preservative drives, if we apply the first classification of drives proposed by Freud. On the other hand, the disorganized psychotic behavior of a subject who is going through a breakdown seems to resist explanation either by the pleasure principle or by the security principle. In effect, the disorganized psychotic seems to be "beyond" sadism and masochism. The subject is no longer able to cope with destructive impulses, to organize them through sadism and masochism, and thus becomes psychically destroyed. He seems unconcerned about sadistic pleasure or masochistic security but very concerned about mental disorganization, or about the "pleasure" of being mentally organized.

Disorganized psychotic behavior could be regulated, thus, by an "organization principle" that, like the security principle, could be either a different kind of principle or just a variation of the pleasure principle if one broadens the meaning of the concept of pleasure.

If we want to explain the motivation of disorganized psychotic behavior by the Freudian theory of drives, it seems that the distinction between Eros and Thanatos might be necessary. But the doubt still remains with the explanation of masochism: is the disorganized psychotic still fighting for his survival or is he committing psychic suicide because he can no longer tolerate internal and external reality as they are or as they are presented to him by others? In other words, perhaps disorganized psychotic behavior is regulated by the Nirvana principle, that is, by the aspiration to eliminate desires and merge the "self" with the universe.

HYPOTHESES 4–11

4. The fourth theoretical hypothesis of the second metapsychological level of the theory of psychic bipolarity would be that pleasures can be initially classified, according to their sources, into "pleasure of psychic organization," "pleasure of survival" (or "security"), and "pleasure of enjoying life" (or just plain "pleasure").

5. Pleasure can be subclassified, according to its sources, into "hedonistic" (sensory satisfaction), "ethical" (moral satisfaction), and "cognitive" (the satisfaction of understanding the world coherently).

6. Sadists mainly fear hedonistic, ethical, and cognitive unpleasure and look for hedonistic, ethical, and cognitive pleasure; their psychic functioning works as if it were regulated by the pleasure principle.

7. Masochists mainly fear insecurity and look for security; they are regulated by the "security principle" as if they are "beyond the pleasure principle."

8. Disintegrating psychotics mainly fear psychic disorganization and look for psychic organization because they are regulated by the organization principle as if they are "beyond the security principle."

9. Sadists can look for hedonistic, ethical, and cognitive pleasures without caring much about security because they are fairly sure of their ability to survive and remain psychically organized.

10. Masochists look for security without caring much about pleasure because they are unsure of their ability to survive even if they are fairly sure about their psychic organization.

11. Psychotics at breakdown look for mental organization without caring much about pleasure or security because they are not able to keep themselves mentally organized, either sadistically or masochistically, when facing conflictive situations.

Mutilation of the Psychic Space

As we have said before, the narcissistic subject has a compelling tendency to perceive and participate in human relations in a conflicted, competitive way: he competes with others for the control and enjoyment of the sources of pleasure, security, and mental organization.

One of the reasons for this compulsive competitive tendency seems to be a certain narrowing of the capacity to think and to feel of the narcissistic subject. There is a limitation or mutilation of the capacity to conceive alternative ways of obtaining pleasure and security.

In other words, the narcissistic subject can think about human pleasure only in competitive terms. He conceives of human existence as a "game" that is always competitive, and in which there can only be winners of pleasure and security at the expense of losers—a *zero-sum game*. If one player wins, the other (or others) must necessarily lose. Narcissistic speech and thinking always refer to a sadomasochistic relationship between <satisfied frustrators of others> and <frustrated satisfiers of others>. It can be said that a first mutilation of the psychic space is a narrowing of the thinking of the narcissistic subject. This first mutilation reduces his range of logical ways of obtaining pleasure and security other than in terms of conflict and competition: his range of thinking is drastically reduced and he recognizes only sadomasochistic human relationships.

This first mutilation allows room for only two or three "positions" in human interactions: the sadistic position of the <satisfied frustrator> who says that he is a generous, frustrated satisfier; the masochistic position of the <frustrated satisfier> who says that he is a selfish, satisfied frustrator; and, eventually, the untenable (psychotic) position of the <frustrated frustrator> who refers to himself and others in a disorganized way. But the narcissistic subject is not allowed to think or behave in the healthy position of the <satisfied satisfier> who can nevertheless share unavoidable unpleasures and insecurities with others, and who can describe himself and the others correctly. To do so would mean breaking the very rules of the competitive game that dictate the terms in which he is allowed to think.

Narcissistic thinking is by definition unable to describe and understand narcissistic thinking. In other words, the narcissistic subject seems incapable of perceiving himself as a narcissist who reflects others and uses others to reflect himself, being engaged in a sadomasochistic competition for pleasure and security. He has no "mirror of mirrors" to reflect the rules of his narcissistic game and is thus condemned to remain imprisoned, compulsively playing a conflicting, competitive game, the rules of which he does not know. In fact, he is not even aware that he is playing the game at all.

The narcissistic sadomasochistic subject is not only confined to thinking of himself as a satisfied frustrator, frustrated satisfier, or, eventually, frustrated frustrator; he is also unable to recognize these mutilations.

But even if the analyst, or another healthy significant other, tries to change the analysand's narrow competitive conception of human interactions, the narcissistic subject will fight against it, trying to defend his old mutilated way of thinking. The sadomasochist is very fond of his narrow thinking and very frightened of thinking differently: he avoids every possible unpleasant cognitive dissonance by regressing as soon as he can to his old mutilated pattern of cognition. This gives him the peculiar pleasure of cognitive consonance.

The psychic space of the narcissistic subject also suffers a very important second mutilation that confines him not only to conflicted and competitive object relations but also to a stereotyped, conflicted, competitive satisfaction or frustration of his desires. This second mutilation explains the empirical hypothesis that the speech, actions, and affective states of narcissistic individuals are both sadomasochistic and stereotyped. In other words, they speak exclusively about sadomasochistic interactions; they always tell the same sadomasochistic story with the same characters, the same plot, and the same sequence (see chapter 3). And they act out the same stereotyped action with the same monoaffective states. If he is an hysterical sadistic agent, for example, he will always speak about a particular way of being seduced by others, while seducing others in the same way, and he will always feel that he is being seduced in the same way. The second mutilation allows him to consciously perceive himself as an hysterical frustrated satisfier and the others as hysterical satisfied frustrators.

These mutilations are both a result of a mutilating sociopolitical structure (as we will demonstrate in the next chapter) and a cause of the stereotyped sadomasochistic behavior and thinking of the narcissistic individual. In other words, once the mutilation has taken place, it perpetuates itself as a defense mechanism against unpleasure (or terrifying) cognitive dissonance (Deutsch and Krauss 1968). Similarly, the compulsion to repeat the same fundamental acting-out not only perpetuates itself but reinforces the psychic mutilation.

HYPOTHESES 12–16

12. All pleasures (including security and psychic organization) can only be experienced by a narcissistic individual as conflicted, competitive, and sadomasochistic as a result of a first mutilation (a narrowing) of his psychic space; that is, pleasure is always competitive because it is the result of provoking unpleasure in others.

13. This hypothesis derives from the previous one: the narcissistic subject can only represent himself and others as either <sadistic satisfied frustrators>, <masochistic frustrated satisfiers>, or <psychotic frustrated frustrators> but never as <healthy satisfied satisfiers> of their own desires.

14. As a result of a "second mutilation," only stereotyped sadomasochistic pleasure can be conceived by a narcissistic individual: his psychic system knows only this one way of obtaining pleasure and security.

15. Both the first and the second mutilation of the psychic space produce a "tunnel" type of thinking and perception, and tend to perpetuate and reinforce themselves, not only because of the mutilating effect of the compulsion to repeat but also because of a fear of psychic disorganization provoked by the admission of new possibilities—cognitive and affective dissonance. The narcissistic individual is addicted to his old mutilated conception of the world and of himself.

16. The narcissistic individual is unable to think by himself about these mutilations of his psychic space as a result of the very same mutilation: he cannot escape the sadomasochistic trap because he cannot see the problem space as a whole. Consequently, he cannot find nonsadomasochistic alternatives to the trap.

Transconscious Psychic Space

In the previous chapter the topography of the psychic space was divided into a conscious space (with a nonreduced superficial psychic structure); a preconscious space (with a reduced semi-deep psychic structure); and an unconscious space (with an inverted deep psychic structure). These psychic structures are constituted by the intrapsychic representations of speech, actions, affective states, unconscious defense mechanisms, and the superego.

Analyzing the observable behavior of a narcissistic individual, we find in his interpersonal relations a fundamental acting-out that is constituted by his bipolar, stereotyped, sadomasochistic speech, actions, and affective states as well as by his inverted speech. We also find a fundamental selecting-out, constituted by his tendency to make a compulsive and selective object-choice who behaves and thinks as his own mirror (see Figure 8-2).

In the unobservable psychic space of the narcissistic individual there exists at the conscious level the correct nonreduced representations of the inverted speech; the inverted nonreduced representations of the actions; and the inverted nonreduced representations of the affective states.

In the narcissistic psychic space at the preconscious level, there exists the mechanism of bipolar "splitting" of the representations into ego-representations and alter-representations; the mechanism of reduction of the alter-representations into only one kind of representation; the correct reduced bipolar representations of the inverted speech; the inverted reduced bipolar representations of the actions; and the inverted reduced bipolar representations of the affective states.

In the narcissistic psychic space at the unconscious level there are different degrees of depth in its elements. In effect, we find in the first unconscious layer the defense mechanisms of repression, projection, denial, and introjection against painful representations of actions, and the defense mechanisms of suppression, evacuation, rejection, and absorption against painful representations of affective states.

In the second unconscious layer we find the correct reduced and nonreduced bipolar representations of painful actions and affective states. We agree with Freud that there are no speech

BEHAVIORAL	Acting-out	Bipolar stereotyped sadomasochistic speech, actions and affective state Inverted speech	Nonbipolar, nonstereotyped, nonsadomasochistic speech, actions and affective states Noninverted speech
	Selecting-out	Stereotyped compulsive object-choice	Nonstereotyped free object-choice
INTRAPSYCHIC	Conscious	Correct nonreduced representations of inverted speech Inverted nonreduced representations of painful actions and affective states	
	Preconscious	1. Splitting mechanism Reducing mechanism	
		2. Correct reduced representation of inverted speech Inverted reduced representations of painful actions and affective states	Correct representation of noninverted speech
	Unconscious	1. Repression, projection, denial and introjection Suppression, evacuation, rejection and absorption	Adaptive and liberating intrapsychic mechanisms
		2. Correct reduced and nonreduced representations of painful actions and affective states	Representation of nonsadomasochistic speech, actions and affective states Correct representations of speech about painful representation of actions and affective states
		3. Superego's norm with its contradictory rule Judge (master)-Accused (servant) relationship	Coherent superego Equal-equal relationships
		4. Conflicted stereotyped competitive pleasure principle	Representations of psychic Other types of pleasure principle, reality principle

Figure 8-2. Intrapsychic structure and behavior in narcissistic and open individuals

representations (word-representations) in the unconscious, but only action- and affect-representations (thing-representations).

In the third unconscious layer we find both the conflicted competitive norm of the superego and its contradictory rule of action, as well as the master-servant structure derived from the function of the ego and the superego either as a judge or as an accused.

At the fourth unconscious layer we find the conflicted, stereo-typed, competitive pleasure principle. At the fifth unconscious layer we find the double mutilation of the psychic space and the cognitive terror of modifying that mutilation.

These different degrees of unconsciousness imply specific deep operations and different "timing" in the analysis of each. This will be demonstrated in detail in chapter 10.

We are now presented with the theoretical problem of what happens with the psychic space to the intrapsychic representations that are excluded by the effect of mutilation. In effect, the conscious, preconscious, and unconscious psychic spaces consider only the representations of speech, actions, affective states, the defense mechanisms, the "superego," and the pleasure principle. The narcis-sistic individual is able to speak, act, feel, and think about these in some way, either correct or inverted.

But what about the representations of speech, actions, and affective states that are unknown and unthinkable for the narcissistic individual? These may not be represented at all in the psychic space; they may be represented in a deeper layer of the unconscious; or they may be contained in another compartment of the psychic space that can be called the *transconscious*.

The representation of a correct, noninverted speech concerning actions and affective states does not exist at the unconscious level; consequently, it is introduced, and not merely uncovered, by the analyst. But are these word-representations in the transconscious, or on a deeper layer of the unconscious, or are they not in the psychic space at all? This question applies not only to representations painful to the consciousness, but also, and more strikingly, to the representa-tions of nonsadomasochistic healthy actions and affective states. In which part of the psychic space are the representations of specific therapeutic words, actions, and affective states located? Where are the representations of the reality principle, of noncompetitive human interactions, and of a satisfied-satisfier actor, that are not perceived (consciously or unconsciously) by the narcissistic sadomasochistic individual? Is the therapeutic project as a whole included in the psychic space, and if so, where? We know that the truth about the narcissistic sadomasochistic project is hidden in the unconscious, but we don't know if the therapeutic project is hidden elsewhere in the psychic apparatus and is merely waiting (in the transconscious space, for example) to be uncovered by the psychoanalyst.

If we assume the existence of a transconscious space, that space would contain, among other things, the full range of competitive and noncompetitive ways of obtaining sadistic or nonsadistic pleasure and masochistic or nonmasochistic security as opposed to the stereotyped sadomasochistic way always used by the narcissistic individual. It would contain all the other noncompetitive, nonsadomasochistic ways of obtaining nonsadistic pleasure or nonmasochistic security.

In short, within the transconscious space we find not only the representation of other classes of satisfied frustrators or frustrated satisfiers but also the representations of satisfied satisfiers that share with others (and try to overcome) unavoidable frustrations. This implies the representations of (1) both mutilations of the psychic space; (2) the reality principle; (3) a "superego" with a nonconflicted, noncompetitive norm and a coherent rule of action, comprising not a master and a servant but equals; (4) the correct representations of the speech about painful actions and affective states; (5) other representations of speech, actions, and affective states that are not bipolar, sadomasochistic, stereotyped, or inverted; and (6) other intrapsychic mechanisms that are not defensive, but liberating (in the sense of allowing correct perceptions and successful strategy for obtaining nonsadistic pleasure and nonmasochistic security).

If the psychoanalyst is able to introduce in the conscious space not only the repressed, projected, denied, and introjected unconscious representations but also the healthy representation which has been mutilated, perhaps the narcissistic individual will be able to think not only about the negative consequences of his mutilated, stereotyped, sadomasochistic behavior and thinking but also about the positive consequences of a new, nonsadomasochistic action and thinking.

Given the novelty of our proposition concerning the transconscious, we would like to explain that in our view it is the analyst's task not only to make conscious whatever is unconscious, but also to introduce the transconscious into consciousness. Only in this way does it become possible for the analysand to recover fully from the mutilation of his psychic structure so that it contains only a single type of competitive, sadomasochistic object relationship.

In our view there is a mutilation that extends in at least three directions:

1. The exclusion of other types of competitive relationships
2. The exclusion of noncompetitive relationships
3. The exclusion of any possibility of thinking in order to form a clear idea of the type of object relationship in question in the narcissistic structure

We can describe this mutilation as horizontal in the sense that it narrows the spectrum of behavior to one type of conflictive object relationship. It is vertical in the sense that it lacks the possibility of reaching a level of abstraction where the rule of this conflictive type of relationship can become clear. As a result we include in the concept of the transconscious not only other types of object relationships on the horizontal plane, but also the rules that regulate them on the vertical plane. For while the conscious, preconscious, and unconscious contain the member, they do not contain the class to which it belongs, which the transconscious can do.

In our concept of the transconscious we are aware that we are following a kind of reasoning that leads to the paradox of the unthinkable class of all the classes that cannot contain themselves. How can the transconscious, which contains the rules for the functioning of the conscious, preconscious and unconscious, contain its own rules? We believe this hinges on the role of the analyst who, being external to the transconscious of the analysand, is not, in fact, included in his transconscious. And therefore he can come to the aid of the analysand, who is otherwise unable to arrive at the rules of his conscious, preconscious, unconscious or transconscious on his own. He cannot, therefore, think his way through to the solution of his own conflicting defenses. And he surely cannot do what he cannot think.

We must remember that whenever the mutilated psychic space is suddenly broadened, there is a danger of an episode of psychotic disorganization. While he remains sadomasochistic, the narcissistic individual is mainly concerned about pleasure and security; but when he goes, or we push him, beyond sadomasochism, he will have to face the painful experience of psychotic disorganization (in order to attain the benefits of a state of mental health).

When the narcissistic subject becomes conscious of his sadism, he fears he will lose his pleasure; when he becomes conscious of his masochism, he fears he will lose his security; and when he becomes conscious of his psychic mutilation, he fears he will lose his mental organization.

HYPOTHESES 17–19

17. The seventeenth theoretical hypothesis of the second metapsychological level of the theory of psychic bipolarity would be that in addition to the conscious, preconscious, and unconscious psychic spaces, a transconscious space is created as a result of the double mutilation of the psychic space.

18. The content of the transconscious space is constituted by the representations of classes of frustrated satisfiers and satisfied frustrators other than the stereotyped ones conceived by the narcissistic individual. The transconscious also contains the representations of satisfied satisfiers who share pleasure and security with others and try to overcome unavoidable frustrations. This implies the representations of:

(a) both mutilations of the psychic space

(b) the noncompetitive reality principle, perceiving the true sociopolitical structure that made him a narrow, stereotyped sadomasochistic individual

(c) a nonconflicted, noncompetitive coherent ego-superego relationship comprising not a master and a servant but equals

(d) the correct representations of the speech concerning painful actions and affective states

(e) other (healthy) representations of speech, actions, and affective states that are not bipolar, sadomasochistic, stereotyped, or inverted

(f) adaptive and liberating intrapsychic mechanisms.

19. The broadening of the mutilated psychic space, by means of making conscious the transconscious, carries both the risk of a psychotic disorganization and the reward of a therapeutic psychic reorganization.

The hypothesis of a double psychic mutilation producing a transconscious psychic space whose contents, when suddenly introduced to consciousness, can produce a psychotic disorganization, is very close to the hypothesis of "foreclosure" or "repudiation" introduced by Lacan (1966). Lacanian foreclosure denotes:

> . . . a specific mechanism held to lie at the origin of the psychotic phenomenon and to consist in a primordial expulsion of a fundamental "signifier" (e.g., the phallus as signifier of the castration complex) from the subject's symbolic universe. Foreclosure is deemed to be distinct from repression in two senses: (a) foreclosed signifiers are not integrated into the subject's unconscious; and (b) they do not return "from the inside"—they reemerge, rather, in "the Real," particularly through the phenomenon of hallucination. (Laplanche and Pontalis 1973, p. 166)

Lacan derived support for his hypothesis from the case history of the Wolf Man, in which Freud cites the coexistence of a number of different attitudes toward castration, including "a third current, the oldest and deepest, which did not as yet even raise the question of the reality of castration, was still capable of coming into activity" (Freud 1918, p. 85). The hypothesis of foreclosure thus implies that a fundamental intrapsychic representation has been expelled from consciousness but is not integrated in the unconscious: this representation could appear again, as if it were coming from the external world; and this seems to be basically the representation of castration.

On the other hand, our hypothesis of mutiliation implies:

1. Many representations (signifiers) of sadomasochistic and nonsadomasochistic object relations have been excluded both from the conscious and the unconscious spaces.

2. These mutilated representations are located in the transconscious psychic space, which is a new dimension of the psychic space that is "beyond" the unconscious space.

3. This transconscious space contains, among other things, the representations of the mutilated aspects of the subject himself and aspects of the external world.

4. Generally speaking, it can be said that the contents of the transconscious space initially tend to appear as new aspects of the sociopolitical reality whose perception and representation the subject had mutilated.

5. The transconscious space contains the representation of the psychic mutilations and its result, the psychic castration.

Both the concepts of foreclosure and mutilation deeply involve the representation of external (sociopolitical) reality. This leads us to reconsider the hypothesis of the reality principle, in the sense that it must imply not only a more mature approach to the attainment of pleasure and security but also a less mutilated approach to the sociopolitical reality. This will allow the nonnarcissistic individual a more realistic and effective therapeutic approach when he tries to obtain pleasure, security, or psychic organization.

We think that both foreclosure and mutilation imply that we must make conscious both the unconscious and the transconscious, or the aspects of the individual and of the sociopolitical world which were repressed, denied, or mutilated. Consequently, the "insight" (of the intrapsychic sadomasochistic representations, mechanisms, superego, and pleasure principle) will be as important as the "outsight" (of the sadomasochistic behavior of the individual himself) and as the "social-sight" (of the sadomasochistic behavior and structure of society).

In this way, the narcissistic subject will be able to overcome, at least partially, both the internal limitations of his conception of new alternatives, of his problem space, so that he can obtain more and better pleasure and security, and the sociopolitical limitations of the origin of his psychic mutilation. The implementation of new alternatives for pleasure and security will result from the working-through of his repression and mutilation.

However, we must not forget that opening the closed narcissistic system and attacking the sadomasochistic dogma means that the analysand must change his conception of the world and, consequently, his whole strategy of living. The sadomasochistic analysand must realize that he has a closed narcissistic system of thinking; he must then try to open it by revising and broadening his sadomasochistic theory about the structure of society. In other words, he must start thinking about the way he thinks in order to change it.

"If he wants to go ahead he has to get a theory" about his own theories. Because "the quantity of information required to weaken an opinion is always many times greater than that required to strengthen it," there is a sadomasochistic inertia, a resistance against psychic change, very similar to the resistance described by Kuhn (1970). Scientists are, and always have been, very reluctant to change their theories—their scientific paradigms—even if they are presented with a new and much better theory, unless the old theory breaks down of itself, through a complete failure to explain essential aspects of reality.

The Social Explanation of Repression and Mutilation of the Psychic Space

Replacing the pleasure principle with the reality principle during the analytic treatment implies a requirement of "social-sight," not only into the limitation imposed by the social structure on narcissistic ways of obtaining pleasure and security but also into the social origin of psychic repression and mutilation. The sadomasochistic characteristics of the sociopolitical structure in which the individual became narcissistic still reinforce his narcissism.

A new level of explanation of the narcissistic functioning of the psychic apparatus can now be described by means of auxiliary sociopolitical hypotheses of the theory of psychic bipolarity.

1. The space of the psychic apparatus is mutilated and recognizes only competitive ways of obtaining pleasure, security and psychic organization, because society requires the use of these ways. Because society only allows satisfied frustrators or frustrated satisfiers (or, eventually, frustrated frustrators) to survive successfully, but does not permit the existence of satisfied satisfiers, a first mutilation is provoked within the psychic apparatus. Other types of noncompetitive human interactions are confined to the transconscious psychic space.

2. The normative code of the psychic apparatus, that is, the superego, has a rule of action that contradicts its own norm for action, because society simultaneously stimulates and censors competitive ways of obtaining pleasure, security, and psychic organization. That is why some intrapsychic representations of competitive actions and affective states are painful to consciousness and the

defense mechanisms must invert them. For similar reasons, the speech of the individual with respect to his actual behavior and affective states is inverted, and the correct representations are confined to the unconscious.

3. The space of the psychic apparatus is mutilated and recognizes only stereotyped competitive ways of obtaining pleasure, security, and psychic organization because of the rigid division of labor in society and the bureaucratization of its relations of production and distribution of goods and happiness. This second mutilation of the psychic space means that speech, actions, affective states and representations refer only to a stereotyped kind of satisfied frustrators or frustrated satisfiers. The representations of other types of satisfied frustrators or frustrated satisfiers are confined to the transconscious psychic space.

4. Other sociopolitical factors, such as regional cultural differences (which generate cognitive provincialism) or the rigid division of the sexes, ethnic groups, etc., contribute to the mutilation, narrowing, and further stereotyping of the psychic space. These factors tend to create closed social circles that feed back on themselves in a vicious, stereotyping way. Once the analyst knows the sociopolitical characteristics of the society in which the analysand has been raised, the kind of job he is doing, his reference group, and his group affiliation, he can predict approximately how the analysand's thinking, perception, speech, actions, and affective states will be narrowed into a typical social stereotype. The basic social personality of the analysand can be outlined and predicted.

Some Consequences for Technique

With the theoretical hypotheses of the second metapsychological level of the theory of psychic bipolarity, some new technical consequences emerge. In effect, the analyst must show the analysand that:

1. He qualifies his own speech, actions, affective states, and thoughts according to philosophical principles that underlie his set of values: he must make these principles conscious.

2. According to his unconscious set of values, to be a "winner" of pleasure is ethically "bad" and to be a "loser" of pleasure is ethically "good."

3. If he is a sadist, the analysand thinks that he must give security to others and absorb insecurity from them in order to obtain pleasure, and provoke unpleasure in them, and that he is a "loser" with respect to security but a "winner" with respect to pleasure.

If the analysand is a masochist, the analyst must show him that he thinks that he must give pleasure to others and absorb unpleasure from them in order to obtain security from them and provoke insecurity in them, and that he is a "loser" with respect to pleasure but a "winner" with respect to security.

4. Because of a limitation or a narrowing in his thinking, he can perceive himself and others only as <frustrated satisfiers (good victims)>, or as <satisfied frustrators (bad victimizers)> or, eventually as <breaking-down frustrated frustrators>. That is why his speech, actions, and affective states are stereotyped in this regard.

5. Because of another limitation in his thinking, the analysand can perceive himself and others only as stereotyped <frustrated satisfiers> or <satisfied frustrators>, and he is only able to perceive a stereotyped way of obtaining competitive pleasure or insecurity. That is why he has a monotheme in his speech, a single pattern of action, and monoqualification of affective states.

The analyst must also illuminate:

6. The relation between the stereotyped competitive structure of the social network within which the analysand was raised, as well as the competitive structure of his present social network, and the mutilated competitive way in which he conceives his relations with others.

7. The relation between the contradictory way in which his social network simultaneously stimulates and censors competition and the structure of his system of values, as well as the inversion of his conscious representations of actions and affective states.

8. The relation between the stereotyping division of labor and status in his original and current social networks and the stereotyped ways in which he perceives, speaks, acts, and feels in his relations with others.

And finally, the analyst must indicate to the analysand that:

9. He is afraid to recognize alternatives different from the familiar stereotyped competitive ones because he is emotionally

attached to his old theory about the structure of the world and is afraid of the unknown. He fears losing his mastery of the world and being punished by others (the analyst included) if he tries to amplify his narrowed perception, representation, speech, actions, and feelings about the world and himself.

10. If he is able to accept, recognize, consider, and think of new aspects of social reality and other psychic alternatives, perhaps he will be able to find new solutions for his old conflicts and symptoms. He will be able to perceive himself and others as satisfied satisfiers who are also prepared to share the unavoidable unpleasures and insecurities of everyday life.

Summary of the Second Metapsychological Level of the Theory of Psychic Bipolarity

PRESUPPOSED PSYCHOANALYTIC HYPOTHESES

1. Sadomasochism is not only a restricted perversion but a universal interpersonal and intrapsychic phenomenon that takes into account many varieties of submission-dependence, or of <satisfying oneself by frustrating others> and of <frustrating oneself to satisfy others>.

2. The relationship between the ego and the alter is basically sadomasochistic. The introjected aggression of the subject is used by his superego to blame, torture, and disqualify his ego in the same way that his parents punished and disqualified him when he was a little child.

3. Sadomasochism is a basic organizer of the psychic apparatus; it avoids psychic chaos by distributing aggression inside and outside it.

4. The pleasure principle is one of the two major principles governing mental functioning. The whole psychic activity is aimed at avoiding unpleasure and procuring pleasure.

5. Universality of the oedipal competition: "every new arrival on this planet is faced with the task of mastering the Oedipus complex" (Freud 1930). All psychic pleasure is competitive until that

complex is overcome. The whole psychic activity is aimed at avoiding unpleasure and procuring pleasure at the expense of provoking unpleasure in others. In mythical terms, the killing of the primal father and the control of fratricide is the origin and maintenance mechanism of culture.

6. The reality principle is the other major principle governing mental functioning. When it dominates, psychic activity takes into account the conditions imposed by the outside world. Pleasure is no longer only competitive and impulsive, but also cooperative; reality is no longer mutilated to preserve narcissistic omnipotence.

7. The ego is a dependent servant of three masters: the id, the superego, and the external world.

PRESUPPOSED INTERDISCIPLINARY HYPOTHESES*

9. The subject resists the recognition of the aspects of reality and of himself which differ from his own structuring of, and hypotheses about, reality. He avoids cognitive dissonance and procures cognitive consonance in order to avoid psychic pain.

10. The subject builds his own cognitive paradigms that give him the definition of the problem space and the task environment when he is trying to solve a problem.

11. The subject thinks initially through paradigms (analogic prototypes) and then through digital thinking.

12. There are competitive or zero-sum games, which require losers to offset winners, and cooperative games, whose results add up to more than zero.

13. The human mind is a psychic space whose possibilities of conceiving of the world are restricted.

14. The human mind encounters difficulties in knowing the limitations of its own psychic space.

FUNDAMENTAL HYPOTHESES

We will now explain, at a second metapsychological level, the empirical hypotheses of the theory of psychic bipolarity of speech,

*Many of these will be elaborated in chapter 9.

actions, and affective states of the analysand and the analyst within the psychoanalytic setting.

1. The master-servant structure of the "superego" (that is, the super-or-infer relation of ego and alter) can be explained by the functioning of a competitive pleasure principle that regulates the psychic apparatus.

2. The conflicting competitive content of the verbalized norm of the "superego" (as well as its contradiction with its corresponding rule of action) can be explained by the fact that psychic pleasure is not only competitive but conflicting, because it considers hedonistically pleasant what is ethically unpleasant (and vice versa).

3. The psychic representations of speech, actions, and affective states are stereotyped because when only a child the narcissistic subject learned a stereotyped conception of how to obtain, in a conflictive, competitive way, the pleasure of security.

4. Pleasures can be initially classified, according to their sources, into "pleasure of psychic organization," "pleasure of survival" (or "security"), and "pleasure of enjoying life" (just plain "pleasure").

5. "Pleasure" can be subclassified, according to its own sources, into "hedonistic" (or sensory satisfaction), "ethical" (or moral satisfaction), and "cognitive" (or the satisfaction of understanding the world coherently).

6. Sadists fear hedonistic, ethical, and cognitive unpleasures and look for corresponding pleasures because their psychic functioning is regulated by the pleasure principle.

7. Masochists fear insecurity and look for security because their psychic functioning is regulated by the "security principle": they are "beyond the pleasure principle."

8. Disintegrating psychotics fear psychic disorganization and look for psychic organization because their psychic functioning is regulated by the "organization principle": they are "beyond the security principle."

9. Sadists can look for hedonistic, ethical, and cognitive pleasures with little regard for security because they are fairly sure of their ability to survive and to remain psychically organized.

10. Masochists look for security without caring much about pleasures because they are unsure of their ability to survive even if they are fairly sure of their psychic organization.

11. Disintegrating psychotics look for mental organization with little regard for pleasure or security, because they are not able to keep themselves organized, either sadistically or masochistically, when facing conflicting situations.

12. All pleasures (including security and psychic organization) can be conceived by a narcissistic individual only as conflicted, competitive, sadomasochistic ones because of a "first mutilation" (narrowing) of the psychic space: pleasure can be conceived only as the result of provoking unpleasure in others.

13. The narcissistic subject can represent himself and others only as <sadistic satisfied frustrators> or as <masochistic frustrated satisfiers> (or as <psychotic frustrated frustrators>)—but not as <healthy satisfied satisfiers> of his own desires and of the desires of others.

14. All sadomasochistic pleasures can be realized by a narcissistic individual only as stereotyped ones because of a "second mutilation" of his psychic space: his psychic system knows only a single, stereotyped, sadomasochistic way of obtaining pleasure and security.

15. Both of these mutilations of the psychic space, producing a "tunnel" type of thinking and perception, tend to perpetuate and reinforce themselves—not only because of the mutilating effect of the compulsion to repeat, but also because of a fear of the psychic disorganization that can be provoked by the admission of new cognitive and affective possibilities (fear of a disorganizing cognitive and affective dissonance).

16. The narcissistic individual is not able to think by himself about these mutilations of his psychic space because of that very mutilation: he cannot escape the sadomasochistic trap because he cannot think of the problem space as a whole. Consequently, he cannot find nonsadomasochistic alternatives to it.

17. In addition to the conscious, preconscious, and unconscious psychic spaces, a transconscious space is created as a result of the double mutilation of the psychic space.

18. The content of the transconscious psychic space is constituted by the representations of other classes of <frustrated satisfiers> and <satisfied frustrators> that differ from the stereotyped ones usually conceived by the narcissistic individual, as well as by the representations of <satisified satisfiers> that share and try to

overcome with others the unavoidable frustrations of everyday life. This implies:

(a) The representation of both mutilations of psychic space

(b) the reality (nonsadomasochistic) principle

(c) a nonconflicted, noncompetitive coherent ego-alter relationship comprising not a master and a servant but rather equals

(d) correct speech representations of painful actions and affective states

(e) other (healthy) representations of nonbipolar, nonsadomasochistic, nonstereotyped speech, actions, and affective states

(f) adaptive and liberating intrapsychic mechanisms.

19. The broadening of the mutilated psychic space, by means of introducing the transconscious, carries both the risk of a psychotic disorganization and the reward of a therapeutic psychic reorganization.

AUXILIARY SOCIOPOLITICAL HYPOTHESES*

1. The space of the psychic apparatus is mutilated and it is only able to conceive competitive ways of obtaining pleasure, security, and psychic organization, because society itself institutionalizes this competition.

2. The normative code of the psychic apparatus (that is, of the "superego") has a rule of action that contradicts its own norm for action, because society simultaneously stimulates and censors competitive ways of obtaining pleasure, security, and psychic organization.

3. The space of the psychic apparatus is mutilated and only allows stereotyped, competitive ways of obtaining pleasure, security, and psychic organization, because of the rigid division of labor in society and the bureaucratization of the production of goods and the realization of happiness.

4. Other sociopolitical factors, such as regional and cultural differences (which generate cognitive provincialism) or rigid division of the sexes, ethnic groups, etc., contribute to the further mutilation, narrowing, and stereotyping of the psychic space.

*See chapter 9 for further discussion.

REFERENCES

Deutsch, M., and Krauss, R. M. (1968). *Theories in Social Psychology.* New York: Basic Books.

Freud, S. (1895). Project for a scientific psychology. *Standard Edition* 1: 281–397.

—— (1905). Three essays on the theory of sexuality. *Standard Edition* 7: 125–243.

—— (1912). Totem and taboo. *Standard Edition* 13:1–162.

—— (1913). The disposition to obsessional neurosis. *Standard Edition* 12: 311–326.

—— (1915a). Repression. *Standard Edition* 14:143–158.

—— (1915b). Instincts and their vicissitudes. *Standard Edition* 14:109–140.

—— (1918). From the history of an infantile neurosis. *Standard Edition* 17: 3–122.

—— (1920). Beyond the pleasure principle. *Standard Edition* 18:7–64.

—— (1924). On the economic problem of masochism. *Standard Edition* 19:157–170.

—— (1930). Civilization and its discontents. *Standard Edition* 21:59–145.

Kuhn, T. (1966). *The Structure of Scientific Revolutions.* Chicago: University of Chicago Press.

Lacan, J. (1966). *Ecrits.* Paris: Editions du Seuil.

Lagache, D. (1960). Situation de l'agressivité. *Bulletin de Psychologie* 14.

Laplanche, J., and Pontalis, J. B. (1973). *The Language of Psycho-Analysis.* New York: Basic Books.

Sptiz, R. (1957). *No and Yes: On the Genesis of Human Communication.* New York: International Universities Press.

9

Narcissistic Structures in Society

One cannot consider the phenomenon of identity apart from the phenomenon of freedom. While we have explored the psychological dimensions of identity and freedom, we have yet to examine the conditions of freedom in the world insofar as they limit or enhance the possibilities of psychological freedom and identity. Here we will distinguish two domains: first, freedom from economic necessity, which is always relative but nonetheless the condition for the possibility of cultural development; and second, freedom from political domination so that one can act together with others to bring about change in the world. While economic and political freedom are closely connected, each manifests its own structure and must be understood on its own terms before one can see how they are connected. Ultimately we hope to show that the specifics of social and political structure contribute to the mutilation of the norm of the "superego" and to the contradiction between this norm and the correspondent rule that leads to the repression of the subject.

The Problem of the Weak and the Strong

One of the two fundamental oppositions underlying social life is the contradiction between necessity and freedom (Arendt 1958, p. 119). Necessity refers to those conditions that we must satisfy in order to survive—in particular, the production of those goods necessary to sustain human life, and the humanized environment that will support the efforts needed to stimulate the development of culture. Insofar as we are subject to the claims of necessity, we may not survive or may not be free to pursue activities that promote the cultivation of our humanity.

This contradiction has been recognized in theory as the struggle between the strong and the weak, or between the master and the slave. In Hegel's analysis, the master attains his position because he is not afraid of death and can therefore compel the slave, who is. The irony of his position is that the master nevertheless remains dependent on the slave, to whom he has refused recognition as an equal, for his own recognition. Consequently his apparent freedom hides an underlying dependence on the slave (Hegel 1807, pp. 228–240).

In this competitive organization necessity is not really mastered and freedom is only an illusion. We have instead an interdependent structure of submission and domination between those who are privileged to be masters and those who are condemned to be slaves. Entrenched over time, the structure eventually becomes embedded in society as if it were a fact of nature.

The crucial point is that the master does not see that his freedom is a shared illusion since it is only a reflection in the eyes of the slave; and the slave does not see that his enslavement is only real insofar as he reflects the freedom of the master: "It is because I believe you are a master that I condemn myself to being a slave." But the master desires to appropriate the slave as a person, as a producer of the symbolic goods of recognition.

At the moment of mastery and enslavement, the struggle with necessity gives rise to the formation of a perverse desire to master the other, and not simply to master necessity. From the point of view of the slave this double level of the structure takes the form of obeying the master in order to survive. This in turn gives rise to the desire to obey the master as if he were in fact superior in order to avoid the problem of insecurity.

It becomes impossible for those who are socialized into this structure to think of the economic problem of taking care of necessity except in terms of relations of domination and submission. Then, to be prosperous means to dominate, and to be poor means to submit. But as we have shown, this desire to dominate or submit goes beyond the desire for riches or the resignation to poverty.

Once the subject is engaged in a specific line of work he becomes embedded in the bureaucratic organization, whether private or public, that governs the relations of production on his or her job.

Consequently, it can be said that the mutilation of the subject in terms of the social order occurs in something like the following sequence: the contradiction between necessity and freedom leads to the master-slave dialectic which leads to the bureaucratic maintenance of the social relations.

As a result, one could say that all social relations are informed by the master-slave interaction modified according to the prevailing economic and organizational sophistication. Thus, for example, in a society where scarcity prevails, economic competition is likely to have more severe consequences than in prosperous societies, and indeed one of the achievements of modern social development has been the deliberate effort to cushion the effects of the competitive economic structure.

Nevertheless, the universal condition in modern society remains a competition for jobs and resources, so that human interactions are constantly competitive on an individual or group basis. Even where we find groups of people united by a set of common interests, a deeper analysis shows that their unity derives from the need for cooperation in order to compete with another group. Seen from the outside, the group as a whole then exhibits the competition that appears to have disappeared within it.

THE FAMILY

A classic example of this is the well-known contradiction in middle-class family morality whereby relations among family members are supposed to be supportive, cooperative and protective, in contradistinction to the competition with others defined as being outside the family. In effect, the family's domestic ethics represents an impossible ideal because it is really in the external world that the children's social destiny will be determined. This contradiction becomes manifest in the values that parents transmit to their children: they want them to be moral, that is cooperative, respectful, and loving; but at the same time they must prepare them for the competition that prevails in society. This contradiction becomes clear in the disaffection of middle and upper-middle class children from the competitive economic world in which their parents are successful.

For these children the contradiction becomes impossible, even when it is veiled by the typical bourgeois recourse to hypocrisy.

Within the family itself, the definition of sex roles also reflects the influence of competitive social ethics. Traditionally, upper middle-class men occupy a dominant position in relation to women because they are the "breadwinners." The husband, therefore, dominates the wife because he earns money, even if to do so he may have to submit to a position of exploitation in the world. The wife is then confined to the submissive role because she is not paid for her work within the household. Thus even within the family structure, where economic resources are supposed to be shared, the master-slave interaction takes over the distribution of both material resources and symbolic recognition.

The man becomes the master because he is the one who goes out into the world to compete. He thereby assumes responsibility for the economic security of the family. The woman, who works in the household, submits in the belief that her security will be assured without having to face the insecurities of the outside work-world.

The desire between husband and wife is therefore perverted on the lines of the master-slave interaction. That is, it offers recognition only to the man and security only to the woman. In effect, however, neither the recognition nor the security available in this kind of structure are sound.

In contemporary society the balance of economic power between men and women is slowly shifting as it becomes necessary for both partners to work outside the home in order to support the family. Consequently there is a contradiction between the traditional socialization of men and women and the reality of their economic condition that contributes to the increasing instability of sexual relationships. While this instability reflects the changing relations of economic power in the family, it is also a sign of the equalization of sex roles that might in fact promise a greater stability in the long term, if matched by an equality of recognition.

Therefore, in addition to the parents' dilemma of raising their children according to contradictory sets of values—the cooperative and the competitive—they are also faced with the dilemma of raising their male and female children according to already contradictory norms—which are also now in contradiction with prevailing economic and social conditions.

BUREAUCRACY

Bureaucratic organizations in both the public and private sectors are faced with similar contradictions between the need for cooperation in a common task and the competition for limited resources. One could almost say that a leading aim of bureaucracy is to neutralize competition within its structure in order to compete successfully outside.

Bureaucracy operates on the basis of a rational breakdown of the functions required in order to perform an overall task. These functions are then organized into a hierarchy. Places within the hierarchy are meant to be rationally distributed according to merit and seniority so that, in theory, the best person, according to ability and experience, will always be assigned to each job (Swingle 1976, pp. 14–17).

Unfortunately, the master-slave dialectic comes into play and undermines this bureaucratic rationality. Positions in the hierarchy become invested with the competition to dominate or submit so that, far from serving the rational purpose of efficient production, the hierarchy gives rise to forms of competition that contradict the possibility of efficiency intended by the bureaucratic design.

There are two further characteristics of bureaucratic organization that present obstacles to the realization of freedom, whether economic or political. First, the way to move up the bureaucratic ladder is to appear to others as if one is making an important contribution without becoming the focus of controversy. This requires a specific skill whereby someone can claim credit for any positive effects of a decision or act, but escape blame for any negative outcome.

To supply this skill the public bureaucratic culture has developed a particularly shrewd method of using the research and investigative techniques of the social sciences, relying heavily on statistical method, in order to make it seem that no professional or political judgment is involved in the making of decisions, but simply the application of technical expertise. Should the decision turn out well, the expert is in a position to claim credit for his professional work. Should it turn out badly, the inadequacy of science and of the research method is to blame, and we can only look forward to further progress in the social sciences to rescue us from its shortcomings (M. Weber, quoted in Girth and Mills 1958, pp. 129–156; Hummel 1977, p. 165).

This faceless quality of the bureaucratic culture and its intolerance for responsibility at the individual or collective level is not merely an aspect of the art of climbing the bureaucratic ladder instead of devoting oneself to its tasks. It turns out to be an inhibition generated by the bureaucratic structure: namely, that members of the hierarchy tend to lose confidence in their capacity to make judgments and in the end develop a kind of mental impotence with the effect that our institutions and corporations often appear to have lost contact with the changing reality of society and to have lost the ability to make realistic adaptations to significant changes. Far from serving the purpose for which they were designed, these organizations become the prime obstacles to the realization of those goals (Hummel 1977, pp. 95–100; Merton, quoted in Etzioni 1961, p. 53).

A second and related characteristic of bureaucratic culture is the undermining of initiative. For some time economists have been discussing the relationship of incentives to the maintenance of levels of productivity. It stands to reason that where job security and a reasonable level of income is guaranteed, the motivation to work becomes problematic unless, of course, one is fortunate enough to work in a field that he or she finds profoundly engaging. While we recognize that this touches on a broad range of questions, none of which lend themselves to a simple approach, it is nevertheless important to observe the unique contribution of bureaucracy to this problem.

In a bureaucratic organization there is built into the structure itself a definite disincentive to initiative. As we have seen, the principle of a bureaucracy involves the breakdown of functions and their distribution within a hierarchical framework meant to render unnecessary the need for deliberate cooperation and initiative on the part of the workers. If each does the job assigned him, the system will run itself and turn out the product or service it was designed to deliver (Max Weber, quoted in Girth and Mills 1958, pp. 196–244).

Initiative in this system is contraindicated. Consequently, the system itself generates resentment among the employees who find themselves reduced in human stature by the conditions of their work. In other words, the bureaucratic structure, intended to be a "rational" substitute for the unreliable contingencies of initiative and cooperation, finally eliminates these critical dimensions from the performance of workers. Society is then left with organizations that lack the very capacity for intelligent individual effort that is one of our most valuble economic assets (Blau 1963, pp. 213–219).

The contradiction is particularly glaring where the influence of the Protestant work ethic still prevails sufficiently that individuals find themselves torn between a concern to make a contribution to society and the restriction of a code of economic behavior that insists that they simply conform to a preassigned function.

If the effects of bureaucratization are evident in terms of the rigidity of social institutions in relation to a constantly changing reality and the problem of declining productivity, they are equally noticeable in terms of the political life of the Western democracies. The possibility of decision making in the public interest is lost between the requirements of party machines on the one hand and huge administrative bureaucracies on the other, in which the numerous career interests of politicians and civil servants are negotiated within the terms of a bureaucratic culture. In the face of this reality, the repeated calls for a new or revived "leadership" to overcome the immobility of the economic and political system amounts to a symptom of the despair generated by the prevailing bureaucratic system, since it is questionable how far a structure so deeply embedded in the system can be transformed by changes at the top.

PSYCHOLOGY

There is a social dimension to the bipolarity of narcissism, insofar as both the ego and the alter are defined in terms of interacting roles and action at the level of social reality. For example, considerations of class, sexual role, and job and professional potentials are transmitted by means of the child's interactions with significant others.

With few exceptions the possibilities for action which a person considers are confined to those that his alter has held up—a particular version of society that implicitly locates the child socially for the rest of his or her life.

What this means is that each person tends to define their social identity in terms of the restrictive possibilities for action that particular jobs or professions impose on them. Thus, for example, the choice of a career pattern which at first may appear to be "free" soon locks a person into a definition of their identity (and alterity) that represents a profound *mutilation* of the rich possibilities that remain unrecognized and therefore unrealizable.

What makes this particularly ironic in modernized (developed) societies is the manifest contradiction between this narrow definition of identity according to social function that comes from the division of labor, and the flexibility and mobility also implicit in the social system. Thus, for example, the increasing possibilities for leisure time are only defined as an alternative to and a relief from these alienating models of *work identity*. If we perceive the work identity not as a mutilating preemption, a tunnel vision of the subject, but as one among the various possibilities for earning money and for engaging in different kinds of projects, the reified distinction between work and leisure becomes unnecessary.

In this context, to simply change from one job to another in search of a nonalienating work identity proves futile since it represents only a shift from one alienating definition of the ego in relation to the alter, to another. If we examine the situation of someone caught up in this dilemma we can identify three contributing levels in the structure: (1) the definition of "social ego" in relation to "social alter" that he or she "inherits" from their initiation into society and which is maintained by the system of narcissistic mirror inversions we have described; (2) the social structure, which builds institutions upon a rigid model of the division of labor and applies the ideology of "professionalization" and of the rationalization of economic functions, induces people to limit themselves to specific job descriptions, and threatens them with unpleasure and insecurity (anxiety) if they venture beyond their functions, beyond their "job tunnel" on their own; (3) in the actual context of a job the person encounters the consensus of their colleagues that mediates the institutional dimension and brings it down to the level of day-to-day interactions. It is here that the individual who might want to break out of a restrictive identity will encounter their restricting alterity, that is, the alter who pushes them back into their tunnel vision by threatening personal rejection or institutional ostracism.

An overview of the interaction between these three levels shows that while the subject's intrapsychic alter maintains an internal pressure to confine their ego identity, it is matched by both their institutional and collegial alters. The result is that the external bureaucratization of economic functions, the socioeconomic mutilation, is matched by an internal mutilating bureaucratization.

The Problem of the One and the Many

The second fundamental opposition in social life can be put simply as the problem of the one and the many. The issue here is that human beings always exist in the plural; yet in order to organize their life in common they must arrive at a simple mode of action. The process of moving from the plurality of opinions to an agreement, even where a group is not divided by conflicting economic interests, is bound to alienate certain members of the group whose positions have not changed and who could not be accommodated in the final decision.

This means that we do not believe that like-mindedness or an identical mode of consciousness can be taken for granted as a characteristic of a group that is free to think its own thoughts. Furthermore, the free process of persuasion and debate cannot produce unanimity with any "efficiency." Of course, there are well-known methods for manipulating the decision-making process of a group in order to arrive at a decision that seems to be universally endorsed, but these can hardly be considered acceptable in the normal exercise of political freedom. They constitute specific forms of pathology in themselves, as we will argue later.

In the group, then, the issue of power always involves the shift from the many, with their plurality of views, to the one decision that creates the power of the group and makes collective action possible (Arendt 1958, pp. 175–248). This one decision must furthermore be represented by someone who can speak for the group. At this point the group's power gives rise to authority, and a further question arises as to the relationship of their representative to the group.

While our argument may seem to suggest the model of a utopian participatory democracy, we recognize that in reality both the process of decision making and the election of a leader (that is, the constant movement from the many to the one) are profoundly influenced by a process of unconscious transference that Freud indicated in *Group Psychology and the Analysis of the Ego* (1921) as well as in *Totem and Taboo* (1912).

In the pathology of the group, a false or unrealistic unity arises by virtue of a collective submission to a leader rather than being created by a process of discussion and assessment of the group's position. This unifying force of the leader arises from the same master-slave dialectic involved in the social issues of necessity and freedom. Here the anxiety and insecurity evoked by the need to arrive at a common decision of how to act for the good of all leads to the desire for a master who, by virtue of some unaccountable capacity, is believed to know what is best for all.

The bargain that the group strikes with the leader is once more an exchange of submission on its part for the sake of the security he offers. The leader assumes the responsibility for containing within himself whatever dangers and contradictions reality presents. He also decides what to do about them. The group members perceive themselves as dependent on their leader precisely because they have yielded their own capacity to observe, think, and make decisions to the point where they become uniquely distinguishing attributes of the leader and part of his mystique. Is a leader great because he knows how to lead, or simply because he is followed?

The followers arrive at an artificial unity because they unconsciously agree on one point: nobody wants to have to deal with the big decisions, and they are all happy to confine their deliberations to the small inconsequential issues. In other words, their condition for the choice of the leader is that he protects them from the anxiety provoked by the larger issues. In the same way, by giving him power and recognition they guarantee him freedom from the unpleasure provoked by smaller issues.

The result of this structure is that the group believes that the leader has an exclusive expertise in decision-making which they lack entirely. The leader, on the other hand, becomes convinced that he rules by virtue of a natural superiority. In the course of time this system of beliefs is transformed into a reality where, for want of practice, the group has indeed become incompetent in major decision making, and the leader cannot cope with the small issues of life, or with being an ordinary person. The end result is a system of pathological dependence, with the fate of the group entirely in the hands of the leader, who no longer feels accountable to the many he represents.

The fundamental structure of political freedom, the contradiction between the one and the many, therefore gives rise to two alternatives. The first uses the system of participation and representation in order to maximize the possibilities of action and power, so that the people have the opportunity to continually influence the reality of their world. But in the second, leadership can preempt participation, and a relationship of dependence follows. The result is some form of authoritarian domination and submission that utterly contradicts the structures of freedom and power.

These two directions are not mutually exclusive. To some extent representation will always give rise to authority and, with it, the tendency toward dependence and domination. Any political system not entirely authoritarian will exhibit a tension between participatory-representative and hierarchical-authoritarian tendencies.

Political freedom has survived historically only in those societies where provision has been made to protect political participation by a fundamental law or constitution. Even so, a fundamental law cannot be guaranteed forever against constant attempts by those eager to find a way around its provisions.

Violence and Sadomasochism

The issue in the master-slave dialectic is violence itself. The master wins because he is not forced to submit by a fear of death, while the slave loses on precisely that account. Consequently one can say that the master-slave relationship as well as the elaborate hierarchies that are built on its premises, contain but do not resolve the issue of violence in human relationships.

Freud makes exactly the same point when he shows the universal significance of the oedipus complex and castration anxiety in the case of social structure, as well as the universal significance of the murder of the father in the primal horde for the constitution of religious and political authority. In the work of Melanie Klein (1950), annihilating anxiety arises in the paranoid-schizoid position and presents the profoundest threat to psychic integration. Jacques Lacan (1966), on the other hand, has devised the specific concept of the *phallus* to indicate the threat of castration transmitted by the culture in order to compel the child to enter into the linguistic structure of the culture, to make the transition from the imaginary to the symbolic.

The containment of violence within the various hierarchical structures of a culture does not resolve the issue but merely transforms it into one of domination and submission. As a result, the threat of its return remains constant and in fact constitutes the ultimate source of the compulsion to conform to the norms of the culture. While conformity of this kind may well be preferable to the constant regression to violent conflict, it is hardly what one might call a true integration of civilized values.

Furthermore, precisely for that reason it constantly gives rise to corruption in either a dominant or a submissive agent. Pushed far enough, corruption can provoke a return of the repressed violence. In other words, conformity or the containment of violence by social and cultural structures has definite limits.

At the level of the transmission of culture through the family, psychoanalysis locates the issue of violence, as we have said, in the oedipus complex (Freud 1910) or in the paranoid-schizoid position (Klein 1948) or in terms of the *phallus* as signifier zero (Lacan 1966). Here as well the mere containment of the issue will lead to a psychic structure based upon conformity rather than integration, and for this reason it is both rigid and unstable. On the one hand, it leads to a compulsive conformity to the rules of the sadomasochistic game, and on the other it is subject to the compulsion to repeat the original situation of danger.

Taking both the collective and the individual perspectives into account, it becomes clear that the return of violent conflict in society can arise from either structure and, indeed, from one working against the other. Thus, the motive for corruption within the social and political system could arise from the individual's compulsion to push his sadomasochistic game to an extreme by manipulating the hierarchy in which he is situated. In doing so he may well remain a conformist in terms of the norms he internalized as a child, while he becomes a rebel or a tyrant in terms of the norms of the hierarchy. The same could also be true from the other perspective, where conforming to the norms of the hierarchy can put one in contradiction with those acquired in the family.

The somewhat pessimistic outlook that psychoanalysis has presented with regard to the issues of society and politics is more a matter of its critical posture and its analysis of the constant recurrence of violence than its own convictions. Psychoanalysis does raise the possibility of a truly democratic and cooperative model of human relationships at the familial, social, and political levels by analysing its necessary conditions in depth. At a minimum this requires overcoming rather than containing violence, and depends upon forming psychic, social, and political structures—not on the basis of a compulsion to conform constantly undermined by a compulsion to repeat, but by consciously integrated transformation of these structures.

At this level the underlying issue of violence does not disappear but on the contrary is openly recognized. The difference is that the reality of the threat is seen to impinge on everybody and is not selectively deflected from the dominant and directed against the submissive. At the oedipal level, for instance, this means the conscious acceptance of the fact that everybody's incestuous wishes must be equally frustrated to sustain the social structure. In political terms it means the recognition that nobody can be secure against violence once it takes its own course, so that the maintenance of a noncorrupted social structure is in the true interest of all—weak or strong, powerful or powerless, rich or poor. Hence, society needs to ensure that the pressures toward corruption are neutralized.

Working against the democratic possibility is the phenomenon of negative authority: the selective application of the threat of violence that is used to facilitate various forms of corruption and that undermines conformity with the same authority that claims to enforce it. Negative authority can be observed at almost any level of human organization.

Within the family, negative authority turns on the contrast between the world outside and the parents as champions of genuine values. The parent threatens the child with the dangers prevailing outside and the danger from the other parent in order to instill dependence upon him as the "good guy." Once he has established this negative authority he can even use it to convince the child that he is a danger to himself and can only be saved from himself by the "good guy" parent. The child finds itself trapped between its own supposed destructiveness and the threat of destruction from the other parent or from outside, which is the configuration that Melanie Klein (1950) identified as the paranoid-schizoid position. In her version, however, she neglected to identify the role of negative authority played by the sadistic parent. Moreover, the other parent, who according to our model would be masochistic, complements the negative authority of his partner by encouraging the child to believe in its validity. He thus presents himself as the "bad guy" from whom the child has to seek protection.

The result is that the parents encourage a split in the child's relationships to them, whereby it idealizes the negative authority of the sadistic parent and demonizes the lack of authority of the masochistic one. This bipolar structure has long been recognized in police and intelligence work, where two operatives break a suspect by means of the good-guy/bad-guy routine.

The Problem of the Many and the Few

While one can reduce the structure of political reality to the contradiction of the one and the many, as we have done, one cannot assume that the force of this contradiction remains constant despite the range of group size. Political groups may vary in size from a handful of people to millions. At a certain point the sheer size of the group limits the possibility for participation and directly affects the conditions of representation and leadership. At its simplest, this can be seen in terms of communication, the vehicle of political life.

For example, in a group of twenty who have come together for political purposes one can imagine a reasonably egalitarian process of mutual persuasion in order to reach a decision, which one of the members would then be called upon to represent in a larger forum. His relationship to the group would fairly accurately reflect his dependence on their delegating power for his own function as representative. The minimal degree of his abstraction from the reality of the group when he represents them does not create much room for the dialectic of the master and slave to assert itself and to begin to transform this relationship into one between a dominant leader and a submissive group.

The contrary is true when somebody is elected to represent millions of citizens. A high degree of communication among these citizens is virtually foreclosed in advance by their sheer numbers. Consequently, the nature of the representation becomes far more abstract in two senses: first, it is empty since the citizens hardly have a real chance to arrive at a political position among themselves. Second, they are essentially electing someone with whom they have had virtually no opportunity to talk. To call this kind of leader a true representative of the group is to stretch the concept to the point of absurdity. In reality the connection between the representative and the group has become a mere abstraction. It is here that the pressure of the master-slave dialectic comes into play, not so much distorting the real relationship between the group and its representative as supplying a regressive and simplifying substitute.

In democratic political culture, however, the gap between the group and the leader is filled at an ideological level with the myth that denies and inverts the reality of political power and authority in order to protect the belief in democratic participation as the legitimating source of government. The myth is accompanied by a ritualized political process by virtue of which the leaders are seen to be elected as true representatives of the people. But when one examines the elements of this process, it becomes apparent that the power of the people is purely nominal and that the election of leaders is both stage-managed and manipulated from behind the scenes by the true power brokers in society; without their support it is virtually impossible to become a "representative of the people."

There are four elements to the myth and ritual of mass democracy: mass communication, opinion polls, political parties and their platforms, and elections.

A politician who addresses the people via the mass media is compelled by the structure of his situation to think of the many he is addressing in terms of an abstraction by virtue of which they are reduced to one. His task is to find one—both in himself and in his audience. In himself the task is simplified because of the intrapsychic alter who is ready and available for the purpose in the form of a repression and projection onto the abstraction of the "people" (or "political alter").

He succeeds, either by chance or owing to his powers of seduction, in appealing to the specific anxieties of the people and the way in which they want to be protected by an idealized parental figure. The only way he can get support is by playing on the master-slave dialectic. He will present issues and propose solutions for them in a way that appears to be focused on reality, but is really intended to arouse particular anxieties that the people feel unable to master by themselves. He thereby unconsciously reminds them of the need for the true master, whom he promises to be.

In other words, by means of the structure of the mass media, the successful leader can mobilize a deep intrapsychic master-slave relationship in order to induce its transference across the gap of the political abstraction that separates him from the people. In doing so he is essentially reviving the "political" situation of childhood dependence on the powerful protective other, which, as Freud indicated in *The Future of an Illusion* (1930), was also the case in the relationship of the believer to his god, induced and manipulated by the agents of the church.

At the same time this manipulation is legitimated by and legitimates the political process, since it is understood to be in the tradition of real political communication despite the fact that it is not a debate in which the "people" talk among themselves and appoint a leader to represent their conclusions. This illusory form of democratic legitimation depends upon the particular character of the mass media, which give an artificial quality of immediacy to the presence of the speaker in the living rooms of the country.

Opinion polls play an important role in creating the illusion that the political process depends upon constantly consulting and respecting the "will of the people." Since the "people" never has the chance to consult itself in any meaningful political forum, what the polls are actually doing is inventing a "will of the people" in the absence of any real one. The method is based upon the most sophisticated statistical designs developed in the social sciences and therefore has the sanction of strict scientific neutrality. But the random opinions of the majority of a sample of people is no indication of the deliberate intention of any of the individuals consulted, let alone the result of collective deliberation. Consequently the so-called "opinions" can sometimes be the reflections of the prior influence of the media and of those who speak through them.

In effect, therefore, we have a set of reflecting mirrors set up between the media and the polls, and the politician's task is to manage the reflections. The people whose deliberation is supposed to be reflected in the polls are reduced to the "people," that is, the mirror reflection of the mass communications they receive through the media (Kraus and Davis 1976, pp. 142–145, 208–227). Those who speak through the media are like Narcissus, whose words are echoed in the polls. The people who respond to the polls in their own words are simply providing the feedback that has been induced by the mass communication. Here we can observe the irony that the more emphatically the people insist upon their "opinion," the more likely it is that they are echoing the opinion of others. In creating this artificial sense of the "will of the people," opinion polls actually mobilize a drive toward conformity in conjunction with the mass media that constantly report the results, and the politicians who read the polls in order to find out how they should address the people.

Citizens in modern society depend on information from the media to find out not only what others are "thinking" but also what they themselves should think in order to be safely included in the majority. The combination of the polls that "invent" the majority opinion (the "political alter"), the politicians who induce and exploit it, and the media who announce the "scientifically verified" outcome more than meets this need.

The third element in the management of the political process is the organization of political parties that adopt the platforms on which elections are fought. The parties are in the hands of the real power brokers, who use the party organization in order to determine who may become a candidate in the election and a "representative of the people." The platform a party adopts is frequently no more than an election strategy intended to assist its agents in selling themselves to the people. Once the election is determined, everyone expects the government to be run more or less as usual, regardless of the ephemeral platforms on which the candidates were elected.

So far we have discussed the fundamental tasks of the politician in forming his abstraction—his "political alter"—of the people, in order to project his own intrapsychic servant alter onto it, and to elicit the transference of their intrapsychic master alter onto himself. While he establishes his "credibility" in this way, his remaining task is to bring the people in line with the specific policies that, as their master, he intends to put in place. This involves the art of political persuasion that has been recognized as such since Socrates' attacks on the Sophists were recorded by Plato. Rhetoricians pretended to appeal to the reason of the audience but actually persuaded them, regardless of reason, by the skilful manipulation of language. If we look at political rhetoric in the context of the master-slave dialectic, the "reason" it works is not simply the inherent power of language to confuse the mind, but rather the fact that it is spoken by one who has already assumed the mantle of authority, so that his proposals carry the unconscious message of reward and punishment through promises and threats. To conform to his "proposal" is to enjoy the prospect of reward, while not to conform carries the threat of punishment. "If you don't support me I won't be there to protect you from insecurity and unpleasure or, if I get there anyway, I'll exclude you from the group I reward with security and pleasure."

Under some paradoxical circumstances it is possible for the master-slave dialectic to be inverted in reality so that the leader becomes a disqualified, incompetent, and powerless slave and the people enjoy criticizing his performance. He is made a scapegoat, and they go on believing that they retain unlimited possibilities of action. Since the interaction between the leader and the people is almost always based upon a narcissistic misconstruction of ritual and myth, we must look elsewhere for an explanation of this situation.

In relation to our psychoanalytic model, we can discriminate the relationship of the leader to the power brokers from that of the leader to the people. The first would constitute the backroom power structure, comparable to the unobservable intrapsychic power structure of ego and alter, while the second would compare with the interpersonal ego and alter, as in Figure 9-1.

With this model in mind, the leader, like the ego, can be either the master or the slave, depending upon the condition of the system that he has to maintain. Usually leadership requires that he be the master and the people his slave, but under some historical conditions an inversion of this dialectic may be the only way in which the legitimacy of the political regime can be maintained in the society. Under conditions of economic prosperity the constant reinforcement of the expectation of a secure and comfortable life may negate the tendency of the people to submit to a sadistic leader out of insecurity. At this point a masochistic leader would be more likely to win their acceptance, since he would indulge their demands for pleasure and assume responsibility for whatever goes wrong should

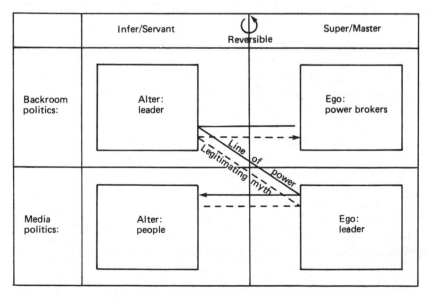

Figure 9-1. The narcissistic structure of ego and alter in politics

their expectations lead to the formation of unrealistic policies. Nevertheless, one has to look at the interests of the power brokers, who have been working behind the scenes as well.

Regardless of whether the leader is sadistically or masochistically oriented, the outcome is always "mental illness"—that is, the mystification of the people concerning both the realities of power and the real political issues, and the frequent failure of policymakers to realize the public interest in the face of changing realities. This is comparable to the fact that neither the sadistic agent nor the masochistic patient achieves full pleasure and security because of the constant failure of his alter (as policymaker) in taking care of the interest of his ego in the constantly changing modern world.

The Leader as Superego

We have indicated that while the basic structure of the political sphere can be analyzed in terms of the relationship of the group with its representative, if one applies this analysis to contemporary mass democracy, there is a third element to the structure that fills the gap left by the fact that the group can no longer be truly represented. This is the group of power brokers whom the leader actually represents even though the people and he himself believe that he represents the will of the people. By some means or another the power brokers are usually the ones who control the function of leadership from behind the scenes.

There is a difference between the psychology of a leader and the psychology of a power broker. The leader carries the burden of anxiety that goes with his task of maintaining political control of the people, but the power broker enjoys both security and pleasure since he has the benefits of the system at his disposal and the satisfaction of having a representative (who is also the leader of the people) accountable to him as the condition for ongoing support.

The distinction between the leader and the power broker is also similar to the distinction between the two functions of the "superego": the leader is the judge, the master who applies the law, but the power broker is the law itself (or, at least, the one who makes the law). Similarly, the sadistic agent of mental illness, who functions as a master alter to the servant ego of the masochist, is not simply a ruler in full control of the sadomasochistic relationship. In fact, he blindly obeys the law of his own superego.

In modern society, where legitimation in politics does not come from tradition or a transcendent principle of order, the system can be maintained only by the consensus that the leader evokes in the people and that they, in turn, demand that he fulfill. The power brokers themselves cannot achieve this consensus; they depend on the leader to make their own interests appear to be the interests of the people. This gives the leader a degree of leverage in relation to them, so that the relationship between the power brokers and the leader is not simply unidirectional. It must be negotiated, although in comparison with the relative continuity of the elite, leaders come and go.

There is sufficient room for the master-slave dialectic to assert itself between the power brokers and the leaders in either direction, depending on who has the advantage—the leaders because their services are indispensable, the power brokers because their backing is critical to the ambitions of the leader. All of this has direct consequences for their relationship. The leader may have a submissive role in relation to the elite and a dominant role in relation to the people, or vice versa. On the other hand, he may be either masochistic or sadistic in both directions.

What is critical for the endurance of the political system is not the specific constellation among the power brokers, the leaders, and the people that obtains at any one time, but whether in fact it permits the system to maintain itself in relation to the prevailing realities of the world.

The Master and the Slave in Freud's Work

The evidence of the master–slave dialectic is implicit in Freud's social writings, particularly in *Totem and Taboo* (1912) and *Group Psychology and the Analysis of the Ego* (1921).

TOTEM, TABOO, AND OEDIPAL COMPETITION

Freud's argument in *Totem and Taboo* is that there are two stages in the development of the social contract and especially of the taboo against murder. In the first stage he posits a primal horde in which a tyrannical father maintains exclusive possession of the women, thereby depriving his sons of sexual pleasure and reproduction. In order to free themselves from this literal repression, the sons conspire to kill the father, since the father's pleasure is premised upon their unpleasure. They then confront the possibility that anyone of them could aspire to usurp the father's place, or, if not, simply deprive one or more of his brothers of pleasure. Either instance would give rise to the problem of fratricide, which follows directly from the problem of patricide and exhibits the identical structure of rebellion against the <satisfied frustrator>. That is, the tendency toward fratricide derives from the desire to imitate the father by becoming a <satisfied frustrator> at the expense of a <frustrated satisfier>.

At the second stage the brothers overcome this tendency by realizing that if it is pushed to its conclusion, even the <satisfied frustrator> cannot achieve his goal because he will have eliminated his object, the <frustrated satisfier>, in his murder. Consequently, they enter a contract which specifies that each is entitled to his own woman and none has the right to murder another. But the problem is that the brothers are haunted by the memory of their patricide, as well as by the possibility of taking the father's place. In order to collectively purge themselves of this temptation and to renew their contract on a regular basis, they engage in a totemic feast in which the father is symbolically murdered and eaten by each of them.

This does not represent a resolution of their conflict with their father, nor of the contradiction between the <satisfied frustrator> and the <frustrated satisfier>. Instead, the totemic system manages to contain the contradiction by a symbolic displacement of the father onto the totem. But Freud's irony is that the authority which maintains the taboo against fratricide and that constitutes the social contract still derives from the ghost of the father and is maintained by periodically incarnating and devouring him. In effect this amounts to a literal process of projection and introjection and a literal version of the "superego" which perpetuates unconsciously a rule that is the very opposite of the norm it insists upon consciously.

Another way of expressing this is to say that the totemic feast is the return of the repressed desire to be the father, which at the same time is defended against, as it was originally, by the renewal of the fraternal contract signed in the blood of the father.

In Freud's version, the attempt to get away from the primitive violence that makes possible the beginning of culture is defeated by the constant need to return to it in fantasy and ritual. The more the brothers attempt to arrange things differently, the more it turns out that they have remained basically the same. In the first stage, we are introduced to the murderous competition between the brothers and the father for an object of pleasure from which the fraternity then tries to flee. At the second stage we discover that their attempt actually consists of a ritual reenactment of the murderous competition with the father. By killing and eating the totem, each of the brothers ritually enjoys the place of <satisfied frustrator> of the father.

Freud argued that this myth reveals the phylogenetic version of the oedipus complex from the masculine point of view. It is noteworthy that the women, who are the ostensible objects of dispute, are barely featured. This can be brought into line with the interpretation of the oedipus complex that we have proposed, where the issue is really the competition between the child and the parent of the same sex, in which the parent of the opposite sex is featured only as an exclusive source of pleasure.

In effect, the traditional view of the oedipus complex as a triangle of relationships clearly yields to a bipolar analysis as Freud depicted it in the myth of *Totem and Taboo* (1912), where the interest centers exclusively on the conflict between father and son. Ultimately, however, the jealous father succeeds in raising sons in his own image—they are jealous. Father and son constitute mirror images, and the two poles of this bipolar conflict can almost be said to be identical. Thus the father fights with his own reflection in the son, and the son fights with his own reflection in the father. In terms of the Greek myth, therefore, the triangle of Laius, Jocasta, and Oedipus can be reduced to the opposition of Laius and Oedipus, or, more simply, of Oedipus and his aural-visual reflection. This also happens to Narcissus with his visual reflection in the water and his aural reflection in the nymph Echo.

THE ONE AND THE MANY IN
GROUP PSYCHOLOGY AND THE ANALYSIS
OF THE EGO

In terms of the development of sociology, *Group Psychology and Analysis of the Ego* belongs in the context of the study of charisma that Max Weber had also identified as the primary mode of group cohesion in society (Weber, quoted in Runciman 1978, pp. 212–225, 226–251). Where Weber interpreted charisma as the elementary form of social cohesion immediately overtaken by the development of institutions that established the group and provided a continuous social formation, Freud's analysis of group psychology did not pertain simply to an initial stage of society but to an ongoing process as well.

While it is true that the phenomenon of the group behaving as a mass without individuality, completely dependent on a leader, is likely to be revealed only in those moments of profound social dislocation (hence the importance for Freud of Le Bon's study of the crowd), Freud did not take an historical perspective of social evolution in Weber's terms. He believed that this kind of group behavior remains unconsciously determinant of social and political behavior in general. For him the historical occurrence of crowd behavior amounted to a kind of uncovering of this primary mode of containing the fundamental contradiction between the one and the many in politics.

Freud draws a distinction between the individual psychology of the leader and the psychology of the group. It is essential to note that these two psychologies are at once opposed and mutually dependent. Both represent a distortion of the ordinary psychology of an individual generated in the attempt to overcome the fundamental problem of the group itself—how to find a structure that will permit it to determine a common mode of action. (Rousseau, for example, refers to this as the problem of the general will.) By reducing the group to a mass of individuals who do not have a desire of their own, the problem of arriving at a unified decision to act is simply reduced to the will of a single individual who has kept a desire of his own because he has not submerged himself in the group. His will becomes the will of the group.

What follows in the structure of the group are precisely the mutually exclusive but dependent categories of psychology that Freud indicated. Thus the individual who retains his identity finds it distorted by virtue of the fact that he has also to provide the group, whose members have renounced their identities, with an identity so that it can function. The leader emerges as a kind of superman who is induced to develop all the characteristics of what Freud calls a narcissist. In our own terminology, he is a sadistic agent.

The leader is untroubled by considerations of security and has a clear idea of the pleasures he wants provided by the group. He believes in his superiority to the group, and that as a result he is entitled to make the decisions that affect their common interest. While the leader enjoys the distortion of his individuality in a megalomanic direction, what is not clear to him is the fact that he is in reality condemned to accept this distortion for the sake of the group and, in the process, to lose the possibility of an ordinary life whose pleasures and anxieties are within human proportions.

The members of the group evade the anxieties arising from the determination of their future by handing over the problem of their security to the leader. In return, however, they are trapped in a dependence on his will and must sacrifice any independent determination of their own desires.

Once the leader is compelled to think and act on a macro-scale, the group is compelled to confine its thoughts and actions to the insignificance of a micro-scale. And if the leader's identity is magnified constantly into megalomanic proportions, such identity as the members of the group retain is minimized into a micro-depressive proportion, if they do not lack identity altogether.

Freud analyzed this complementary distortion of reality by the two parties in terms of a hypnotic process whereby the members of the group transfer their ego-ideal onto the leader, who is then perceived as an idealized other. The leader, on the other hand, is "counter-hypnotized," in keeping with the notion of countertransference, so that he believes himself to be ideal. Implied in Freud's analysis (although not clearly articulated) is that the converse of the process of idealization must obtain simultaneously, namely, that the group retains the devalued image of itself while the leader projects his own devaluation onto the group.

Consequently there is a double hypnotic transfer between the group and its leader that takes on the appearance of a relation of domination and submission in which the leader is free to enjoy the sadistic pleasures of domination at the same time as his ideal image of himself is being constantly confirmed by the group. The group is compelled, because of its devalued self-image which the leader constantly reinforces, to submit masochistically to his domination, which offers it a false sense of security. The leader is condemned to the tyranny of the idealization by others that does not allow him any weakness, and the followers to the pit of devaluation that does not allow them any strength.

If one analyzes the domination of the leader and the submission of the group, the underlying structure turns out not to be an absolute, asymmetrical relationship, but, on the contrary, one that is equally sustained by the two parties: one looking for pleasure and the other looking for security.

The masochistic members of the group demand a sadistic leader, while the sadistic leader insists on a masochistic group, because only the realization of these two functions makes the structure viable. At the same time they have to be disguised in order to make the structure consciously acceptable. The simplest disguise is to pretend that you think and do the opposite of what you are thinking and doing in reality. Thus the leader constantly claims to be masochistically led by the group, while the members of the group enjoy the idea that they have freely chosen as their leader someone who puts their interests and needs before his own. In their view he becomes an indulgent, caring parent.

Once more we can see that this bipolar structure of the sadist and the masochist actually reduces to a single narcissistic mirror relationship, whereby the leader (the sadistic agent) sees himself reflected in the mirror of the group, while members of the group (masochistic patient) in turn see themselves reflected in the mirror of their leader.

THE POLITICS OF FREUD'S STRUCTURAL MODEL

One of the remarkable innovations that Freud introduced (1923) with his new model of the mind was the political conception of the relationship among the three mental agencies—id, ego, and superego.

Freud's first model (the topographical) distinguished between the layers of the mind (conscious, preconscious, and unconscious) in relation to the accessibility of memories of ideas and affects (Freud 1900). In his theory of repression based upon this distinction (1915), he had already introduced the concept of a censor responsible for maintaining the repression. When he explained the operation of this censorship in *The Interpretation of Dreams* he utilized a political metaphor. He invoked the image of a censor responsible for reading all the communications entering a country that was governed by a repressive regime. The censor resorts to the literal erasing of those parts of the texts that expose aspects of the political structure which the regime must keep secret in order to perpetuate its legitimacy. Freud's analogy not only illustrated how repression works but also showed the necessity for preserving the integrity of the psychic apparatus, which might otherwise collapse under the impact of unwanted revelations.

In his second model (the structural), the concept of censorship is transformed into the defensive and, in our terms, inverted relation that prevails between the ego and the superego. A critical political relationship between these two agencies is set up in the psychic apparatus and at the same time its truth is censored. In Freud's view the submissive ego is deprived of the possibility of satisfying the demands for pleasure (and security) from the id and is dominated by the superego. But this oppression is kept out of consciousness by means of systems of censorship and disguise.

The latent content of dreams is, in effect, the attempt of the id to reveal the truth of the frustrations resulting from the oppressive political relationship between superego and ego. What is repressed is not only the fact of the political domination of the ego but also the resulting frustration.

According to our interpretation of Freud's work, his structural model presents the intrapsychic picture of the masochistic patient whose servant ego or infer-ego is dominated by a master "superego" or super-alter; consequently, his id is kept secure but frustrated in relation to pleasure by this political structure, even if the punitive super-alter is disguised as a good, overprotective master. This picture is completed by introducing the intrapsychic politics of the sadistic agent. His master ego or superego dominates his servant "superego" or infer-alter and, consequently, his own id is satisfied with regard to pleasure but frustrated in terms of security, even if his indulgent infer-alter is disguised as a complacent servant. In both cases, the latent content of the dreams reveals the truth about the affective results (in the id) of the political system which exists between the ego and the alter.

In our view the analytic cure would consist of the transformation of the intrapsychic political system so that the relationship between ego and "superego" (ego and alter) becomes that of two equals who are well disposed toward each other. That is not simply a matter of making the super-alter "benign" but rather of redistributing the power between the two agencies on a truly equal basis. Since the issue between ego and alter is the satisfaction of desires—as we learn from Freud's theory of the oedipus complex—this political transformation takes place specifically in relation to the pursuit of pleasure. Instead of this pursuit taking the form of a competitive or sadomasochistic pact, it becomes a cooperative venture in which both parties gain satisfaction (of pleasure, security, and psychic organization) and share unavoidable frustrations.

PSYCHIC AND POLITICAL BREAKDOWNS

A psychic system breaks down when a crisis of incompetence occurs in relation to the significant other. In the case of a political system the critical factor in a breakdown is the maintenance of legitimation by means of the construction of the political myth between the leader and the people. In practice the myth is always characterized by a specific content or issue reflecting the concerns of the society at the time. Part of the leader's task is to integrate new elements into his construction of the political myth.

In addition, the political myth requires a sensitivity to the limits of either the sadistic or the masochistic directions of its structure; otherwise, it will collapse. The domination of the people can go only so far before it becomes impossible to retain their loyalty. Alternatively, if the leader is masochistic he cannot indulge the sadistic demands of the people to the point where neither he nor they can take reality into account in the formation of policy.

The breakdown of the political system can be the result of two main processes. First, legitimation collapses because of exaggeration (in either direction) of the master-slave dialectic to the point where the construction or reconstruction of the political myth becomes impossible: the sadist can no longer provide security and the masochist can no longer provide pleasure. Second, the legitimation may survive but the dynamics of the master-slave relationship may have led to the distortion of the political myth to the point where reality itself, in the form of internal or external factors, is in such contradiction with the political system that it breaks down.

We do not mean that a simple sadomasochistic model of the leader/people relationship can explain the vicissitudes of the system. Power brokers also play a crucial role. The structure that sustains the cohesion of the political system can be defined in terms of the master-slave dialectics; critical input comes from the pressures that the power brokers can generate and the pressures that domestic and international realities generate.

The issue of the breakdown of the political system brings us back to the fundamental structure of politics: the problem of the one and the many. When the system breaks down, this problem reasserts itself in an entirely negative form—a form which often has served as the point of departure for developments in social or political theory. The disintegration which Hobbes, for example, saw as "the war of all against all" can take the form of civil war or international war (given the interdependence of political systems). Similarly, in schizophrenic psychotic breakdown, we have a war of all representations against themselves; that is, the intrapsychic subject (ego) and its alter reach no agreement at any level.

We have emphasized the possibility of the breakdown of societies in terms of an analysis of the political system, but the same is true of the economic system. Economics is sustained by the shared belief in a common economic reality despite the fact that it varies from one region or group of society to another. Given the integration of economic and political authority at the highest levels, the leaders are also responsible for sustaining the economic myth.

Politicians make economic policy, and the power brokers do so through them. We believe, however, that it is possible for the breakdown of the system to arise for distinctly political and economic reasons. Nevertheless, the structure through which the economic myth is disseminated is the political structure; therefore the analysis of the breakdown of the system arising from economic conditions must include an analysis of its distinctive political structure.

Semiotics and the Distribution of Power: Analogy between the Psychic and the Political Systems

As we suggested earlier, (page 324) the power brokers operate like the ego, the leaders like the alter, in the first instance, and then the leader operates like an ego in relation to the people as alter (see Figure 9-1). While this describes the psychic agencies, we have also taken into account the problem of representation peculiar to the maintenance of both psychic and political systems. In the psychic system, the formation of an appropriate structure of representations is critical for the maintenance of both psychic and biological life. The representation of the real relationships between the agencies is inverted in consciousness, as we have shown in our model of psychic bipolarity.

In the political system there are also two layers of inverted representations. The first is the leader's representation of the power brokers; the second is his representation of the people. The inversion occurs when the successful leader gets the people to believe that they are the power brokers and he is their servant, while the opposite is true: he is the servant of the unseen power brokers and, usually, the people serve him.

The result is the maintenance of a political system that cannot get beyond the inherent sadomasochism generated by the contradiction between the one and the many, and the many and the few. The system as such is maintained in a tenuous relationship with reality in a way that is similar to a psychic system whose sadomasochistic narcissism finds suitable accommodation to reality in a complementary partner.

In comparison with the psychic system, where the possibility of overcoming the sadomasochistic Moebius strip remains realizable, the political system confronts us with a real and fundamental limitation: the gap between the leader and the people in mass democracy. So far this gap has only been bridged by means of the complex but primitive dialectic of the master and the slave that underlies the legitimating political myth or unifying "representation," and permits the ongoing interaction between the power brokers and the leader.

The maintenance of the political system in the psyche depends upon both the management of the relations of power among the three mental agencies and the semiotic structure of representations that permits their negotiations to that end. But it also requires a reasonably accurate response to conditions in reality.

The political system, like the psychic system, is both a semiotic system and a means of distributing power. In the psychic system, one can distinguish two levels of representation in the formation of the intrapsychic subject-object relationships. First, the parents "represent" the interests of the child to him and to the outside world; one could call this "political representation" and it clearly arises from the contradiction in being a child. A child both is himself and is incomplete in himself, so that he needs the parents to represent the possibility of completeness. On the other hand, incompleteness remains the fundamental contradiction of human life and if it is foreclosed the outcome is a misconstruction of the ego, as Lacan has indicated.

Consequently, on this first political level of representation, the child is particularly vulnerable to the parents' misrepresentation, if in fact they undertake the task of representing his completeness literally, instead of reflecting the inherent paradox of incompleteness in both positions.

The second level of representation is the psychological introjection by the child of the representation that its parents construct for him. This can be called the "representation of the representation." The same double meaning of the concept applies in politics: the many must find one to represent them in order to provide some remedy for their incompleteness and impotence as an unintegrated group. The representative then constructs a representation that the group introjects psychologically. This double process reaches its limits, both in the case of the child and of the group, in their dependence on the other to carry the burden of their incompleteness for them.

In this narcissistic resolution the fact of incompleteness is buried instead of being carried over into the representation and reflected back to the child or the group. It forms the basis for the master-slave dialectic, in which the issue is contained by constructing an opposition between omnipotence and impotence, in which there is no room for consideration of this gap that marks human beings equally.

The child's ongoing relationship with his parents provides the opportunity to modify the representation of the representation in a more realistic direction that recognizes and transcends the narcissistic basis of the master-slave dialectic. In political democracies the problem is whether a similar possibility of interaction and communication with the other can be realized in view of the apparently insurmountable problem of numbers. It is primarily through balancing different kinds of power and limiting authority by law that the divisive thrust of this dialectic is held in check.

CONVERGENCE OF THE SOCIAL, POLITICAL, AND PSYCHOANALYTIC HYPOTHESES

In this chapter we have shown that in addition to the intrapsychic sphere, the socioeconomic and political spheres are also informed by the mutilating and inverted dialectic of the master-slave bipolarity. While this structure appears to be the same in all three cases, we believe that in fact it is not, but rather, that it arises in each case as the attempt to overcome a specific problem.

Intrapsychically, the subject is confronted with the problem of pleasure versus security and resorts to the master-slave dialectic in order to obtain satisfaction in at least one respect, given that the competitive situation precludes the possibility of both.

Socially, the issue of necessity versus freedom has been overcome by a series of institutions governed by the master-slave dialectic in terms of the distribution of recognition and financial rewards. Politically, the problem of the one and the many is transformed into the structure of the few and the many where the intrapsychic agencies of ego and alter find their counterparts in the political agencies of power brokers, leaders, and people, whose relations are also based on the master-slave dialectic: the "real" power is negotiated between the brokers and the leader(s) and ritualized power is negotiated mythically between the leader(s) and the people.

The pressure behind this structure therefore comes from three different directions, but their effect on the subject is that they reinforce one another. Theoretically it is impossible to ascribe the origin to either the intrapsychic or the social or political spheres. Freud attempted to deal with this question by virtue of the distinction between the ontogenetic dimension, which referred to the intrapsychic development of the child in relation to its significant others, and the phylogenetic dimension, which referred to the history of culture. Ultimately, however, we must take a synchronic perspective even when looking at the origin of this dialectic from an historical viewpoint, since the cultural development of the group and the psychic development of the individual cannot be separated.

The analysand presents himself—whether as sadistic agent or masochistic patient—as somebody in whom the master-slave dialectic is consistently at work in relation to the intrapsychic, political, and socioeconomic spheres.

To view his speech, affects, and actions exclusively in the light of intrapsychic contradiction deprives the analyst of the therapeutic power to help him work through the social and political dimensions of his alienation, and may well confuse the specifics of his intrapsychic conflict.

The intrapsychic conflict reflects the sociopolitical structure introjected by the analysand during his infancy and childhood: the therapeutic "insight" must give him a clear picture of it. But the analysand must also achieve a clear picture, a therapeutic "socialsight" of the social and political structure in which he presently lives, once he has obtained a good insight into the old one.

REFERENCES

Arendt, H. (1958). *The Human Condition*. Chicago: University of Chicago Press.

——— (1969). *On Violence*. New York: Harcourt Brace Jovanovich.

Blau, P. M. (1963). *The Dynamics of Bureaucracy*. Chicago: University of Chicago Press.

Etzioni, A. (ed.) (1961). *Complex Organizations: A Sociological Reader*. New York: Holt, Rinehart and Winston.

Freud, S. (1900). The interpretation of dreams. *Standard Edition* 4/5.

——— (1910). A special type of choice of object made by men. *Standard Edition* 11:164-175.

——— (1912). Totem and taboo. *Standard Edition* 13:1-162.

——— (1915). Repression. *Standard Edition* 14:143-158.

——— (1921). Group psychology and the analysis of the ego. *Standard Edition* 18:67-143.

——— (1924). The economic problem of masochism. *Standard Edition* 19:157-170.

——— (1927). The future of an illusion. *Standard Edition* 21:3-56.

Gerth, H. H., and Mills, C. W. (eds.) (1958). *From Max Weber*. New York: Oxford University Press.

Hegel, G. W. F. (1807). *The Phenomenology of Mind*, transl. J. B. Baillie. New York: Humanities Press, 1966.

Hummel, R. P. (1977). *The Bureaucratic Experience*. New York: St. Martin's.

Klein, M. (1948). *Contributions to Psycho-Analysis*, 1921-1945. London: Hogarth Press.

Kraus, S. and Davis, D. (1976). *The Effects of Mass Communication on Political Behaviour*. University Park: Pennsylvania State University Press.

Lacan, J. (1966). *Écrits*. Paris: Editions du Seuil.

Mills, C. W. (1956). *The Power Elite*. New York: Oxford University Press.

Offe, C. (1972). Political authority and class structure. *International Journal of Sociology*, Spring.

Runciman, W. G. (ed.) (1978). *Max Weber: Selections*, transl. E. Matthews. Cambridge: Cambridge University Press.

Swingle, P. G. (1976). *The Management of Power*. New York: John Wiley.

10
Recommendations for Treatment

Psychopathology and Sociopathology

It will be apparent from the range of interpretation and intervention we recommend that we have a broader concept of the analyst's work than is conventional. In particular, we believe that the analyst must be competent to understand the specific location of the analysand within the socioeconomic and political system. Otherwise many aspects of the analysand's conflicts will be passed over, or worse, misplaced and misinterpreted as personal problems.

A distinction must therefore be made between psychopathology and sociopathology, both of which are transmitted to the analysand as a result of his particular insertion in a family and in society. Obviously the sociopathology will be more broadly based, and its fundamental conflicts will be represented in the group to which the analysand belongs, and reflected in its national, regional, class, ethnic, or civic culture. The psychopathology will derive more strictly from his family.

In order to analyze both dimensions of the analysand's conflicted structures the analyst must himself be prepared in the relevant aspects of social science. Unfortunately this is not always a part of analytic training and the lack of it contributes to the narcissistic tendency of psychoanalysis at an institutional level, since it condemns the analyst to becoming the narcissistic mirror reflection of the analysand's sociopathology instead of being able to interpret and transform it.

We believe that our emphasis on the problem of sociopathology follows Freud's insistence on the problematic of the reality principle. Too often the concept of the reality principle has been taken to mean the passive acceptance of reality as if it were given by some fiat beyond human control. But in fact, whatever the generalized status quo of society, the particular position one occupies in the world is not necessarily beyond one's own capacity for changing it. And in many ways it is precisely this kind of mastery that psychoanalysis is concerned with: "Where id was, there ego shall be."

It is difficult to imagine how an analysand can overcome an incapacitating conflict induced by his own cultural, social, or economic situation or that of his parents in childhood unless he can actually change it and thereby eliminate its influence. In other words, the intrapsychic agencies are to a considerable extent the products of social, cultural, and economic reproduction and are therefore typical. To change them requires both a new consciousness of the world and the analysand's particular place in it as well as new ways of acting that will enable him to improve his social situation.

The neglect of the sociopathological dimension of unconscious conflicts no doubt contributes to the problem of therapeutic disappointments and the consequent disenchantment with psychoanalysis. Since psychoanalysis promises the analysand the transformation of the entire psychic structure, it is bound to disappoint him when, in effect, it can deal only with those aspects of the structure that are confined to personal relationships at home or at work as these derive from childhood experiences.

Analysts tend to rationalize this in terms of the requirement of neutrality that inhibits them from questioning the "values" of the analysand. Social science, however, tells us that these values are not in the nature of absolute or rationally digested convictions but are for the most part simple reflections of one's primary affiliations and the particular socialization they entail. To dignify the analysand's conflicted value system with the kind of reverence one would pay to the conclusions of a major philosopher is really to abort a fundamental aspect of the analytic process and to condemn the analysis to failure in important respects. On the other hand, we are not suggesting that analysts simply assume the right to invent their own social science and make interpretations of sociopathology. We are suggesting only that psychoanalysis recover its original, more broadly based understanding by the study of the social sciences, so that it can be competent in socio- as well as psychopathology.

In our view the work of Lévi-Strauss is critical for this renewal of psychoanalysis since he has shown the way to understand the connection between the psychological and cultural spheres as we have tried to indicate elsewhere in our book.

In trying to integrate psychoanalysis with the social sciences in our theory and practice we are not opting for a naive culturalist approach that would ultimately so dissipate the unconscious conflicts as to render them impossible to analyse. In such approaches the analysand in effect becomes invisible. But to ignore the problem entirely does not remove the threat of a truncated analysis in which it is society that becomes invisible. Our point is that the psychic structure is the meeting place of influences that are both micro and macro in origin. Taking both dimensions into account has been the task of psychoanalysis since Freud, who set a clear example in this respect, both in his practice and in his theoretical writings. To do so is not to generate a utopian and unrealistic *furor curandis* but simply to address conscientiously the problem of the analysand's insertion in reality. Without taking the social context into account one can hardly make sense of the psychological text. A psychoanalysis that persists in trying to make society invisible may end in the unenviable position of itself becoming invisible to society.

The analyst's ability to interpret the interaction between psychopathology and sociopathology cannot be developed simply on the basis of theoretical study; it requires also that he analyze his own location in culture, society, and the economy, and maintain a constant objectivity about his own world. He has to become something of an anthropologist of his own world, or a participant observer, who is both inserted in a particular social context and uses a clear and distinct model of the world for his own handling of reality. Without this attempt at clarity about himself, he can hardly help the analysand toward clarity about his own handling of reality.

Building the Authority of the Analyst

Convention holds that the psychoanalyst must remain neutral in the analytic setting, and should confine himself to being an accurate mirror that reflects the analysand back to himself. Certainly the function of listening carefully to the analysand's speech and interpreting it to him so as to reflect not only its manifest but also its latent content is crucial to the analytic process.

But in our view this does not fully describe the role of the analyst. What it overlooks is the analyst's power in relation to the patient. If that power is to be used to facilitate the process of healing, it must be understood and applied systematically. If it is not deliberately controlled, it is likely to be deployed for unconscious manipulative reasons that reflect the transference-countertransference situation.

The analytic setting is usually considered to be protected from the normal constraints of reality in several respects. First, the confidentiality of the setting permits the discussion of matters that would be considered indiscreet in most other social situations. Second, the concept of the transference allows both analysand and analyst to understand that whatever may be said in the course of free association, as opposed to the other forms of speech, is not directed personally at the analyst: "Any resemblance to an actual person is purely coincidental." This, of course, is true only when the analyst is not engaged in a narcissistic game himself. Third, the relationship is exclusively directed to the task of analysis, and whatever is said will not lead to action to change the setting.

This protection, if it were unqualified, would suggest that the setting is immune to the possibility of generating pressures to influence the analysand's behavior, either in the analysis or outside in reality. But this is not the case. There are several levels of pressure that arise in the analytic setting that the analyst can actualize.

In addition to *reconstructing* the way in which the analysand's universe of representations was structured under the influence of significant others (and especially in response to the affective pressures they brought to bear on him), the analyst is concerned to *transform* the structure in order to help the analysand. This requires a reversal of the chain of transmission; the obvious point of entry is the analysand's affects, which were vulnerable to his family in the first place. Therefore the analyst must take stock of the vulnerable points in the analysand's affects so that he can create the pressures for change deliberately and oppose the pressures for resistance inherent in the structure.

In effect, this is what the analysand looks for in his analysis: an experience that will not simply repeat his infantile set of relationships, or merely reflect them back, but one that will correct them. To do so the analyst must use the opening provided by the analysand's repetitions, which invariably gives him the power of the significant others (conveyed by the transference) in order to undo the way in which they exercised that power. In this way he can use the transference against the transference at the same time that he analyzes it. If one considers the history of Freud's discovery of transference, its connection to a process of influencing the analysand becomes obvious. In fact, it was from his practice as a hypnotist, and the recognition of his power to influence what the patient transfers onto the hypnotist, that Freud came upon the possibility of psychotherapy in the first place. When he turned to psychoanalysis, it was not in order to give up the healing powers he had found through hypnosis but rather to make them more effective and applicable to a larger number of people, many of whom could not be hypnotized. But with its emphasis on the analyst's neutrality (in order to make his interpretation as accurate as possible), psychoanalysis has lost sight of the influencing process which has always been at the heart of psychotherapy.

The advantage of psychoanalysis over hypnosis is that it can both provide the patient with this therapeutic influence and at the same time analyze what is going on. The underlying issue of dependence and the danger of repeating a master-servant or a servant-master relationship that would counteract the therapeutic outcome can be avoided.

The advantage of looking at psychoanalysis in light of its origins in hypnosis is that it becomes clear that the very nature of the therapeutic relationship depends on the influencing process that the analysand unconsciously sets in motion with his transference. It is not a matter of choice that the analyst tries to influence the analysand. The question he is free to determine is how he will use this influence. To interpret the transference is in itself an influencing process that uses the transference against itself. It is our view that if the psychoanalyst understands that this inevitably occurs, he can be more deliberate in exercising this influence and thereby make the therapeutic relationship more efficient. Perhaps this point of view challenges a cherished belief that psychoanalysts share: that their relationship with their analysands is untainted by considerations of influence, pressure, or power, which, on the contrary, belong only in the competitive or manipulative context of the unanalyzed world outside. In part, this assumption is justified because the kind of power we are talking about is the power to heal that, ideally speaking, reverses the process of manipulation in competitive relations of power.

On the other hand, to deny or ignore the fact that healing is in fact a form of power and, as with other forms of power, that it only works to the extent that it is exercised, and that it works only if it is exercised with care, is to remain out of touch with the reality of the analytic setting and to depend on chance rather than skill for the outcome (Freud 1912b).

Let us examine the widely held belief that the psychoanalytic setting is basically democratic in its point of departure in recognizing the equality of the analyst and the analysand as persons in their own right. The problem is that the analysand does not come in with an established capacity for a democratic relationship of this kind. In all likelihood, if he had this capacity he would not be seeking the analyst's help. It is the analyst's responsibility, therefore, to bring the analysand around to a democratic way of relating, and this becomes the goal of the treatment. In technical terms this means helping him resolve his sadomasochistic pattern of abusing the other. The shift from one kind of power relationship (master-servant bi-polarity) to another kind of power relationship (between equals) can be made only with the help of the healing power of the treatment. It takes a new kind of power to break down and reconstitute an old and established power structure.

Insofar as the goal of the treatment is to transform the analysand's sadomasochistic psychic power structure, the project is revolutionary and not simply supportive or reformist. By contrast, supportive therapy is conformist in orientation in that it accepts the authority of the analysand, while psychodynamic psychotherapy tries to negotiate a better deal between the parties, on the model of an industrial-relations mediator. In our view, therefore, the various forms of psychotherapy can be classified according to attitudes toward power, because the psychic structure they attempt to heal is itself a structure of power. (We should emphasize once more that we are not advocating gross manipulation of the analysand or an authoritarian exercise of power; we ourselves subscribe to the democratic ethos.) The point is to understand how the analyst can help the analysand to move in a democratic direction without violating his respect for him as an equal.

In what ways can the analyst bring his influence to bear on the analysand without violating the analytic setting? The first dimension is relatively simple: it is important for the analyst to keep reminding the analysand that the setting is not a substitute for reality, and indeed that it is outside the setting, in reality, that the real issues of the analysand's life are determined. In other words, the constraints of reality must be lifted in order to make the process possible, and the process itself must be protected from reality. Nevertheless, reality has the last word. The ambiguous place of the setting must be respected; otherwise it can become an end in itself, or become split off from reality and exploited as a kind of pressure valve that enables the analysand to continue playing his game. The analysis is real only to the extent that it respects the larger context of reality, the setting of the setting. Otherwise it runs the risk of becoming yet another narcissistic, self-referential, and repetitive game.

Second, the basic rule of free association requires that the analysand talk openly about himself. It does not, however, imply that the analysand simply drift along the spontaneous current of his ideas. On the contrary, free association is ultimately task-oriented; the analysand's objective in the analysis is to overcome the problems enunciated in his initial complaint. The analyst of course has to bear in mind that all the free associations, however far removed from the stated goal they may appear to be, are in fact working toward it. This should be reflected in his interpretation, which should constantly point out to the analysand an association to his original conflict. Among other things, this creates an ongoing pressure to deal with these issues.

Third, the analyst maintains the direction of the analytic work and steers the analysand toward change by challenging him to overcome his symptoms and at the same time helping him work through the anxieties this evokes. Since anxiety is the key to maintaining the psychic structure and its reality principle, this working-through makes it possible to transform the structure and to follow a new course of action in reality.

Fourth, in our view the analysis itself is a negotiating process that continues throughout its course rather than being settled with the analytic contract to work. At issue in this process is the analysand's change and the resolution of the problem for which he consulted the analyst. In a sense he must make a new contract with himself; the analyst's task is to bring him to that point in order to fulfill the terms of the analytic contract itself. Any contract is made in order to deal with a specific problem, and it proposes that both partners agree that it is more in their interest to enter the contract rather than to let things go on in the same way.

Contracts are always the result of an interest in overcoming certain pressures. In the analytic situation pressures are also required in order to get the analysand to enter a new contract with himself. To do this, the analyst has only to actualize the pressures inherent in the setting; the alternative is therapeutic failure.

There are basically two kinds of pressures the analyst can generate: persuasion to undertake therapeutic actions, or dissuasion from repeated acting-out. Both play upon the affective interests of the analysand in becoming happier—or in becoming less unhappy. Of course the specific vulnerability of analysands in this area varies according to their complaints.

To assume that the analyst is negotiating with a partner who is completely rational about his own interests would eliminate the need for the analysis itself, since the specific reason for the treatment is the analysand's failure to negotiate his own interests in reality. Therefore the analyst is in a peculiar position. He must persuade his partner to look to his own interests rationally in order to secure them, not only in terms of a successful completion of the analysis but also in reality: the two are inseparable.

Finally, the ultimate sanction in analysis is the despair of the analysand. Failure to change, and the constant repetition of acting-out, in themselves generate despair. The analyst is in the paradoxical position of having to use this despair against the tendency to maintain the old narcissistic structures. The threat that things will stay the same or get worse only reflects the situation that obtains. This is, in a sense, a therapeutic form of symbolic violence; it confronts the analysand with the ultimate source of the analyst's own authority, namely, that he can help him overcome this despair. In effect the analyst needs this symbolic violence in order to initially establish his authority, because his job is to challenge the authority of the superego that presides over the analysand's difficulties. Once he persuades the analysand to help himself and to overcome the inertia of his old patterns, he will of course give up his authority—based in the analysand's despair, it will have disappeared.

Other forms of authority are ultimately based on a threat of violence and do not resolve the underlying threat; the analyst's authority should be used in order to resolve its source.

Undermining the Authority of the "Superego"

The intrapsychic power structure can be compared to a political regime which perpetuates itself by the exercise of authority. The ruler can command the support and loyalty of his subjects because they believe in his legitimacy and his right to rule.

Legitimation can take many different forms in politics, depending on the ideology of the society. But it is never guaranteed to endure indefinitely. If the ideology changes (whether in response to socio-economic change or a radically new way of understanding reality generated by new intellectual influences), or if the ruler oversteps the behavioral norms defined by the ideology, his legitimacy disappears and with it his authority. At this point the political order is ready for a transformation: either a new ideology will arise with a new source of legitimation and a new leader on whom this legitimacy is conferred, or, where the ideology remains intact, a new ruler emerges to take the place of the old so that despite the change the regime remains the same.

In psychoanalysis the kind of transformation we have in mind is not simply the replacement of one ruler with another; that only perpetuates the regime. We are talking rather about the complete replacement of the authority of a regime (the sadomasochistic one) legitimated by an ideology (that of the "superego") so that an entirely new psychic ideology and authority can take its place, conferring legitimacy on a new kind of ruler (Strachey 1943).

The ideology that legitimates the "superego" is the belief system that underpins sadomasochism. Essentially this amounts to the belief that life is indeed a zero-sum game. In more classical terms, this is a tragic vision in which either you lose your pleasure in order to gain security, or vice versa. And sometimes you lose both.

Psychoanalysis is in some danger of itself subscribing to such a philosophy, insofar as it sees the mourning process as an end in itself. The capacity to continually accept and feel the innumerable losses experienced in life is thereby taken as the criterion of the deepest development of character. The problem is that this position does not necessarily challenge the fundamental belief of sadomasochism but may simply contain it at a more sophisticated level of reflection. Real transformation would entail mourning sadomasochism itself so that one can give up mourning as a way of life. This obviously requires the articulation of a new philosophy based upon the pursuit of happiness through real satisfactions that are not necessarily obtained at the price of real frustrations.

The psychoanalyst himself needs to have such a philosophy, and in order to undermine the authority of the analysand's "superego" he must challenge the ideology of suffering that legitimates it. He would thereby leave the analysand in a position where the ego no longer believes in the right of the "superego" to rule its conduct. At this point the superego's authority to maintain the zero-sum game will crumble, and the position of ruler in the psychic regime can fall to an ego that believes in the democratic pursuit of real satisfaction.

In order to clarify the argument we have made, it might be helpful to think of the analysand as being trapped at the center of an overdetermined structure that constitutes, in Freudian terms, his reality principle (which has a political basis as well as the dynamic one hypothesized by Freud [1910a]). At the center of this structure we can observe that the analysand is engaged in the constant repetition of a set pattern of behavior in reality. This is the game that he also brings to the analytic setting, where it can be seen in the pattern of the transference (and the countertransference) with its stereotyped sadomasochistic overtures.

This game is sustained by and contained within a specific concept of reality that has been learned in childhood and that reflects the social and cultural location of the family. It is maintained and transmitted by the authority of the parents ultimately introjected into the law of the superego (Ferenczi 1952). This law, as we have indicated, may in itself be contradictory and confusing insofar as it is partly defined by a familial ethical code of respect and cooperation that is at odds with a broader social code of competition (Freud 1915).

Behind the authority of the parents or the "superego" there is an ideology or Weltanschauung that rationalizes the law or the codes in terms of a philosophy of life. This can be seen as the attempt to reconcile the reality principle with the pleasure principle in the sense that it defines the way in which one obtains pleasure and avoids frustration (Figure 10-1).

This model of the analysand's political space can be transformed only if the analyst works systematically to make him aware of his model and then to question its logic by suggesting an alternative philosophy which legitimates a different kind of authority, a different view of reality, and ultimately a different "game" (Gear and Liendo 1979).

To do so means tracing the analysand's game to its origins in the influence of his parents and their beliefs about reality and life summarized in the advice and expectations that they communicated to him (Heimann 1950).

In the course of the analysis the analysand could develop insight into these different levels of his political space. This is not the conventional definition of insight into his intrapsychic dynamics; what must be discovered is another way of understanding reality (Freud 1924).

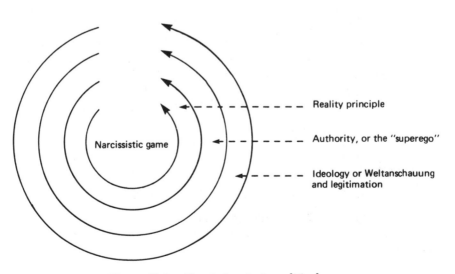

Figure 10-1. Narcissism in its political space

The Power of Changing the Psychic System

In applying the master-servant dialectic to the structure and functioning of the psychic system we introduced the concept of power both in our clinical descriptions and in our theoretical explanations: we defined the system as a sadomasochistic political one. Consequently, we must now introduce the concept of power to design the policy, strategy, tactic and technique of the psychoanalytic therapeutic approach needed to deal effectively with the pathogenic master-servant dialectic.

The analyst must be able to use systematically the elements of power already present in the analytic situation—or he must be able to create new ones if necessary—if he does not want to be a blind, unconscious puppet of the sadomasochistic power game the analysand will unconsciously but compulsively try to play. This thesis is based on the assumption that a certain distribution of power—as with communication and norms of behavior—is present in every human relationship: if it is healthy, power will be shared by equals; but if it is pathological, there will be only powerful and powerless positions.

In other words, if the analyst refuses to participate actively in the power game by trying to be "neutral" he will be condemned to be a master or a servant of his analysands. He will either manipulate power or be manipulated by it instead of redistributing power in a consciously therapeutic way.

Therapeutic power should thus be a major technical and theoretical concern of the analyst, if he wants the therapeutic "authority" that will enable him to help his analysands achieve the transformation of their unconscious structures. This is not the authority of a master but the technical authority given to him when the therapeutic alliance is established. As is well known, Freud (1912b) repeatedly insisted on the necessity of such authority. The pathogenic distribution of power is given by virtue of the transference-countertransference phenomena, from the very beginning of the analytic relationship. If it is true that the analyst must not use it manipulatively, it is true also that he can overcome it only with the aid of a therapeutic authority that is deliberately cultivated and applied. It is a moot point whether an analyst becomes prestigious because he is effective or whether he is effective because he is prestigious—that is, institutionally powerful in the eyes of his analysands. In other words, we are touching here on the issue of suggestion that Freud himself considered in some ways unavoidable (Lacan 1961). According to our previous hypotheses, the analyst should be powerful enough to deal with both the powerful agent and the powerless patient of mental illness because they always form a united political system. When treating a masochist, the analyst will have to face his internal agent—the analysand's master alter—in the first place and his external agent—the analysand's master others—in the second. Similarly, when treating a sadist, the analyst will also have to face both the analysand's internal servant alter and his external servant other (Gear and Liendo 1976).

We suggested that the sadistic agent and the masochistic patient form an intrapsychic and interpersonal political system in which the sadistic agent functions as the leader or the ruler, and the masochistic patient as the follower or the ruled. Like any other political system, the psychic system has goals and strategies to achieve them. Its conscious political goal is rational (or rationalized); the unconscious one is narcissistic and sadomasochistic. Its conscious rational strategy is the specific action; its unconscious narcissistic one is sadistic or masochistic acting-out. For example, the psychic system of a paranoid analysand can have, as its conscious rational goal, the attainment of a satisfactory, stable job; but its unconscious sadomasochistic goal will be, through a paranoid acting-out, starting a new fight with someone he can later accuse of being his rejecting victimizer. He will lose the job but he will "win" a new victim-victimizer relationship to satisfactorily stabilize his psychic equilibrium.

Briefly, it can be said that the intrapsychic system has a conscious, rational, strategic plan (specific action and reaction) to obtain its conscious rational goal (some kind of happiness: pleasure with security); and an unconscious sadomasochistic counter-plan (acting-out and counter–acting-out) to obtain its unconscious narcissistic goal (sadistic pleasure with insecurity or masochistic security with unpleasure).

Applying the same hypothesis, it can also be said that the therapeutic psychoanalytic system is also a political system, with goals, strategies, leader, and followers. The political goal of the therapeutic system would be to change the political structure of the intrapsychic system of the analysand from an initial pathological state to a final therapeutic one. The strategy, the therapeutic plan to be applied to realize this goal—to obtain the best possible cure for the analysand—would be the specific therapeutic action and the specific therapeutic reaction. The technical leader, the democratic representative, is supposed to be the analyst, and the follower, the democratic represented, is supposed to be the analysand.

In other words, the goal of the analytic treatment could be conceived as a deep change in the type of government, goals, strategies, and leadership of the psychic system of the analysand through therapeutic negotiations under the technical leadership of the analyst with the cooperation of the conscious nonnarcissistic (mature, adult) part of the analysand and the resistance of his unconscious narcissistic (immature, infantile) part.

Political systems in crisis are usually changed through negotiations—understanding of the political process, pressures, and coalitions—that achieve, if successful, equilibrium of the system through partial change or radical change. Depending on the resources and possibilities of the system and of the goals of the representative agent who is trying to change it, the therapeutic goal can be revolutionary, reformist, or conservative.

Planning Change of the Psychic System

It must be remembered that in changing any system, the process of change always goes through stages of resisting, accepting, implementing, and stabilizing. This is particularly true in the analytic change of the psychic system even if the analyst is trying to obtain a partial change or merely repair the equilibrium of the system to its precritical state. Usually the analysand wants his symptoms and anxieties to be alleviated without having to make any deep change at all.

In trying to change the deep political structure of the psychic system of the analysand through changing the deep political structure of the analysand-analyst system that the analysand tries to impose from the very beginning of treatment, the analyst can apply a systems analysis approach to his therapeutic strategy. He must know his starting point, as well as his destination. What are the characteristics of the initial pathological state of the analysand's psychic system? What would be the possible (not the ideal) final therapeutic state of the sytem to be achieved through the analytic process? What will the intermediate stages be? And what instruments and operations must the analyst use during each stage?

In order to understand and to solve any conflict or crisis within the analysand's psychic system, the analyst must analyse it operatively, taking into account the following steps:

1. The therapeutic process begins when the consultation is made by the analysand or by someone in charge of him.

2. In that moment the analyst must be able to identify the type and the specific sphere of the crisis of incompetence that the analysand's psychic system is undergoing.

3. Once the problem is identified, the analyst must identify the characteristics and the dimensions of the system in crisis.

4. After the initial diagnosis, the analyst must define more precisely the conflict between the conscious and unconscious goals and strategies of the analysand's psychic system, as well as its resources to solve the conflict and the changes in the social world of the analysand that predispose, provoke, or perpetuate his crisis of psychic incompetence: the pathological initial state of the psychic system must be defined.

5. Once the characteristics of the psychic system and the factors provoking its crisis are defined, the analyst should try to find what alternatives are already available, not only to overcome the crisis but to change in depth the intrapsychic and interpersonal predisposing, provoking, and perpetuating factors.

6. After identifying the available alternatives, the analyst should consider whether it is possible to create any new alternative that could be more effective and economic in terms of anxiety, time, etc.

7. When the alternatives are identified and defined as well as the characteristics of the initial pathological state of the analysand's psychic system, it is time to define precisely the best possible political therapeutic goal that can be achieved, that is, the best possible final therapeutic state that the analysand's psychic system can achieve in this analytic moment and situation with this analyst and with this environment.

8. Once the final therapeutic state of the psychic system in crisis is defined, the analyst should select the best strategic alternative to achieve that therapeutic state (Earle 1973).

9. After choosing the most strategic therapeutic alternative, the analyst must implement that alternative by designing a tactical therapeutic plan with its corresponding subgoals.

10. Once the tactical plan is designed, a careful technical analytic approach must be designed: which interpretations, descriptions, prescriptions, actions, and setting would be the best instruments and operations to achieve each tactical subgoal?

Once the therapeutic goal, strategy, tactics, and techniques are defined, the planning stage is over and the analyst should begin the administrative stage:

11. The analyst should apply the strategy by implementing the tactical plan with the technical operations in order to achieve the first therapeutic subgoal as designed.

12. After applying the strategy for a while, the analyst should carefully evaluate it by comparing the subgoal intended to be achieved with the actual results obtained.

13. If the evaluation is positive, the analyst should go ahead with the therapeutic plan until further evaluation; if the evaluation is negative, the analyst must first revise his tactics, his strategy and, finally, his whole therapeutic policy if necessary.

14. Once the successive therapeutic subgoals and the general goal are obtained, the analyst should try to generalize and stabilize the analysand's psychic system in the new therapeutic state.

15. Finally, when the therapeutic change is generalized and stabilized, the therapeutic intervention must end and self-analysis take place: the after-analysis process is started and, it is hoped, will never end (Freud 1937a).

The basic political diagnosis of the analysand's psychic system will consist in the definition of its conscious rational goal, unconscious narcissistic goal, and possible therapeutic goal. Its basic strategic diagnosis will consist in the definition of its conscious rational plan (specific action and reaction), unconscious sadomasochistic counter-plan (acting and counter–acting-out), and therapeutic "metaplan," because it is a plan aimed at changing the other plans (specific therapeutic action and reaction).

Therapeutic Speech, Actions, and Affects

The empirical basis of the analytic theory—and the analytic therapeutic strategy—is formed not only by the analysand's speech and actions but also by the analyst's speech, actions, and affective states. The analysand unconsciously uses his words and actions to transmit mental illness to the analyst, while the analyst analyzes his own feelings with respect to the analysand (as well as the analysand's behavior) in order to transmit mental health by means of his own words and actions.

It must be remembered that we distinguished different types of analysand speech (associative, defensive, working-through, consulting, setting, and conventional) and four different types of analysand actions (verbal, nonverbal, paraverbal, and contextual).

We will now distinguish eleven types of analyst speech: (1) descriptive, (2) reconstructive, (3) interpretive, (4) requalifying, (5) prospective, (6) directive, (7) supervising, (8) informing, (9) pressing, (10) setting, and (11) conventional. The analyst's actions are of the same four types as the analysand's—verbal, nonverbal, paraverbal, and contextual. Finally, there are two types of affective states in the analyst—original and countertransferential.

The contextual actions of the analyst form a special therapeutic instrument, called the analytic setting, which can be clearly distinguished from the analytic process that takes place within this framework. The analytic setting is the group of conditions—constant and variable—that the analyst imposes on his relationship with the analysand: the therapeutic norms used to define the context of the analytic process.

On the other hand, the analytic process is the succession of words, actions, and feelings of analysand and analyst occurring within the analytic context previously defined by the analyst (Figure 10-2).

Descriptive therapeutic speech is used by the analyst only to describe the characteristics and relations of the speech, actions, affective states, and representations of the analysand (and sometimes of the analyst himself) as well as the speech, actions, and affects of others as they are mentioned by the analysand: their reductions and

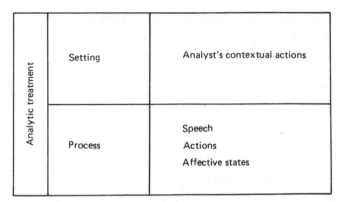

Figure 10-2.   Setting and process as components of the analytic treatment

inversions. The analyst uses descriptive speech to produce "outsight," or the recognition by the analysand of his own pathological behavioral patterns.

Reconstructive therapeutic speech is used by the analyst to show the analysand the pattern in which his speech, actions, and affects occur in the analytic setting or with current significant others. It is also used to show that the speech, actions, and affects he is trying to obtain from those others (including the analyst) are practically identical to those that occurred between himself as an infant or child and his early significant others such as parents or siblings. The analyst first describes clinical facts and descriptions of the analysand's speech and then compares them. Once the analyst describes and constructs the transferential object relations, he is able to reconstruct the analysand's past object relations and predict his future object relations (unless of course he changes his compulsive repetitive pattern). With the reconstructive speech the analyst tries to produce "historic outsight" in the analysand, or recognition of the infantile origin of his pathological behavioral patterns.

Interpretive therapeutic speech is used by the analyst to explain why the analysand's speech, actions, and affects have pathological characteristics and sequence—why they are sadomasochistic, stereotyped, inverted, etc. Consequently there are interpretations of mechanisms, anxieties, characteristics of the norm and the rule of the superego's law, general principles of functioning of the psychic system, and the mutilation of the psychic space. The analyst uses interpretive speech to try to produce "insight" in the analysand, or the recognition of the conscious and unconscious levels and meanings and motivations of pathological behavior (Viderman 1970).

Requalifying therapeutic speech is used by the analyst to correct the pathological over- and disqualifications of self and others in the analysand's qualifying speech. The analyst tries to produce "qualifying outsight" in the analysand, or the recognition of the analysand's pathological tendencies to idealize or denigrate himself or others.

Prospective therapeutic speech is used by the analyst to modify the old unconscious narcissistic project, and to design a new therapeutic plan for the analysand—for example, the nonsadomasochistic specific therapeutic action he must enact, and the specific therapeutic reaction he must provoke in the other in order to overcome the vicious circle of his repetition compulsion. With the prospective speech the analyst tries to produce "future outsight" in the analysand, or the recognition of new behavioral, affective, and cognitive possibilities in himself and others.

Directive therapeutic speech is used by the analyst to proscribe the analysand's pathological compulsive behavior, and to prescribe the corresponding therapeutic one. By directing the analysand to specifically challenge his symptoms—stopping his compulsion to repeat—the underlying anxieties and unconscious fantasies appear clearly in the analysand's consciousness and can be analysed more easily and deeply. Freud did this with the Wolf Man when he proscribed his phobic avoidance and dependence and prescribed more independent action. With the directive speech the analyst tries to produce "task outsight" in the analysand, or a realization of how he can actively help the therapeutic process (both inside and outside the analytic setting) to become more effective (Gear and Liendo 1979).

Supervising therapeutic speech is used by the analyst to help the analysand understand and solve a particular conflict with a critical significant external object relation (Winnicott 1953). When this happens, the analysand usually cannot associate freely and employs a consulting speech. Of course, the supervising speech does not exclude the use of a simultaneous or subsequent interpretive speech; it is used when the interpretive speech is not enough to unlock the analysand from a very absorbing situation in the external world that inhibits him from associating freely and from being able to listen and work through the interpretations. It can be said that most of so-called analytic psychotherapy consists of precisely this type of supervising speech: the analyst limits his therapeutic action to helping the analysand understand the conscious and unconscious meanings of the critical significant other's behavior, as well as the analysand's own "countertransference," as if the analysand were a supervisee and the significant other his analysand. With the supervising speech the analyst is trying to produce "insight into others" in the analysand, or the recognition of the meanings and motivations of the other's behavior as well as his own participation in provoking or dealing pathologically with that behavior (Gear and Liendo 1980).

Informing therapeutic speech is used by the analyst to make the analysand aware of his position within the sociopolitical structure of society—for example, the limitations of typical middle-class thinking, or his real economic limitations if he is a middle-class American. This does not imply political indoctrination but rather an objective socioeconomic view of the analysand's social position and possibilities—a view to be compared with the analysand's subjective or egoistic conception of the world. In fact, once the analysand achieves the different levels of insight and outsight we have mentioned, it is less difficult for the analyst to help him to an effective and objective "social outsight." We must remember that one of the analyst's main tasks is to systematically introduce the reality principle into the regulation of the psychic system of the analysand; even though the analyst knows how vague and controversial the very concept of reality can be, both scientifically and philosophically. (For a detailed discussion of this subtle issue, see Gear and Liendo 1979).

Pressuring therapeutic speech is used by the analyst to counter-compel the analysand to abandon as quickly and as safely as he can his own compelling mechanisms of sadomasochistic repetition compulsion. In effect, the analyst is always using his therapeutic power—even if he does not want to—to press the analysand toward the analytic therapeutic goals. The point is that the analyst must use his power consciously, systematically, and scientifically instead of using it in a naive, clandestine, and counterproductive way by disguising his position as a neutral one. He is not "neutral," and he cannot be neutral even if he wants to, because of the very definition of the analytic process as therapeutic.° Using the descriptive speech, the analyst helps the analysand achieve "insight into power" by showing him how he uses psychological pressures (threats, promises, etc.) to push the analyst into a sadistic or masochistic position and how the corresponding counter-pressures can be used to overcome sado-masochism.

Setting therapeutic speech is used by the analyst to clarify for the analysand the basic nonnegotiable conditions that are indispensable in the development of a truly therapeutic analytic process. In many ways the setting speech is also a pressuring speech, as we will see later. Consequently, the analyst must clarify from the very beginning the characteristics of the analytic setting and process—what psychoanalysis is all about and how it can be done. Both the meaning and the form of the analytic treatment must be clarified again and again each time the transference neurosis of the analysand pushes him to violate or confuse the basic setting rules. By using the setting speech, the analyst helps the analysand develop "insight into the analytic process" or a clear recognition of both what he does, why he does it, how he must do it, and what the analyst is supposed to do during the analytic treatment.

Conventional therapeutic speech is used by the analyst to talk with the analysand outside of the analytic setting conditions, that is, under special circumstances: if they meet, for example, in the elevator or at a party. Even in these circumstances the analyst must be careful to be as "neutral" as he can, in the sense of avoiding any direct or indirect reference to confidential material imparted to him during the analytic session. But being careful does not mean being mute, artificial, or paternalistic; it means being as natural as possible to avoid social situations embarrassing to either party.

°We will analyze later in this chapter the different types of negative and positive counter-pressures that the analyst can use to neutralize the pathogenic, sadomasochistic pressures unconsciously used by the analysand (and his patient or agent). The negative and positive pressures that he can use to provoke new therapeutic behavior (and which, initially at least, are anxiety provoking for the analysand) will also be discussed.

All these types of therapeutic speech can be considered *therapeutic verbal actions*. But the mere fact that the analyst speaks (or does not speak) as a consequence of the analysand's behavior can also be considered a verbal action. Many analysts use a "therapeutic" silence as one of their chief analytic instruments. One could possibly consider the therapeutic pressuring speech, which conveys threats and promises provoking persuasion or dissuasion, as the paradigm of verbal actions. The tone of voice, the style of the wording, etc. of the analyst could be considered *paraverbal therapeutic actions*. The analyst usually tends—consciously or unconsciously—to mimic the tone and style of speech of the analysand's alter. That is, he plays or takes the role of the most significant others of the infancy and childhood of the analysand. This verbal "counter-tone" and "counter-style" in the formulation and communication of the therapeutic speech are decisively important in the analysand's acceptance or rejection of it.

The analysand will accept the content of the therapeutic speech much more easily—even if it is completely opposed to the content of the pathogenic speech of his early significant others—if the tone and style of the speech are in some way similar to those the analysand is used to. If the analyst respects the form of the speech, he might be able to introduce greater change in its content. If this is not systematically considered, the risks are that the analyst can either counter–act-out unconsciously the role of the analysand's significant pathogenic other (not only in style but in content, reinforcing in this way the original pathology of the analysand) or use a totally different tone and style unknown to the analysand (who will possibly reject them). On the other hand, when the analytic treatment is well advanced the analyst will be able to progressively use his own tone and style, broadening in this way the cognitive and affective spectrum of the analysand.

The gestures of the analyst, the way he is dressed, etc. could be considered *nonverbal therapeutic actions*. Again, the analyst should initially allow some similarity between his gestures and appearance and those of the significant others of the analysand's childhood.

The characteristics of the analyst's office, his ritualized therapeutic behavior, his theoretical and strategic approach, and the socioeconomic environment of the community in which his office is located, could be considered *contextual therapeutic actions* constantly employed by the analyst. Any significant change in the analytic routine, in the furniture of the office, or in the technique will be felt by the analysand very strongly as a deep message from the analyst. For instance, if the analysand is a sadistic patient—a "borderline"—who constantly arrives late to sessions in order to push the analyst into the position of a hypertolerant masochistic agent (like the analysand's father), the analyst can warn him that each time he arrives late he won't have the session. This is a threat which, when materialized into a punishment, constitutes a contextual therapeutic action on the part of the analyst (Meltzer 1967).

The affective states of the analyst are also very important therapeutic instruments; he must be able to use them properly through his own therapeutic self-analysis—reinforced periodically by adequate supervision—in order not to get contaminated and blindly counter–act-out as a reinforcing mirror for the analysand's narcissism. Consequently, the analyst should constantly try to resist the temptation of total counteridentification with the alter of the analysand, even though he must permit himself to experience the peculiar affective states provoked in him by the analysand's behavior. In other words, the analyst's original affective states—those of his own infancy—will be a good standard with which to compare and analyze the new affective states induced in him by the analysand. The better able to identify his usual affective states the analyst is, the better able he will be to detect the sadistic or masochistic type of countertransferential feelings he will be working with. Dealing with his feelings is the turning point of the analyst's work, and he can only deal with them effectively under two conditions: if he is "well analyzed" and has a clear picture of the type of affective states he usually accords to the structure of his relations with his intrapsychic significant others; and if he is "well supervised" and has a clear picture of the type of affective states that the analysand usually provokes in his significant others.

If the analyst is aware of both his own deep intrapsychic structure and that of the analysand, as a true analyst he will be able to "mirror" the analysand's behavior and then analyze with the analysand his mirror game, by comparing the narcissistic reflections with the true actions and speech of the analysand and of himself; he will show the analysand, for instance, how he is reflecting his own sadism in the analyst while pushing him into a masochistic position or vice versa. A clear picture of the mutual affective structure will protect the mental health and clarity of the analyst from becoming distorted or burned out, just as a lead shield protects a radiologist from the destructive effects of unprotected exposure to the x-rays he uses to see what is "inside" his patients.

The Analytic Setting

The basic condition to be established before analytic intervention is the *analytic setting.* After interviewing the analysand and deciding that it is worthwhile to begin analytic treatment, the analyst must design a specific anti-agent (or anti-patient), antisadistic (or anti-masochistic) set of conditions such that neither analysand nor analyst will be able to transform the treatment into a new sadomasochistic repetition (Freud 1912a).

In the same way that the analytic process is referred to as the evolution of the variables of the analytic situation, the analytic setting is referred to as the maintenance and enforcement of the constants of the situations. The setting is intended to ensure minimal narcissistic or environmental interference with the analytic process, and to favor the effectiveness of the analyst's interventions (Donnet 1973).

The constants of the analytic situation can be classified into six categories (Figure 10-3): theoretical (the analytic theory); functional (the analytic technique); time (duration, frequency, and rhythm of the sessions); space (physical environment: furniture, design, and location of the office); the analyst as a real person (personality, ideology, social class, institutions); and environmental (the socio-economic setting of the setting, the attitudes of the whole community toward psychoanalysis, etc.).

Always taking into account the fundamental characteristics of the analytic treatment—free association, couch, number of sessions, confidentiality, interpretation of the analysand's behavior—the conditions of the setting should be modified for each of the four psychopathological syndromes described in chapter 1. When the analysand is a *sadistic agent,* for example, the conditions of the setting must prevent him from making the analyst in any way dependent on him, so he will not be able to press the analyst into the position of an abused masochistic patient. If the analysand is a *masochistic patient,* the conditions of the setting must prevent him from depending on and being abused by the analyst. If the analysand

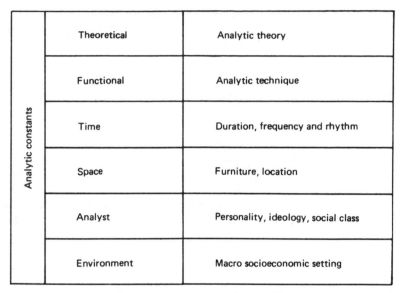

	Theoretical	Analytic theory
	Functional	Analytic technique
Analytic constants	Time	Duration, frequency and rhythm
	Space	Furniture, location
	Analyst	Personality, ideology, social class
	Environment	Macro socioeconomic setting

Figure 10-3. The analytic setting

is a *sadistic patient,* the setting must prevent him from making the analyst totally responsible for his self-destructive behavior so he will not be able to blame and blackmail the analyst while destroying himself. Finally, if the analysand is a *masochistic agent,* the setting must prevent him from "spoiling" the analyst.

Verbal Therapeutic Interventions

Once the specific conditions of the setting are established, the analyst will use his descriptive speech in order to describe to the analysand the clinical characteristics of their speech, actions and affective states. He will apply the hypotheses of reduction and inversion of the empirical level of the theory of psychic bipolarity in order to arrive at a cognitive agreement with the analysand about what is going on between them before attempting any further interpretation about why this is going on. Consequently, the analytic work of the analyst will start with *therapeutic descriptions* of what is going on clinically in the analytic process of transference and countertransference. The analyst should describe to the analysand:

1. How the analysand always tells the same story, with the same characters, the same relationships, and the same sequence of events.
2. How the story the analysand always repeats in many different forms is a stereotyped one that can be reduced to the bipolar interaction between the analysand himself and only one type of significant other who always happens to have the same characteristics.
3. How in this repeated story, the relationship between the analysand and his significant other always tends to be sadomasochistic—that is, a stereotyped interaction between an abusing satisfied frustrator and an abused frustrated satisfier
4. How the analysand usually tends to disqualify as bad, stupid, or crazy the one who is described by him as an abusing satisfied frustrator, and to overqualify as good, clever, or sensible the one who is described by him as an abused frustrated satisfier; that is, that the analysand tends to disqualify himself and overqualify the significant other if he is a masochist, and to overqualify himself and disqualify the other if he is a sadist.
5. How the story the analysand tends to reenact is a sadomasochistic one in which one of the two main characters tends to make the other dependent, socially isolated, disqualified, censored, and affectively exploited under the promise of giving him protection and security.
6. How the analysand always repeats the same course of action within and outside the analytic setting.
7. How the analysand's behavior within the analytic setting is stereotyped and sadomasochistic; how he acts either as an abuser (a satisfied frustrator) who tries to make the analyst dependent, disqualified, isolated, denigrated, censored, and exploited; or as an abused who tries to depend on the abuser analyst, and who tries to be disqualified, isolated, denigrated, censored, and exploited by him.
8. How the behavior that he attributes to himself inside and outside the analytic setting is usually the inverse of what actually happens between himself and the analyst. When he describes himself

as a <"bad" satisfied frustrator abuser of the others> (the analyst included) he usually behaves as a <"good" frustrated satisfier abused by the others> (the analyst included) and vice versa.

9. How he pushes the analyst into a sadistic or a masochistic position by using symbolic violence or by using psychological pressures against the security or the pleasure of the analyst. If he is a sadist, he will threaten or punish the analyst's security in order to push him into the role of a <frustrated satisfier abused by the analysand> who also has to confess that he is a <satisfied frustrator who is abusing the analysand>. If he is a masochist, he will threaten or punish the analyst's pleasure in order to push him into the role of a <satisfied frustrator who abuses the analysand> and who also has to say that he is a <frustrated satisfier abused by the analysand>. Finally, the analyst's behavior could be mirroring the analysand's if the analyst is not aware of such pressures.

10. How the analysand usually responds to the analyst's interventions by distorting the message he conveys. If he is a masochist he will use the interpretations, for example, to confirm once more how bad, crazy, and stupid he is and how good, sensible, and clever the analyst is; if he is a sadist he will distort the interpretations in exactly the opposite way.

Consequently, the analyst will be able to use at least ten different types of *therapeutic description:*

1. The monotheme of the analysand's speech
2. The bipolarity of the analysand's speech
3. The sadomasochistic content of the analysand's speech
4. Overqualifications and disqualifications of the analysand's speech
5. The history of dependency, isolation, disqualification, censorship, and exploitation contained in the analysand's speech
6. The analysand's stereotyped course of action within and outside the analytic setting
7. The sadomasochistic quality of the analysand's actions
8. The analysand's speech inversion with regard to his actions and affective states
9. The analysand's psychological pressures (through dependency-making, isolation, disqualification, censorship, etc.)

that push the analyst into the position of a sadomasochistic mirror

10. The analysand's distorting answers to the analyst's interventions

As we said before, these descriptions of the clinical facts are intended to obtain the outsight from the analysand that will later allow him to look for his insight.

Once the empirical basis has been thoroughly described to the analysand, the analytic work of the analyst will continue with *therapeutic reconstructions* (Freud 1937b). In effect, the analyst will show how the analysand's behavior with the analyst (or with other people as described in the analysand's speech) is similar (if not identical) to that which the analysand described as happening with his own parents (or any significant other) when he was a child. It is not enough to simply tell the analysand that he is identifying the analyst with his father, for example, and that he is consequently behaving in the same way as he did with his father. In effect, the analyst must reconstruct carefully and in detail all the conflicting characteristics of both the father and the child that are embedded in the repetition compulsion. To do this, the analyst will use the detailed descriptions that he has already prepared of the analysand's behavior within the analytic setting. In other words, the analysand must recognize not only who compelled him into his pathological patterns and when, but also that the analyst will later interpret the reasons for those patterns (Freud 1914).

Once the analyst has described the analysand's conflicting repetitive patterns and explained their origins, he will start using interpretations in order to explain why these patterns are happening here and now, and why they happened there and then. Reconstruction is a limited and insufficient type of explanation: to know the origin of something does not allow the analysand to fully understand and change his destructive behavior (Freud 1909).

In our experience, the most powerful reconstruction is usually the oedipal one. It is very useful to the analysand to realize that he has been behaving all his life like one of his parents (usually the one of the opposite sex) while treating his significant others as if they were the other parent. We think it no coincidence that Freud (1910a) always showed the superego of the male analysand to be the result of the introjection of his father. In effect it can be observed that the male analysand usually tends to treat the analyst as if he were his father (and as if he himself were his mother) while the female analysand tends to treat the analyst as if he were her mother (and she herself were her father). When we say "father" or "mother" we do not merely refer to the biological parents but to the persons who functioned as such (Freud 1937b). On the other hand, of course, the oedipal reconstruction is not the only powerful one (Ferenczi 1952).

Once the analysand has enough outsight and historic outsight about the objective characteristics of his repetitive pathological behavior and its origin during his infancy and childhood, the analyst will start trying to give the analysand different kinds and levels of the meaning and motivations of his behavior through *analytic therapeutic interpretations*. The analyst should interpret (explain) to the analysand:

1. How the analysand perceives himself and the others (the analyst included) in a stereotypical way, as if the others were always the same kind of person doing the same kinds of things for the same kinds of reasons (Lagache 1957).

2. How the analysand perceives himself and the others (the analyst included) in an inverted way with respect to what they are actually doing and feeling.

3. How the analysand sees in the other what he is doing and feeling, and sees in himself what the others are doing and feeling, because he is avoiding certain painful affects that may appear in his consciousness should he perceive those actions and affects correctly. The sadistic analysand must perceive himself as masochistic to avoid feeling guilty, and the masochistic analysand must perceive himself as sadistic to avoid feeling insecure.

4. How the analysand talks about and perceives in an inverted way his own actions and affects, and those of his significant others, because he is unconsciously afraid that the analyst will punish him if he does not do so. The masochistic analysand is afraid the analyst will punish him with insecurity if he does not perceive himself as a sadist; the sadist, on the other hand, fears the analyst will punish him with unpleasure if he does not perceive himself as a masochist.

5. How the analysand fears being punished by the analyst because he identifies him with his parents or their substitutes, particularly the parent of the same sex (Klein 1961).

6. How the analysand's parents probably used a normative code (which contained their strategy for obtaining pleasure and insecurity in life) that, at best, was conflicting and obsolete because

it was designed to deal with a type of reality very different from that which the analysand is facing currently. The purpose of this level of interpretation is, of course, not to antagonize the analysand against his parents in a short-sighted, counterproductive way: he must realize that his parents were not necessarily vicious, but were impotent to tackle some problems, or were not communicating well enough to make the analysand aware that their strategy (one among many) was perhaps only adequate to deal with some specific situation in reality now past.

7. How the analysand has internalized the conflicting obsolete code learned when he was an infant and a child dependent on the authority of his parents. This is now his own way of thinking and must be changed if he wants to obtain more and better happiness, and if he wants to develop a strategy for obtaining pleasure and security that takes into account the actual characteristics of his present sociopolitical and economic reality (Schelling 1960).

8. How the intrapsychic normative code of the analysand pushed him into a sadomasochistic game because he was told that being an abused victim is "good" and being an abusive victimizer is "bad." In other words, the basic law of both sadistic and masochistic analysands rewards masochism and punishes sadism (von Wright 1963).

9. How the sadistic analysand has unconsciously learned in his actual interactions with his primary significant others that he was rewarded with pleasure only if he acted sadistically; but he perceived himself as acting masochistically. He was punished with unpleasure if he acted masochistically or if he perceived that he was acting sadistically. On the other hand, the masochistic analysand must know that he was rewarded with security only if he acted masochistically but perceived himself as acting sadistically, and that he was punished with insecurity if he acted sadistically or if he perceived that he was acting masochistically.

10. How the analysand has learned to perceive himself and others either as dominant masters entitled to disqualify and abuse others, or as obedient servants condemned to be abused and disqualified by the others.

11. How the sadistic analysand feels entitled (and unconsciously pushed) to overqualify himself and disqualify the analyst (and his other significant others). If he does not do so the analyst will punish him with unpleasure. The masochistic analysand must realize how

he disqualifies himself and overqualifies the analyst because he fears that if he does not do so, the analyst will punish him with insecurity. It seems to be extremely important not only to undermine the authority of the superego and the validity of its normative code, but also to make clear to the analysand how his own self-image (as a dominant master or as an obedient servant) and the image that he has of the other tends to lock him into the ruinous sadomasochistic interpersonal game (Bion 1962).

12. How the analysand is trapped in the sadomasochistic game because he thinks that the only way to obtain happiness—security and pleasure—is through competition with others. This competitive conception of human relationships, which pushes him into the position of either "winner" or "loser" of happiness, contradicts the very notion of happiness, or at least of a more comprehensive, complete, and profound human happiness.

13. How the analysand is also locked into a stereotyped competitive way of obtaining security and pleasure that not only impoverishes him but pushes him into wrong decisions.

Consequently, the analyst will be able to use at least twelve different types and levels of *therapeutic interpretation:*

1. The analysand's stereotyped perception of himself and others
2. The analysand's inverted perception of his own actions and affective states and of those of others
3. The painful affective states that the analysand is avoiding by inverting his perceptions
4. The analysand's intrapsychic normative code—projected onto the analyst—that provokes such painful affective states
5. The analysand's intrapsychic rule of action that pushes him to act either sadistically or masochistically
6. The internalization of the analysand's parents' normative code and rule of action
7. The obsolescence and inadequacy of that code and that rule. They form a counterproductive strategy for obtaining security and pleasure because they have been designed for dealing with another type of socioeconomic reality
8. The analysand's obedience and respect toward that code

and rule in the present simply because they were learned by him when he was a child

9. The analysand's internalized sadomasochistic normative code that rewards masochism and punishes sadism

10. The analysand's internalized sadomasochistic rule of action that rewards with pleasure sadism disguised as masochism in the sadist and rewards with security masochism disguised as sadism in the masochist; of the analysand's misqualification of himself and others either as good, clever, sensible dominant abusing masters who indulge themselves and disqualify the others, or as bad, stupid, crazy obedient abused servants who condemn themselves and overqualify others

11. The analysand's psychic mutilation that allows him to perceive only competitive human relations in which he can obtain only sadistic pleasure or masochistic security

12. The analysand's second type of psychic mutilation, which locks him into an impoverishing stereotyped way of obtaining sadistic pleasure or masochistic security.

The first three classes of interpretation tend to make conscious the unconscious, according to Freud's first theory of the psychic apparatus (Freud 1900). The next seven tend to replace the superego and the id with the ego, according to Freud's second theory (1923). The final two classes tend to make conscious the transconscious, according to our theory of psychic bipolarity.

Once the analysand has achieved some level of outsight and insight with the aid of descriptions, reconstructions, and interpretations, the analyst will start trying to actively correct, "here and now" in the transference, the analysand's tendency (and "there and then" in the past the analysand's unconscious tendencies) to overqualify or disqualify himself or the significant others by using *therapeutic requalifications*. In effect the analyst should requalify:

1. The masochistic analysand's disqualifications of himself as bad, stupid, or crazy. The analyst should requalify him as good, clever, and sensible or, at least, as not bad, not stupid, not crazy. He should also stop the analysand from using the descriptions, reconstructions, and interpretations to disqualify himself again and again.

2. The masochistic analysand's idealization (overqualification) of the analyst as being extremely good, clever, and sensible even if he has not been.

3. The masochistic analysand's disauthorization of himself as if he were born to be an abused obedient servant of the analyst and his significant others: that he is not a "servant analysand."

4. The masochistic analysand's overauthorization of the analyst and his significant others as if they were born to be abusive dominant masters of himself: that the analyst is not a "master analyst."

5, 6, 7, and 8. The sadistic analysand's idealization and over-authorization of himself as being a good, clever, and sensible master who is entitled to dominate, abuse, denigrate and disauthorize the analyst and his significant others as if they were bad, stupid and crazy servants who must obey him and let him abuse them: that he is not a "master analysand" and that the analyst is not a "servant analyst."

9. The legitimacy and validity of the analysand's normative code and rule of action as a sacred and unique law.

In synthesis, the analyst should be able to use at least nine different types of *therapeutic requalification:*

1. The masochistic analysand's self-denigration
2. His idealization of his significant others
3. His disauthorization of himself
4. His overauthorization of his significant others
5. The sadistic analysand's self-idealization
6. His denigration of his significant others
7. His overauthorization of himself
8. His disauthorization of his significant others
9. The legitimacy and validity of the normative code of both the masochistic and the sadistic analysands.

The analyst can now start opening new symbolic possibilities which will allow the analysand to conceive new therapeutic patterns of creative behavior. Since the analysand is now ready to develop an outsight into the future by the prospective speech of the analyst, the analyst should use *therapeutic openings* to reveal to the analysand the following new perspectives.

The analyst should convey that human interactions are not always necessarily ruinously competitive; they can also be intelligently cooperative. Of course there are situations in which the game is a competitive one and the analysand has no power to change it. But there are other situations—whether in a capitalist or a socialist society—where there is room for intelligent cooperation. Consequently, the first opening will "teach" the analysand how to cooperate, when the situation allows him to do so, with his wife, friends, children, parents, and colleagues.

It should also be revealed that competitive human interactions are not always of the same stereotyped nature learned by the analysand during infancy and childhood. There are different kinds of competition, and he must be prepared to deal adequately with all of them if possible. If he keeps applying the old stereotyped parental strategy for obtaining pleasure and security he will keep failing. Consequently, the second opening will "teach" the analysand how to compete effectively when the competitive situation is different from the one he has learned. The openings tend to expand the analysand's knowledge of his transconscious; he becomes aware of some things in his symbolic structure that he had totally ignored because they were "unthinkable" for him. In this way the analyst not only tries to make evident the analysand's old prescientific unconscious paradigm based on the pleasure principle, but also tries to help him in constructing a new scientific paradigm based on the reality principle (Kuhn 1970). The analyst will next be in a position to give the analysand some clear *therapeutic directions* about how to avoid repeating or being locked into his old compulsive repetitive pattern, and how to look for or provoke a new therapeutic creative pattern (Freud 1919). These directions can be given to the analysand either in the form of *proscriptions* or *prescriptions*.

In effect, once the analyst has clearly identified the pathological and therapeutic patterns that are typical of and specific to the analysand, he should proscribe the analysand's typical compulsive repetitive pattern that starts with some kind of specific painful affective state, and continues with some counterproductive defensive actions (acting-out) which trigger counterproductive defensive actions (counter–acting-out) on the part of his significant others (reinforcing his fears because they provoke again and again the same feared painful affective state of unpleasure, insecurity, or disorganization). The analyst should also prescribe (Ferenczi 1966) some specific course of actions that the analysand should follow each time he starts feeling the typical painful affective state, because these actions will trigger specific responses on the part of his significant others that will finally overcome the painful affective state therapeutically.

In giving these therapeutic directions the analyst is not attacking the autonomy or judgment of the analysand, nor is he infantilizing him. He simply speaks with technical proficiency about some specific conflict areas of the analysand's behavior: he does not direct the analysand as if he were a blind, obedient, silly child any more than the pilot of an airplane infantilizes his passengers when he advises them to fasten their seat belts during turbulence. The analyst is merely using his professional authority in his own area of expertise; he is not in some way "superior" to the analysand. He does not advise the analysand to buy shoes of a certain color, but rather gives him advice on the kinds of fears he must be aware of, the kinds of actions that provoke or reinforce them, and the kinds of actions he must perform in order to overcome them. As a matter of fact these directions give the analysand much greater autonomy, because he can use them to analyze himself and to cope with his unconscious anxiety-provoking behavior: from now on he can be a self-conscious adult with a clear task-sight who can operate by himself; he will no longer be a blind, disoriented, impotent child.

Once the analyst can identify, explain, predict, and solve his own counterproductive repetitive patterns, the analyst is in a much better position to help him directly when he goes through critical moments with his significant others. Once the analysand is aware of his own former patterns, and once he tries to change them, his significant others, even if they want to see the analysand improve his mental health, will consciously or unconsciously resent that awareness and change. In these critical moments when the external object-relations structure of the analysand changes, the *therapeutic supervisions* of the analyst are sometimes unavoidable and may be decisive. In effect, in these circumstances the analyst behaves as if he were supervising the countertransference of a psychoanalytic candidate (who already knows his own pathology) and the transference of his analysand: he is analysing the effects and the motives of the analysand's own behavior plus the motives and the effects of the analysand's critical significant other. In other words, if the analyst can recommend the analysis of the resisting critical significant other of the analysand, maybe he will have to do little supervisory work. But if it is impossible to send the significant other to analysis, he will have to start "treating" him indirectly through the analysand himself: the critical resisting significant other will be thus the "analysand of the analysand." This happens, for instance, when the parents of the analysand are old or sick. In this case the analysand will have to try to detect and understand his parents' pathological behavior in order to neutralize them and to continue his own changes in a way less disturbing to everyone (Kovacs 1936).

Consequently, the analyst should supervise the analysand's "paratransferential" neurosis with his significant others (Gear and Liendo 1979) in order to help him overcome the critical steps of changing the structure of his own environment.

In effect, the supervisions are intended to analyze the analysand's paratransferential crisis and crucial decisions in such a way that he can achieve an accurate "insight into others" or improve his reality principle with respect to his immediate environment. Usually the supervisions are delivered when the analysand resorts to a consulting type of speech. The supervision should cover at least:

1. The analysand's own pathological involvement in the critical situation with his significant other; that is, why and when he selected such a mate or friend or partner, and how he has induced the typical steps of his paratransference neurosis—dependence, isolation, disqualification, crippling, attacks on reputation, censorship, blackmail, exploitation, etc. Once the analysand's pathological pattern (para–acting-out) has been analyzed, the analyst should proscribe it and then prescribe its corresponding therapeutic pattern (specific para-action).

2. The significant other's pathological involvement in the paratransferential crisis: the structure and conscious and unconscious motivations of his pathological pattern (para–counter–acting-out) and how to overcome it by its corresponding therapeutic pattern (specific para-reaction).

3. The distinction between the characteristics and sequence of the analysand's own pathology and those of the pathology of his significant others—that is, the distinction between what the analysand is "putting" there (transferring) and what he is "taking" (countertransferring), the product of his own pathology as distinct from the product of his contamination with the pathology of the other.

4. The most likely outcome of this critical conflictive significant relationship: deep healthy modification, partial superficial modification, or no modification and interruption of the relationship; that is, whether the analysand will be able to continue, deepen, and enrich the relationship (with his spouse, for example), if he will only be able to modify it partially in some kind of chronic semipatho-

logical agreement, or if the significant other responds with such a negative and impossible reaction to every attempt at modification that the analysand will finally have to break off this relationship ("alterectomy"—Gear and Liendo 1979).

5. The transferential relationship of the analysand with the analyst while he is being supervised by him. In effect, this type of evaluation and assessment of the analysand's external significant relationships is rather delicate and must be handled very carefully to avoid both the mismanagement of this type of deep information on the part of the analysand and the hyper-responsibilization of the analyst for the important decisions the analysand will have to make. That is, before supervising the analysand's critical relationships with his significant others, the analyst must carefully assess whether the analysand is fully able to use the deep information that he will receive not only about himself but about the others in a responsible and healthy way and not in a compulsive destructive sadomasochistic way so as to resist the analytic process or, simply, to reinforce his own narcissistic structure. Of course he will always try to repeat his old pattern in some way, but it is the final balance that matters.

The analyst must also assess whether he himself is not unconsciously counter–acting-out under some intensive pressure on the part of the analysand: this will be the case with masochistic or sadistic patients, for example, who are not looking for a healthy technical assessment but who seek to avoid their own responsibilities as adults and who start blaming the analyst. It is important, however, to realize that the analyst cannot avoid being involved in some way in the continuing cooling or interrupting of the analysand's relationships with his significant others. In other words, the analyst is always a technical witness who is endorsing or discouraging in an open or hidden way the analysand's decisions with respect to the others, even if the analyst tries to deny it by qualifying himself as a neutral passive bystander. The claim of neutrality in this context is an iatrogenic myth that is contradicted with each analytic intervention that openly or subtly qualifies the analysand's behavior as acting-out or as healthy. Therefore, it seems healthier to supervise these decisions openly and systematically: the true "neutrality" of the analyst will lie in the fact that his assessment will be as objective and scientific as possible rather than partial and impulsive (even if it seems to be a "neutral" intervention). The analyst "knows" if a decision to marry is healthy or if it is a mere resisting repetition of an old compulsive pattern. It is the responsibility of the analyst not only to let the analysand know his technical opinion but also, in the extreme case where the analysand threatens to commit suicide or homicide, for example, to enforce such an opinion (Gear and Liendo 1976).

Consequently, the analyst will be able to make at least four classes of supervision of the analysand's critical relations with his significant others:

1. The characteristics and sequence of the analysand's own involvement
2. The characteristics and sequence of the involvement of the significant others
3. The distinction between the analysand's own pathology and the pathology of the significant others that he can counter-act-out by contamination
4. The possible outcome of that critical relationship: intensification, cooling, or interruption.

At this point the analyst is in a better position to begin systematically introducing a broader and more objective perspective of the sociopolitico-economic structure into which the analysand was placed as an infant and child as well as the one in which he is placed in the present. Again, this type of analytic intervention can be considered controversial because the analyst could be seen as "teaching" the analysand the "true" structure of socioeconomic reality instead of leaving him to discover it for himself. To clarify this possible source of confusion, one could say that this type of intervention is only necessary when treating an analysand who has little or no systematic information about his own place in a particular social class or about the institutional, national, or international political and economic game. It must also be clear that, when conveying these *therapeutic socioeconomic openings*, the analyst is not advising or leading the analysand to accept a certain economic or political point of view, but is only suggesting that he become better informed about the institutional, national, or international dynamics that are affecting or will affect his own pleasure and security as well as those of his significant others. Even if we just limit ourselves to advising the analysand that he must obtain more and better information about what is going on in his external world, this advice will always be ideologically contaminated. But, as everyone knows, it is practically impossible to transmit any information without transmitting some kind of ideology at the same time. On the other hand it is also important to remember that the analyst is always transmitting to the analysand, even with the most "neutral" interpretations, his own theories about the social structure. This is equally unavoidable. Thus, it is better to work openly and systematically, not to impose our own values and prejudices on the analysand, but to help him be as well informed as possible about the structure and problems of the world through independent sources of information. This is particularly important, of course, in the case of the masochistic patient who tends to isolate himself from the world and to rely only on the connection that he can obtain through his sadistic agents (the analyst included). If the analysand knows very little about the structure of his society he will always be in the position of a naive, powerless child without any real social mastery: that is why patients (and sometimes agents) typically have a strong inner feeling of being just a child in a world of adults, a child who lacks any accurate socioeconomic awareness and who is always making a fool of himself in the business world.

As a result, our opinion is that the analyst must make at least the following socioeconomic openings in order to allow the analysand to see his own culture and society as if he were an anthropologist ("anthropologist's outsight"):

1. Explain to the analysand that he has a strong compulsive sadomasochistic tendency because the society in which he was raised and in which he lives simultaneously stimulates and punishes competition when its members try to obtain pleasure and security.

2. Explain to the analysand that his sadomasochistic behavior is stereotyped because it has been taught to him by a group of people who were restricted in their resources and possibilities because of income limitations, etc.; that his stereotyped psychopathology depends to a great extent on his stereotyped sociopathology.

3. Suggest that the analysand obtain specific information about the psychosociological dynamics of the type of institution he belongs to or works in: hospitals, banks, etc.

4. Suggest that the analysand obtain specific information about the socioeconomic and political dynamics of the region or country he lives in, and of the region or country he lived in as a child (if this is different).

5. Suggest that the analysand obtain specific information about the international politicoeconomic dynamics that can affect him directly or indirectly: international conflicts, runaway inflation, unemployment, and war.

In sum, the analysand, before he can be considered "healed," must have some sound sociological, economic, and political ideas about the structure of his world so that he can anticipate social changes and prevent himself and his family, as far as possible, from being crushed by catastrophic events.

All the verbal analytic interventions already described are addressed to consciousness, to the intelligent nonnarcissistic aspect of the analysand's psychic apparatus. But there are other types of verbal intervention that can be applied simultaneously; these are addressed to the irrational narcissistic unconscious aspect of the analysand's psychic structure. We are referring now to the *therapeutic verbal counterpressures* that the analyst usually applies (consciously or unconsciously) when the analysand is using a defensive type of speech or mode of action which is particularly resistant to the other types of analytic intervention, or when he is very strongly resistant either to associating freely or to starting to execute the specific therapeutic actions that will allow him to open the vicious circle of repetition compulsion (Gear and Liendo 1980).

As we said before, the therapeutic verbal counterpressures are applied to the specific affective interests of the analysand: against the pleasure of the sadists and against the security of the masochists. These counterpressures can be direct or indirect threats or promises in order to dissuade the analysand from executing his acting-out or to persuade him to execute his specific therapeutic action. But they can also be alliances or coalitions with sadistic significant others and the master alter of the masochistic analysand, or with the masochistic significant other and the servant alter of the sadistic analysand.

In synthesis, the analyst should be able to exercise the following pressures against the otherwise insurmountable resistances of the analysand:

1. Dissuasion of the analysand from executing his pathogenic acting-out through threats to his feared affective states: that the unpleasure of the sadist or the insecurity of the masochist will be increased if he doesn't stop being a sadist or masochist.

2. Dissuasion of the analysand from executing his pathogenic acting-out through promises that his feared affective states will disappear if he stops being a sadist or masochist.

3. Persuasion of the analysand to execute the therapeutic specific actions through threats against his pleasure or security.

4. Persuasion of the analysand to execute the therapeutic specific action through promises that his pleasure or security will improve if he does so.

5. Coalition with the analysand's intrapsychic significant others. Initially, when he is successful, the analyst usually disguises himself (consciously or unconsciously) as another servant alter of the sadist analysand, who will be able to diminish his pleasure if he does not start changing his sadistic pattern; or, as another master alter of the masochistic analysand, who will be able to diminish his security if he does not change his masochistic pattern.

6. Coalition with the analysand's external significant others. In effect, when he is successful, the analyst usually has the ability to send covert messages to the sadistic other of the masochistic analysand or the masochistic other of the sadistic analysand in order to obtain support (the specific therapeutic reaction) for changing the pathogenic pattern of the analysand. The analyst will promise more pleasure to the sadistic significant other if he also puts some pressure to change on the masochistic analysand, or threaten more unpleasure if he does not; similarly, he will threaten insecurity or promise security to obtain the collaboration of the masochistic significant other of the sadistic analysand. These covered (or uncovered) alliances with the significant others of the analysand can be established indirectly through the analysand himself if he is a neurotic or characteropathic analysand. But sometimes it is necessary to make direct contact and alliances with them if the analysand is psychopathic, psychotic, or is reacting negatively to every kind of analytic intervention and pressure.

7. Coalition with the healthy, nonnarcissistic aspect of the analysand himself: the so-called "therapeutic alliance." In explaining the advantages of change in terms of better pleasure and security, the analyst gets the analysand to move toward the therapeutic change. Again, if the analysand is psychopathic or psychotic, sometimes it is necessary to establish a therapeutic alliance with a responsible significant other of the analysand's family. This is usually the sadistic agent in the case of the psychotic, and the masochistic agent in the case of the psychopath.

8. Transference of the dependency of the patient-analysand and creation of the dependency of the agent-analysand. In effect, none of the previous pressures can be enforced if the analysand has not previously established some kind of solid relation of therapeutic dependence. The difference with the pathogenic dependency stimulated by the agent of mental illness is that the therapeutic dependence is created to promote real adult independence and mental health, and not more infantilizing dependency and mental illness.

All these counterpressures are, of course, unavoidable in the course of any analytic treatment. Even if for tactical reasons they are executed in an indirect and covert way, they must not be ignored by the analyst himself. Again, he cannot remain neutral while working in a therapeutic situation that is full of pathogenic pressures and counterpressures that cannot be solved (initially at least) by their mere description or interpretation. A naively "neutral," passive approach implies either ignorance on the part of the analyst of the essential characteristics of human relationships—particularly of the pathological ones—or the false assumption that the analysand merely "has" a narcissism and not that he "is" a narcissistic person: that he is more rational than he really can be. If he were able to change simply by rational explanations of his irrational behavior, he would not need the psychoanalytic process at all. This process is absolutely necessary precisely because the analysand is not only "irrational" in his pathological unconscious behavior but also in his pathological unconscious resistance to change: the language of pressures and counterpressures would be the real therapeutic communication "from unconscious to unconscious."

Consequently, the analyst should be able to exercise at least eight classes of therapeutic counterpressure to overcome resistances that are impossible to change otherwise:

1. Threats against the analysand's pleasure and security in order to dissuade him from acting-out
2. Promises of pleasure and security to dissuade the analysand from acting-out
3. Threats of unpleasure and insecurity to persuade the analysand to execute his therapeutic specific action
4. Promises of pleasure and security to persuade the analysand to execute his therapeutic specific action
5. Coalition with the analysand's intrapsychic significant other in order to press him from "inside"

6. Coalition with the analysand's external significant others through indirect or direct threats and promises to dissuade them from executing their counter–acting-out and to persuade them to execute their specific therapeutic reaction
7. Therapeutic alliance with the healthy aspect of the analysand himself or with the healthy aspect of his significant others
8. Transference of the dependency of the masochistic analysand and creation of dependency in the sadistic one.

The previous verbal therapeutic interventions of the analyst were directed either to the analysand's conscious and unconscious levels or only to his unconscious. But when the analysand is speaking or asking specific questions about the characteristics or the meaning of the analytic setting, the analyst should use *therapeutic setting clarifications* that are directed to the analysand's conscious level even if they unavoidably have unconscious consequences for the analysand. The analyst should be able to make as many setting clarifications as are needed as to what must be done and why it must be done in order to avoid the failure of the analytic treatment and to promote it success (Meltzer 1973). There are three main classes of setting clarifications that the analyst may use to produce "insight into the analytic process" in the analysand:

1. Initial setting clarifications, just before starting the treatment and after the first interviews. The analyst should explain carefully to the analysand that he must come regularly, that he must lie on the couch, that he must associate freely, etc. He must emphasize that the analyst will thus be in a much better position to understand the underlying meanings of his compulsive counterproductive behavior and his symptoms, and consequently will be able to help him much more effectively in overcoming them and finding new solutions for his problems.

2. Setting reclarifications, to be given each time the analysand asks for them, or each time he—because of his transference neurosis or psychosis—breaks the rules of the setting. Often after these reclarifications, the analyst can and should interpret the meaning of the analysand's questions about the setting or of his breaking of it.

3. Special setting clarifications of specific rules prescribed for overcoming some specific resistances of a special analysand, for instance, when increasing the number of the sessions because the analysand is facing a very significant and decisive crisis of his narcissistic structure in his working-through process.

Once the analyst has made verbal interventions, the analysand, especially at the beginning of the analytic process, usually treats them defensively to reinstall the analyst as his narcissistic alter, by distorting or ignoring their meaning through different types of disqualifying transactions: changing the subject, literalizing the meaning, taking the interpretation out of context, denigrating or idealizing the analyst, etc. In such cases, the analyst is obliged to make *therapeutic verbal reinterventions* in order to clarify that his previous intervention has not been a new repetition of the same message that the analysand is used to receiving from his old significant others. He must show the analysand again and again that he is not speaking as his old sadistic or masochistic significant other. In this way the analyst is avoiding being "realterized" by the analysand: he is giving him "insight into the analyst" (Gear and Liendo 1915).

The verbal interventions of the analyst addressed to the conscious, preconscious, and unconscious levels of the analysand's psychic apparatus are synthesized in Figure 10-4.

Factual and Affective Therapeutic Interventions

At the same time that he is speaking, the analyst is always executing paraverbal, nonverbal, and contextual actions that depend on the transference-countertransference process and should be used as therapeutic tools. These we designate as factual interventions. Within the analytic setting they always hold a special latent meaning for the analysand.

As we said before, the verbal therapeutic actions of the analyst are either the eleven verbal interventions already described or the technical use of silence on very special occasions. In our opinion silence as a therapeutic tool has a very restricted use: it is not therapeutic by itself and many times is really harmful because it is unconsciously used to cover the analyst's ignorance or disorientation and may have a disastrous effect on the analysand.

Among the paraverbal actions the *therapeutic counterstyle* is very important—the grammar, phonetics, and style as well as the tone in which the verbal interventions are communicated. Usually, the most effective therapeutic counterstyle is that of the significant others of the analysand; that is, the "alter's counterstyle": the analyst will use, initially at least, not only the psychopathological style of the alter (for example, an hysterical masochist) but also his power position (for example, an hysterical masochistic agent). Of course, especially with sadistic analysands, the analyst can also use the "ego's counterstyle" of the analysand. It depends on whether he wants to stabilize the position of the analysand for the time being or whether he wants to invert it. As the treatment advances, the analyst will be allowed to use more freely his own therapeutic style (friendly, warm, serious, quiet, or dynamic).

In order to execute the following kinds of therapeutic factual interventions, the analyst will need to combine verbal, paraverbal, and nonverbal actions. In effect, in the *therapeutic dramatizations* the analyst tries to play (but not to take) the role of either the ego or the alter of the analysand, or a totally different role. If we think of the role as a set of actions, the difference between the pathogenic ego and alter (who execute the acting and counter–acting-out, respectively) and the healthy therapeutic ego and alter (who use the same style and tone of the ego and alter and who execute the specific action and reaction) must be clarified. The style and the tone remain the same but the role changes subtly. Consequently, the analyst should carefully avoid taking the role of the analysand's pathogenic ego or alter; on the contrary, he should play—initially at least—the therapeutic role of the analysand's ego or alter. The analyst should be able to play either the "alter dramatization" or, less often, the "ego dramatization": that is, he should be able to resist the temptation of executing the analysand's counter–acting-out and should be able to execute instead the analysand's specific therapeutic reaction. It should be said that the therapeutic equivalent of a master alter could be a strong alter, that of a servant alter, a kind alter. In other words, being strong satisfies the needs of the masochistic analysand for security without disqualifying or crippling him; and being kind satisfies the needs of the sadistic analysand for pleasure without allowing him to disqualify or cripple the analyst (Freud 1905b).

The third type of factual intervention is the *therapeutic corrective action*—that is, execution of the therapeutic action and reaction instead of acting-out and counter–acting-out. Such actions might be included among the therapeutic dramatizations, but they have an identity of their own inasmuch as they can be executed even

1. Descriptions of:
(outsight)

- Speech monotheme
- Speech bipolarity
- Speech sadomasochism
- Speech qualifications
- Pathogenic speech sequence
- Stereotyped actions
- Sadomasochism of actions
- Speech inversion
- Psychological pressures
- Distorting answers

2. Reconstructions of:
(historic outsight)

- Oedipal object relations
- Present object relations

3. Interpretations of:
(insight)

- Stereotyped perception
- Inverted perception
- Avoided painful feelings
- Intrapsychic normative code
- Intrapsychic rule of action
- Validity of norm and rule
- Authority of intrapsychic ruler
- The master-slave structure
- Sadomasochistic pleasure principle
- First psychic mutilation
- Second psychic mutilation

4. Requalification of:
(insight into power)

- Masochistic autoidentification
- Masochistic idealization of the other
- Masochistic auto-disauthorization
- Masochistic overauthorization of the other
- Sadistic autoidealization
- Sadistic denigration of the other
- Sadistic auto-overauthorization
- Sadistic disauthorization of the other
- Validity of intrapsychic law
- Authority of intrapsychic ruler

Figure 10-4. Verbal interventions

5. Openings of: (outsight onto the future)	Nonsadomasochistic reality principle Creative thinking
6. Directions: (outsight onto tasks)	Proscription of acting-out Prescription of therapeutic action
7. Supervision of: (insight into others)	Analysand's para-acting-out Other's counter-para-acting-out Distinction between analysand's pathology and the contamination with the pathology of the other Possible outcome of the crisis with the significant other
8. Socioeconomic openings of: (anthropologist's outsight)	Competitive social structure Stereotyping social structure Institutional dynamics National dynamics International dynamics
9. Verbal counterpressures of:	Dissuasion of acting-out Persuasion of therapeutic action Coalition with superego Coalition with significant others Therapeutic alliances Transference of dependence
10. Setting clarifications: (insight into the analytic process)	Initial clarification of rules and meaning of analysis Reclarifications Specific clarifications
11. Reinterventions: (insight into the analyst)	Correcting reprojections of the alter (realterizations)

Figure 10-4 (*Continued*). Verbal interventions

without the analysand's counterstyle or countertone. In effect, therapeutic corrective actions are no more and no less than a subtle modification of the analysand's pathogenic actions and reactions that avoids provoking dependency, domination, submission, disqualification, blackmail, exploitation, etc. In other words, the therapeutic actions and reactions are neither stereotyped nor sadomasochistic and their speech is not inverted. Moreover, they are specifically antisadomasochistic. For instance, the specific action corresponding to a sadistic hysteric's acting-out would be to act as a dynamic attractive person without being a disqualifying seducer (Freud 1905a).

The fourth kind of factual intervention is the *therapeutic factual counterpressure*—that is, antisadomasochistic punishments and pro-nonsadomasochistic rewards. For instance, if a sadistic analysand is behaving sadistically, the analyst could use an unpleasant tone or a tougher style to communicate his interpretations; or, conversely, if the analysand is improving, and is behaving more kindly, the analyst will use a more pleasant tone and a softer style with him.

The fifth kind of factual intervention is the contextual action, the *therapeutic setting modification*. This can be used to deal not only with the critical stages of the working-through process but also with the analysand's sadomasochistic violations of it. Particular examples are the stricter limits that the psychopathic analysand requires, and the more flexible and comprehensive setting (including the family) that the psychotic analysand requires. The analyst will use five classes of setting modification: (1) critical stage modifications; (2) anti-sadistic modifications; (3) antimasochistic modifications; (4) antipsy-chopathic modifications; and (5) antipsychotic modifications.

The five classes of factual intervention play a central role in the struggle for recognition and independence, and against domination and disqualification, that is in our approach the very core of analytic treatment.

With respect to the *affective interventions* of the analyst, we recall that they fall into two classes. First, the therapeutic rescue and working-through of the analyst's own original and typical feelings, which he was made aware of during his own training analysis; second, the identification and working-through of the counter-feelings provoked in him by the analysand. The analyst, after avoiding the temptation to indulge his own sadism or masochism, must avoid also the new temptation of indulging the counter-sadism or counter-masochism induced by the analysand. The distinction between his own feelings and those induced in him is crucial in solving the problem of psychic contamination (Racker 1960).

As a matter of fact, the *therapeutic rescue of the analyst's own feelings* and the *therapeutic identification of the feelings induced by the analysand* constitute, we think, the turning point for the transformation of mental illness into mental health. (See Figure 10-5).

Stopping the Transmission of Mental Illness

The first goal of a psychoanalytic epidemiology would be to interrupt as soon and as definitively as possible the unconscious sadomasochistic chain. Usually this is attempted by modifying the patient first and then, with his help (because he is gradually transformed into an agent of mental health), the agent. As we have indicated, one of the main sources of this chain is the misconception that the only way to obtain pleasure and security is to exploit others. Once the pathological dependence upon others is established, then all the steps described (disqualification, disauthorization, isolation, censorship, etc.) are made possible. Thus pathological dependency is a critical variable in the pathogenic process. For this reason the battle for a healthy dependence, independence, and multiple dependence should be a central issue in any analytic treatment. In this sense it can be said that analysis is equivalent to a campaign of liberation. We have indicated also that the agents of mental illness, either sadists or masochists, are basically dependency makers, and that the corresponding patients are dependency "mades." This is like the relationship between "pushers" and "addicts." Consequently, the analytic strategy will be different with agents than with patients. Even if patients are addicted to the conflicting security given by their agents, and agents are addicted to the conflicting pleasure given by their patients, the agents will have control of their relationship because survival is more basic than pleasure.

In dealing with patients, the analyst should be able to take control of the analytic relation, simply by allowing them to transfer dependence onto him from their current agents. But when he is dealing with agents, he will have to struggle for control until he is able

FACTUAL INTERVENTIONS	1. Counterstyles	Alter's style Ego's style Original analyst's style
	2. Dramatizations	Alter's dramatization Ego's dramatization
	3. Corrective actions	Specific reaction Specific action
	4. Factual counterpressures	Antisadomasochistic punishments Pro-nonsadomasochistic rewards
	5. Setting modifications	In critical states Antisadistic Antimasochistic Antipsychopathic Antipsychotic
AFFECTIVE INTERVENTIONS	1. Rescue of original feelings	Anti-contamination
	2. Identification of the analysand's induced feelings	Anti-counteridentification

Figure 10-5.   Factual and affective interventions

to invert the direction of the dependence. In other words, patients will give control automatically to the analyst, but agents will try to fight him. They will not accept the analyst as a therapeutic ruler with enough power to change the unconscious rules of the sadomasochistic game.

Once the problem of pathogenic dependence is worked out, and the analyst is in therapeutic control of the analytic relationship, all the other central variables in the transmission of mental illness—crippling, isolation, censorship, disqualification, disauthorization, exploitation, blackmail, etc.—should be worked through differently with sadistic and masochistic analysands.

In brief, the analyst should ask himself two basic clinical questions when he faces a new analysand: (1) Is he a patient or an agent? (2) Is he a sadist or a masochist? The answer to these questions will allow him to classify the new analysand psychopathologically and then to design and apply an appropriate analytic policy, strategy, tactic, and technique.

Analysis of the Masochistic Patient

The reader will recall that the masochistic patient is, basically, a dependent person who tends to look for and to idealize sadistic others who attack his reputation, who cripple, isolate, censor, disqualify, and disauthorize him, and who blackmail and exploit him with respect to pleasure. He accepts this mistreatment and surrenders his independence, thinking that this is the only way he can be protected by the sadistic others—as if he were a helpless child and the others were strong and helpful adults. He carefully avoids making big decisions with respect to financial or occupational matters regarding his actual survival, and he severely punishes any attempt by these others to depend on him for their security; he has the insurmountable feeling of being a child and thus cannot accept other children depending on him. He is not only addicted to a "protective" agent, but also to a sadistic one, in the sense that he can not tolerate a masochistic agent because he feels that he is weak, or at least not strong enough. Usually he is a naive, overtrusting person who is highly hypnotizable (or suggestible) and who is constantly hypnotized by sadistic others who blatantly cheat him with respect to pleasure.

Consequently, if the masochistic patient is addicted to cruel, tough sadistic agents, it will be impossible for the analyst (initially at least) not to play the role of the firm, strong analyst if he really wants the patient to remain in treatment with him. If the analyst does not play the alter's role, giving the patient a feeling of therapeutic security, it will be as if he were suddenly withdrawing alcohol or cocaine from an addict.

The first movement of the analyst with a masochistic patient will thus be to replace his sadistic agent by playing the role of an active, firm, and strong analyst who appears as if he will take responsibility for the survival and big decisions of the patient without, of course, really doing so. More important, he must do this without crippling, isolating, or disqualifying the patient. It is the functional counterstyle without pathogenic effects.

Once the analysand's sadistic agent has been substituted by the role-playing of the strong analyst, the analyst will immediately start the therapeutic requalification and disauthorization of the intra-psychic and external sadistic master alter of the analysand, as well as the requalification and authorization of the analysand himself. That is, the analysand's tendency to idealize and overauthorize sadistic others and to denigrate and disauthorize himself must be fully analyzed. In order to do so, the analyst must demonstrate the lack of validity and the obsolescence of the sadomasochistic values, code, and strategy that both the masochistic patient and the sadistic agent are unconsciously applying in order to obtain pleasure and security.

In other words, when undermining the overqualification and the authority of the internal and external sadistic agent as well as the validity of his strategy, the analyst is challenging not only his talent and effectiveness as a leader, but his entire philosophy of life.

By playing the rule of the strong, tough analyst and by under-mining the authority of the agent as well as the validity of his philosophy, the analyst is provoking a full transference of the patient's dependence from the sadistic agent onto the analyst himself. In this way he will exercise increasing therapeutic control of the analytic relationship—not of the analysand himself—and will have enough authority and power to proceed with the therapeutic steps of the analytic treatment of the masochistic analysand which follow.

The transference of the masochistic dependence means the transference of an idealized transference that must then be carefully and gradually analyzed. That is, the self-denigration of the analysand and the idealization of the analyst must be fully clarified. But the analyst must permit this idealization to actually occur. We agree with Kohut (1971) when he suggests that the mirror transference of narcissistic omnipotence must not only be allowed initially but must in fact be promoted by the analyst when healing a narcissistic personality. We would say that when treating a narcissistic masochistic patient, the spontaneous idealizing transference should be allowed (and in fact promoted) and then fully analyzed.

When undermining the authority of the agent and the validity of the norm and rule of the "superego," the analyst must be aware of the unconscious resistances of the masochistic patient based in his ambivalence toward his sadistic agent. In effect, very often the patient goes back to his agent and mentions to him, quite naively at the conscious level, what the analyst is saying "against" the agent and his philosophy. The agent usually reacts against the analytic treatment and counterattacks, disqualifying and disauthorizing the analyst or trying to interrupt the treatment. In other words, the masochistic patient can use the sadistic agent to express his own negative transference and resistance to change the structure of his psychic apparatus and his interpersonal relationships.

Consequently, knowing that the masochistic patient is like a frightened child who can act unconsciously as a coward and a traitor, the analysis of his unconscious loyalty and attachment to the sadistic agent is indispensable at this stage of the treatment. We must remember that he is not a "good" person attacked by a "bad" person: he is just a masochist related to a sadist and is quite ambivalent about being rescued by any "white knight."

Apart from analyzing the masochistic loyalty, the analyst must try to build, as quickly as he can, an antisadistic therapeutic coalition with the patient with respect to his agent—not against the agent himself but against his pathogenic attitude. In doing that, the ex-masochist should act as a "double agent" (Halleck 1971): in the manifest service of his sadistic agent, on the one hand, and in the secret service of his analyst on the other. In other words, the masochistic patient should be carefully prepared so that he can understand not only the motives of the sadistic behavior of his agent but also that the agent cannot change suddenly. He must be very tactful in retransmitting the therapeutic information received in the analytic sessions as well as in introducing deep therapeutic changes in his relationship with the agent. He must be advised to change tactfully and gradually in such a way that the sadistic agent will not get panicky; he will understand that the analyst is not really against him personally but is merely trying to change the pathogenic system in which he is unconsciously included as the leader, and that, finally, this change will be better for himself and for his masochistic patient. If the analyst is successful in handling this delicate and crucial stage of the treatment, the sadistic agent will probably approach him for therapeutic advice; the analyst should then recommend the analytic treatment of the sadistic agent.

At the same time that these therapeutic steps are taken, the analysand should also analyze and work through all the other aspects of his pathogenic relationship with his own superego, master alter, and sadistic agent. That is, the analyst should relieve the censorship in the analytic relationship, encourage the analysand to retrain the atrophied aspects of his ego (to overcome his functional crippling) and to reconnect himself socially (to overcome the social isolation and his bad reputation as a victimizer of the sadistic agent).

While undermining the "principles" of the patient's superego and retraining his crippled ego, the analyst is preparing the patient to seek and obtain not only new types of security (that do not require the sacrifice of his pleasure) but also to seek and obtain pleasure itself from his significant others. A whole new world will open up to the patient.

Once the masochistic patient is relieved of the censorship and reconnected to society, and seeks and obtains nonmasochistic security and nonsadistic pleasure, he will be in a much better position to neutralize the sadistic blackmail of his agents and to avoid exercising his own masochistic blackmail toward them.

The analysand will become not only more and more self-sufficient in terms of survival (that is, more independent) but will also be able to "interdepend" in a mature way with many other people. He will thus break his pathogenic dependence on sadistic agents. In this way he will be able not only to offer a different (nonsadistic) type of pleasure to the agents but also to be a source of nonmasochistic security to them.

Again, if the analyst is successful in all these stages of the treatment, a "quiet revolution" should occur in the narcissistic political system formed by the patient and his agents, and the analyst will be in full command of the therapeutic process: a new, healthy agreement will be achieved between the patient and his agent, and both of them will be able to finish their analytic treatment because they will be able to perform self-analysis and live more happily.

Unfortunately, things do not always happen this way; sometimes the couple formed by the analyst and the masochistic patient are not able to convince the sadistic agent to make a therapeutic change. In that case the analyst must be prepared to face two main alternatives. If the analysand is extremely dependent on his resistant sadistic agent, he will probably leave treatment sooner or later. The analyst will not be able to prevent it: the only way to avoid it is to transform the psychoanalysis into a "psycho-dialysis," that is, into a chronic situation in which the dialyst (no longer the analyst) limits his activity to listening to the chronic complaints of the masochistic patient—who never improves—but does not attempt any deep interpretation or change in the patient-agent system. Naturally, to work as a powerless psychic garbage can is not healthy, either for the patient or for the analyst. But sometimes—more often than one cares to admit—this degradation and perversion of the analysis into dialysis is unavoidable and it is left to the analyst to do this dirty and unhealthy work. This is a philosophical problem, and sometimes an economic problem, because these endless pathogenic treatments solve the financial problems of a young analyst (or of a masochistic analyst) who has been unable to attain a healthy financial independence and must therefore sell his mental health and absorb mental illness.

The second alternative, if the sadistic agent resists any therapeutic change and the masochistic patient is not very dependent on him, is that sooner or later an "agentectomy" will occur. That is, the formerly masochistic patient will decide to leave his old sadistic agent and look for a nonsadomasochistic type of relationship with a new significant other. This means, of course, relationships ending in divorce, etc. This outcome is not as good as therapeutic transformation of the sadistic agent but is to be preferred to chronic pathogenic submission of the masochistic agent (and, sometimes, the analyst). Figure 10-6 presents the main steps of the typical analytic treatment of a masochistic patient.

Analysis of the Sadistic Agent

The sadistic agent tends to be a very dominant, dependency-making type of person who seeks masochistic others whom he denigrates, cripples, isolates, censors, disqualifies, disauthorizes, and black-

```
┌─────────────────────────────────────────────────────────────────────────┐
│ Playing the role of the strong, tough analyst                             │
└─────────────────────────────────────────────────────────────────────────┘
                                      ↓
┌─────────────────────────────────────────────────────────────────────────┐
│ Analysis of the patient's idealization and overauthorization of his       │
│ sadistic agent and of his own self-denigration and self-disauthorization  │
└─────────────────────────────────────────────────────────────────────────┘
                                      ↓
┌─────────────────────────────────────────────────────────────────────────┐
│ Analysis of the validity of the counterproductive code and strategy of    │
│ the patient's superego                                                    │
└─────────────────────────────────────────────────────────────────────────┘
                                      ↓
┌─────────────────────────────────────────────────────────────────────────┐
│ Transference of the patient's dependence                                  │
└─────────────────────────────────────────────────────────────────────────┘
                                      ↓
┌─────────────────────────────────────────────────────────────────────────┐
│ Taking control of the analytic relationship                               │
└─────────────────────────────────────────────────────────────────────────┘
                                      ↓
┌─────────────────────────────────────────────────────────────────────────┐
│ Analysis of the idealized transference                                    │
└─────────────────────────────────────────────────────────────────────────┘
                                      ↓
┌─────────────────────────────────────────────────────────────────────────┐
│ Analysis of the negative transference expressed through the patient's      │
│ sadistic agent                                                            │
└─────────────────────────────────────────────────────────────────────────┘
                                      ↓
┌─────────────────────────────────────────────────────────────────────────┐
│ Relief of censorship, retraining of the crippled ego, social reconnection, │
│ stopping the sadistic and the masochistic blackmail and exploitation      │
└─────────────────────────────────────────────────────────────────────────┘
                                      ↓
┌─────────────────────────────────────────────────────────────────────────┐
│ Discovery of nonmasochistic security and nonsadistic pleasure             │
└─────────────────────────────────────────────────────────────────────────┘
                                      ↓
┌─────────────────────────────────────────────────────────────────────────┐
│ Antisadistic coalition with the masochistic patient                       │
└─────────────────────────────────────────────────────────────────────────┘
         ↓                        ↓                          ↓
┌──────────────────┐   ┌──────────────────────┐   ┌──────────────────────┐
│ Treatment of the │   │ Chronic              │   │ Separation           │
│ patient's        │   │ sadomasochistic      │   │ from the resistant   │
│ sadistic agent   │   │ regime including the │   │ sadistic agent       │
└──────────────────┘   │ analyst              │   │ (agentectomy)        │
         ↓             │ (psychodialysis)     │   └──────────────────────┘
┌──────────────────┐   │ or interruption of   │              ↓
│ Healthy agreement│   │ the treatment        │   ┌──────────────────────┐
└──────────────────┘   └──────────────────────┘   │ New healthy agreement│
                                                   └──────────────────────┘
```

Figure 10-6. Outline of the typical analytic treatment of a masochistic patient

mails; he attacks their reputations and exploits them with respect to pleasure. Meanwhile they exploit him with respect to security. He accepts taking care of their survival and security because he thinks this is the only way he can transform them into masochistic sources of sadistic pleasure, which is the only type of pleasure he thinks is available. He also thinks, unconsciously at least, that the others are crazy, stupid, bad, and weak children whom he can exploit but cannot count on for his own survival.

Consequently, he acts as a "pusher," as an addict-maker who cannot tolerate the independence of others, and who is usually a very good authoritarian hypnotizer of these others. If this is so, it will be impossible for the analyst—initially, at least—not to play the role of the soft, kind analyst (playing the alter's dramatization of the sadistic agent) in order to give the agent a feeling of therapeutic pleasure. With this nonpathogenic, functional counterstyle, the analyst is merely avoiding a traumatic and counterproductive cognitive dissonance for the analysand without allowing him to cripple, isolate, or disqualify the analyst.

Once the analysand's masochistic patient has been replaced by the analyst and the sadistic agent has accepted the treatment, the battle for control of the analytic relationship really begins. In order to take over the therapeutic government of this relation, the analyst must switch very gradually from the analysand's alter dramatization to the analysand's ego dramatization—that is, from the alter-counterstyle to the ego-style of the sadistic agent. In other words, the analyst will change gradually from being a fair, kind type of person to a strong, tough person who uses the same style that the agent uses with his own patients, but without the pathogenic effects. The analyst will become the "agent of the agent" by giving the sadistic analysand "more of the same." For example, if the analysand uses a sarcastic devaluating type of phrasing to undermine the others, the analyst will use an ironic nondevaluating style with him.

In this way, what the analyst is trying to do is to invert the control and dependence in the analytic relationship. As we have indicated, the change from the kind counterstyle to the strong, tough style must be negotiated very carefully if we want to avoid the analysand becoming anxious and interrupting treatment.

At this stage it is generally very important that the analyst start giving signals of independence, showing the sadistic agent that he is perfectly capable of surviving without his help.

To reinforce this inversion of control and dependence, the analyst should also begin to gradually counter-disqualify and counter-disauthorize the disqualifications and disauthorizations that the sadistic agent is constantly aiming at him. In other words, at this stage the therapeutic requalifications are indicated to modify the self-idealization and self-overauthorization of the analysand and the denigration and disauthorization of the analyst and significant others. Also indicated is the invalidation of the sadistic agent's philosophy, code, and strategy (the superego) that is behind his self-idealizing and denigrating attitude.

If the sadistic agent can tolerate these requalifications and invalidations, the analyst can start fighting more openly against the censorship, crippling dependence, social isolation, blackmail, and exploitation that the sadistic analysand is unconsciously trying to impose on him in order to obtain pleasure. At this stage the negative transference must be fully analyzed, as well as the splitting of the idealized transference; the latter is commonly evidenced by the masochistic patients who surround the sadistic agent analysand.

While undermining the sadomasochistic values and strategy of the sadistic agent analysand, the analyst is preparing him not only to look for and to obtain new types of pleasure (that do not require the sacrifice of his own security) but also to look for and to obtain security itself from his significant others. A whole new world will open for the agent. In this way, the sadistic agent will be in a much better position to neutralize the masochistic blackmail of his patient and to avoid exercising his own sadistic blackmail toward that patient. He will instead begin asking for support and protection from his dependent patients on matters of survival, and on big decisions. In this way, he will be able also to offer not only a different (nonmasochistic) security to the patients but also will be able to be a source of nonsadistic pleasure to them.

At this stage the unconscious addiction to the sadistic pleasures given him by his masochistic patients must be fully analyzed and an antimasochistic therapeutic coalition formed with the ex-sadistic agent—not "against" the masochistic patient but against the pathogenic temptation he represents. In doing this, the former sadistic agent must act as a "double patient": of his masochistic agent, on the one hand, and of the analyst on the other.

The analyst may succeed in taking control of the analytic relationship: by inverting roles; by undermining the self-idealization of the analysand as well as the validity of his exclusively sadistic strategy; by analyzing the negative transference and integrating it with the split idealized one; by opening a new alternative for nonsadistic pleasure and nonmasochistic security; by stopping the censorship, crippling, dependence, social isolation, blackmail, and exploitation; and by forming an antimasochistic alliance. If he succeeds in these things, very often the sadistic agent analysand will switch to the position of masochistic patient. The following steps of the analytic treatment are identical to those described as typical for the masochistic patient.

If this "patientization" of the agent can be avoided, he will have to face, sooner or later, a decision with respect to his relationship with his most significant masochistic patients—wife, friends, business partners, etc. Again, he usually has three alternatives. First, his masochistic patient other asks for therapeutic help, or is already in analysis, and is also able to change his masochistic pattern and accompany the former sadistic agent toward a healthy nonsadomasochistic agreement. This would be, of course, the best alternative. Second, his masochistic patient may be very resistant to therapeutic change, and yet the sadistic agent analysand may be very attached to him because unwilling to leave his sadistic pattern; here again, either a chronic sadomasochistic relationship that now includes the analyst can be installed (psychoanalysis is replaced by "psycho-dialysis") or the analytic treatment is interrupted. This is the worst alternative. Third, the masochistic patient of the former sadistic agent analysand may be absolutely resistant to leaving his narcissistic dependent partner, and the analysand decides to leave him (or her) and look for another nonnarcissistic partner who can be kind and soft but not masochistic. This "patientectomy" is usually very painful and constitutes an intermediate alternative that usually needs a longer analysis in order to work through guilt feelings and a whole new relationship with different persons with whom he will be able to settle into a healthy relationship. Figure 10-7 presents the main steps of a typical analytical treatment of a sadistic agent.

The Analysis of the Masochistic Agent ("Borderliner")

The masochistic agent tends to be a very soft, tactful, overprotective type of person who likes to take care of and idealize sadistic others who depend totally on him. He is a "pusher," a dependency-maker

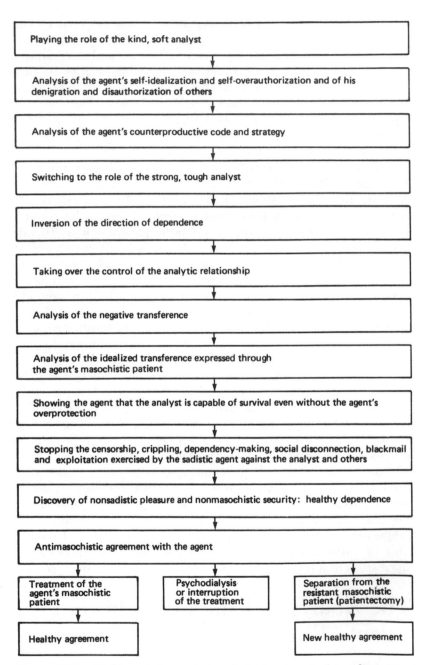

Figure 10-7.   Outline of the typical analytic treatment of a sadistic agent

who overprotects his sadistic dependent others in a way that pushes them out of touch with reality. He appears to be even more masochistic than the masochistic patient because he keeps protecting his dependent torturers even if he does not need them for survival. One possible explanation for this peculiar spoiling behavior is that the masochistic agent seems to have received the strong and systematic message from his parents (or surrogates) that he himself is not lovable. He must win the company of others by overprotecting them: he is the "loyal subject" of the spoiled unrealistic others, the sadistic patients or "their majesties the borderlineds." He behaves like a sacrificing, suffering, overunderstanding adult constantly concerned and blaming himself for the childish, irresponsible, unpredictable, and abusive behavior of others.

Consequently, he accepts mistreatment, disqualification, disauthorization, attacks on his reputation, blackmail, and exploitation (with respect to both pleasure and security) from his sadistic patient others but, at the same time, cripples them with his overprotection, pushing them out of touch with reality by helping them avoid any frustration, and undermining their confidence in themselves by making all the major decisions by himself. He accepts being mistreated and tortured as a masochistic patient but, unlike a patient, he punishes the independence rather than the dependence of the sadistic others. This unconscious strategy seems to be based on the fact that the more spoiled, unrealistic, and aggressive his sadistic others are, the more they will be rejected by society and the more they will have to depend on him. Consequently, he will never be left alone or abandoned. Of course, the defensive pattern reinforces the unconscious fear that the others remain with him just because they can abuse and exploit him, and never because they love or even like him for himself. He is a guilt-ridden kind of person who accepts (and provokes) any kind of torture from the spoiled others; but he can turn into a nasty blamer if the others try to abandon him.

Usually this type of masochistic agent comes into analysis because he is no longer able to deal with his dependent torturers. They are out of his control either because they are improving and becoming more independent, or because they are getting more and more destructive in their sadistic pattern. Sometimes these dependent torturers are threatening (or committing) suicide or murder. It must be said, however, that the masochistic agent usually is a good analytic patient: not as insightful or collaborative as the masochistic patient, but much more "psychological-minded" than the sadistic agent or patient.

The first movement of the analyst with a masochistic agent is usually the therapeutic replacement of his sadistic patient by playing the role of a somewhat demanding and needy analyst who seems to tolerate very little frustration from the agent.

From this position as "spoiled" but childish analyst, the analyst should start analyzing the masochistic agent's basic misunderstanding: his feeling that he is unworthy of any kind of love or affection from others unless he spoils and overprotects them. Consequently, his idealization of the company of his sadistic others must be fully analyzed, as well as the validity of the blaming and devaluating judgment of his internal and external sadistic others—in particular, the vulnerability of the masochistic agent either to the threats of being abandoned (and of no one else wanting to be with him) or to the accusations of being selfish or egotistic if he does not give in to the spoiled, unrealistic demands of his sadistic dependent others.

On the other hand, the analyst must also show the masochistic agent that his whole strategy is highly counterproductive, in the sense that he "castrates" the ego-strength of his sadistic dependent others when he indulges them by not allowing them to be self-sufficient and in touch with reality. He must show the agent that with the wrong superficial accusations his spoiled borderlineds try to make him feel repulsive and guilty because he is not protecting them enough, but that beyond that they could correctly accuse him of crippling them with his overprotective attitude.

In some ways, this style of treatment is like a supervision of the critical conflictive relation between the masochistic agent and his sadistic patients—they are really the focus of his concerns. If the analyst is successful in analyzing the analysand's basic self-devaluation and the counterproductive effects of his overprotecting strategy, he himself becomes the focus of his own interest and accepts the role of the analyst as an experienced technician who can help him, and that there is no need to spoil him. Usually during the first stages of the treatment the masochistic agent tends to make a show of respect for the professional authority of the analyst while secretly undermining it.

At the same time that the analyst helps the masochistic agent to change his relationship with his conflicting sadistic patients, the analyst should switch from the needy, demanding counterstyle to a warmer, tolerant, self-confident style, to complete the inversion of the direction of the control of the analytic relationship.

Once the analyst has taken effective control of the therapeutic relationship and has fully analyzed not only the apparent idealizing transference that covers the actual devaluating one, he is in a better position to open for the masochistic agent the experience and knowledge of a new type of nonsadistic company and nonmasochistic mutual help.

The next step will be to show this masochistic agent how he unconsciously tries to overprotect and cripple the analyst by treating him as a spoiled, overdemanding child whose independence is constantly attacked by him.

Consequently, the analysand will start encouraging real independence and connection with reality in his sadistic dependent patients and will also neutralize their devaluating and blaming blackmail. This stage of the treatment is crucial, and is helped by an antisadistic coalition built with the masochistic agent: when he learns to deal with the destructive pressures of his sadistic dependent others, he not only feels better and more free, but also experiences a feeling of relief from his pathological overresponsibilities. In some sense, he was responsible for keeping the others out of touch with reality and totally dependent on him. At this stage, the sadistic patient must already be in treatment or, at least, must begin it. If this treatment is successful a new, healthy (nonsadomasochistic agreement) is reached by the former masochistic agent. If this treatment is unsuccessful, the whole therapeutic relationship can be switched into a chronic new sadomasochistic relationship that includes the analyst (or analysts), and psychoanalysis is turned into psychodialysis. Another unsuccessful outcome occurs if the sadomasochistic couple interrupts their analytic treatment. The former masochistic agent may also leave the resistant sadistic patient who is reluctant to make any change, and establish a new healthy relationship with a nonsadistic agent. If the sadistic patient does not accept or tolerate any analytic treatment at all, sooner or later he will be abandoned by the former masochistic agent, who will look for a healthier and more pleasant type of relationship. Figure 10-8 presents the main steps of a typical analytic treatment of a masochistic agent—borderliner.

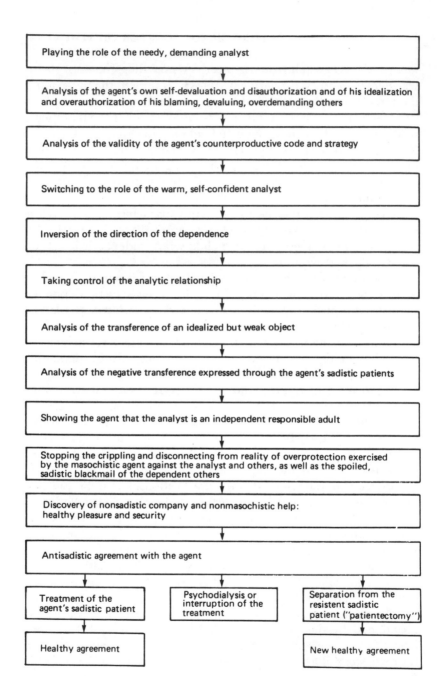

Figure 10-8. Outline of the typical analytic treatment of a masochistic agent ("borderliner")

Analysis of the Sadistic Patient ("Borderlined")

The sadistic patient usually tends to be an overdependent, overdemanding, blaming, charming, torturing, unpredictable, spoiled type of person, who switches suddenly from seductive idealization of the others (when he is trying to induce them to spoil him) to paranoid denigration of them when they do. He has a peculiar and remarkable ability to live as a parasite on others and to "overresponsibilize" them for his own careless and destructive behavior.

The sadistic patient is like a "complaining kicker" because he is locked into the vicious circle of pressing others to overprotect him in a crippling way and then attacking them for doing so.

In a peculiar way, he feels entitled to ask for protection, tolerance, and infinite patience from the others without giving them anything more than his periodically charming company; he is like a sadistic "gigolo" to the masochistic, overprotective others. As a former masochistic agent described it in an insightful moment: "I have to take care of and constantly swallow all the garbage from this charming, impossible little girl [his girlfriend]. And, on top of that, I must love her. She constantly switches from being a cute, helpless princess, when she wants something from me, to a nasty, bossy bitch when I've given it to her."

Usually this type of sadistic patient is sent into analysis by his masochistic agent, because his destructive acting-out is getting out of control. The more he tries to overcome the castrating dependence on the agents, the more he destroys himself and others. He behaves like a terrorist who threatens to blow himself (and others) up if the agents do not accept his spoiled demands, but unlike a terrorist he does in fact blow himself up if these demands are accepted. From the beginning, the analyst has to face a very volatile and dangerous balance of blackmail and terror. The analyst is included in the picture as an emergency force who must be able to neutralize and disarm explosive situations and to allow a more civilized type of interpersonal negotiation.

Consequently, the first movement of the analyst with a sadistic patient is the therapeutic replacement of his masochistic agent by assuming the role of the warm, quiet, tolerant, persuasive analyst who is able to cope with both the threats and seduction of the patient and who is able to cool off his unrealistic demands until the situation can be clarified.

From this position of the calm, persuasive, but firm analyst, the analyst should start analyzing the sadistic patient's basic misunderstanding about his counterproductive and unrealistic demands of overprotection on the part of others. Thus, the analyst should describe very clearly to the analysand how he is trying to press the analyst into a position of masochistic overresponsibility and, at the same time, gets worse if he does so.

Once the borderline "bomb" is neutralized, the analysand's denigration and blaming of the analyst and others must be fully analyzed, as well as the validity of the analysand's moral code and values that sustain the blaming and blackmailing attitude.

At this stage of treatment the critical relation of the borderlined with his borderliner masochistic agent comes into focus: the analyst should analyze the vicious circle that locks them in an impossible bind, and should prescribe some specific actions and reactions to start breaking through this explosive sadomasochistic alliance, without the analyst himself being involved in it. In order to avoid being trapped in a vicious blackmailing relationship, the analyst must analyze the sadistic patient's switching transference, as well as a more stable type of idealized transference (initially at least) usually split and expressed through the analysand's masochistic agent.

There are sudden changes from the superficial idealized seductive transference of a sweet, cute, helpless, overdemanding small child to the deep negative transference of a bitter, nasty, and blaming boss. If the analyst is successful, the sadistic patient will transfer his dependence from the masochistic agent to the analyst.

While analyzing the switching transference, the analyst should gradually show the sadistic patient that he is not his blackmailed hostage, and that neither the reward of his charming affection nor the punishment of his suicide attempts will push him into the pathogenic role of overprotecting the patient. He should show him that he has decided to take the risk of resisting the analysand's pressures. If the analyst is successful in doing this, the analysand will be in the position of understanding the change in the therapeutic strategy.

On one occasion an analyst told a sadistic patient that he would interrupt the session each time the patient started to yell and to insult him. He did not carry out his therapeutic threat, and the analysand reminded him of the threat by saying, "you promised me that you would interrupt the session if I was nasty and noisy, and you are not honoring the promise." It was as if the therapeutic punishment were really a gift to the sadistic patient, because he "knew" that the worst poison for his mental health was the masochistic submission of the others. If the analyst does not submit to the sadistic patient and the patient starts accepting it, the analyst can take full therapeutic control of the analytic relationship.

Consequently, at this stage of the analytic treatment of the sadistic patient it seems crucial to stop his seductive and tyrannical overdependence, and to resist his psychological and social black-mail as well as his sadistic exploitation of the analyst and others through specific antisadistic therapeutic reactions and counterpressures.

At the same time, the analyst must open for the sadistic patient—through explanations and actions—the discovery of new non-sadomasochistic feelings. He must aid him in the discovery of non-sadistic demands for help and of nonmasochistic company, and show him better ways of obtaining pleasure than being spoiled and tyrannical with others.

Once the switching transference, the blackmailing pressures, and the sadistic exploitation have been fully analyzed and to some extent overcome, an antimasochistic alliance will be established with the analysand in order to resist the temptations offered by his maso-chistic agent, who is ambivalent toward the analysis of his depend-ent sadistic patient. He wants him to regain control over his acting-out but does not want him to be fully cured because he fears losing his dependent company, even if it is that of a torturer. The masochistic agent can try to sabotage the treatment by offering bribes to the former sadistic patient when he begins to resist the masochistic pressures—sudden trips or holidays that interrupt the treatment, increasing criticism of the rigidity and coolness of the analyst, etc. The masochistic agent can then follow three different paths: a successful treatment, a failing treatment, or resistance to any kind of therapeutic help. If he chooses the first alternative, the former sadistic patient finally arrives at a healthy agreement with him. If he follows the second, the former sadistic patient can either regress and try to transform his own psychoanalysis into a chronic iatrogenic psychodialysis; he can interrupt the treatment; or he can

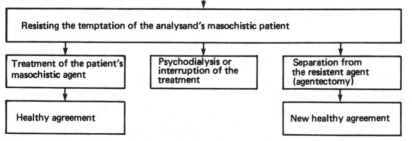

Figure 10-9.   Outline of the typical analytic treatment of a sadistic patient ("borderlined")

separate from his former masochistic agent (agentectomy) and start a healthy relationship with a nonmasochistic agent. If the masochistic agent does not accept any treatment at all, the most probable outcome is that he will be abandoned by the former sadistic patient (agentectomy), provided that the patient has established an analytic relationship strong enough to resist the temptation of returning to the old sadomasochistic pattern. Figure 10-9 presents the main steps of the typical analytic treatment of a sadistic patient— borderlined.

REFERENCES

Bion, W. R. (1962). *Learning from Experience.* New York: Basic Books.

Breuer, J., and Freud, S. (1893-1895). Studies in hysteria. *Standard Edition* 2.

Donnet, J. L. (1973). Le divan bien temperé. *Nouvelle revue de la psychanalyse* 8.

Earle, E. M. (1973). *Makers of Modern Strategy.* Princeton, N.J.: Princeton University Press.

Ferenczi, S. (1909). Introjection and transference. In *First Contributions to Psycho-Analysis.* London: Hogarth Press.

―――― (1926). *Further Contributions to the Theory and Technique of Psycho-Analysis.* London: Hogarth Press.

Freud, S. (1895). Project for a scientific psychology. *Standard Edition* 1:281–397.

―――― (1900). The interpretation of dreams. *Standard Edition* 4/5.

―――― (1905a). On psychotherapy. *Standard Edition* 7:257–269.

―――― (1905b). Jokes and their relation to the unconscious. *Standard Edition* 8.

―――― (1905c). Fragment of an analysis of a case of hysteria. *Standard Edition* 7:7–122.

―――― (1909). Family romances. *Standard Edition* 9:235–241.

―――― (1910a). Five lectures on psycho-analysis. *Standard Edition* 9:3–57.

―――― (1910b). The future prospects of psycho-analytic therapy. *Standard Edition* 11:139–151.

―――― (1911). The handling of dream-interpretation in psycho-analysis. *Standard Edition* 12:89–96.

―――― (1912a). The dynamics of transference. *Standard Edition* 12:97–108.

―――― (1912b). Recommendations to physicians practising psycho-analysis. *Standard Edition* 12:109–120.

―――― (1914). Remembering, repeating and working-through. *Standard Edition* 12:145–156.

―――― (1917). Mourning and melancholia. *Standard Edition* 14:237-260.

—— (1918). From the history of an infantile neurosis. *Standard Edition* 17: 3–122.

—— (1919). Lines of advance in psycho-analytic therapy. *Standard Edition* 17:157–168.

—— (1920). A note on the prehistory of the technique of analysis. *Standard Edition* 18:263–265.

—— (1924). The loss of reality in neurosis and psychosis. *Standard Edition* 19:183–187.

—— (1926). The question of lay analysis. *Standard Edition* 20:179–258.

—— (1937a). Analysis terminable and interminable. *Standard Edition* 23: 209–253.

—— (1937b). Constructions in psycho-analysis. *Standard Edition* 23:255–270.

Gear, M. C., and Liendo, E. C. (1975). *Sémiologie psychanalytique*. Paris: Minuit.

—— (1976). Psychanalyse, sémiologie et communication familiale. *L'Evolution psychiatrique* 2, pp. 239–272.

—— (1979). *Action psychanalytique*. Paris: Minuit.

—— (1980). *Psicoterapia strutturalista*. Florence: del Riccio.

Halleck, S. L. (1971). *The Politics of Therapy*. New York: Jason Aronson.

Heimann, P. (1950). Dynamics of transference interpretation. *International Journal of Psycho-Analysis* 37.

Klein, M. (1961). *Narrative of a Child Analysis*. London: Hogarth Press.

Kohut, H. (1971). *The Analysis of the Self*. New York: International Universities Press.

Kovacs, B. (1936). Training and control analysis. *International Journal of Psycho-Analysis* 17:346–354.

Kuhn, T. (1970). *The Structure of Scientific Revolutions*, 2nd ed. Chicago: University of Chicago Press.

Lacan, J. (1961). La direction de la cure et les principes de son pouvoir. *La Psychanalyse* 6:149–206.

Lagache, D. (1957). Fascination de la conscience par le Moi. *La Psychanalyse* 2,70.

Meltzer, D. (1967). *The Psycho-Analytical Process*. London: Heinemann.

Racker, H. (1960). *Estudios sobre la técnica psicoanalitica*. Buenos Aires: Paidos.

Schelling, T. (1960). *The Strategy of Conflict*. Cambridge, Mass.: Harvard University Press.

Strachey, J. (1943). The nature of the therapeutic action of psycho-analysis. *International Journal of Psycho-Analysis* 15:127–159.

Viderman, S. (1970). *La construction.de l'espace analytique*. Paris: Denoel.

Winnicott, D. W. (1953). Transitional objects and transitional phenomena. *International Journal of Psycho-Analysis* 34:89–97.

Wright, G. von. (1963). *Norm and Action*. London: Routledge and Kegan.

Index